WHAT GOD HAS WROUGHT

Bishop Neil L. Irons

WHAT GOD HAS WROUGHT

*A History of the Southern New Jersey Conference
of
The United Methodist Church*

by
Robert B. Steelman

published by
The United Methodist Church
Southern New Jersey Annual Conference
Commission on Archives and History
Pennington, New Jersey

ISBN 0-914960-56-3
ISBN 0-914960-60-1 (cloth)
Library of Congress Catalog Card No. 86-70275

Copyright © 1986
by Southern New Jersey Annual Conference,
The United Methodist Church

Printed in the United States of America
by Academy Books
Rutland, VT 05701-0757

EDITOR

    Dr. J. Hillman Coffee

MEMBERS OF THE EDITORIAL COMMITTEE

    Dr. Andrew C. Braun*
    Lloyd E. Griscom
    Betty Hawk
    Penny Moore

MEMBERS OF THE ADVISORY COMMITTEE

    Dr. Andrew C. Braun*
    Dr. J. Hillman Coffee
    Rev. J. Wesley Day
    Alice Detwiler
    Betty Hawk
    Rev. Herbert J. Smith*

    * Deceased

Cover depicts SNJ Conference
Sesquicentennial Banner
designed by
Harry Norcross of
First United Methodist Church
Moorestown, N.J.

CONTENTS

List of Illustrations viii
Forewords ix
Preface xii
Acknowledgements xiv

1. Methodist Origins (1738-1775) 1
2. The Early Years (1776-1799) 19
3. Circuits—Circuit Riders—Class Leaders (1800-1829) 35
4. A New Conference Is Born (1830-1839) 51
5. The Pre-Civil War Era (1840-1859) 64
6. The War Decade (1860-1869) 79
7. A Flourishing Church (1870-1899) 91
8. Camp Meetings in Southern New Jersey 110
9. Entering a New Century (1900-1914) 129
10. World War I and the Turbulent Twenties (1915-1929) 142
11. The Methodist Church Is Born (1930-1939) 159
12. The Methodist Protestants 171
13. Ministering to Children and Youth 186
14. War and Peace (1940-1949) 201
15. Women's Role in Southern New Jersey Methodism 217
16. The Methodist Church (1950-1967) 235
17. Our Ethnic Churches 251
18. Institutions of the Church 263
19. The United Methodist Church (1968-1986) 281
20. Looking Back — Looking Ahead 295

Abbreviations	299
Notes	300
Appendix I Conference Sessions (1837-1985)	320
Appendix II Methodist Protestant Conference Presidents	323
Appendix III District Superintendents	325
Appendix IV Delegates to General and Jurisdictional Conferences	329
Appendix V Conference Women Presidents	333
Appendix VI Conference Lay Leaders	335
Appendix VII Conference Youth Presidents	336
Bibliography	338
Index	346

LIST OF ILLUSTRATIONS

Bishop Neil L. Irons	ii
Statue of John Wesley	xvi
Captain Thomas Webb	7
Joseph Toy's Home	10
Bishop Francis Asbury	15
Rev. Thomas Ware	24
Head of the River Church	32
John Walker's Ordination Papers	44
Azail Coate Home, Lumberton	48
Father Henry Boehm	57
Bishop Levi Scott	59
Rev. Charles Pitman	71
Rev. William Roberts	73
Dr. John McClintock	87
General Clinton B. Fisk	103
Seaville Camp Meeting Grounds	114
Ocean Grove Auditorium	118
Rev. Jacob B. Graw	127
Dr. Harold Paul Sloan	144
Harry P. Bennett	146
Methodist Unification Proclaimed	163
William S. Stockton	173
Christ M. P. Church, Atlantic City	183
Rev. Daniel P. Kidder	187
Wallace "Uncle Wally" McKeag	193
C. Austin Miles	203
Francis A. Stanger, Jr.	213
Mrs. Bessie Larkin	220
Mrs. Clinton (Jeannette) Fisk	232
St. Andrew's Church, Cherry Hill	237
Methodist Relay, First Issue	243
Bishop Prince A. Taylor, Jr.	246
Mt. Hope Church, Salem	252
Rev. C. Albert Tindley	255
Pennington School	265
United Methodist Homes	272
Neighborhood Center	276
Tumethca	279
Evangelical Church, Clarksboro	285
Bishop C. Dale White	290
Memorabilia from SNJ Conference Archives	296

FOREWORD I

From circuit rider to city pastor, from camp meeting to the high-steeple church, from the Atlantic Ocean to the Delaware and Raritan Rivers, from the 18th Century to the present our spiritual mothers and fathers have spread the Gospel with warm hearts and sturdy spirits. Francis Asbury traveled thousands of miles to reach souls with a disciplined and joyous faith. His heirs have done the same in German, Korean and Spanish communities. History has been made and it is exciting reading.

The recording of Christian history is both a necessity and an opportunity. The necessity arises from the Church's responsibility to tell the stories of the men and women who have done Christ's work. Without these stories, we cannot properly put into perspective our own Christian service. Much has been bequeathed to us and we dare not be unfaithful in our stewardship of gifts from the past. Christian history offers the promise of opportunity as well. When one learns the paths walked by the disciples of the Lord, it is easier to discern spiritually what the Holy One is now about. In other words, the Church does not start new paths unrelated to the old. Rather, the Church continues the journey in which God leads us by fiery pillar and towering cloud.

You, the reader, are about to embark upon a journey into the past of God's people in Southern New Jersey. United Methodists and their different Wesleyan roots have left a strong imprint on the soul of our state. In reading their stories, you will find the prelude to the work of The United Methodist Church to be accomplished in Southern New Jersey during the closing years of the 20th Century.

NEIL L. IRONS
Bishop

FOREWORD II

Since before 1770, Methodism has been an active, exciting, and important influence in the section of our country now known as the state of New Jersey. New Jersey has always been a corridor state for many purposes. Methodism developed early in New Jersey because of this fact. The early, itinerent preachers proclaimed the power of God in New Jersey as they traveled between Philadelphia and New York by way of this corridor. As a society and then as a church, Methodism quickly spread throughout the state. The story of the many branches of Methodism in New Jersey has never been fully written. With the publication of this book, *What God Has Wrought,* we now have that story in great detail.

The Southern New Jersey Annual Conference has authorized the writing of its history to commemorate its sesquicentennial. The conference selected the Reverend Robert Bevis Steelman, the conference historian, to research the material and to author this history. This excellent choice has been proved as Reverend Steelman has conscientiously pursued his task. After many months of researching, outlining, writing the first draft, revising, and writing the final draft, he finally relinquished the manuscript to the printer. All Methodists, but especially those of the Southern New Jersey Conference, are greatly indebted to Reverend Steelman for his scholarly, informative, and enjoyable book.

This book will be meaningful not only to us in the present time but also to those of the future as a vital history of the Methodists in southern New Jersey.

Dr. J. Hillman Coffee
Editor

FOREWORD III

History is a terrible thing to waste. It is our link with the past — the story of our roots. For the Christian (and United Methodist) history tells us who we are as well as Whose we are. Unfortunately, too many people today suffer from amnesia. They have little or no knowledge of the past. Some insist only that which is current is relevant to life and faith. Herein lies our problem. In order to appreciate where we are and where we are going, we need to know from where we have come. It is little wonder that some United Methodists suffer from an "identity crisis."

The Southern New Jersey Conference of The United Methodist Church celebrates one hundred fifty years of service to Jesus Christ, the Church, and the world in 1986. To commemorate this event Robert B. Steelman, Conference Historian, has written the history of our Annual Conference entitled *What God Has Wrought*. In this book the reader will be brought face to face with the men and women who helped build our great church. The lives of great people, both laity and clergy, will challenge us to serve our Lord more faithfully. The stories of great churches and ministries will remind us that the Spirit of God guides us as we proclaim the Wesleyan message of grace and freedom. Though our church cannot live on past glories, there is encouragement that our Lord still has work for His people called United Methodists. We are part of an unbroken chain dating back to May 24, 1738 and stretching to the future. Since the day John Wesley put his trust in Jesus Christ and found his heart "strangely warmed" to the present, the history of United Methodism has been written. We are all part of it. As you read *What God Has Wrought,* you will begin to feel a part of that history whatever your background. We are indebted to the Reverend Robert B. Steelman for helping put our lives into proper perspective and reminding us of our heritage as United Methodist Christians. It remains for us, the spiritual children of Wesley, Asbury, Otterbein, and Albright, to continue the writing of this history through our lives and faith remembering in Wesley's words, "The best of all is, God is with us."

> WALTER JESUNCOSKY III
> *Chairman,* Commission on
> Archives and History

PREFACE

It has long been the goal of the Commission on Archives and History to publish the history of the Conference. The only previously published history is *The Methodist Trail in New Jersey,* published in 1961 for the 125th Anniversary of the Conference. That volume was basically a capsule history of the churches of the Conference. The new history was envisioned as a history of the Conference itself.

The project was set in motion by the adoption of a recommendation at the 1975 Conference which called for the exploration of the possibilities of publishing such a history for the 150th Conference Session in 1986. Work on the history began in earnest with the appointment of an Advisory Committee in late 1978. The first meeting was held in Ocean City on March 27, 1979 with Alice Detwiler, Betty Hawk, Herbert J. Smith, J. Wesley Day, Hillman Coffee and myself attending.

Research continued for the next five years. The Advisory Committee met twice yearly, served as a sounding board for the author's ideas and assisted with the research. The Commission on Archives and History, chaired by Dr. J. Hillman Coffee, served as the Editorial Committee making the numerous decisions which moved the history project along. Assistance and support was rendered by the Task Force on Historical Celebrations originally appointed by Bishop C. Dale White.

As the summer of 1984 neared, a separate Editorial Committee consisting of Dr. J. Hillman Coffee, Editor; Lloyd E. Griscom, Penny Moore, Betty Hawk and Dr. Andrew C. Braun was appointed. A new Commission on Archives and History, chaired by the Rev. Walter Jesuncosky, III, was elected and charged with the responsibility of overseeing the history's publication and sale. The author, with the approval of the Cabinet and Old First United Methodist Church, West Long Branch, was given a three month summer study leave. During this time, the first draft of the history was completed.

Each member of the Editorial Committee read the first draft during the fall of 1984. Following a meeting of the Editorial Committee in Central Church, Bridgeton, January 3, 1985, the final draft of the manuscript was prepared, passed through the scrutiny of our English scholar, Mrs. Miriam Coffee, and was typed by the author's wife, Eileen. The last writing is being done on this warm July day, long set as the date for the completion of the manuscript.

The Southern New Jersey Conference cannot boast of being one of the great Conferences of United Methodism. Our boast is in the Lord. We are not a large Conference, as Conferences go, yet it is unlikely that many Conferences have permeated their area as has this Conference in southern Jersey. There are few towns and villages where there is not a United Methodist Church.

This history attempts to tell the story of what these people called United Methodists have been up to as they met in classes, built churches, sent sons and daughters into the ministry of Christ's Church and as missionaries to far away places. It tells the story of some of our mothers and fathers in the faith, lest they be forgotten. It reminds us of the witness that was borne, the Christian principles upheld, the crusades waged and the struggles endured. It will be a story well told if it can inspire us to be faithful in our time to Christ and The United Methodist Church.

To this writer whose family roots are nearly three centuries old in southern New Jersey and whose Methodist roots here go back nearly to the beginnings of Methodism in our state, the writing of this history has been a labor of love. It was decided that this book would not have a particular dedication. If there was I would dedicate it to my children and yours in the hope that this will be their story too.

ROBERT B. STEELMAN
Bridgeton, N.J.
July 15, 1985.

ACKNOWLEDGEMENTS

In a publication such as this one, numerous persons deserve to be thanked. It is not possible to remember each one who made a contribution but some must be praised. I beg the forgiveness of any who may be overlooked.

First, I want to thank my uncle, Walter B. VanSant, long a member and consultant of the Commission on Archives and History and Historical Society of the Conference, and an outstanding Conference layman. He has been an inspiration and a support in all my historical endeavors. At the age of ninety-two he still pursues his historical interests and his love for his Church.

Second, thanks goes to those who have served for the last ten years on the Commission on Archives and History and have been behind this project all the way. In fact, it is their project. Those most active include: Dr. J. Hillman Coffee, Chairman, 1976-1984; Rev. Walter Jesuncosky, III, Chairman since 1984; Louis J. Barbour, Doreen Dyer, Lloyd E. Griscom, Rev. William J. Kingston, Jr., Edna Molyneaux, Penny Moore and more recently John Ebner, Walter Jones and Esther B. Simpson.

The members of the Advisory Committee have rendered invaluable service. They are: Dr. Andrew C. Braun, Dr. J. Hillman Coffee, Rev. J. Wesley Day, who researched Methodist Protestant roots; Alice Detwiler, our expert on women's history; Betty Hawk, who did the research on ministry to children and youth, particularly our Conference Camps and Institutes; and the late Rev. Herbert J. Smith, who inspired us all and we trust is pleased with the results.

The work of the Editorial Committee deserves the highest accolades. They never faltered in their support, were lavish in their praise, consistent and honest in their criticisms, and did everything they were asked. Thank you Hillman Coffee, Andrew Braun, Lloyd Griscom, Betty Hawk and Penny Moore.

My friends, Hillman and Miriam Coffee need to be thanked first and last. Hillman has been a co-worker throughout this entire venture. Without his assistance this history would never have been written. Hillman also gathered all the pictures for the book. Miriam Coffee is our English expert. She read and corrected the entire manuscript. If there are still errors, it is probably because I did not do what she suggested. Miriam and Hillman did another thing. The summer of 1984 they made available to my wife, Eileen, our daughters Sue and Lynda, and myself, their lovely "Sneaky Hollow" Cottage in the foothills of the Allegheny Mountains of Pennsylvania. There the first draft of this history was written and typed. It is an experience we will always remember.

To the two churches and congregations I pastored during this venture, I say thanks. Old First United Methodist in West Long Branch and Central

United Methodist in Bridgeton were agreeable to the extra time it took their minister to work on this history and were supportive of him in this endeavor.

The Library and Staff of Drew University and the United Methodist Archives Center, especially Dr. Kenneth Rowe and Mrs. Louise Capron were most helpful on numerous occasions.

Special thanks to the New Jersey Historical Commission. A grant awarded in 1984 paid nearly the entire cost of typing the first draft of this history.

Rev. Walter Jesuncosky, III, assumed the Chairmanship of the Commission on Archives and History in June of 1984. He has had the job of seeing that the funding for publication was available and to the sale of the book once published. I appreciate his support and help.

The Conference has been most gracious to their Historian. Support and encouragement have come from many sources: Council on Finance and Administration, Bishop C. Dale White, Bishop Neil L. Irons, Task Force on Historical Celebrations and its two Chairmen, Rev. Robert J. Williams and Rev. Fred W. Price; and numerous individuals, many of whom sent information in answer to the author's queries.

E. Farley Sharp is a fine publisher. This south Jersey native is also a personal friend. He has done much to make available and publish United Methodist history. His publishing skills are seen in this work. Thank you, Ed.

My family, Eileen, Fred, Sue, Bert and Lynda must be thanked for putting up with the time it took to get this done. I have saved my last thank you for my wife, Eileen. She typed this entire manuscript, not once but twice. That is no small feat. Besides that, she somehow manages to put up with me and still love me. Thank you, Eileen. I love you.

ROBERT B. STEELMAN

STATUE OF JOHN WESLEY
City Road, London, England

Chapter 1

METHODIST ORIGINS

1738-1775

April 21, 1777, John Wesley preached while standing on a stone. The stone's brass plate was inscribed: "This was laid by Mr. John Wesley on April 21, 1777. Probably this will be seen no more by any human eye, but it will remain there until the Earth and the works thereof are burnt up." That stone is the cornerstone of Wesley's Chapel on City Road, London, England, a Chapel destined to be the Mother Church of World Methodism.

Wesley preached from the text in Numbers 23:23, "What hath God wrought!" In his sermon, Methodism's founder declared, "Methodism is not a new religion, but the old religion of the Bible . . . of the primitive Church . . . of the Church of England . . . no other than the love of God to all mankind." Wesley could then look back on nearly fifty years of Methodism in Great Britain. He could rejoice that it had spread across the Atlantic to America.

Methodism in New Jersey is over two centuries old. The Southern New Jersey Conference is celebrating one hundred and fifty years of service to Christ. As the story of its deeds are told we shall see what God has wrought. Far more important than a recital of names, dates, and official Conference actions is what God has done and is doing, often in spite of ourselves. As the ritual for receiving new members into The United Methodist Church puts it: "The Church is of God and will be preserved to the end of time, for the conduct of worship and the due administration of his Word and Sacraments, the maintenance of Christian fellowship and discipline, the edification of believers and the conversion of the world. All of every age and station stand in need of the means of grace which it alone supplies."

What is the origin of Methodism? Bible moths! Religious fanatics! Methodists! Zealots! Holy Club! Such derogatory names were heaped upon a small company of serious students of Oxford University who wanted to live only to the glory of God. Charles Wesley started the meetings of these few friends in 1729. John Wesley, returning to Oxford, from which he had graduated, to assume his duties as a Fellow of Lincoln College, became their leader.

The name Methodist stuck. It was given because of the methodical way this group of zealous, young Christians sought to live and discipline their lives for God.

John Wesley was born in the rectory of Epworth, England, June 17, 1703. Charles, his hymn-writer brother, was born December 18, 1707. John was his parents fifteenth child; Charles, the eighteenth. Samuel Wesley, the father, was the Anglican rector of the parish church in the little town of Epworth. Samuel was scholarly and rigid in matters of church doctrine, practice, and moral standards. The mother, Susanna, daughter of the non-conformist minister Samuel Annesley of London, was beautiful, talented and John's spiritual mentor throughout her life. Susanna, the twenty-fifth child of her father and the twenty-fourth of her mother, gave birth to nineteen children, ten of whom lived to maturity, seven girls and three boys.

A disastrous fire completely destroyed the Wesley home in 1709. All but little Jacky quickly escaped. Suddenly, he appeared in a window. Just as quickly a townsman jumped on the shoulders of another and pulled the frightened child to safety as the roof was falling in. Susanna exclaimed, "A brand plucked from the burning."[1] She resolved to be particularly careful about this child's training, for she believed God had saved Jacky for some special purpose.

His mother was John's first teacher. He did not attend a formal school until he became a student at Charterhouse in London at the age of ten. Six years later, he became an Oxford student at Christ Church College where he earned both the Bachelor of Arts and the Master of Arts degrees. John was ordained to holy orders in the Anglican Church, a church he never left, for he believed Methodism to be but a Society within the established church.

The disciplined living and loving service to their fellowman inculcated in the Holy Club served as a model for Methodism in the years to come. Also, life-long friendships were formed there. Particularly noteworthy was the friendship with George Whitefield.

Both John and Charles accepted the offer of General James Oglethorpe to assist his work in the colony of Georgia in America. It was John's hope to minister to the British settlers, to preach to the American Indians, and to save his own soul. Charles stayed only a few months. John's visit lasted almost two years, but was frustrating, to say the least. He was frustrated in his ministry to the colonists, frustrated in his lack of any real opportunity to preach to the Indians, and frustrated by an unfortunate love experience with Sophie Hopkey. He returned to England, not even sure of his own soul's salvation.[2]

Back in England, John continued to wrestle with the lack of the assurance of salvation. Then came the experience that gave birth to Methodism. The date is May 24, 1738. Wesley described it in his *Journal:*

> In the evening I went very unwillingly to a society in Aldersgate Street, where one was reading Luther's preface to the Epistle to the Romans. About a quarter before nine, while he was describing the change which God works in the heart through faith in Christ, I felt my heart strangely warmed, I felt I did trust in Christ, Christ alone for salvation, and an assurance was given me, that he had taken away my sins, even mine, and saved me from the law of sin and death.

Charles had experienced a similar spiritual awakening a few days earlier. The two brothers were now spiritually prepared for their life's work.

This Aldersgate or heart warming experience made a new man, a God-born man of Wesley. It also brought to England through Wesley and his Methodist cohorts the fires of an evangelical revival and a vital piety which transformed a nation and soon spread across the Atlantic to a new continent.

An English historian credits the Wesleyan revival with saving England from the bloodshed that marked the French Revolution.

Wesley's work was not easy. It precipitated attacks, persecution, and riots that lasted a decade. In the end, Wesley became one of the best known and most revered men of his time. For over fifty years, he traveled the roads of England, toured Scotland twenty times, visited Wales twenty-four times and Ireland twenty-one times.

The work John Wesley accomplished was equivalent to the labors of many men. It is estimated that during his itinerant ministry he traveled over a quarter of a million miles, mostly on horseback. He preached over fifty thousand times, organized and actively superintended hundreds of societies, wrote over two hundred books and pamphlets besides editing some two hundred more. He kept a daily journal of his ministry, carried on a huge correspondence, organized relief for the poor and the unemployed, and started schools and dispensaries. In addition, he always had time to talk and to pray with any who needed him.

John Wesley knew how to do effectively and in a unified ministry what we now struggle with and hold in tension. That is, Wesley was an evangelist who knew how to bring souls to Christ. He was also a social activist who fought to right the wrongs of society and did so in effective ways. There was no dichotomy in his ministry between evangelism and social concerns.

He worked and preached until he died. His last letter was written six days before his death to William Wilberforce urging him to continue his efforts to eradicate slavery. "Go on in the name of God and in the power of His might, till even American slavery (the vilest that ever saw the sun) shall vanish away before it."

John Wesley died March 2, 1791. He was "father Wesley" to his spiritual children.

A friend of Wesley's from Holy Club days, although their friendship went through many stormy times, was George Whitefield. The most prominent Holy Club member, George Whitefield, son of a Gloucester, England, innkeeper, was born December 16, 1714. It was Whitefield who initiated field, or open-air, preaching which became a mark of the evangelical revival.

Whitefield is a hard man to categorize. He was a member of the Holy Club and a friend and co-worker with Wesley. He was a Methodist in the broad sense of that term coming out of his Oxford University days and broadly applied to all devotees of the evangelical revival. He was not, however, a Wesleyan Methodist. He never placed himself under the aegis of Wesley's direction or command. In theology, they differed widely. Wesley was an Arminian; Whitefield was a Calvinist, yet they were the leading evangelists of their day. George Whitefield's contributions cannot be ignored in studying Methodist origins.

Whitefield was best as an open-air preacher. He drew enormous crowds. His effects as an orator were devastating. It is said that by merely pronouncing the word "Mesopotamia" he could bring tears to the eyes of his listeners. Seven times he visited America. Following Wesley to Georgia, Whitefield established an orphanage, still in existence, at Bethesda. Worn out with preaching, George Whitefield died at Newburyport, Massachusetts, September 30, 1770.

The account of his visits and work in New Jersey needs to be told as a background for organized Methodism and for the light it throws upon colonial religion in New Jersey. George Whitefield played a very important role in the Great Awakening that swept the colonies in the 1740's. The New Jersey leaders were the Dutch Reformed minister, Theodore J. Frelinghuysen of the Raritan Valley, and the Presbyterian Tennent brothers, Gilbert of New Brunswick and William, Jr. of Freehold. The New England leader was Jonathan Edwards of Northampton, Massachusetts. Whitefield came to know them all and because of his itineracy throughout the colonies helped spread the revival. Winthrop Hudson calls him "The Grand Itinerant."[3]

George Whitefield's first visit to New Jersey was in 1739 on his second voyage to America. Monday, November 12, he left Philadelphia and preached in Burlington. The following evening he preached in New Brunswick in Gilbert Tennent's meeting house. One week later he again preached in New Brunswick.

He returned to New Jersey in the spring of 1740. Monday, April 21, he preached to about fifteen hundred in Greenwich, Gloucester County and the next day to about the same number in Gloucester. Leaving Philadelphia on Friday, April 25, he preached at Amwell. Saturday and Sunday he preached at New Brunswick and took an offering for his Georgia orphanage. Nearly seven or eight thousand, he says, heard him preach on Sunday. Monday, he preached at Woodbridge and Elizabeth on his way to New York. On his return to Philadelphia he preached at Amboy on May 5, and the next day to about three thousand each at Freehold and Allentown.

Later in 1740 he was in Boston. Heading south in early November, he records preaching at Newark, Baskingridge, in Mr. Cross' barn about two miles from Baskingridge, New Brunswick, and Trenton.

November 17 to 20, going out from Philadelphia, he made a quick tour of southern New Jersey. His Journal records:

> Monday Nov. 17 I preached at Gloucester; but found myself weighed down, and not able to deliver my sermon with my usual vigour. However, there was an affected meeting, and several (as I heard afterwards) who had been in bondage before, at that time received joy in the Holy Ghost. . . .
> Tuesday Nov. 18 Was somewhat better in the morning. Preached at Piles Grove,[4] in the afternoon, to about 2,000 people.
> Wednesday Nov. 19 Had two precious meetings today at Cohansie.[5] Preached to some thousands, both morning and afternoon. . . . At this place Mr. Gilbert Tennent preached some time ago.
> Thursday Nov. 20 Salem. Preached twice here this day: in the morning in the Court House; in the afternoon, in the open air, before the prison, to about 2,000. Both times God was with us.[6]

It was to be another twenty years before Methodism would become established in America. In 1760, the estimated population was just under two million. The churches were growing. The number of churches in the colonies more than doubled between 1740 and 1780 when there were about three thousand churches in the land. One could find Congregational, Presbyterian, Baptist, Anglican, Lutheran, German and Dutch Reformed, Quaker, and a few Roman Catholics.[7]

Methodism in America owes its origin to Irish lay immigrants who had been converted and became Methodists in the old country. It is interesting that the three principal figures in Methodist beginnings in America—Robert Strawbridge, Philip Embury and Barbara Heck—all arrived about 1760.

Robert Strawbridge and his wife Elizabeth from County Leitrim, Ireland, settled on a fifty acre farm on Sam's Creek south of New Windsor, Frederick County, Maryland. Almost immediately he started to preach to his neighbors in his own two-story log home. Soon a Methodist Class was organized, the first in America.[8] The date may have been 1762. A log meeting house was built later about a mile from his home, possibly in 1764.

Strawbridge traveled in ever widening circles. He preached in Leesburg, Virginia and elsewhere in Fairfax County; Frederick, Maryland, and on the Eastern Shore. In 1770, he preached at St. George's Church in Philadelphia. Records of First United Methodist Church Trenton show that Strawbridge was paid three pounds twelve shillings for travel expense when he preached there in 1774. Henry Boehm states in his *Reminiscences* that Strawbridge preached "at my father's house in 1781" near Lancaster, Pennsylvania.

There can be little doubt that Strawbridge was the first to organize Methodism in America. There is also little doubt that he was a maverick. He insisted on administering the Sacraments and did so when others were forbidden prior to the Christmas Conference. He was even made an exception to the rule. At the first Conference of Methodist preachers in America, held at Old St. George's, July, 1773, a rule was adopted which stated:

> Every preacher who acts in connection with Mr. Wesley and the brethren who labor in America, is strictly to avoid administering the ordinances of baptism and the Lord's Supper.

A qualifying clause was added according to Asbury:

> Except Mr. Strawbridge, and he under the particular direction of the Assistant.[9]

Strawbridge, the farmer preacher, died in the summer of 1781. Today his body lies buried in "The Preachers Lot" near the grave of Francis Asbury in Mount Olivet Cemetery, Baltimore.

Philip Embury and Barbara Ruckle Heck, cousins from Ballingrane, Ireland, arrived in New York aboard the ship Perry on Monday, August 11, 1760.[10] Both were Methodists, along with other Irish friends. Embury had been a class leader and local preacher in Ireland, but finding no Methodists in New York, Embury and his friends joined the Lutheran Church. There is no evidence they did anything to practice their faith as Methodists until 1766.

One fall day in October of 1766, Barbara Heck returned home to find some friends playing cards at her kitchen table. Incensed at their "fall from grace," she scooped up the cards, threw them into the fire, and warned one and all that if they did not repent, they would all perish. Marching over to Philip Embury's, she insisted, "Philip, you must preach to us, or we shall all go to hell together, and God will require our blood at your hands!" To his hesitant, "Where shall I preach?" came the swift answer, "In your own house!" "But who will come?" "I will." The time was fixed. Barbara gathered a small congregation consisting of her and her husband Paul, Betty, their black servant, and John Lawrence, one of the card players. Embury, the carpenter, preached. A class was formed. The congregation grew and a rigging loft was secured for services. Within two years, the first Wesley Chapel, predecessor of the present John Street Church in New York City, was dedicated by Embury, October 30, 1768.

By the time Wesley's first preachers arrived in the new world, the Emburys, Hecks and others had moved north to the Camden Valley area between Cambridge, New York, and Arlington, Vermont. There, Philip helped start the Ashgrove Society. He died suddenly in 1773. A large monument now marks his grave in the cemetery at Cambridge. His widow married John Lawrence. When war broke out with England, they moved to Canada where they helped establish yet another Methodist Church, one of the first in Canada.

Barbara Heck died at the age of 70 in 1804 and is buried with her husband Paul in the Old Blue Church Cemetery on the banks of the St. Lawrence River near Brockville, Ontario.

To the story of Strawbridge, Embury, and Heck, must be told the story of another whose role was most significant in the formative development of early Methodism in America and in New Jersey. His name is Thomas Webb, Captain Thomas Webb of His Majesty's army. He has been called the number one layman in early American Methodism.

While there is some evidence that Webb preached in Albany, New York, prior to 1766, it was not until he made his appearance at one of Philip Embury's meetings in the rigging loft in New York that his presence was felt in Methodist circles. One night while Embury was conducting services, the Methodists were surprisingly joined by this British army officer. Not knowing whether he was there to spy on them, arrest them, or join them in worship, they were quite taken aback. Upon being assured the Captain was there to join them in worship, being a Methodist himself, they were overjoyed. Would he like to preach? Of course. The Captain, attired in the red coat of an army officer, stepped to the pulpit. His green eye patch covering an eye lost at the Battle of Montmorency, Quebec, in the French and Indian War, made him an imposing figure. He removed his sword, laid it across the pulpit and began expounding the Word of the Lord.

Captain Webb was born in 1725. About the age of nineteen or twenty, he enlisted in the 48th Regiment of Foot. October 29, 1754, the twenty-nine year old Webb was commissioned Quartermaster. A year later while serving in America, he was promoted to Lieutenant. A year after he lost his eye, he married Mary Arding of a fairly well-to-do family from Jamaica, Long Island. They had one son, Charles.

Capt. Thomas Webb

Webb was also an author. In 1759, he published *A Military Treatise on the Appointments of the Army*. General Washington used this book when he wanted a treatise on military discipline. Washington's copy is now in the Boston Athenaeum.

In 1764, when his regiment was recalled to Ireland, Webb elected to stay in America and resigned his Commission even though he was recommended for the rank of Captain. In retirement, he received a Lieutenant's half-pay and out of courtesy was called Captain. He soon was appointed Barrack Master at Albany.

About this time, his wife died, and Webb, a troubled man, was soon back in Bristol, England. On Passion Sunday, 1765, he was converted under the preaching of a Moravian minister. Soon he joined the Methodists and determined "to live and die with them." It was not long before he began to preach, and preach he could! John Adams once heard Webb preach at Old St. George's and remarked, "He is one of the most fluent, eloquent men I ever heard."

Webb returned to America and soon began his work. His preaching in New York brought crowds, won converts and soon led to the building of Wesley

Chapel, his name heading the subscription list. He also preached in 1767 on Long Island and in Philadelphia where he organized a Class of Whitefield's followers into a Methodist Society and assisted in the purchase of Old St. George's Church. Webb preached the opening Sunday morning sermon in the chapel on November 26, 1769. His work was not confined to the two cities. He preached in New Jersey, Wilmington and New Castle, Delaware, and later in Maryland.

In 1772, Webb returned to England to appeal to Wesley for preachers in America. He stayed almost a year. While there he was married by the Rev. John Fletcher of Madeley to Miss Grace Gilbert, whose brother, Nathaniel, was the pioneer Methodist of Antigua. A son Gilbert and daughter Mary were born to the Webbs.

On April 9, 1773, the Webbs sailed for America with Thomas Rankin and George Shadford, the preachers he sought and whose fares he paid.

If anyone can be called the founding father of New Jersey Methodism it would have to be Captain Webb. Trenton, Burlington and Pemberton all claim him as their founder. All point to 1769 or 1770 as their founding date. Each would like to claim the honor of being the first Methodist Society in New Jersey, a claim which cannot be substantiated at this late date. Oh, if Captain Webb had only left us a diary! It does, however, seem likely that he had preached in each place by 1769. There was an army barracks in Trenton, and he could have preached there earlier. Gout, which was a periodic problem with Webb, did confine him to New Jersey's capital during much of the winter of 1771-1772, prior to his return to England. Yet, he wrote, "Thank God . . . I have been able to preach in my lodgings. I have large congregations and sinners are convinced and turn from the error of their ways." Exactly when the first class was formed in Trenton cannot be said. What we do know is that sometime in 1771, Joseph Toy moved from Burlington to Trenton and became class leader there.

Webb's preaching in Burlington seems to have been in the market place and in the court house. There, Toy heard him preach on justification by faith and was converted. Webb induced Toy to form and lead a class. This class was formed December 14, 1770.[11]

When The Captain returned to America in 1773 with his bride Grace, they moved into a rented home "on the Green Bank," a high spot on the Delaware River in Burlington. They were favored by having such fine Quaker neighbors as the Morrises, Dillwyns and Anthony Benezet. The Webbs spent about three years in Burlington. Grace was often left alone while her husband was off preaching someplace. Baltimore was one of those places. Webb and Francis Asbury share the responsibility for building Lovely Lane, the first Methodist meeting house in Baltimore. Asbury laid the foundation stone in April, 1774. In October, Webb preached the first sermon in the building.[12]

In 1776, Webb moved his family to the more rural and secluded area of Pemberton, then known as New Mills. The war may have had something to do with the move. This must have been another rented home as no deed to any property Webb owned can be found. His friend, Thomas Rankin, frequently visited him in Pemberton, sometimes staying for long periods. Webb sometimes accompanied Rankin on his preaching trips. During the spring of 1776, Rankin appointed Webb to supply the Trenton Circuit. He promised to do it "in the best manner he could." At this time the Trenton Circuit included such preaching places as Burlington, Trenton, Mt. Holly, Pemberton, Black Horse, Bordentown, Hopewell and Pennington.

The Captain's homes in Burlington and Pemberton were frequently visited by Methodist preachers. Thomas and Grace were congenial hosts. While William Duke served on the Trenton Circuit the latter half of 1775, he often visited Webb who helped him learn Latin and Greek. Webb gave Duke his Greek New Testament.

From his home in New Jersey, the venerable Captain went forth to preach salvation in Christ in many places. There are other churches in this State which trace their roots to Webb. They are in such widely scattered places as Pennington, Manahawkin, Hazlet and Newport. No definite proof can be pointed to verifying this fact, but strong tradition, coupled with much circumstantial evidence, makes it a plausible conclusion.

The Revolutionary War brought to an end Webb's work in America. Webb loved America and its people. He loved his Country in whose service he had fought. He loved the Methodist people in America. These were loyalties that could not be reconciled. To add to his difficulties, as a former British Officer and even as a Methodist, colonists suspicioned his loyalty. They may have been right about his loyalty to the colonial cause. No one, however, could question his loyalty to Christ or to the people called Methodists.

Webb moved his family back to Burlington to live with friends in the spring of 1777. On May 7, he was arrested. Cleared of some trivial charges, he was held on the more serious charge of spying for the British government. On May 26, he and his family were taken prisoners to Bethlehem, Pennsylvania. There they were befriended by the Moravians. Allowed freedom of movement within a radius of six miles, Webb preached often to other prisoners and their guards. Imprisonment lasted some fifteen months. Eventually, he was permitted to go to New York in a prisoner exchange. On October 18, 1778, the Webbs sailed for England.

Finally settling in Bristol, Webb continued to preach, helped build churches, and be as useful as he could. He never returned to America. He died December 20, 1796, and was buried in a vault under the communion table of Portland Chapel in Bristol, a church he had helped to build.

Captain Webb's body was reinterred from its burial place in Portland Chapel to the New Room in Bristol, May 22, 1972. Some confusion existed over which grave was actually his. The confusion was cleared when in one of the suspected graves was found the green eye patch. His green eye patch, sealed in a jar, is now on display in the New Room.

Captain Thomas Webb deserves to be called the father of New Jersey Methodism.[13]

Joseph Toy's old home still stands facing the Delaware in Palmyra, N.J.

While Webb is the father of New Jersey Methodism, others who were sons, brothers or co-workers in the faith, had much to do with establishing Methodism in this state in those formative years. Joseph Toy has already been mentioned. A bit more needs to be said about this man who has been called "the first Methodist of New Jersey."[14] Toy was born in Palmyra, New Jersey, April 24, 1748, and attended school in Burlington. It was in Burlington at the age of twenty-two that he was converted and became a class leader in 1770. Married a few months later to Frances Dallam of Maryland, they moved to Trenton in 1771. There he taught school and served as class leader in his own home. In 1773, Asbury induced Toy to become a trustee for the building of a church in New Mills. About this same time he began to preach.

The Toys left New Jersey and moved to Abingdon, Maryland where Joseph taught school, continued to preach, and was instrumental in building a Methodist meeting house. One of his converts was his father-in-law, Colonel Richard Dallam, an American Army officer, who became a friend and confidant of Bishop Asbury.

When Cokesbury College was started in Abingdon in 1785-1786, Mr. Toy was named instructor of Mathematics and English Literature. When the school burned in 1795, Toy moved with it to Baltimore. A year later, a second fire ended Cokesbury's days. Toy resumed his preaching career. He served numerous circuits in the Maryland-Virginia area. Joseph Toy died January 26, 1826.

Three other laymen of note played important roles in early New Jersey Methodism, though on a more limited scale. Two were Irish Methodists. John Early was born in Ireland in 1738. As a young man, he and his brothers were partners in a wood-working trade. Converted by John Wesley during one of his preaching tours to Ireland, John became a Methodist. Disowned by his family for leaving the Catholic faith, Early emigrated to America in 1764. He settled in what was known as the "Irish Tenth," comprising parts of the present counties of Gloucester, Camden and Atlantic. He bought acreage along "Still Run Creek" in Greenwich Township, Gloucester County, and later two-thirds interest in a saw mill. Later he bought the remaining third.

How soon and under what circumstances Early began to practice his Methodist faith and witness to Christ is not known. At his death in 1828, he was said to have been a Methodist for sixty years. That would make the date 1768. It is known that he was among the founders of Bethel Church, Hurffville, and Aura Church near where he lived. His home was a preaching place of Richard Sneath and others on the Bethel Circuit prior to the building of Aura Church. His name is listed on deeds as a trustee of Bethel and Aura Churches and also the Adams or Stone Meeting House near Swedesboro and the Friendship Church near Monroeville. In time, his eldest son William became a traveling preacher.[15]

The other Irishman who played a role in early New Jersey Methodism was Squire Thomas Murphy. The records of St. John's Church, Hazlet, show that Captain Webb preached in the home of Squire Murphy at Bethany prior to the Revolution. It is believed he and Webb had a prior acquaintance. If so, could it have been at John Street or perhaps on Long Island or Staten Island, places where Webb also preached? One wonders if the Squire was another of John Wesley's Irish converts. Other preachers are also believed to have stopped at the Squire's home as they traveled between Philadelphia and New York. The Bethany Society, oldest in that part of the Conference, out of which came the present St. John's Church in Hazlet, stems from the work of Squire Murphy. The Squire lived on Pig Street, now Hazlet Avenue, and his home is still standing.

The third layman of note is William Budd of New Mills or Pemberton. William Budd was a member of the noted Budd family of that place, many of whom played important roles in Methodism in various parts of the State. William Budd was one of those who welcomed Asbury to New Jersey in 1771. He had a hand in the building of the first meeting house in New Mills in 1776 and throughout a long life continued as a faithful Christian. He served for a long time as a local preacher in many places. Bishop Asbury last saw his friend William Budd on April 18, 1807. He says, "I found old grandfather Budd worshipping, leaning upon the top of his staff—halting, yet wrestling like Jacob. Ah! we remember when Israel was a child; but now, how goodly are thy tents, O Jacob, and thy tabernacles (camp meetings), O Israel!"[16]

The work these extraordinary laymen did in establishing Methodism in New Jersey cannot be overstated. The foundations they laid were built upon and enlarged as Wesley's preachers arrived to do their work.

Richard Boardman and Joseph Pilmore were the first missionaries to be sent to America by John Wesley. Their appointment read "America." They landed at Gloucester Point, New Jersey, October 21, 1769.

Gloucester Point, opposite Philadelphia, is an historic New Jersey landmark. It has been an annual meeting place of the West Jersey Proprietors since 1688. It was the headquarters of the famed Gloucester County Fox Hunting Club, organized in 1766, the oldest hunting club in America. Betsy Ross was married in Hugg's Tavern in 1773. Hugg's Tavern was headquarters for General Lord Cornwallis during his siege of Gloucester in 1777.[17]

A call for John Wesley to send some preachers to America was given at the Bristol Conference of 1768. The decision was deferred until the following Conference to give the preachers time to reflect upon it. Accordingly, when Wesley next met his preachers at Leeds, August 1, 1769, the question was raised:

> Q. 13. We have a pressing call from our brethren at New York (who have built a preaching house) to come over and help them. Who is willing to go?
>
> A. Richard Boardman and Joseph Pilmoor.
>
> Q. 14. What can we do more in token of our brotherly love?
>
> A. Let us make a collection amongst ourselves.
>
> This was immediately done. And out of it 50 pounds were alloted for the payment of their debt and about twenty pounds given to our brethren for passage.[18]

Both men were about thirty when they arrived in America. Boardman had been preaching about six years and Pilmore four. Earlier in 1769, Boardman had lost his infant daughter and five days later his wife. It was out of this tragedy in his life that the divine call came to go to America.

Monday August 21 they boarded the ship *Mary and Elizabeth* for their nine week trip across the Atlantic. As soon as they had landed, they sang the Doxology and gave praise to God for their deliverance. After resting awhile at Hugg's Tavern, they went to Philadelphia. Who should meet them there but Captain Webb.

J. B. Wakely, Methodist historian, in his centennial sermon at Gloucester Point in 1869 said of Gloucester Point:

> Here they ended their voyage. Here their feet pressed American soil. From that day Gloucester Point is immortal, immortal as the first place in America, where Wesley's first Missionaries landed. It deserves a conspicuous place in the Annals of American Methodism. It should be embalmed in Methodist History.[19]

Richard Boardman was designated Wesley's assistant in charge of the American work. The day following his arrival in Philadelphia, he preached his first sermon in America at the Society's meeting place in Loxley Court.

Then, leaving Pilmore in Philadelphia, he made his way to New York. Stopping in Trenton, he preached his second American sermon to British soldiers in the Presbyterian Church. His real work began once he arrived in New York.

As Wesley's assistant, Boardman insisted that he and Pilmore change stations at least three times a year in the spring, summer and fall. Pilmore did not like this idea, but went along with his friend's plans. Not only was it Boardman's plan to move frequently, but also to make New York and Philadelphia merely the base of operations into the nearby towns and villages. Because Boardman left no Journal, we have only fleeting glimpses of his work. We do know he preached in Trenton, Burlington and Princeton, New Jersey as well as in places around New York and Philadelphia, in Chester, Pennsylvania, and on the western shore of Maryland.

It was also Boardman's plan that sent Pilmore on a year's preaching tour through the south as far as Savannah, Georgia. He himself went to New England where he preached in Providence and Boston. That was in 1772. Asbury's criticism of the preachers' staying in the cities at the expense of the countryside seems a bit harsh.[20]

Joseph Pilmore left a *Journal* so we know much more about him. His first American sermon was preached in Philadelphia. Pilmore liked Philadelphia and was reluctant to leave it as often as Boardman wanted.

Pilmore enjoyed his ministry in America. He says, "God has opened a great and effectual door in this place for the preaching of His Gospel. Of all that I have seen in England and Wales where I have travelled, nothing was equal to this! The Word runs from heart to heart, and from house to house in such a manner that I am filled with wonder and praise."[21] He preached the first sermon in Old St. George's Church, Friday, November 24, 1769. He also celebrated the first love feast in Philadelphia at Old St. George's on Friday, March 23, 1770.

Pilmore's *Journal* records frequent preaching in New Jersey. On his way to Philadelphia from New York in 1770, he preached his first New Jersey sermon in Bordentown, on July 26, in the Baptist Church. The following morning he preached in the town hall at Burlington. Other places he preached in New Jersey were Gloucester Court House, Trenton, Princeton in the College Chapel, Greenwich (Gloucester County), Pennington Presbyterian Church, Somerset, Mount Holly in the Presbyterian Church and the Baptist Church at Pemberton.

The first of January, 1774, Boardman and Pilmore boarded ship at New York and returned to their native land. Boardman resumed his work as a Methodist preacher until his death at Cork, Ireland, September 29, 1782.

Pilmore, too, continued to receive appointments by John Wesley until 1785. That year he suddenly appeared in America where he was ordained Deacon by Bishop Samuel Seabury of the Protestant Episcopal Church, somewhere in Connecticut. Two days later he was ordained Priest. He became rector of three parishes near Philadelphia, Trinity, All Saints and St. Thomas. From 1789 to 1794 he was assistant at St. Paul's in Philadelphia. For ten years, he served Christ Church in New York before being elected rector of St. Paul's, Philadelphia, in 1804. He resigned in 1821 and died July 24, 1825. He was buried in a crypt beneath St. Paul's Church on south Third Street. Although he became an Episcopalian, he remained friendly to the Methodists until the last.[22]

What can be said of these first two Methodist preachers in the United States? First, Boardman was the first appointed leader of American Methodism. Second, they unified the scattered Methodist societies. Third, they instituted Wesley's itinerant plan in America. Fourth, through their travels, Methodist preaching was heard as far north as Boston and as far south as Savannah.

Pilmore records in his *Journal* for Sunday, October 27, 1771, "In the afternoon Messrs. Asbury and Wright, two of our Preachers arrived from Europe to help us in the great work of the Lord."

Francis Asbury is the patron saint of American Methodism. It would be impossible to say too much about him or his work. In the next chapter his work in New Jersey will be told. Here, let us concentrate on a few remarks of a biographical nature and indicate his first work in our State.

His appointment read "America." They called him "this man that rambles through the United States." It was said of him that "he printed the map of his ministry with the hoofs of his horse." He deserves the accolade, "Prophet of the Long Road." Shortly before his death, he told a British correspondent that his mailing address was simply "America." Any postmaster would know that he would soon pass that way.

For forty-five years, this pioneer, circuit-riding bishop was the moving force behind American Methodism. When he set foot in Philadelphia in 1771, there were less than 1,000 Methodists in all the colonies. When he died in 1816 there were more than 200,000.

During his American itinerant ministry, Asbury traveled some 270,000 miles or 6,000 miles a year, mostly on horseback. He rode the circuits from Maine to Georgia, from New Jersey to Kentucky and Tennessee. He preached a total of between 16,000 and 17,000 sermons, an average of one a day. He presided over no less than 224 Annual Conferences and ordained more than 4,000 preachers.

Francis was born August 20, 1745, in Handsworth, Staffordshire, England, near Birmingham, to Elizabeth and Joseph Asbury. Joseph was a middle class farmer and gardener who moved his family to West Bromwich, just west of Birmingham, when Francis was a small boy. The house is still standing. One other child, a daughter, was born to Joseph and Elizabeth. She died at an early age and Franky, as they called him, was raised an only child.

His education was meager, but he loved to read; good books, especially the Bible, were always his friends. He learned to read the Scriptures in their original tongues.

When he was thirteen and a half, Francis was apprenticed at an old Forge owned by a Methodist named Foxall. Soon afterward, Francis was converted. He and his parents joined the Methodists. Francis began publicly to read the

BISHOP FRANCIS ASBURY
"The Lost Portrait"

Bible, pray and occasionally expound Scripture when attending one of his mother's prayer groups. At twenty-one he began to preach. He served in Staffordshire and other adjoining shires, Bedfordshire Circuit and Salisbury Circuit before volunteering to go to America.

Aboard ship, the twenty-six year old Asbury wrote the following: "I will set down a few things that lie on my mind. Whither am I going? To the New World. What to do? To gain honour? No, if I know my own heart. To get money? No! I am going to live to God, and to bring others so to do."[23]

Asbury preached his first sermon in America at Old St. George's Church, October 28, 1771. When he first arrived, Asbury was under the direction of Richard Boardman. About a year later, October 10, 1772, he received a letter from Wesley naming him the assistant in charge. About eight months later he was disappointedly replaced by Thomas Rankin as Wesley's assistant. When Rankin returned to England in 1778, the job as Methodism's number one leader in America was his for keeps for the remaining thirty-nine years of his life.

Francis Asbury established classes, strengthened societies, built churches and encouraged the work of God in scores of places in New Jersey. His first preaching in the state occured while enroute to New York at Burlington on November 6, 1771. "Preached in the court house to a large, serious congregation." Returning to Philadelphia, he preached again in the Burlington Court House on Sunday, March 29, 1772, and the next day in the New Mills Baptist meeting house.

While stationed in Philadelphia in the spring of 1772, he preached often in New Jersey at Burlington, Greenwich (Gloucester County), Thomas Taper's (near Mantua), Isaac Jenkins, Gloucester, New Mills, Haddonfield, Mantua, Trenton, Turner's, Joseph Thorne's, and Amboy.

In the spring of 1773, Asbury again visited the area of Jersey near Philadelphia and remarked in April about seeing the foundation of the new preaching house in Trenton. The first Conference of preachers in America called by Thomas Rankin was held at Old St. George's, July 14 to 16. Asbury was stationed in Maryland. At the second Conference in May of 1774, he was sent to New York. Asbury next preached at Burlington in late November 1774. Most of 1775 he spent in Maryland and Virginia. Asbury's work in America as well as his work in New Jersey was well underway.

The story of one more of Wesley's men in America needs to be told and his work in New Jersey delineated. Thomas Rankin is probably less known by Methodists in America than any of the other early leaders. Even the *Encyclopedia of World Methodism* dismisses him with a very brief paragraph. He surely deserves more because for five years he was Wesley's assistant with the oversight of the Methodist work in America.

By birth, Rankin was a Scotchman. An itinerant preacher for twelve years before coming to America, he was a stern disciplinarian, a fact seen by Wesley as a necessity to give form and stability to the work.

An older man than Asbury and more experienced, Rankin did good work. Within six weeks after his arrival, he summoned all the preachers to Philadelphia for American Methodism's first General Conference which became, through the Annual Conferences, a yearly event. As assistant, Rankin stationed the preachers while remaining himself free to rove about. He was God's man for the time until the Revolution sent him and all the other British preachers home, except Asbury. Rankin returned to England in the spring of 1778 where he served until his death in 1810.

Rankin preached often in New Jersey. Like Asbury, he first preached in Burlington. Wednesday, March 2, 1774, "I set off in a stage boat for Burlington in my way to New York. I preached in the Court House where many of the members of the assembly attended and appeared to hear with Divine seriousness."

His next visit was to a Quarterly Meeting at Mantua Creek, West Jersey. Since this is the first record of a Quarterly Meeting, which we now call Charge Conference, in the state, here is the record as preserved in Rankin's *Diary*:

> Monday. Aug. 15th (1774): I set off, in company with a friend to the Quarterly Meeting at Mantua Creek, West Jersey. I preached in the evening and many were much affected.
>
> Tuesday. Aug. 16th: We began our temporal business early, and at 12 o'clock I preached to a large congregation. After dinner we finished the rest of the business and concluded the day with a love feast. The presence of the Lord crowned our assembly, and many declared what great things the Lord had done for their souls. A blessed work has the God of love wrought in these parts.

The next day Rankin preached in the Greenwich Church. On August 29, he presided over a Quarterly Meeting in Trenton. The next few days he preached "to a genteel congregation near Pennington . . . to a large number in the Baptists Meeting House at New Mills," in the Presbyterian Meeting House in Mount Holly "to an attentive congregation . . . rode to Burlington and preached in the evening. . . . This has been a pleasant excursion to the Jerseys and I hope profitable also."

In November, he again attended Quarterly Meetings at Jesse Chew's near Mantua and at Trenton "for our upper circuit in the Jerseys."

The latter part of May and June 1775, he was again preaching in Jersey. Among other places, he mentioned Hopewell Township about twelve miles from Trenton. In September, he again held Quarterly Meeting at Jesse Chew's and at Trenton in late November.

At various times in 1776, he preached in New Jersey. Late in that year and early in 1777, Rankin spent time with Webb in New Mills because of the "dins of war" about which he constantly complained. In the spring of 1777, while Rankin was in Baltimore, Webb was arrested and Rankin made plans to return to England. The war created much difficulty for American Methodists.[24]

After ten years of Methodism in America, Methodist Societies could be found in New York, New Jersey, Pennsylvania, Delaware, Maryland, and Virginia. The principal meeting houses were John Street in New York, St. George's in Philadelphia and Lovely Lane in Baltimore. Captain Webb had a hand in all of them.

Lay Methodists, principally those converted under Wesley or Wesley's preachers in Ireland, laid the foundation for Methodism. Captain Webb cemented the work together. The preachers who came as Wesley's missionaries to America, chiefly Boardman, Pilmore, Asbury and Rankin, brought unity and order to the work. Circuits were organized, preachers stationed, annual Conferences of preachers started, quarterly circuit meetings arranged, and much preaching done by itinerant circuit riders. The work expanded through the end of 1775.

New Jersey Methodism started about 1769 through the preaching of Captain Webb in Trenton, Burlington and New Mills. It expanded mainly along the Delaware River from Pennington in the north to Mantua in the south. There was Methodist preaching in other places and beginnings of movement farther inland, out from Trenton, Burlington and Greenwich. The state of Methodism in other places where Webb is purported to have preached is not known. The outbreak of the Revolution brought many changes, but the place of Methodism in America and New Jersey was secure. The days of its origin were past.

Chapter 2

THE EARLY YEARS

1776-1799

The Revolution hit New Jersey hard. Because of its strategic location between New York and Philadelphia, it was the arena for contending armies throughout the war. The State has been called the "Cockpit of the Revolution." During three winters, Washington and his army were quartered in New Jersey. On its soil were fought major battles at Trenton, Princeton, Red Bank, Monmouth and Springfield. Numerous other minor skirmishes were fought. It has been said that "no other state so generally and continuously felt the impact of the struggle for independence."[1]

New Jersey was also a divided state. Loyal patriots were in abundance: the men who signed the Declaration of Independence, burned the British Tea at Greenwich in Cumberland County on the night of December 22, 1774, served in the Continental Army or the State Militia, or distinguished themselves as privateers who harassed British shipping. It is estimated that some four thousand men saw service with the Contenental troops and some ten thousand more saw duty with the State Militia.

The King had his Loyalists, too. Tories they were called by the patriots. In fact, one of the bitterest sides of the struggle for Independence was this fratracidal struggle that divided neighbors, churches, and even families. While no estimate can be given as to the actual number of those who sided with the British, "there is basis for belief that New Jersey had as high a proportion of active Loyalists as any other state."[2]

The War was difficult for the Methodists in America. John Wesley in 1775 wrote a tract, "A Calm Address to Our American Colonies." In it he strongly supported the cause of the British government. His conclusion was that the liberty for which the colonists were contending was a liberty from obeying their rightful sovereign and from keeping the fundamental laws of their country. The tract was widely circulated on both sides of the Altantic. Methodists were already suspected of toryism because of their allegience to Wesley in England. Now they were even more suspect.

By 1778, the last of the British preachers had sailed for home. Only Asbury remained, but for two years from 1778 to 1780, he was in virtual seclusion at the Delaware home of Judge Thomas White. Responsibility fell upon the few American preachers to carry on the work as best they could. Although Asbury decried his many "dumb Sabbaths," there were many other times he did preach. Souls were saved through his ministry, and he kept in touch with his preachers. Asbury remained the leader, although a leader-in-exile.

Even the American preachers suffered. Freeborn Garrettson was threatened with personal assault in North Carolina, beaten by a mob in Delaware, and imprisoned in the Maryland town of Cambridge. Philip Gatch was tarred by a mob. Benjamin Abbott barely escaped such a plot in south Jersey. Jesse Lee was drafted into the army and was threatened with court martial for refusing to bear arms. He escaped that fate by offering to do non-combatant service.

The amazing fact is that for most years there was an actual growth in membership in the Methodist Societies. From an approximate membership of three thousand in 1775, there was an increase to five thousand in one year and to almost seven thousand in 1777. A decrease of one thousand showed in the reports in 1778, but thereafter growth was evident.

New Jersey, however, did not fare so well. The first recorded membership statistics for the state in 1773 showed two hundred Methodists. By 1775 there were three hundred. The next year there were only one hundred and fifty, and but ten more in 1777. There are no figures given for 1778 or 1779 and only one hundred and ninety-six recorded for 1780. The following year showed an increase to five hundred and twelve. By 1783 there were over one thousand members in New Jersey.

Rankin's *Journal* relates some of the difficulties brought on in New Jersey by the War. December 1, 1776, he comments: "The noise and tumult occasioned by the British Army marching through the province, and the American Army retiring before them, threw everything into confusion; and made it unsafe for me to travel." Later in December he writes, "This whole month was spent in battles, skirmishes between the British troops and the American. . . . It is a painful time for me, and numbers of pious persons of different denominations." In early 1777 he says, "Had it not been for the noise and din of war, with the confusion that the British and American Armies made, wherever they came, there was before the most pleasing option of doing good in those parts of the Jerseys I had ever seen before."

The one man largely responsible for keeping alive the flame of Methodism in New Jersey during the dark days of the Revolution was Benjamin Abbott. Abbott, in fact, is one of the most unique and important contributions from New Jersey to early American Methodism.

Benjamin Abbott was forty years of age when he was converted by the preaching of Abraham Whitworth in John Murphy's home at Friendship, Pittsgrove Township, Salem County. The date was October 12, 1772.[3] The following February, Philip Gatch, perhaps the first regular itinerant in the state,[4] organized the Methodists of Pittsgrove into a class and appointed Abbott as the leader. The class met in John Murphy's home near where a log meeting house was soon erected, the predecessor of the present Friendship Church. From Pittsgrove, Methodism moved out, largely through Abbott's work, into Salem, Cumberland, Cape May, Atlantic and Ocean Counties.

Prior to his conversion, Abbott, by his own admission, was a drinking, gambling, fighting, swearing man. "I lived," he says, "in sin and open rebellion against God. . . . Yet I worked hard and got a comfortable living for my family." Abbott was born in 1732 in Hunterdon County, New Jersey, the son of Benjamin, Sr. and Hannah Burroughs. As a boy he lived on Long Island and in Pennsylvania. Apprenticed to a hatter, he soon moved to New Jersey to work on his brother's farm. After his marriage to Mary Snook,[5] he rented his own farm near Daretown in Salem County.

Abbott was an unusual man. He had very little education. All he knew was the Bible, and he cared to know little else. He could not speak proper English, but he knew how to bring sinners to Christ. Divine power attended his preaching. His diary is replete with such phrases as "the slain lay all around the house." These things may seem strange to modern ears, but all sorts of physical manifestations accompanied the preaching of Abbott. Sinners would scream for mercy. Men and women would fall prostrate as though dead. Others would run away in dread. The result was that the most wicked sinners were converted. Abel Stevens says, "He crowded the Methodist classes of New Jersey with such souls, reclaimed, purified, and not a few of them for years after his death, models of purest Christian life."[6]

Abbott was not only a hell fire and damnation preacher, but a preacher of holiness. When God saved his soul, he became as much a model of holiness as before he had been of unholiness. He is described as an "uncommon zealot for the blessed work of santification."

After his conversion, Abbott worked for his livelihood during the day, held prayer and class meetings at night, and preached on Sundays. From 1772 to 1789, he was a local evangelist in New Jersey, Pennsylvania and Delaware. In 1789 at the age of fifty-seven, he entered the ranks of the itinerant preachers. He served on the Dutchess, Newburg and Long Island, New York Circuits; the Trenton, Salem and Freehold, New Jersey Circuits; and the Cecil and Kent Circuits on the Eastern Shore. While serving on the Dutchess Circuit one of his converts was the nine year old Elijah Hedding, later a bishop of the Methodist Episcopal Church.

Abbott died on Sunday, August 14, 1796. His last words were "Glory to God! I see heaven sweetly opened before me!" He is buried in the churchyard at First Church, Salem.

One of Abbott's most extensive tours as a "war time evangelist" in New Jersey was in 1778.[7] He began at Port Elizabeth where he says, "we had a powerful time; the slain lay all through the house, and round it, and in the woods, crying to God for mercy; and others praising God for mercy."[8] He preached at Peter Cressy's near Cape May Court House, Nathaniel Champion's and Mr. Smith's near Tuckahoe and at Esquire Champion's and Samuel Hewes near Mays Landing. At the latter Champion's he says, "The meeting began at eleven o'clock in the morning, and lasted until about midnight: before it was over, seven found peace with God, and joined the society."[9]

It is impossible to tell every place Abbott preached. Often he just says, "at my next appointment." He does speak on this 1778 tour of preaching at Waretown, Goodluck and Esquire Akin's on Toms River. He also preached at Trenton, New Mills, Morrestown and at Jesse Chew's on Mantua Creek. Whether the latter were all on the 1778 tour or not is hard to tell.

If the date of 1778 for this preaching tour is correct, Abbott was the first Methodist preacher to preach in Cumberland, Cape May, Atlantic and Ocean Counties.

One other example of Abbott's work is the summary of his accomplishments during the six months he served on the Salem Circuit in 1792.

> I left the circuit after six months, having received eighty-five members into society, and had seen about fifty sanctified, by the mighty power and grace of God, and many others that had been justified. There was a great revival among the classes; may the Lord be mindful of them, and preserve them in his holy fear.[10]

1780 was the year Methodism became firmly established in the southern part of New Jersey which now comprises the Southern New Jersey Conference. In that year, William Gill, John James and Richard Garrettson were appointed to New Jersey.

The War was still on, but Methodism was beginning a new day. The loyalty of the American preachers was no longer suspected. Asbury was able to leave his Delaware hiding place, hold a Conference in Baltimore and visit the southern states. Methodism was set to move forward.

Prospects in New Jersey did not look good, but God was ready to bless. Atkinson in his *Memorials of Methodism in New Jersey* says:

> The condition of the country was not such this year as to render the prospects of religion much more favorable than they had been during the war; the American army of the north being quartered at Morristown in deep privation and distress, and the spirit of the war being rife throughout the province. The winter was terribly severe, so that 'the earth was frozen so deeply that in many places the ground opened in vast chasms, of several yards in length and a foot wide, and three or four feet deep.' It was also difficult to obtain provisions, 'the rivers, creeks, and other waterways were frozen almost to their bottom, so that oxen, and sleds loaded, passed over the water as on solid ground. The birds and the wild animals of the West Jersey forests died in vast numbers.' Notwithstanding the unpropitiousness of the circumstances, the work advanced gloriously this year, and a brighter day than it had ever known dawned upon the infant Methodism of the province. At the close of the year, five hundred and twelve members were reported, which was an increase of three hundred and sixteen, and almost treble the number reported the previous year.[11]

It was probably about the first of May when the three preachers reached New Jersey from Baltimore. The terrible winter was over and the dawn of a new life for Methodism about to begin. William Gill was an eminent preacher mostly in Maryland, Delaware and Virginia. He served from 1777 until his death in 1788. Being the senior of the three preachers, he must have been in charge. Little is known of his work in 1780, but he probably served the area along the Delaware, including Trenton, Burlington and New Mills.

John James was the newest of the three. This was his first year as a preacher and after one more year in Virginia his name disappears from the Minutes. James served that vast area from the Mullica River to the point of Cape May. Since he was serving a sparsely populated and largely new area for Methodism, James is purported to have proceeded like this. Letting his horse take his own course, upon reaching a house, he would tell the family he had come to tell them and their neighbors to prepare to meet their God. If they would invite their neighbors to come on such a day and hour, he, James, would be there with a message from God. As many as would cooperate found him a man of his word.

An often repeated story is the time James reached the house of Captain David Sairs. It was late afternoon and snowing when he arrived to ask for a night's lodging. Realizing the stranger was a Methodist preacher, the Captain paused a long time before replying: "I hate to let you stay the worst of any man I ever saw; but as I never refused a stranger a night's lodging in all my life, you may stay." The preacher stayed. During the course of the evening, the preacher several times rebuked his host for failing to say grace before supper and for swearing. The next morning, James prayed with the family before leaving. However, when he left, the Captain was a converted man. A class was soon formed which in 1792 built the Head of the River Church, today the oldest Methodist Church building in New Jersey.

The third preacher was Richard Garrettson who served as a Methodist circuit rider from 1778 to 1783. He was a brother of the more famous Freeborn Garrettson. Richard served the area between the Mullica and Raritan Rivers and introduced Methodism to the north Jersey shore area. It was at a service held in Job Throckmorton's barn near Adelphia that the first Methodist class in Monmouth County was formed.

Lednum says that Monmouth County preaching places about this time were at Justice Aiken's on Toms River, Long Branch, Freehold and Leonard's. Later, there was preaching at Tuckerton, Squan River, Shark River, Mount Pleasant and Shrewsbury.[12]

The work in New Jersey had sufficiently grown that in 1781 there were two circuits established for the state, the West Jersey and the East Jersey. Caleb B. Pedicord and Joseph Cromwell were appointed to West Jersey. The East Jersey Circuit preachers were James O. Cromwell and Henry Metcalf. It is not now possible to describe the bounds of these circuits. They are named after the old dividing line of the province of New Jersey, although it is certain the circuits did not follow that old political line which went from just north of Tuckerton to a point on the Delaware River opposite Dingman's Ferry, Pennsylvania.

Two interesting incidents occurred in 1781 through the ministry of Caleb Pedicord. The first was the conversion of Thomas Ware. Thomas Ware heads the list of charter members of the New Jersey Conference. Born in Greenwich, Cumberland County on December 19, 1758, he was the son of Thomas and Margaret Reed Ware. A patriot, he saw service during the Revolution as a private in the State Militia. He was converted in Mount Holly under the preaching of Pedicord who later introduced him to Asbury. Asbury gave him his first appointment in 1783 on the Dover, Delaware Circuit. For the next forty-two years, "Father Ware" as he came to be called, served faithfully and well as a circuit rider, missionary to east Tennessee and southwestern Virginia, presiding elder in eight states and from 1812 to 1816, Book Agent of the Church.

REV. THOMAS WARE

Ware attended the Christmas Conference and every succeeding General Conference through 1832. He was the last surviving member of the Conference which organized the Methodist Episcopal Church. He retired in 1825 to his home in Salem, New Jersey, where he died on March 11, 1842. He is buried in the cemetery of First Church, Salem, not far from the grave of Benjamin Abbott. He was married to Barbary Miller of Strasburg, Pennsylvania. They had four children: Frances Lurana, Thomas Asbury, Ann Amanda and Thomas Edwin.

The second incident in connection with Caleb Pedicord in 1781 was quite different. For some years, Joseph Mulliner had earned a reputation as the "bandit of the pines." He and his gang of ruffians terrorized the territory. Mulliner, however, had two weaknesses. He liked women and he liked to dance. He broke into one too many dances. One of the men at the dance left, rounded up a posse, and Joe Mulliner was captured. Taken to Mount Holly, he was imprisoned, tried for his crimes, found guilty and hung. Today at a lonely spot in the pine barrens, a few miles below Batsto, is a solitary grave marker which reads:

> Joe Mulliner
> Hung
> 1781

What the usual stories of Joe do not tell is that in prison, he was visited by Caleb Pedicord and William Budd. They told him of Jesus and his power to save even the vilest of sinners. Joe listened and responded. He died, the preachers testified, a regenerate man.

Through all these early years, Methodism was a religious society, not a church. A few preaching houses or meeting houses were built, but they were not called churches. The preachers were only laymen. Not even Asbury was ordained. The Lord's Supper could not be served, nor could baptism be celebrated. It had been expected by John Wesley that the Methodists would attend the Episcopal Church to receive the Sacraments.

Since the beginning of the Revolution, there were few Episcopal Churches for the Methodist people to attend. Deveraux Jarrett in Virginia and Uzal Ogden in northern New Jersey were about the only two Episcopal priests sympathetic to the Methodist cause. Most Methodists were either denied the Sacraments or else left the Methodists to join another church. Methodists wanted to receive the Sacraments from their own preachers, the very ones who had led them to Christ.

The preachers in the south where Methodism was strongest were especially adamant about serving the Sacraments. They even drew up a plan for their own ordination. Asbury had all he could do to delay them until some definite word and advice could be received from Wesley.

Finally, Wesley acted. Once the Revolution was over, Wesley had a change of heart. He accepted the American victory as a sign of God's providential approval. He believed that since the Americans were now politically free from England, they should have ecclesiastical freedom also. He felt they should have their own church with an ordained ministry, although he firmly expected to be able to give orders as long as he lived.

Wesley tried his best to get one of the English bishops to ordain a man for America. He failed. Accordingly he took it upon himself as a "Scriptural episcopus" to ordain Richard Whatcoat and Thomas Vasey to the orders first of deacon then of elder and to ordain Thomas Coke, already an ordained elder in the Anglican Church, to the office of Superintendent. He would not call him a bishop and did not like it later when Coke and Asbury called themselves by that name.

What Wesley did in addition to the ordinations was to provide for his American friends a form of church government and a revision of the *Book of Common Prayer* into what he called the *Sunday Service*. The *Sunday Service* also included a revision of the Thirty-Nine Articles of Religion which he reduced to twenty-four. Wesley also added *A Collection of Psalms and Hymns for the Lord's Day*.[13] All of these were sent with Coke, Whatcoat and Vasey to America along with a letter addressed "To Dr. Coke, Mr. Asbury, and our Brethren in North America." In this letter he explains what he has done and why and concludes:

> As our American brethern are now totally disentangled both from the State and from the English Hierarchy, we dare not entangle them again either with one or the other. They are now at full liberty simply to follow the Scriptures and the primitive church. And we judge it best that they should stand fast in that liberty wherewith God has so strangely made them free.[14]

Coke and his friends arrived in New York, November 3, 1784. Eleven days later, they met Asbury at Barratt's Chapel, Frederica, Delaware, where Coke administered the first official Methodist Communion Service in America. Coke informed Asbury of Wesley's plans for American Methodism which included Asbury's appointment as joint superintendent with Coke. Asbury refused to accept Wesley's appointment unless it was confirmed by vote of the American preachers. Coke finally agreed. Christmas Eve was set as the date for the Conference to be held in Baltimore at Lovely Lane Meeting House. Freeborn Garrettson was sent out "like lightning" to summon the preachers to Baltimore. He says, "My dear Master enabled me to ride about twelve hundred miles in about six weeks."[15] Jesse Lee, upset at not receiving notice, complained that Garrettson preached too much along the way.

The Christmas Conference met as planned, December 24, 1784 to January 2, 1785. Wesley's letter was read and accepted. Asbury and Coke were elected joint superintendents over the Methodists in America. They soon called themselves bishops. At John Dickins' suggestion, the new church was named the Methodist Episcopal Church. *The Sunday Service of the Methodists in North America,* Wesley's *Prayer Book* revision with its orders and ritual, was accepted, along with the Articles of Religion. To the Articles was added one entitled "Of the Rulers of the United States of America." *A Book of Discipline* was to be drawn up and published by the two bishops.

Three deacons and thirteen elders besides Asbury were elected and ordained. Asbury was ordained deacon on Christmas Day and elder the next. On December 27 he was set apart for the office of superintendent by Coke, assisted by Whatcoat and Vasey and, at Asbury's request, his friend Philip William Otterbein, pastor of the German Church in Baltimore.

Among other decisions, the Conference passed a motion against slaveholding by members of the church and set about the business of organizing Cokesbury College.

No definite list of those present exists. There were probably about sixty, including Thomas Ware from New Jersey. Benjamin Abbott may also have been present.

Methodism in America was now a church, the Methodist Episcopal Church. In the name of the church and the Lord of the church, the preachers went forth from Baltimore to preach the gospel, "reform the continent, and spread Scriptural-holiness over these lands."[16]

Who was this Thomas Coke, Wesley's emissary and newly elected general superintendent with Asbury of Methodism in America? Thomas Coke was born in Brecon, Wales, on September 9, 1747. A graduate of Jesus College, Oxford University, he became an Anglican priest. In 1777, he joined the Methodists and became Wesley's trusted assistant.

Between 1784 and 1803 he made nine visits to America, no small feat in itself. None of his visits were long. He presided over the Christmas Conference, but Asbury usually saw to it that Coke only assisted him in other Conferences when he was in America. He served effectively to link British and American Methodists and was much respected by his American friends. On his last visit to America, he preached before the Congress of the United States. He was a worthy leader who deserves a high place in the annals of Methodism.

In England, Coke became a leader of Methodism after Wesley's death. He served repeatedly as the Conference Secretary and twice as its President. Among other publications, he authored a *Commentary on the Bible* and a *History of the West Indies*. Known as the "Father of Methodist Missions," he died on May 3, 1814, while on a voyage to take Christ to India. He was buried in the Indian Ocean.

After the meeting of Coke and Asbury at Barratt's Chapel prior to the Christmas Conference, Asbury sent Coke with black Harry Hosier as his guide on a preaching tour of the Delmarva Peninsula. Thomas Ware met Coke there and made this observation:

> Dr. Coke, on his way to the Christmas Conference, passed through our circuit. I met him at Col. Hopper's, in Queen Anne's, on the Eastern Shore of Maryland, and was not at first sight at all pleased with his appearance. His stature, his complexion, and his voice, were those of a woman rather than of a man; and his manners were too courtly for me. . . . He had several appointments on our circuit, to each of which I conducted him; and before we parted I saw many things in him to admire, and no longer marvelled as at first, at the selection the father of the Methodists had made of a man to serve us in the capacity he sustained.[17]

Not all of the *Journals* of Coke are available. From those that are, we have a record of several visits to New Jersey.

> Monday Jan. 7, 1785. I left New York: and on Tuesday 8, reached Trent-Town (State of Jersey). There I had but a small congregation, and about 20 hearers in the morning. Wednesday 9. I went to Burlington. The Vestry opened to me the church [St. Mary's], and some of the first men of the State came to hear me. Mr. S- R- formerly one of our Trenton preachers, and a very zealous man, but now a prophesier of smooth things, has been appointed a reader and preacher in this church by the convention of the clergy of the Church of England. He expects to be ordained as soon as they have a Bishop.
> Thursday 10. Mount Holly. Here is another preacher appointed by the Convention who was also formerly one of our travelling-preachers, (Mr. Sprague), a genuine Christian.

> Friday 11. New Mills. My congregation in this Chapel was not large, but very serious. Surely this place will have much to answer for.[18]

In 1789, Coke attended a Conference in Trenton.

His other visit to New Jersey occurred on Thursday, November 29, 1792. "I preached in the Church of Mr. Ogden of Newark, New Jersey, a truly pious clergyman of the Church of England."[19]

Four weeks after George Washington had been inaugurated President of the United States, a Methodist Conference was held in New York City. Asbury asked "Whether it would not be proper for us, as a church, to present a congratulatory address to General Washington in which should be imbodied our approbation of the constitution, and professing our allegiance to the government." It was agreed. Thomas Morrell, who knew Washington personally, and John Dickins made arrangements for the visit and accompanied Asbury and Coke on June 2 to see the President. Morrell tells us that Asbury read the address "in an impressive manner," and the President delivered his reply "with fluency and animation."[20]

A few days before the visit to Washington, Bishops Asbury and Coke attended the first Methodist Conference ever held in New Jersey at First Church, Trenton. The Conference was held on Saturday and Sunday, May 23 and 24, 1789. Probably only the New Jersey preachers were present as a Conference in Philadelphia preceded and one in New York followed. We do know that Benjamin Abbott and Richard Swain were received on trial at the Trenton Conference.

Asbury's brief comments are: "Friday, 22. We rode to Trenton; and on Saturday, 23, opened our conference in great peace. We laboured for a manifestation of the Lord's power, and it was not altogether in vain.

"Sunday, 24. We had an abundance of preaching."[21]

Coke says a bit more.

> In our Conference which began in Trenton, on the 23d, for the State of New Jersey, all the preachers seemed full of love. The few friends we have in this town, did everything, I believe, that they could conceive, to make us comfortable: but, alas! the work is, and ever has been, at a very low ebb in this place. The numbers in Jersey are 1,751: here also has been a decrease of 295. This will necessarily happen sometimes in so extensive a work; yea, where the ministers have been most faithful. Rotten members, be they ever so numerous, must be lopped off, or we should soon become like other men. We have three Indians in this district: and who knows but they are the first fruits of a glorious harvest among that people.[22]

These three were the only Indian members listed for the entire church.

The appointments for the year were for the following circuits: Salem, Trenton, Burlington, Flanders and Elizabethtown. Salem had the most members, 680 white and 24 colored.

The only other Conference of record in New Jersey prior to 1800 was at Burlington, September 27-30, 1790. Asbury said the Conference was in great peace and harmony. He preached at least three times and presided over a love feast. He speaks of revival in most of the circuits. There was also trouble as a mob broke out the windows of the meeting house on Tuesday night. Asbury said, "It is well my head escaped the violence of these wicked sinners."[23]

A Conference was called for New Mills, July 12, 1792. Asbury was in the vicinity on that date, but says nothing about a Conference.

Methodism continued to grow in New Jersey. At the time of the Christmas Conference there were 963 Methodists recorded in the state. At the century's end, there were 2,725 white and 167 colored members for a total of 2,892. Methodism was expanding across New Jersey as this table of Circuits shows.

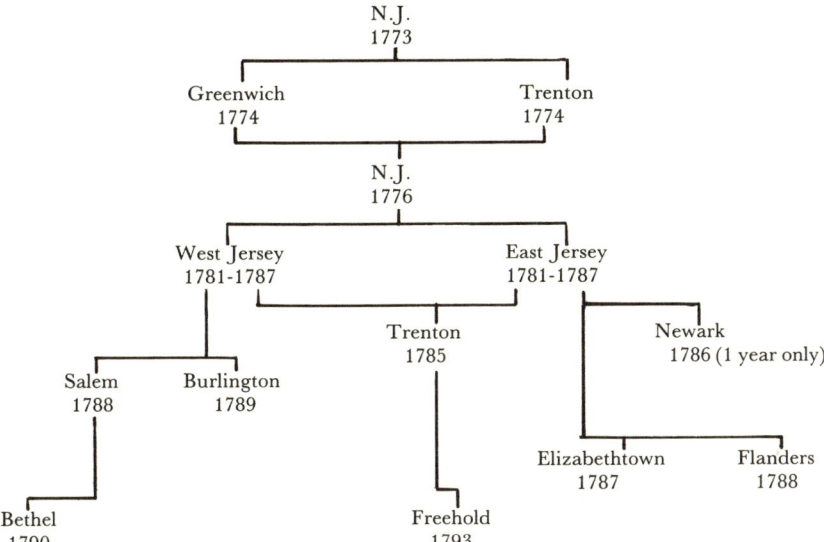

Membership Statistics in 1799 for the area now comprised by the Southern New Jersey Conference were:

Circuit	White	Colored
Bethel	741	27
Burlington	569	30
Freehold	328	29
Salem	504	57
Trenton	167	13
Total	2,309	156

THE EARLY YEARS / 29

In northern New Jersey there were two Circuits:

Circuit	White	Colored
Elizabethtown	201	7
Flanders	215	4
Total	416	11

Ezekiel Cooper preached on the East Jersey District in 1786. George Phoebus in *Beams of Light on Early Methodism in America* quotes extensively from Cooper's diary and lists twenty-seven preaching places on the circuit. At least seven of them were in New York State's Orange County, which later became the nucleus of the Newburg Circuit. Some of the places were at persons' homes not now identifiable. We do know Cooper preached in the following places: Flanders, Basking Ridge, near Clinton, near Blairstown, near Dover, Vernon Township, Wantage, Frankford Plains, Newton, Lockwood, Hackettstown, Finesville and Everittstown.[24]

The following year the twenty-four year old Cooper was preaching on the Trenton Circuit. He was one of the giants of early Methodism. He preached on circuits, pastored churches and served as a presiding elder from South Carolina to Massachusetts. For ten years, he was Book Editor of the Church, a very important position. Living to be eighty-four, he was supposed to be, at the time of his death, the oldest Methodist preacher in the world.

There were forty-eight preaching places on the Trenton Circuit where Cooper and his associate, Nathaniel B. Mills preached. It was a six week circuit. That means it took each preacher six weeks, preaching at least once a day, to make a complete round of the circuit. Since they would usually rest a week or two after completing a circuit, preaching only in the area around the Delaware, that meant the more distant parts of the circuit, such as along the shore, would see a preacher only about once every four weeks.

This vast circuit included what is now Mercer, Burlington, Ocean and Monmouth Counties plus parts of Middlesex and Hunterdon. There was preaching at Burlington, Crosswicks, Freehold, Kingston, Princeton, Titusville, Pennington, Hopewell, Wrightstown, Trenton, Burlington, Mount Holly, New Mills, Browntown, Speedwell Furnace, Bodine's, Batsto, Tuckerton, Manahawkin, Waretown, Good Luck, West Long Branch, Colt's Neck, Bass River, Toms River, Cranbury, Shrewsbury, Pleasant Valley, Middletown Point, Adelphia and Hightstown.[25] Other places could be identified if it were known where the people lived.

Cooper describes a quarterly meeting (what we now call Charge Conference) held in Manahawkin, Saturday and Sunday, February 9 and 10. The Sunday Service began with a love feast between nine and ten o'clock and lasted until after eleven.

Then the sacrament of the Lord's Supper was administered; public preaching began after twelve o'clock. We had a glorious time, especially in the close of our meeting. The power of God came down in the most powerful manner that I have ever seen in the State of New Jersey. It is said to have been the greatest time that has ever been known in this circuit. All ranks appeared to be in tears; many were overcome in such a manner that they could scarcely stand; some found Jesus, one man crying out to the congregation to help him to praise the Lord, for he had found him whom his soul loved. This increased the flame, and it ran through the house as fire among stubble. Soon as he ceased to speak a boy of about sixteen years of age broke out in prayer, after which we concluded our meeting.[26]

The oldest circuit record in New Jersey and one of the oldest to be found anywhere is the Steward's Book for Salem Circuit, May 17, 1789 to March 26, 1814. It records the collections received at the Quarterly Meetings from the classes and societies of the Circuit. In 1789, Salem Circuit comprised all of what is now Salem, Gloucester, Camden, Cumberland, Cape May and Atlantic Counties. Joseph Cromwell, John Cooper and Nathaniel Mills were the preachers. James Oliver Cromwell was the presiding elder. Most of the classes are listed by a person's name. Many, but not all, can be identified. In 1789, Methodism could be found in these places: Salem, Stow Creek, Woodruff, Newport, Port Elizabeth, Mays Landing, Delmont, Eldora, Cape May Court House, Tuckahoe, English Creek, Friendship near Monroeville, Malaga, Bethel Hurffville, Clonmell, Greenwich in Gloucester County, Deerfield, Sharptown and Penns Neck.

When Bethel Circuit was formed in 1790, the classes in Atlantic, Gloucester and Camden Counties were removed from the Salem Circuit.

Extant diaries of two circuit riders help us fill in some important gaps in our knowledge of south Jersey Methodism. Rev. Richard Sneath, born in Ireland, December 2, 1751, came to America in 1774 and became a Methodist in 1782. In 1796, at the age of forty-five, having a large family, he began his work as a preacher. His diary is published in *The History of Bethel M. E. Church, Hurffville*. It covers his work of 1798-1799 on the Bethel Circuit and 1799-1800 on the Burlington Circuit.

His route while on the Bethel Circuit went down the Tuckahoe Road to Doughty's Tavern, over to Mays Landing, down to English Creek, Bargaintown and Absecon to Port Republic, then up to Batsto, through Egg Harbor and up the present Route 30 to Tansboro, Williamstown and Bethel. From there he traveled to Barnsboro, Clonmell, Sandtown, Swedesboro and Clarksboro.[27]

The Burlington Circuit traveled by Sneath took in Burlington and Ocean Counties. This large circuit traversed the pine barrens. His first tour of the circuit took him from Moorestown, Burlington, Lumberton, Mount Holly, to Buddtown, Browns Mills, Pemberton, then to Bodines (Wading River), Lower Bank, New Gretna and Tuckerton. Sneath then moved up to Manahawkin, Waretown, Good Luck, Toms River and Silverton. From there the circuit rider rode back to Pemberton and on to Burlington for a quarterly meeting.[28]

The other circuit rider's journal is that of Richard Swain. He is a descendent of an old Cape May County family and grew up in the Head of the River area. Born in 1763, he was converted at the age of nineteen and was received into the ministry on trial with Benjamin Abbott at the Trenton Conference of 1789. He served circuits mostly in New Jersey until 1803. He purchased a home on the old Cape Road near Cumberland where he died in 1808, three days short of his forty-fifth birthday. Richard, his wife Charity, and their daughter Hannah, are all buried in the Port Elizabeth Methodist Cemetery.

The Archives of the Southern New Jersey Conference contains the *Journal* of Richard Swain from November 4, 1791 to May 13, 1793. The portion containing his six months on the Salem Circuit in 1792 has been published by the Conference Historical Society. Salem, Cumberland and Cape May Counties comprised the circuit then. It is a valuable first hand account of an early circuit rider.

He tells of the building of Head of the River Church near Tuckahoe, and the dedication of Murphy's new church at Friendship. He talks about his family, of being lost in the glade near Heislerville, contending with the Calvinists in Fairton, beset with swarms of south Jersey mosquitoes, a hail storm near Bridgeton which broke fifteen thousand to sixteen thousand panes of glass, his correspondence with Charity Miller whom he later married, and his scores of preaching opportunities from Penns Neck to Cape May.

HEAD OF THE RIVER CHURCH - 1792
Oldest United Methodist Church Building in N.J.

Head of the River Church, built in 1792, is today the oldest Methodist Church building in New Jersey. Others, however, were built before it. Where were these early Methodist Churches? Trenton, Greenwich near Clarksboro, and Bethel Hurffville all claim dates of 1772 or 1773. Pennsville, New Mills and Pennington also built churches in the 1770's and there may have been one at Friendship in Salem County. The 1780's saw churches built at Centerton, Salem, Port Elizabeth, Burlington and Crosswicks. The 1790's witnessed churches erected at Head of the River, Auburn, Cumberland, Sharptown, Old Stone Church near Swedesboro, Smithville in Atlantic County, Adelphia, New Brunswick, Emley's Hill, Wrightstown, English Creek, and Etra near Hightstown. Bargaintown had a church as did Pleasant Mills, though they were not erected by the Methodists.[29]

In the northern part of Jersey, Methodist churches were built prior to 1800 in Frankford Plains, Flanders, Asbury and Waldwick.[30]

Francis Asbury continued to visit New Jersey. Altogether he crisscrossed the state many times and spent some 511 days here. He did not always like what he found such as the mob in Burlington who broke out the church windows. In 1782, he wrote of Trenton, "Ah, poor Gospel-hardened Trenton! But a few have been converted of late." Traveling through the pine barrens in September of 1786 he writes, "Since this day week we have ridden about one hundred and fifty miles over dead sands, and among a dead people, and a long space between meals." On that same trip, in Cape May County he complains, "My soul is under deep exercise on account of the deadness of the people and my own want of fervour and holiness of heart."

On a visit to the Jersey Shore in September of 1795, Asbury writes under the date of the 28th:

> I was shocked at the brutality of some men who were fighting, one gouged out the other's eye; the father and son then beset him again, cut off his ears and nose, and beat him almost to death. The father and son were tried for a breach of the peace, and roundly fined; and now the man that hath lost his nose and ears is to come upon them for damage. I have often thought that there are some things practiced in the Jerseys which are more brutish and diabolical than in any of the other States: there is nothing of this kind in New England: they learn civility there at least.

Yet many good things merited Asbury's praise. There was a revival of religion in the 1790's. September 5, 1791, he writes, "There is some stir among the people, at Long Branch, within eighteen months, as I am informed, nearly fifty souls have professed conversion." At New Brunswick in 1797, he "rejoiced to hear that God had kindled a living fire here."

Two of Asbury's more extensive early tours in New Jersey were in 1785 and 1791. In 1785, he left New York on September 7. That evening he preached in an unfinished Presbyterian Church in Elizabeth. Two days later he attended a funeral in the Tennent Presbyterian Church near Freehold. The next day, a Saturday, he preached at Monmouth, probably in Adelphia. For the next week, there are no journal entries. Asbury must have traveled down the Jersey coast, through Batsto and Atlantic County for his next appointment on the 17th is at "Morris's River," or Port Elizabeth, Cumberland County. Saturday and Sunday he preached in an unfinished church there.

On Wednesday the 21st, he rode to brother Fisler's, probably in Clayton, where "I received my wagon for forty-four pounds. Will it not bring me into trouble in traveling, and in getting horses?" Asbury bought a "Jersey Wagon" to travel in. Forty-four pounds was a sizable sum of money. Friends must have contributed to its cost, and no doubt urged him to take it. He didn't keep his wagon long. On November 9, he sold it in Annapolis, Maryland.

After Clayton, Asbury preached at Salem, Stow Creek, and stopped overnight at Gloucester. He says, "I plunged H. T. and S. M. in Salem Creek: this unusual baptismal ceremony might, perhaps, have made our congregation larger than it would otherwise have been."

Asbury's 1791 tour again found him riding down the coast. He preached on September 5 in Monmouth County and September 6 at Kettle Creek or Silverton. The next day he was at Potter's Church or Good Luck Chapel between Lanoka Harbor and Forked River. Two days later, he preached at Tuckerton. Saturday he "rode a dreary, mosquito path, in great weakness, to Batsto works." Sunday, he preached there and "advised the people to build a house for the benefit of those men so busily employed day and night, Sabbaths not excepted, in the manufacture of iron — rude and rough, and strangely ignorant of God."

From Batsto he went to Mays Landing and then to Bethel Hurffville. There he preached and administered the Sacrament. Asbury was fulfilling his motto, "Live or die, I must ride." Nearly all the circuit riders felt the same way.

Methodism in New Jersey had become firmly established and was growing. The next three decades would see smaller circuits and even some stationed churches. Days of revival and camp meetings were coming. Glorious days were ahead. Some wonderful things would be wrought by God.

Chapter 3

CIRCUITS - CIRCUIT RIDERS - CLASS LEADERS

1800-1829

The early decades of the nineteenth century were the years of the presidencies of Jefferson, Madison and Monroe, known as the Jeffersonian era. The purchase of Louisiana from France in 1803 more than doubled the size of the United States. Vast sections of the country were opened for the pioneer settlers. Peace was interrupted by the war with the Barbary Pirates in the early 1800's and the War of 1812. The promulgation of the Monroe Doctrine in 1823, making clear that America would not tolerate any outside interference in the Western Hemisphere, made the United States a nation with whom others had to reckon.

Population grew slowly but steadily during these years. The wave of immigration was in the future. America was still a largely agrarian nation. Until 1815, most of our manufactured goods were imported from Europe since almost all American manufacturing was done in the home. After 1815, small factories were built. Most of these were operated by waterpower.

The population of New Jersey in 1800 was only a little more than 200,000 which included over 12,000 slaves. By 1830, the population increased only about 100,000. There were still over 2,000 slaves. New Jersey was still largely a rural state. The state had a reputation for having the worst roads along the Atlantic seacoast. It was not until 1829 that the legislature passed an act establishing the first common schools.

Methodism grew phenomenally during this period. By 1830, the Methodists and the Baptists both had about 2700 churches, far outdistancing the other denominations. In 1800, there were 64,894 Methodists in twenty states, territories and Canada. By 1830, the increase was nearly eight fold, to over 475,000 members, not including Canada. New Jersey reported in 1800 a membership of 2857 white and 173 colored. Thirty years later there were 13,711 white and 488 colored members in the state. However, over half of all the New Jersey Methodists were on the West Jersey District which comprised Burlington and Ocean Counties and those to the south.

Wallace Jamison in his book, *Religion in New Jersey,* bears out the fact that

> It was in South Jersey that Methodism made its greatest advance. The mobility of the circuit system, the informality of worship, the joyous quality of its hymnody appealed to the rural inhabitants and made possible the establishing of chapels where other denominations hesitated to penetrate. Even more important, the practice of training preachers during the course of their ministerial service meant that the Methodists could expand the number of their ministers much more rapidly than either the Presbyterians or Episcopalians.[1]

Methodists have always been known for their organizational genius. It was their way of organizing and getting at things that contributed markedly to their strength and was a decided asset in their growth.

In spite of the individualism inherent in Methodism, the fact remains that in practice Methodism was essentially social. Christian fellowship was always stressed. There developed, therefore, within Methodism, certain definite institutional forms whose purposes were to create, develop and deepen the expressions of Christian fellowship. These organized units of fellowship within the church were the Class, the Society and the Band; and they were usually formed in that order. Sometimes, though, a Society would be formed first and then divide into Classes.

Every Methodist belonged to a Class, small groups of Christian believers who met weekly at a stated time, usually in some member's home. Under the direction of the leader appointed by the circuit rider, the members would testify, pray, and exhort one another, each concerned with "how does your soul prosper?" Frequently, offerings would be received to defray some of the expenses of the larger Society. The Class thus not only aided the members' spiritual growth, but provided mutual support and assistance in any time of need. The Class Leader assumed a role of prominence in early Methodism. Collectively, the Class Leaders knew what was happening within the local Society. If the circuit rider did not have time to meet individually with the Classes, he would meet with the Class Leaders. Within this period there developed the Leaders and Stewards Meeting, forerunner of the present Administrative Board. It needs to be born in mind that in seeking to establish the beginning date of Methodism in a particular locale, the thing to look for is the establishing of the first Class out of which came the Society.

The Society was the officially organized group to which a member belonged. Often, in the early days, as the size of the Class grew and more Classes were formed, the Classes together would make up and form the Society. Even long after the establishment of the Church in 1784, the local unit was still called a Society. The earliest definition of a Methodist Society was "a company of men having the form and seeking the power of godliness." The members were united to "help each other to work out their salvation." It was the Society which would in time elect trustees and build a church.

The Bands were never so popular nor as widespread as the Classes. They were meant to be an inner fellowship of the Society, composed of those zealously striving after holiness or Christian perfection. No Band was to have fewer than five nor more than ten members. Men, women and unmarried persons were to be in separate Bands.

This, then, was the local unit of Methodism. The Society was divided into Classes with every member a member of a Class, and Bands to which those who chose could belong.

In addition to the Class Leader, there were also Exhorters and Local Preachers. Exhorters were licensed yearly by the Quarterly Conference. The Exhorter could lead prayer meetings, give brief messages and assist the preacher much as a lay speaker does today. Often it was the first step for a young man entering the Christian ministry.

If an Exhorter felt called to preach he could apply to the Quarterly Conference for a license to preach, called a Local Preacher's License. A Local Preacher could be ordained as a Local Deacon or Elder and many were. They were, however, but part-time preachers. They would engage full time in their secular livelihood and preach on occasion when called upon. In early Methodism the Local Preacher or even Exhorter would fill in for the circuit rider the appointments on his circuit he could not fill.

In early Methodism the role of the layman was an important one. He filled the office of Class Leader, Exhorter and Local Preacher and along with the circuit preacher and the elected circuit stewards constituted the membership of the Quarterly Conference, the official business meeting of the entire circuit. They met quarterly under the leadership of the presiding elder. Men also served locally as trustees.[2]

Some examples will help show the role certain families played in early New Jersey Methodism. First is the Murphy family of Pittsgrove and Cumberland County. Mention has already been made of John Murphy, an outstanding Christian layman. An elder in the Pittsgrove Presbyterian Church at Daretown, he was the first from that vicinity to open his home to the Methodist itinerant. It was at his home that Abraham Whitworth preached the sermon that became the means for the conversion of Benjamin Abbott. It was in John Murphy's home that the first class in Salem County was organized. On land owned by Murphy, the Murphy Meeting House was erected. He was licensed as a local preacher soon after the Revolution.

Murphy's daughter Sarah married Michael Swing. They moved to Cumberland County about 1790 and settled in the Fairfield area now known as Fairton. The following year, 1791, Michael was licensed to preach by John Merrick, the presiding elder. He was later ordained deacon and then elder. The record of the many Cumberland County marriages he performed is on file at Fairton Church. John Murphy moved to Fairton to live with his daughter and son-in-law.

These two local preachers, Murphy and Swing, began preaching in the area around Fairfield and Bridgeton. They organized a class in New Englandtown, another old name for Fairton, in 1791. The class met in the Swing home. Later, a church long known as the Swing Meeting House was built on his property.

These two men were the first, besides Francis Asbury, to preach in Bridgeton. As a result of their labors, particularly that of John Murphy, a class was organized in Bridgeton in 1804 and a church built four years later. Michael Swing was a trustee of this, the First Methodist Episcopal Church of Bridgeton.

John Murphy was the founding layman of Methodism in Pittsgrove and Bridgeton. Michael Swing was the same in Fairton and was also for many years one of the leading layman on the old Cumberland Circuit.

A second family is the Blackman family of Atlantic County. Andrew Blackman, a cordwainer and staunch Presbyterian, deeded the ground for the Blackman Meeting House. Later, it became Methodist and was located on the property of what is now Zion Church in Bargaintown. Andrew had a son David who married Mary Scull. David was one of the earliest Methodists of Atlantic County. He and his wife, Mary, had ten children, three of whom, Nehemiah, Learner and Sarah, along with their father, made significant contributions to Methodism in Atlantic County and elsewhere.

There is no record of how David became a Methodist. However, his home in English Creek was a favorite preaching place for all the early Methodist itinerants. Benjamin Abbott preached there. It was a station on the Salem and Bethel Circuits. Bishop Asbury also preached at David Blackman's and was entertained by this gracious host.

David and Mary's eldest son, Nehemiah, was, according to local tradition, converted at about the age of thirteen at his father's home by Francis Asbury. He married Sarah Smith, daughter of Captain Micajah Smith of Wrangelboro, now Port Republic, and moved there. Following a revival in 1796, a class was formed with Nehemiah as leader. For the next fifty-two years, Nehemiah Blackman served as a leader of Methodism in Port Republic.

A much more famous son was Learner. Learner Blackman was converted by the first sermon ever preached by his brother-in-law, the Rev. John Collins, in 1797. In 1800 he became a Methodist preacher and served on the Kent and Dover Circuits in Maryland and Delaware, the New River and Holston Circuits in Virginia and Tennessee, the Lexington, Kentucky Circuit and the Natchez, Mississippi Mission. In 1806, at the age of twenty-five, Asbury appointed him a presiding elder. He served on the Mississippi, Holston, Cumberland and Nashville Districts. He was the first presiding elder ever to appear in the states of Mississippi, Louisiana, Alabama and Florida. Learner drowned while crossing the Ohio River from Cincinnati in 1815.

Bishop Asbury said of Learner Blackman, "He has been raised up from small appearances — possibly, to very considerable consequences." This son of New Jersey was a leader of early Methodism in the west, one of the founders of Methodism in Mississippi and Louisiana, and one of the founders of the Holston and Tennessee Conferences.[3]

David and Mary Blackman's daughter, Sarah, became a Methodist preacher's wife. Not long after her marriage to John Collins of Smithville, Atlantic County, John was called to preach. The conversion of Learner Blackman at his first sermon sealed for John the reality of his call. In 1803, John and Sarah moved to Clermont County, Ohio, not far from Cincinnati. While maintaining his home there and raising a family, he preached and served as a presiding elder. He is credited with founding Methodism in Cincinnati and is to be listed as one of the founders of the Methodist Church in the Northwest Territory.

Another family of note in south Jersey Methodist circles is the Swain family who lived in the vicinity of Head of the River. Head of the River is in Atlantic

County at the juncture of Cape May and Cumberland Counties. Four sons of Richard Swain played an active role in early Methodist history in Head of the River, Maurice River Township, Cape May County and beyond.

Judah was the eldest of the four Swain boys. He continued to live at Head of the River and was a trustee of the church there when it was built in 1792.

A second brother, Joab, lived in Leesburg. His home was a preaching place on the Salem Circuit in 1791. When the Society was organized a few years later it, too, met in his home. In 1811, he and his wife Phebee sold to the trustees of the Society for a nominal sum the ground for the building of the Leesburg Church.

The other two brothers, Richard and Nathan, are better known. Already mentioned is Richard's work as a circuit rider. He preached mostly in New Jersey, but also in New England.

Nathan Swain, too, became a preacher of the Gospel in New Jersey. He served as a preacher from 1799 to 1816. After retiring from traveling as a preacher, he continued to serve his Lord until his death twenty-nine years later.[4]

Another layman of particular prominence was Captain James Sterling of Burlington. Atkinson says, "Probably no layman in the State ever did more to advance the cause of religion and Methodism than Mr. Sterling." He and Benjamin Abbott, who led him to Christ, were particularly close. They sometimes traveled together. At one time he was mayor of Burlington and a leading merchant of that city. Sterling contributed much toward the building of Methodist churches in New Jersey and his name frequently appears as a trustee.

In his funeral sermon, Ezekiel Cooper says of James Sterling:

> It is supposed and believed that he has entertained in his house and contributed towards the support of more preachers of the gospel than any other man in the State, if not in the United States; and that he has done as much, if not more, in temporal supplies towards the support of religion, than any other man in the circle of our knowledge. . . . His heart, his purse, and his house were open to entertain, not only his acquaintences, but, to show hospitality to strangers; particularly to those who came in the name of the Lord.[5]

This chapter has been dealing with what we call the structures of Methodism or the Methodist way. We have dealt with the Class, Society and Band, have touched upon the role of the Class Leader, Exhorter and Local Preacher, and have illustrated the role of the layman.

Methodism has always regarded itself as a connectional church; that is, no Methodist Church stands alone. Each one is related to every other. When a person becomes a member of a local United Methodist Church, she or he also becomes a member of United Methodism. This fact was very clear in early Methodism. There was no such thing as a church having its own pastor in New Jersey until Trenton became a stationed church, 1818 to 1820. In 1821 it was linked with Bloomsburg. In 1823, Bridgeton became a stationed church with Charles Pitman as minister. Salem became a station in 1825. Trenton again became a station in 1827 with William Thatcher as minister. Previous to that, every society was part of a much larger circuit. One, two and sometimes three preachers, circuit riders, so called because they rode the rounds of the circuit on their horse, were assigned to the circuit.

Each circuit was part of a district presided over by what we call a district superintendent, but who then were known as presiding elders. Ever since the Christmas Conference, each elder was assigned to supervise so many circuits and their preachers. These elders were first called presiding elders in 1789, but not again until 1797. It was not until 1801 that the districts were named. All of New Jersey that year was one district, the New Jersey District, with Solomon Sharp as the presiding elder.

Districts make up an Annual Conference. Asbury held yearly conferences with his ministers in various parts of the connection. Only at the 1796 General Conference were six Annual Conferences established and their bounds defined. The six original Conferences were New England, Philadelphia, Baltimore, Virginia, South Carolina and Western. New Jersey remained a part of the Philadelphia Conference until 1836. It was and is to the Annual Conference that every preacher is accountable. Methodist ministers' church membership is in the Annual Conference, not in a local church. Annual Conference was for most of Methodist history a conference of ministers only. Laity could and did attend public worship services, but only the clergy had a voice or vote in the business sessions.

The meetings that brought large gatherings of Methodists together were the Quarterly Meetings led by the presiding elder. These would usually be held for two or three days. Besides the business sessions the meetings included a love feast and the celebration of the Sacrament plus other preaching. In time, one of the Quarterly Meetings would continue for a longer period of time in the form of a camp meeting. It is difficult to imagine now the excitement and the enthusiasm of a Methodist Quarterly Meeting. It was not unusual to find hundreds of people traveling many miles for the fellowship and the inspiration of these Quarterly Meetings.

Methodism has always been an organized way. More importantly, Methodism has been a way of experience—Christian experience. To John Wesley, the vital center of the Christian religion was a conscious, dynamic, verifiable experience. The message of early American Methodism was a message of God's grace and freedom in Jesus Christ that led to conversion, assurance and perfect love.

Methodism was evangelistic. "You have nothing to do but to save souls," Wesley said to his preachers. The only condition required of those seeking admission to the Methodist Societies was "a desire to flee from the wrath to come and be saved from their sins." The Methodist preacher was always preaching for conversion. He was equally ready to give an account of his own soul's salvation.

Bishop Asbury says, "On a certain time when . . . I was praying in . . . my father's barn . . . the Lord pardoned . . . my sins and justified . . . my soul."[6]

Thomas Ware found Christ through the preaching of Caleb Pedicord at Mount Holly. He says:

> Mr. Pedicord returned again to our village. I hastened to see him, and tell him all that was in my heart. He shed tears over me, and prayed. I was dissolved in tears. He prayed again. My soul was filled with unutterable delight. He now rejoiced over me as a son—'an heir of God, and a joint heir with Christ.' I felt and knew that I was made free. And, as I had been firm in my attachment to civil freedom, I did hope that I should be enabled to stand fast in the liberty wherewith Christ had made me free.[7]

There was power in the personal testimony of one who had found Christ and had been saved from all sin. It was the dynamic of this preaching of free grace to all that won for Methodism a hearing everywhere. It was true, the Methodist preacher proclaimed, that everyone was lost and needed to be saved; but unlike the Calvinist preachers who taught that only some could be saved, the Methodist with one voice announced that all could be saved. Methodism had no aristocracy consisting of the few who could be saved. There might be only a few saved, but everyone needed to know he could be saved. It was by this means of conversion that most early Methodists entered the fold of the church. Circuit riders reported the numbers of their conversion. Well into the twentieth century the presiding elders in their report to Annual Conference told the number of conversions in the churches of their District.

Methodists believed that everyone could be saved. They also believed that everyone could be sure of their soul's salvation. It is the blessed doctrine of assurance. "The Spirit himself bearing witness with our spirit that we are children of God."[8] For many, this assurance was simultaneous with their conversion. For others, it was a later work of grace. Yet, it was part of the experience of Methodism that God's grace would confirm to each of his children the assurance of the salvation of their soul.

Nor was this all. Once having entered into the life of faith through conversion, the believer was encouraged to consider the yet more glorious privileges offered to him in the gospel. Perfect love, sanctification, holiness of heart and life were ever urged on the believer. No one should be satisfied merely claiming an experience of salvation. There was more. There was a deeper work of grace. As Wesley said, one should strive to be not "almost a Christian," but "altogether Christian!"

Learner Blackman of New Jersey wrote to Bishop Asbury from his Lexington Circuit in Kentucky, March 20, 1804: "The work is still spreading in that part of the circuit. The old professors in general are stirred up to seek for perfect love. I have frequently tried to preach on it latterly. Numbers have obtained it, and are now flaming in religion, while others are pressing after it."[9]

Richard Whatcoat, first after Asbury to be elected bishop of the Methodist Episcopal Church, says that it was in his twenty-fifth year on March 28, 1761 that the coveted gift came:

> Suddenly I was stript of all but love. I was all love, and prayer and praise. And in this happy state, rejoicing evermore, and in everything giving thanks. I continued for some years; wanting nothing for soul or body, more than I received from day to day.[10]

Twenty-nine years later he could testify to the reality of the same experience. He wrote, "I bless God. For almost an uninterrupted peace and communion with God" through the course of the last year. The Methodists believed God's grace could bring all to that same experience.

The dynamics of early Methodism was in its preaching of God's free grace in Jesus Christ to everyone. Its strength lay in its organizational ability to link its converts together, organized, as one has put it, "to beat the devil." The person who was the key in all of this and who made it happen was the circuit rider.

The story of the circuit rider is a thrilling one, not only in the annals of Methodism but also in the history of America. Everywhere he went, the Methodist Circuit Rider was recognized as such. His typical garb was a round-breasted coat, long vest with corners cut off, short breeches, and long stockings.[11] In his saddlebag he carried his Bible, hymn book, discipline and literature to be sold or given away. In all kinds of weather, he felt compelled to keep to his appointed rounds. It became a proverbial expression in foul weather that "nobody would be out but crows and Methodist preachers." President William Henry Harrison, who had witnessed their labors in the West for almost forty years said he looked upon them "as a body of men, who for zeal and fidelity in the discharge of the duties they undertake, are not exceeded by any others in the world. . . . They are men whom no labor tires, . . . no danger frightens in the discharge of their duty."[12]

To the scattered settlements and isolated cabins of the frontier, the circuit rider brought news of the world beyond, sometimes the only reading material to be had, the joy and peace of the gospel and, in time, a settling and moralizing influence on the wild frontier.

The excessive labor and constant exposure to all kinds of weather and situations including incredibly bad roads or no roads demanded a terrible toll from the circuit rider. During the first fifty years of the Methodist Church in America, more than one-half of all the circuit riders preached less than fifteen years and died before reaching their thirty-fifth birthday. It was their indomitable spirit that caused Theodore Roosevelt to pay them this tribute, "nameless and unknown men who perished at the hands of savages, or by sickness and in flood and storm. . . ."[13]

> What do we owe to those,
> That brave and patient band,
> Who blazed the wilderness for Christ
> And followed His command?
> By lonesome trails that led
> O'er hill and rolling river,
> Their spirits still go marching on
> Forever and forever.
>
> To cabin homes they went,
> To give the living bread,
> They left their own and journeyed forth
> As they were Spirit led,
> And counted not the cost,

> Constrained by love to be
> The heralds of the living God
> The spokesmen of the free.
>
> In perils oft by land,
> In hunger and in cold,
> It mattered not, as messengers
> The story must be told.
> The pioneers of peace,
> The builders of the years,
> Upon foundations they have laid
> The finished work appears.
>
> I see them ride at last
> Before the great white throne,
> A gallant company of Christ,
> His faithful and His own,
> With saddlebags laid down,
> And every hardship done,
> And followed by a mighty host,
> The souls they had won.[14]

Bishop Asbury was the one who led the way. He was constantly on the go, sick or well, and he was often very unwell. The saddle was more his home than any place else. He preached nearly every day. He stayed wherever he happened to be. He was equally at home in the homes of the great—like Governors Van Cortland of New York, Bassett of Delaware and Tiffen of Ohio, as he was in the cabins of the pioneer. Yet more than once he was constrained to complain of the poor lodgings and the rigors of travel. He would be up north in the summer and down south in the winter, but almost always on the go.

We cannot today conceive of the hardships of his incredible journeys, but they are all described in his *Journal*. On his first visit to Nashville, Tennessee, Asbury had to sleep in the jail. Once he slept with sixteen adults and several children in seven beds in one vermin-infested room.

It is said that Asbury traveled more, knew more people, and had a better knowledge of the roads and trails, towns and villages, than any man in the land.

One example is his Episcopal tour for the year 1809. January 1, he left the site of the just held South Carolina Conference in Georgia. Traveling with him for the entire year was Henry Boehm, who was to become one of the charter members of the New Jersey Conference. Bishop William McKendree on his first round of episcopal visits traveled part of the time with Asbury.

During the year, Asbury held Conferences in Tarboro, North Carolina; Harrisonburg, Virginia; Old St. George's Church, Philadelphia; John Street Church, New York; Monmouth, Maine; met the Western Conference in Cincinnati; and the South Carolina Conference in Charleston.

What a tour for a man of sixty-four. Sick or well, Asbury seldom rested. Because of his infirmities, he sometimes rode in a kind of sulky, but mostly on horseback. He traveled through nineteen states from Georgia to Maine and on to Ohio, Kentucky, Tennessee and back to South Carolina.

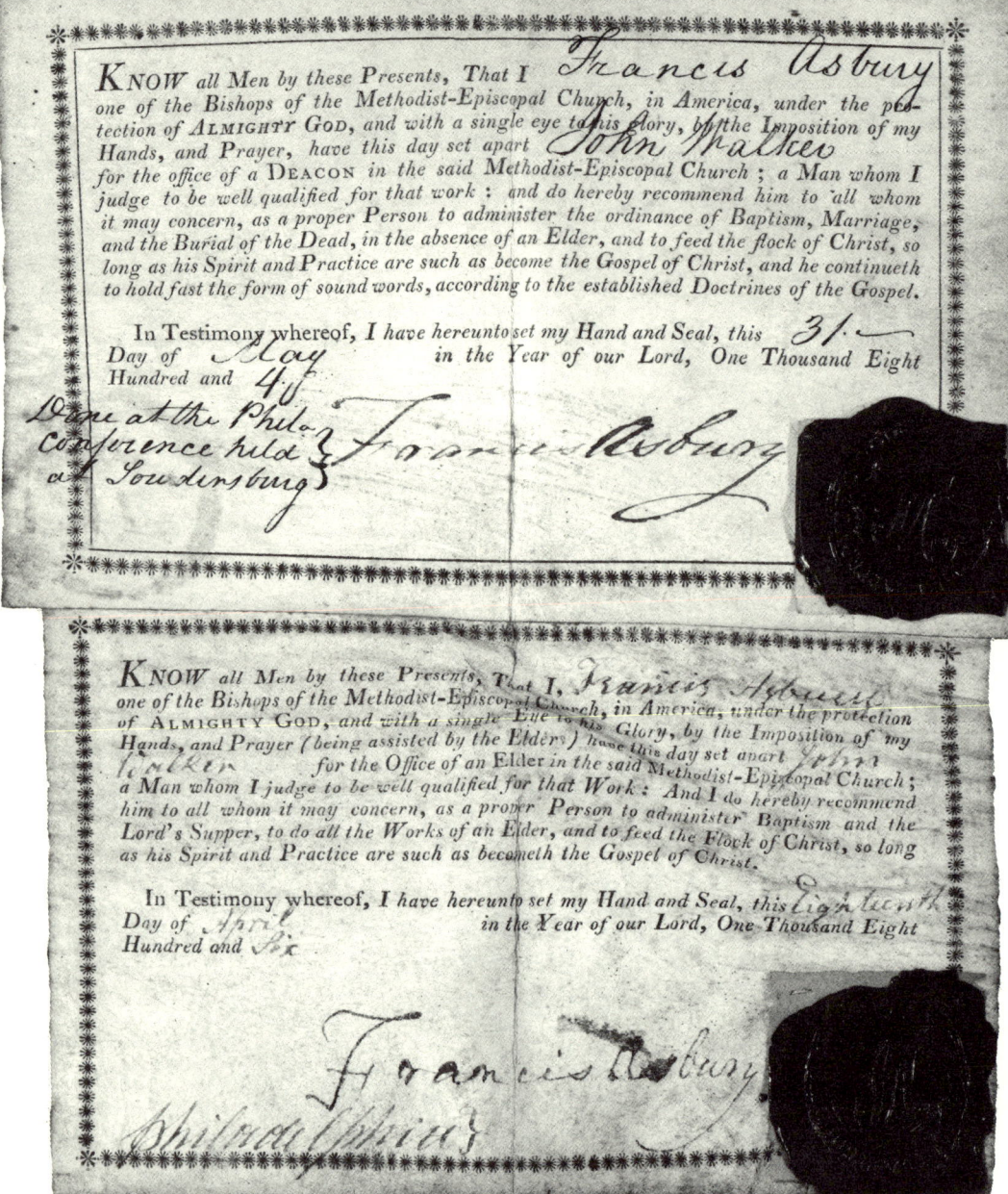

John Walker's Ordination Certificates signed by Bishop Asbury
Top, his Deacon's Certificate dated May 31, 1804
Bottom, Elder's Certificate dated April 18, 1806
Original in SNJ Conference Archives, a gift of Rev. Walker's great grandson,
Carl Walker Gaskill of Bridgeton.

Imagine in 1809, when roads were poor at best and often mere trails, crossing the White Mountains of New Hampshire and the Green Mountains of Vermont, roaming through the Poconos, crossing the Alleghenies from Lancaster to Pittsburg and Wheeling, West Virginia and skirting the Smoky Mountains as he crossed from Tennessee to North Carolina. No wonder he said, "I have need of patience and courage for the roads and weather." Bad roads or no roads, snow or rain, seldom detained the bishop from his appointed rounds.

In March, while riding through Delaware, he wrote: "I have suffered incredibly by the cold in the last hundred and thirty miles: souls and their Saviour can reward me, and nothing else! Lord, remember Francis Asbury in all his labours and afflictions!"

On his visit to Captain Beal at Fort Wolcott near Newport, Rhode Island, on May 29, he said, "I preached to the soldiers; baptized some children; visited the school; prayed with the sick in the hospital; exhorted the poor sinners to turn to God; but I might have said and done more."

He had quite some experiences. At Beverly, Massachusetts, he said, "My host did not quite understand praying in the daytime."

During an eight day span in New York state in July, he preached on Monday in Hampton Church, Tuesday in Dr. Lawrence's store to about five-hundred, Wednesday in M'Gready's barn, next day in a barroom, Sunday in a woods to about one thousand and next day in Favill's barn. Any place was good enough for Asbury to expound God's Word and preach Jesus.

One night near Manlius, New York, Asbury and Boehm stopped at a one room cabin where only a lady was present. Wrote Asbury, "I lay along the floor, in my clothes. There was a lady in the corner, and brother Boehm in bed, LIKE A GENTLEMAN. The female could not possibly occasion reproach, and so I was persuaded; but I wished I was somewhere else: my fear was not commendable."

The Western Conference met for the first time in Cincinnati on October 1. Learner Blackman preached the opening sermon. Asbury had stayed in April at Learner's father's home in English Creek. At the same Conference, Learner's brother-in-law, John Collins, was ordained elder. He, too, was a New Jersey native.

Of particular interest for New Jersey history was Asbury's twenty-three day visit to the state from April 9 to May 1, 1809. Leaving Philadelphia, he preached at Carpenter's Bridge (Mantua) and stayed overnight with father John Early. The next day, Wednesday, he preached at Union Chapel (Aura), "it is a neat building, two stories high, forty by thirty-six feet, built on the plan I furnished them." He preached at Pittsgrove on Thursday, Centerton on Friday and reached Bridgeton on Saturday. Sunday morning and evening he preached in First Church, Bridgeton.

Monday, he preached at Port Elizabeth where he evidently discussed with Dr. Benjamin Fisler the building of an Academy which was soon opened. Tuesday, after an absence of twenty-nine years, he preached at Head of the River Church and dined with Nathan Swain. The bishop wrote, "I feel the heat and labour, and painful weary nights appointed to me; but God, even my God is with me! I hear of several spots where the work of the Lord is reviving powerfully."

From Head of the River, Asbury and Boehm rode to Mays Landing, then to English Creek, where they stayed at David Blackman's. Absecon and Pleasant Mills were next. They stayed in the Batsto Manor House. Friday, April 21, Asbury dedicated the present church at Pleasant Mills. Saturday, they rode along the Mullica River to Tuckerton where Asbury preached Sunday morning and afternoon.

Traveling up the coast, the bishop preached at Waretown and Good Luck. At Good Luck, he must have discussed the purchase of the Old Good Luck Church built by Thomas Potter in 1766. Soon after Asbury's visit, the Methodists took title to this old church. He then preached in Polhemus Chapel at Silverton, at Squan River, where he said, "My host here, Derrick Longstreet, has been married twenty-four years: his wife once had twins, and she has made him the father of sixteen children, all of whom are alive and well."

Asbury next preached at Newman's on Shark River near the present Hamilton Church, Neptune, then at Peter White's near Ocean Grove. He rested at White's on Saturday. Sunday, April 30, he preached the first sermon ever preached at Old First Church in West Long Branch. Sunday afternoon, he preached in Christ Episcopal Church, Shrewsbury. Asbury and Boehm then rode through Matawan and New Brunswick to Staten Island. This was one of Asbury's most extensive tours through New Jersey.[15]

Asbury continued to make yearly visits to Jersey through 1815. In 1814, he visited New Jersey again in April, preaching at Woodbury, Perkintown, Penns Neck, Salem, Bridgeton, Pitts Grove, Aura, Bethel and finally reached Lumberton. For twelve weeks, Asbury was seriously ill at the home of Azail Coate. From his post as presiding elder of the Schuylkill District of the Philadelphia Conference, Henry Boehm spent much time with his beloved bishop and helped nurse him back to health. The Azail Coate home is still standing south of Lumberton.

Bishop Asbury continued to travel as long as he lived. His last *Journal* entry was made at Granby, South Carolina, on December 7, 1815. He was sick, but he traveled on. He did not make the South Carolina Conference nor the Virginia one, though he traveled when he could. He hoped to make the General Conference set for May 1 in Baltimore. Fearing he might not make it, he wrote his Episcopal Address which was read posthumously by Bishop McKendree.

Asbury died at the home of an old friend, George Arnold, six miles south of Spottsylvania, Virginia, on March 31, 1816 — full of confidence and hope, trying in the gathering mists of death to take up a missionary collection — a preacher to the end.

The death of Asbury marks the end of an era. The Father was gone. The mantle of leadership now fell to his spiritual children, and the work went on.

Circuit riders of note served in New Jersey during this period of growth. Ezekiel Cooper, Thomas Ware and Henry Boehm continued to serve. Rev.

Alexander Gilmore in what must be the first history of the New Jersey Conference written in 1866[16] mentions some.

John Walker is one. From 1802 to 1834, he served in the circuit ranks, twenty-four of those years in his native state of New Jersey. His ordination certificates signed by Bishop Asbury are in the Conference Archives.

Peter Vannest was an even more noted circuit preacher who entered the ranks in 1796. He closed his ministry in Pemberton in 1821 and continued to reside there and do much good until his death in 1850. He served as a pioneer preacher in Canada and upper New York state as well as in New Jersey and elsewhere.

Manning Force entered the ministry in 1811. He pastored Old St. George's Church and in Baltimore. Mostly, he served in New Jersey, particularly in the northern part of the state. He served twice as presiding elder and was elected to six General Conferences.

Richard W. Petherbridge served from 1815 to past mid century. He was Presiding Elder of the West Jersey, Trenton and New Brunswick Districts, served as financial agent of Pennington Seminary and in retirement continued to live and serve Christ in Pennington.

Charles Pitman was the most noted minister to enter the ranks of New Jersey Methodism during this period. Native of Cookstown, he joined the Philadelphia Conference in 1818. For the next eleven years, he served on the Bergen and New Brunswick Circuits, as the first stationed preacher in New Jersey at Bridgeton in 1823 and 1824, at Old St. George's in Philadelphia in 1825, and as presiding elder of the West Jersey District from 1826 to 1829. More will be said in the next chapters about this servant of Christ who became a builder of churches, noted camp meeting preacher, presiding elder and for nearly ten years served in the distinguished post as Secretary of the Missionary Society of the Methodist Episcopal Church.

Methodism continued to grow in New Jersey. At the end of 1829 there were over 7,000 members on the West Jersey District, 3,200 in East Jersey and 2,200 on the New Jersey part of the Asbury District. As membership increased, circuits were reduced in size and Bridgeton, Salem and Trenton became stationed appointments.

Some important circuit changes took place. Bethel Circuit became Gloucester Circuit in 1803 and encompassed Gloucester, Camden and Atlantic Counties. In 1828 the Bargaintown Circuit included all the stations in Atlantic County.

The Salem Circuit was reduced when the Cumberland Circuit was formed in 1807. This Circuit embraced Methodism in both Cumberland and Cape May Counties. The New Mills Circuit was formed from a division of the Burlington Circuit in 1811. That same year, the Jersey District was divided into the East and West Jersey Districts. An Asbury District was formed in 1829 which included some circuits in northern New Jersey, but mostly in contiguous areas of Pennsylvania and New York. A New Brunswick Circuit was added

Azail Coate Home in Lumberton where Asbury
recovered from a serious illness in 1814.
The home is still standing.

in 1818. Others came along after 1823. Similar developments occurred, but not so rapidly in the northern part of the State.

In 1829, the following appointments were made in New Jersey: West Jersey District: Burlington, Tuckerton, Pemberton, Bargaintown, Cumberland and Cape May, Bridgeton, Gloucester, Salem Circuit, Salem Station, Woodbury, Woodstown, Toms River, Juliustown, Medford; the East Jersey District included New Brunswick, Freehold, Trenton Circuit, Trenton Station, Essex, Morristown, Belleville, Newark, Elizabethtown and Rahway; the newly formed Asbury District included the Asbury, Warren, Hamburg and Paterson Circuits in New Jersey.

A new phenomenon, the Camp Meeting, made its appearance early in the nineteenth century. Camp meetings were the product of the frontier. The first one held anywhere was probably in Logan County, Kentucky, led by the McGee brothers, John, a Methodist local preacher and William, a Presbyterian minister. An even more famous one was at Cane Ridge, Kentucky, in 1801. Hundreds of people would converge on a camp meeting from miles around. They would pitch their tents and erect a preacher's stand and sometimes a shed or tabernacle. Religious emotion would be at a high tide. Asbury frequently talked of camp meetings and their results with one hundred, five hundred or even one thousand converted, numerous others sanctified, many becoming members of the church, and the spiritual level of the people lifted to a high plane.[17]

It did not take New Jersey Methodists long to adapt to camp meetings. Gilmore, in his Centennial address, describes one held on the Salem Circuit in 1809 as described by Rev. James Newell, a local preacher of Salem County. The meeting was held in Brewer's Woods.

> Rev. Samuel Coates among other preachers was there. One sermon he preached I shall never forget; it was on the resurrection and the judgment, the appearance of the white throne, etc. He sounded the trumpet and the trembling earth gave forth its unnumbered millions, while the ocean rolled its inmates to the shore, Death and Hell gave up their victims, all taking their course toward, and standing before the great white throne, all trembling to hear the fiat of God, the terrible Judge. The grandeur, the sublimity, the eloquence of this description of the scene at the last days can never be forgotten. All eyes were fastened upon him, streaming tears attested the depth of feeling, while he threw open the portals of the mansions of bliss, and crowned the happy righteous with glory—gave them palms of victory and harps of melody—then moving toward the front of the stand the preacher began to drop the wicked into hell; and at last with a mighty effort plunged the whole of the condemned into the abyss, the bottomless pit of eternal woe. Such an effect I never witnessed before or since. Such screams and cries for mercy; such praying and shouting all over the vast assemblage of the camp ground; from all classes—for all were affected. Many of the Society of Friends were there. Charles Jones, a Quaker, became soundly converted and sprang upon a stump and preached to the people. The most respectable persons were down on the ground, rolling among the leaves, or prostrate among the seats; and a general surrender to the Lord seemed to prevail throughout the encampment. At the close an old Friend turned to me and said, 'Thee has some great speakers in thy society; I never heard the like before.' This was a great day for Methodism; it took a position in Salem County and the counties adjoining never occupied before; not merely among the poor and illiterate, but the educated and influential.[18]

The period from about 1797 to about 1830 has been called the Second Great Awakening. It would be hard to prove whether on the frontier the camp meeting was an outgrowth of the Awakening or the cause of it. However, on the frontier, and to a lesser extent in New Jersey, revivals and camp meetings, evangelism, and expressions of religious enthusiasm were a hallmark of the period.

All was not as harmonious in Methodism as one might think. Frederick A. Norwood in *The Story of American Methodism,* makes clear one of the continuing tensions within Methodism. It is the tension between authority and freedom, between strong centralized leadership and democracy.

Methodism, without the authority of Wesley and Asbury, could never have achieved its amazing growth. It was the disciplined corps of preachers moving out under Asbury's command that gave Methodism its tremendous energy and efficiency in an ever expanding nation. At the same time, the church depended on the loyalty of its large band of local preachers, exhorters and class leaders, the local Methodists, to achieve the new community of faith. The result was tension. This tension is part of the genius of Methodism. Its price was periodic conflict.[19]

Conflict broke out at the General Conference of 1792 when James O'Kelly offered a motion that if any preacher did not like his appointment, he could appeal to the Conference. If the Conference approved his objections, the bishop should appoint him to another circuit. When his motion was defeated, O'Kelly left the Conference and the Methodist Church. The appointive power of the bishop was secure.

This did not put an end to conflict, however. As early as 1812, there was agitation to elect presiding elders. This proposal actually was approved by the 1820 General Conference, but the bishops raised so much furor that the rule was suspended and was not passed again. This lessened authority of the bishop and elected presiding elders came to be tied in with more lay rights in District, Annual and General Conferences where no laity had representation. It was promoted as a democratic ideal at a time when democratic idealism was sweeping the country. Those heralding such ideas in the church were called "Reformers."

Between the 1820 and 1828 General Conferences the Reformers appealed to Methodism to adopt their views. A paper, "Wesleyan Repository" was published in Trenton, New Jersey, by a layman, William S. Stockton. Later, it became known as the "Mutual Rights." Union Societies were organized in many places to promote these reform ideas. Even earlier, a group calling themselves "Independent Methodists" withdrew from the Methodist Episcopal Church in Monmouth County centering in the area around West Long Branch and Wall Township.

The 1828 General Conference was decisive. Every reform motion was soundly defeated. Seeing there was no hope to advance their position within the church, many reformers withdrew and formed the Methodist Protestant Church. The full story of the Methodist Protestants will be told in Chapter twelve. Here, let it be said that this division did have some effect on New Jersey Methodism. Some members withdrew; several Methodist Protestant societies and churches were organized. New Jersey was represented at all the important founding conferences of the Methodist Protestant Church. Three of their early leaders, the layman editor, William Stockton; his preacher son, Thomas H. Stockton, and the eloquent Quaker-bred Asa Shinn, were all from New Jersey. There is, however, no evidence that the withdrawal of the Reformers lessened the advance of the Methodist Episcopal Church in New Jersey.

The settling of the dispute, even though by a division in the Church, cleared the way for an even greater advance. In the decade of the 1830's, the Methodist Episcopal Church came into its own in New Jersey.

Chapter 4

A NEW CONFERENCE IS BORN

1830-1839

The 1830's have long been described by historians of the United States as the "Jacksonian Era" or "Rise of Democracy." The old breed of politician from Virginia or New England no longer was in control. Andrew Jackson was a man from the west. He was a man from the people and of the people. In the 1830's Jackson was the outstanding figure in a "golden age of American individualism." The frontiersmen elected their man.

Jackson was not a Methodist, but he knew Methodism first hand. He chose Learner Blackman as chaplain for his troops on his first attempt to go to New Orleans in the War of 1812. During that experience, Blackman made the comment that Jackson "is a good General but a very incorrect divine."[1] Blackman knew the general and his wife well and frequently visited in their home. After such a visit he says, "Lodged with General Jackson, he used us well. The Lord grant that he may embrace religion. His wife seems to be seeking it."[2]

In New Jersey life was beginning to change. The first railroad, Camden and Amboy, was chartered in 1830 and opened for service between Bordentown and South Amboy in January of 1833. Others soon followed, but mostly in the north. The Morris Canal started operations in 1831 and the more successful Delaware and Raritan in 1834. The railroads and canals greatly facilitated transportation and helped immensely in the early industrial growth of the state and in building the cities of New Jersey such as Newark, Jersey City, Trenton, New Brunswick and Camden.

Methodist growth continued in the 30's. The Conference reported a membership at decade's end of 20,506 whites including 123 local preachers and 496 colored for a total of 21,002. This was an increase during the 1830's of over 7,000 members.

The real story of the 1830's so far as New Jersey Methodism is concerned is that this was when Methodism in the state came of age. By action of the 1836 General Conference, the New Jersey Conference of the Methodist Episcopal Church was born.

Seventeen thousand six hundred does not seem like many members for an entire Conference. Yet, the Conference covered the whole state of New Jersey, Staten Island and some adjacent areas of southern New York and northeastern Pennsylvania. While seemingly small in numbers, it still amounted to over 6% of the state's population which at the time was not over 300,000. It was a large area that was becoming established as a great stronghold for Methodism.

Considerable discussion lasting several days was held in the 1836 session of the Philadelphia Annual Conference over the question of the division of the

Conference. There seemed no doubt in the members' minds that a division should take place and that it should include the state of New Jersey. The exact boundaries of the proposed division and the Conference membership and financial responsibility for the retired ministers or Conference claimants as they were called, were the matters of chief discussion. The following report was adopted and submitted to the 1836 General Conference:

1. *Resolved,* that in the judgment of this committee it is expedient to obtain a division of the Philadelphia Annual Conference.
2. *Resolved,* that this conference memorialize the General Conference to allow this conference to divide itself by such line as it may judge best at any of its subsequent sessions between 1836 and the sitting of the General Conference in 1840 under the sanction of the Bishops presiding or present at the time such division is resolved on.
3. *Resolved,* that in case the General Conference should not grant this request of this conference, then this conference prays the General Conference to divide this conference by the Delaware River and Bay excepting so much of the territory west of the Delaware River as is now included in the Asbury District which territory shall belong to the eastern division, and that the eastern section of the division be called the New Jersey Conference, and that this New Jersey Conference meet at Newark. And that the western section of the conference be called the Philadelphia Conference.
4. *Resolved,* that a committee of one from each district be appointed to report the claimants on the conference funds that shall be assigned to each conference in case this conference be divided.
5. *Resolved,* that in case of a division of this conference the privileges, responsibilities, obligations and patronage of that portion of the work lying within the conference at present or in its present form as they now exist be secured and continued in favour of Dickinson College and in favour of the Subscribers to the same, both in reference to the College and Education Fund of the present Philadelphia Annual Conference.
6. If the above take place, a committee of 6, 3 from each conference be appointed to carry out resolution 5.[3]

General Conference met in 1836 in Wesley Chapel, Cincinnati, the first time it convened west of Pittsburg, during nearly the entire month of May. Wesley Chapel was the first Methodist Church established in Cincinnati. It grew out of the first Class formed in Cincinnati by John Collins of New Jersey. Rev. Leaner Blackman of New Jersey, whose last sermon was preached from its pulpit, was buried in its grave yard. The leading topic of the Conference was slavery, but the Conference refused to take any position on slavery except to uphold the status quo. Seven new Conferences were established: Black River, Erie, Michigan, New Jersey, North Carolina, Arkansas and Liberia in Africa.

The memorial from the Philadelphia Conference to divide the Conference was referred to the Committee on Boundaries. When the Committee's report was presented, a motion was made to add the North Philadelphia District to the New Jersey Conference. When the question of boundaries was taken up the next day, the motion to allow the Philadelphia Conference to divide itself was lost. All other amendments to the Boundary Committee's report were laid on the table. The following action forming the New Jersey Conference was adopted:

New Jersey Conference shall include the whole State of New Jersey, Staten Island and so much of the state of New York and Pennsylvania as is now included in the Asbury District.[4]

The New Jersey Conference was born.

The new Conference's first session was held in the Halsey Street Methodist Epicopal Church, Newark, April 26 to May 2, 1837. Bishop Beverly Waugh presided. Conference opened on Wednesday with the reading of II Timothy 2, singing, and prayer by the bishop. The first item of business was the election of a secretary, the Rev. William A. Wilmer. After deciding that daily sessions would be held from eight o'clock in the morning until one o'clock in the afternoon, a series of committees were chosen. Those committees were:

Appointment of Preachers for Sunday Preaching
Sunday School
Periodicals
Education
Post Office
Rules Committee
Formation of Missionary Society
Formation of a Preacher's Aid Society
Examination of Preachers Taking the Course of Study
Reception of Contributions from the Book Room

Five Conference Stewards were elected: Henry Boehm, John Knox Shaw, Waters Burrows, Anthony Atwood and Edward Page.

Conference was then ready for business. The rest of Wednesday and most of Thursday were spent dealing with ministerial relations. Deacons and elders were elected, characters of all the ministers were considered individually, the relationship of the retired ministers was considered, persons were voted as members of the Conference on trial or as full members. These actions took a long time. In fact, it was not until Saturday that all these questions were settled. In these reports, one finds such interesting and often baffling names describing retired ministers as supernumerary, superannuated and worn out preachers. The superannuated were those who because of age or affliction were unable to preform ministerial work. For many years they were known as the "worn out" preachers. They, their widows or children had a claim upon conference funds as today they receive a pension. They were the Conference Claimants. Supernumerary ministers were those who were temporarily disabled or retired, but ready to serve when called upon or able. These men were Conference Claimants only upon vote of the Annual Conference.

Another ministerial concern, which sometimes took up considerable time during Conference, was a trial of someone accused of doing wrong. At this first Conference a special session Monday afternoon, May 2, was held to deal with the appeal of John Dow, a local Elder who had been suspended by the Belville Quarterly Meeting. The Minutes do not say why he was suspended; however, when the appeal was heard, the decision of the Quarterly Meeting was reversed. Brother Dow's character was passed and his right to continue serving as a local Elder affirmed.

Among significant actions taken by that first session was the adoption of a Constitution of the New Jersey Missionary Society, action leading to the formation of a Preachers' Aid Society, a resolution to establish a Seminary of Learning within the Conference, agreement to continue the support of Dickinson College, a motion that parsonages or "a preacher's house" be built and furnished for every circuit and station where it had not yet been done, a pledge of support for the Colonization Society to send slaves back to Africa, and the passage of a strong temperance resolution.

Nathan Bangs and others organized, in New York in 1819, the Missionary Society of the Methodist Episcopal Church. May 26, 1820, General Conference gave its approval and adopted the Society's Constitution.[5] It was the intent to organize Auxiliary Societies in every Annual Conference and Branch Societies in circuits and stations. Accordingly, the New Jersey Conference Society was organized May 1, 1837, "to assist the several Annual Conferences to extend their missionary labours throughout the United States and elsewhere." Anyone could be a member by the payment of at least one dollar annually. Life memberships cost ten dollars. The presiding bishop was President of the Society. Manning Force was elected Vice President.

Within the Conference, mission work was established at New Germantown and Somerset, Quarantine, Fort Lee and Cohansey.

It was significant that this first Conference session took steps to establish a school, for public education was not strong in New Jersey. Conference resolved:

> That the Presiding Elders be a committee to receive proposals for the Establishment of two Seminaries of Learning within the bounds of the New Jersey Conference, viz. a male and female academy, and to obtain information in reference to Academies, and to report to the next Conference. But if in the judgment of this Committee a favorable offer should be made for immediate occupancy, they are authorized to pledge to it the patronage of this Conference.

Hackettstown made an offer, but it was not accepted. The 1838 Conference decided that the "Jersey locality offering the largest subscription for the school would receive it." Hackettstown, Pemberton and Pennington sought the prize. Rev. John Knox Shaw, pastor at Pennington secured the most subscriptions, and the 1839 Conference chose to put the school in Pennington where it has remained. The cornerstone was laid in May of 1839.

New Jersey Methodists have long been staunch foes of the evils of alcohol. This first Temperance report spoke the mind of the Conference:

> Resolved that in the opinion of this Conference it is the imperious duty of the Ministry and membership of the Christian Church to promote both by precept and example, a cause which contemplates the glory of God and good will to man by using their influence to induce all people wholly to abstain from all intoxicating liquors as a drink and that it is incompatible with the Spirit of Methodism for any of its Ministers or Members to participate in any way whatever in the manufacture, sale, or use of intoxicating drinks, except for medicinal purposes in extreme cases.

An interesting event at Conference was the receipt of a letter from blind Mary Collins of the Bargaintown Circuit. It was addressed to the aged ministers of the Conference. Blind Mary, by her own efforts, had collected seventy-two dollars for the worn out preachers, ten of which were for John Walker. This gift induced a member of the Halsey Street Church to make a contribution to raise the collection to one hundred dollars.

At the close of the Conference, eighty-six ministers were appointed to sixty churches, circuits and four districts. Rev. John McClintock, Jr., was appointed to Dickinson College as Assistant Professor of Mathematics. The former East Jersey, West Jersey and Asbury Districts were realigned into four districts:

Newark, Manning Force, Presiding Elder
Paterson, Waters Burrows, Presiding Elder
Trenton, Richard W. Petherbridge, Presiding Elder
Camden, Thomas Neal, Presiding Elder

Conference adjourned on the evening of May 2.[6]

The New Jersey Conference was now established. There were four districts across the state and a growing membership. A Preachers Aid Society was organized and a Missionary Society was functioning. The "worn out" ministers, widows and children were being taken care of; in fact, at Conference there was an additional $300 distributed among the most necessitous. Conference made its first official statements regarding two evils of society: slavery and the drinking of alcoholic beverages. By far, the most ambitious undertaking was the decision regarding a Conference school. More will be written about all of these in subsequent chapters.

Let us now take a look at some of the principal charter members of the Conference. Ten "worn out" preachers head the list. Thomas Ware is first. He has already been named as a participant in the Christmas Conference. He was a Revolutionary War veteran, native of Greenwich, Cumberland County, longtime presiding elder, leader in the church from south to north and for four years Book Editor of the church. His autobiography, *Sketches of the Life and Travels of Rev. Thomas Ware,* published in 1839, is a classic in the history of early American Methodism. It was reprinted twice in 1984, the Bicentennial year of American Methodism, by the Holston Conference and by Mr. E. Farley Sharp of Academy Books, Rutland, Vermont.

Second on the list is Thomas Morrell. He was another Revolutionary War soldier, serving the 4th New Jersey Brigade as Captain, then Major. Major Morrell became an intimate friend and correspondent of Bishop Asbury. He was also acquainted with President George Washington. It has already been told how he arranged with the new president an audience with Bishops Coke and Asbury. Morrell's home was in Elizabeth, New Jersey. He continued to serve his church long after his itinerant days were over. Another of the charter members was a son of Thomas Morrell, Francis Asbury Morrell. He, too, was a noted Conference leader. His mother is said to have been a member of Philip Embury's Class in New York City.

James Campbell, third on the list, became a minister in 1790. Native of Ireland, he lived a long time in Pemberton from where he went to be with his Lord.

Daniel Fidler is another New Jersey native who ended his life in Pemberton. During the later years of his active life, he served circuits in New Jersey. Prior to that, he served for three and a half years on the western frontier. From the west, he went to Canada. He served in Nova Scotia 1792 to 1794, in New Brunswick, Canada, for a year, then three more years in Nova Scotia. He was truly a pioneer, truly a missionary.

Next comes David Bartine who traveled the circuits from Canada to the Delmarva Peninsula, though most of his ministry of forty-one years was on circuits within Jersey.

James Moore began to preach in 1796. Another native of Ireland, he made New Jersey his adopted state. He died at Medford in 1842. His list of circuits served includes many in Pennsylvania, Maryland, New York and Delaware as well as New Jersey. His last appointment was to the Bargaintown Circuit in 1828 and 1829. The spirit of a man like James Moore and many of these other old time preachers is captured in a note he wrote while on the Salem Circuit dated June 3, 1809.

> I was born in Ireland, in the county of Tyrone, 1760; joined the Methodist Society in 1786; came to America 1792; joined the Philadelphia Conference in 1794, now in the fortieth year of my age; still bound for heaven; happy in my soul this morning. All glory to God.
> James Moore[7]

Peter Vannest is the last of the seven charter members who began serving before 1800. Born in Hunterdon County, he spent the last thirty years of his life in useful retirement in Pemberton. Although born in New Jersey, it was in Bristol, England, that he was first licensed to preach. He soon returned to this country and joined the Philadelphia Conference. This father of the faith found his labors for the Master taking him to New England, upper New York State and Canada, as well as to circuits in his native state. Twice he was a presiding elder, first on the Cayuga, New York District, then from 1811 to 1814, on the East Jersey District. Peter Vannest was active to the last. In his ninety-second year he could often be seen going from house to house, inquiring with great interest about the family's temporal and spiritual welfare.

Father Henry Boehm is number eight on the list. He was a son of Martin Boehm, one of the founders of the United Brethren Church. He was a native of Lancaster County, Pennsylvania, and often preached to the Germans in their native tongue. He was one of Bishop Asbury's traveling companions and his ministry took him across virtually the entire church of his day. In New Jersey, he served the Burlington Circuit, 1828 and 1829. The next two years he served the Pemberton Circuit, 1832 he was at Bargaintown, 1833 at Tuckerton, 1834 New Egypt and the last two years of his active ministry, 1835 and 1836, he had the whole of Staten Island for his circuit. In retirement, he lived near Woodrow Church on Staten Island. Henry lived to celebrate his one hundredth

FATHER HENRY BOEHM
Bishop Asbury's Traveling Companion
Charter Member of the N.J. Conference

birthday and to preach his centennial sermon before the session of the 1875 Newark Conference, April 2, in Trinity Church, Jersey City. Another centennial celebration was held later in Trinity Church attended by the mother of President Grant and Fanny Crosby, who wrote a hymn to celebrate the event.

There were two more "worn out" circuit riders who complete that part of the list of charter members. John Walker and William Smith both joined the Conference in 1804. Bishop Asbury ordained John Walker. Through the years his family has proudly kept as a family heirloom his ordination papers signed by Asbury. Nearly all of this man's ministry of twenty-five years was served on circuits within his native state. Born in Burlington County, he died in 1849 at the age of 85 at Clarksboro.

It is not known where William Smith was born, but he died at Long Branch in 1854 and is buried beside the church this writer served in West Long Branch. William Smith's early ministry took him to northern New York and Canada, but chiefly he labored in New Jersey. Shortly before his death, speaking of his minister friends of the conference, he said, "I shall meet with them no more on earth, but I rejoice in the prospect of meeting them in heaven."[8]

What can be said about these numerous other names on the list of the Conference's Charter Members? Altogether there are seventy-seven, including six who transferred at the first Conference session in 1837 and another who located, voluntarily left the ministry for honorable cause, at the same session. Some cannot be ignored.

Levi Scott served only 1836 in the Conference at Franklin Street Church in Newark. He took a prominent role at the 1837 Conference, serving on the important Rules and Education committees. He then transferred to Ebenezer Church, Philadelphia. Levi Scott was an important figure in the Methodist Episcopal Church. Native of Odessa, Delaware, in 1834 he was appointed presiding elder of the Delaware District. He later served as Principal of Dickinson Grammar School, Carlisle, Pennsylvania, and was the Assistant Book Agent of the Church. In 1852, he was elected a bishop. As bishop, he presided over five sessions of the New Jersey Conference and dedicated numerous Conference churches.

Isaac Winner, five times elected by his Conference as a delegate to General Conference, three times appointed presiding elder, served with distinction across the Conference. He was also one of the founders and fosterers of Pennington Seminary.

George F. Brown and John S. Porter each served four times as General Conference delegates. It is a mark of distinction to be accorded this election by your colleagues. Both men also served four times as presiding elders on four different districts of the Conference. In addition, George Brown was a Chaplain in the State Prison.

Twelve other men among the ranks of charter members served in the presiding eldership, a leading position in the Conference. These men are Thomas Neal, noted preacher, revivalist and early Conference leader who was a Philadelphia Conference delegate to General Conference three times and was elected by the New Jersey Conference in 1844. Manning Force served three times as presiding elder before transferring to the newly formed Newark Conference in 1857. Richard W. Petherbridge is an often noted preacher, presiding elder, financial agent for Pennington Seminary and delegate to General Conference. Daniel Parish served in many places across the church before ending his ministry and his life serving on the Trenton and Newark Districts.

John Knox Shaw's ministry was distinguished in every way. He was a preacher, scholar, church builder, administrator, and a man of sterling character. He was twice a presiding elder and twice a delegate to General Conference, but John Knox Shaw is best known as the founder of Pennington School.

Waters Burrows was another preacher who often appeared on New Jersey circuits. At the 1837 Conference, he was appointed to the Paterson District

BISHOP LEVI SCOTT
Charter Member of the N.J. Conference

and later served the Rahway District. He transferred to the Newark Conference in 1857.

Thomas McCarroll, of Scotch parentage, was elected to the 1852 General Conference and became elder of the Newark District in 1856, before joining the Newark Conference at its inception one year later.

Others of the presiding elders are Jefferson Lewis who died in 1895. He was Conference Secretary for fourteen years, Trustee of Pennington Seminary for eleven years, twice presiding elder and General Conference Delegate. William A. Wilmer was the first Conference Secretary and twice led districts. Charles T. Ford, Isaac N. Felch, and Benjamin Day were the other presiding elders from among the class of charter members.

Other charter members whose names should be remembered are Joseph Chattle, first minister of St. Luke's Church in Long Branch. His son, Dr. Thomas G. Chattle, became a noted Monmouth County educator and temperance leader. John L. Lenhart became a United States Navy Chaplain and lost his life at sea during the Civil War. George A. Raybold was the first historian of New Jersey Methodism. The books he wrote and some of the material he collected are still vital sources of early New Jersey Methodism.[9] James Buckley, brother of John Buckley, another charter member, was the first New Jersey Conference member to be called home to God, dying in 1838 at the young age of 28. His brother followed him to the grave and to heaven only four years later.

To paraphrase the book of Hebrews, time would fail me to tell of others who pastored churches, rode the circuits, preached the gospel, evangelized the masses, ministered to the poor, served the sick, visited the prisons, married the young, baptized the children, buried the dead, suffered for the cross, and in all things served their Master.[10]

There were several important matters in the 1830's that concerned the Methodists of New Jersey. The strong temperance stand taken by the first Conference session has already been told. One of the most prominent temperance leaders in those days was Thomas Sovereign. A native of Canada, Rev. Sovereign joined the Philadelphia Conference in 1827 at the age of twenty-six. Although he had already served churches in this Conference, he did not become a Conference member until 1838. He was destined to be a leader in the Conference in years to come. Even in the 1830's, he spent much time preaching and lecturing on the evils of intemperance. He compiled a temperance spelling book which was used in our public schools possibly as early as 1838.[11] Some twenty years later he became a full time temperance agent.

Dr. Robert J. Williams, in his definitive study of the attitude of New Jersey Methodists to racial justice, *A Century of Compromise,* shows the support given to the colonization idea. The American Colonization Society was organized in 1816. It grew slowly with its peak years in the 1830's. The resolution of the 1837 Conference in favor of colonization has already been told.

April 24, 1832, the Rev. Henry Bascom of Pittsburg, later a bishop of the Methodist Episcopal Church, South, spoke in Halsey Street Church, Newark, as an agent of the American Colonization Society.[12] His presence would seem to indicate at least some degree of support from the pastor, if not the congregation of one Methodist Church.

In 1827, the Rev. Joseph Holdich, young pastor of the Methodist Episcopal Church in Elizabeth, was elected a director of the New Jersey Colonization Society. On that occasion, he spoke out strongly for the emancipation of the black, even though it might be a gradual emancipation.[13]

The *Methodist Recorder,* weekly paper published in Trenton in 1824 and 1825, gave strong support for colonization, although it combined its concern for the blacks with that of the American Indians, seamen and other benevolent causes.[14]

Williams provides us with the names of a few New Jersey Methodist clergy serving as officers of the state or auxiliary colonization societies. The Rev. Samuel Doughty of New Brunswick served on the Board of Directors of the State Society in the 1820's. Two Methodist pastors of Newark, Thomas McCarroll and James Ayres, were elected officers of the Newark Auxiliary at its founding in 1838. Rev. Anthony Atwood of Trenton was an official delegate at the reorganization of the New Jersey Society in Trenton on July 10, 1838. John Lenhart of Mount Holly and George A. Raybold of New Brunswick both were officers of local Societies organized in 1839.[15]

There is no way of telling how the laity of the Conference felt about emancipation, colonization and the like. Also, it would be difficult to determine now whether even this interest in colonizing the blacks was due to an inherent desire for complete emancipation, or a concern to merely get rid of the blacks. There was probably some of both feelings present.

Camp Meetings in the 1830's were still a means of arousing religious fervor, winning converts to the faith, and bringing the saints to a closer union with Christ. Charles Pitman was one of New Jersey Methodism's greatest camp meeting preachers. At one camp meeting in the pines of south Jersey, he preached three times with such remarkable power that three hundred-sixty persons professed conversion.[16]

Another camp meeting held near New Brunswick in 1831 at which Pitman preached is described by Gilmore:

> He preached with great power, and at the close the people were so overwhelmed that a death like stillness prevailed. Tears copious and glistening gushed up from every heart. The heaven-inspired minister himself, removed almost beyond the power of utterance, motioned to one who sat near him to pray. The congregation knelt, and for five minutes not a voice was heard. Eventually a prayer meeting was commenced, and 'then came a sound from heaven as a rushing mighty wind.' Believers were sanctified, and sinners were brought to the foot of the Cross. Two preachers, Brothers Petherbridge and Bull fell prostrate to the ground, and lay in a state of apparent unconsciousness for several hours.[17]

One of the highlights of the 1830's was the celebration of the Centenary of Methodism, harkening back to John Wesley's Aldersgate experience. A committee of Charles Pitman, Jefferson Lewis, James Ayars, Anthony Atwood and Thomas Sovereign made the following report to the 1839 Conference:

1. October 25, 1839 — set by the British — be the day for celebration by religious exercises.
2. The exercises should consist of a prayer meeting at sunrise — public discourse at 11 o'clock — love feast at night. Let the 'day be kept as a holy day throughout our bounds.'
3. A thank offering be received.
4. We urge every member to set apart a suitable portion of the substance God has given him or her 'as a holy offering to God.'
5. The collection shall be divided:
   One half for the relief and support of superannuated and supernumerary preachers and widows and orphans of deceased.
   Four tenths for the cause of liberal education to go to the trustees of the education fund.
   One tenth to the 1840 General Conference for the Mission cause.
6. All subscriptions under $50 are to be paid that day. All over $50 by April 1, 1840.
7. The Committee to be the preachers at Trenton, Bordentown, Burlington and Pennington plus the trustees and stewards of their respective charges. The Trenton preacher to be the chairman.
9. Trustees and stewards of each church or circuit be the committee with the preacher as chairman.[18]

That the celebration was successful is born out by subsequent reports which show that $6,375.82[19] was received from the Centenary offerings, one half of which went for the support of the retired ministers. This was the original corpus of funds for the Centenary Fund and Preachers Aid Society officially organized in 1841. This Society is still in existence for the support of the retired preachers.

The first published Conference Minutes was for the 1838 session held in Bridgeton, the first Conference session held within our present Conference bounds. Compared with our present day published Minutes of over 300 pages, the 1838 Minutes had only sixteen pages and was only four by six and a quarter inches in size, but the vital statistics of the Conference are there, showing a membership increase of 1651. The first report of the Sunday Schools was given. There were 137 Sunday Schools in the Conference with 8,308 scholars, 156 superintendents, and 1,124 teachers for a total of 9,588. That is an average of 70 per school.[20]

As a matter of information and record the following is a list of churches known to have been a part of the Conference when it was established in 1836. No pretense is made that this list is entirely accurate and complete. It is taken from *The Methodist Trail in New Jersey* plus other records in the files of the author. The listing is by former districts:

1836 CHURCHES OF THE NEW JERSEY CONFERENCE

BRIDGETON DISTRICT

Alloway	Leesburg
Auburn	Logtown (Harmersville)
Aura	Marmora (Beasley's Point)
Bridgeton: First	Monroeville: Friendship
Cape May	Millville: First
Cape May Court House	Mullica Hill
Cedarville	Newport
Center Square	Pennsgrove: Emmanuel
Centerton	Pennsville
Clayton	Petersburg
Cumberland	Porchtown
Dividing Creek	Port Elizabeth
Eldora	Salem: First
Erma	Salem: Mt. Hope
Fairton	Sharptown
Friendship: Buena	South Dennis
Glassboro	Swainton: Asbury
Goshen	Tuckahoe
Haines Neck	Williamstown
Harrisonville	Willow Grove
Head of the River	Woodruff (Pleasant Grove)
Heislerville	Woodstown

CAMDEN DISTRICT

Absecon
Bargaintown
Barnsboro: Mt. Zion
Blackwood
Camden: First
Catawba
Clarksboro: Zion
Cross Keys
English Creek
Estellville
Gibbstown (Clonmell)
Glendora: Chews
Gloucester City: First
Haddonfield
Hurffville: Bethel
Lawnside
Magnolia
Mantua
Mays Landing
Paulsboro: St. Paul's
Port Republic
Repaupo
Smithville: Emmaus
Swedesboro: Old Stone
Weymouth
Woodbury

NEW BRUNSWICK DISTRICT

Adelphia
Barnegat
Bass River (New Gretna)
Brookville
Cassville
Chapel Hill
Cheesequake
Farmingdale
Forked River
Freehold
Good Luck
Green Bank
Hamilton: Neptune
Hazlet: St. John's
Keyport: Calvary
Little Silver
Lower Bank
Manahawkin
Matawan
New Brunswick: First
Silverton
South Amboy
Squankum
Tinton Falls
Toms River: First
Tuckerton
Wall
Waretown
West Creek
West Long Branch

TRENTON DISTRICT

Allentown
Amwell: Old Rocks
Bordentown
Burlington: Broad Street
Cinnaminson: Asbury
Clarksburg
Cranbury
Crosswicks
Emley's Hill
Englishtown
Groveville
Hightstown
Indian Mills
Juliustown
Lambertville
Lumberton
Medford
Moorestown
Mt. Holly
New Egypt
Pleasant Mills
Pemberton
Pennington
Tabernacle
Titusville
Trenton: First
Vincentown
Winslow
Wrightstown

A New Conference Is Born / 63

Chapter 5

THE PRE-CIVIL WAR ERA

1840-1859

To set the scene for these two decades we need to know what broad things were happening in the United States and New Jersey, in the midst of which we see the church at work. These were the years of the Mexican War and the California gold rush. It was the era of the great waves of westward movement as our nation sought to realize its manifest destiny. Cities were growing, railroads were reaching out and the industrial revolution was bringing changes.

The temperance movement was making headway as people were becoming very concerned about the evils of alcoholic drinking. Maine became the first state in 1851 to have a statewide prohibition against the sale of liquor. Twelve more states followed in the next ten years.

However, it was slavery that was the major issue of the times, and sectional strife seemed ever more imminent. By 1846, every state north of the Mason-Dixon Line had abolished slavery, though, as in New Jersey, full freedom had not yet come. Abolitionism was becoming increasingly popular. William Lloyd Garrison became head of the American Anti-Slavery Society in 1840 and led the way.

Meanwhile in New Jersey, a new State Constitution was adopted in 1844 containing a strong bill of rights guaranteeing religious freedom, free speech, free press, and freedom from search and arrest except on warrant. Population increased 300,000 in these twenty years despite the exodus of those moving west. While the attitude of New Jerseyans toward slavery was ambiguous, the State, led by the Quakers, played an important role in the Underground Railroad which carried fleeing slaves to freedom.

The big happening in Methodism during these years was the division of the Church in 1844 into the Methodist Episcopal Church and the Methodist Episcopal Church, South, a division that was to take nearly a century to heal. Yet, in spite of division, the church in each section grew and expanded. By the outbreak of the Civil War, "each of the two bodies that had separated in 1844 had become the largest and wealthiest Protestant Church in its geographic area, and the members of each church were widely dispersed in the general population of its area."[1] It was also a time when missionaries were sent by the church to the western part of the country and to Africa, South America and China as well.

As we continue to tell the story of New Jersey Methodism, we need first to see the attitudes and reactions of New Jersey Methodists to the church's division and the slavery question. The second big event was the division of the Conference in 1857 into the Newark and the New Jersey Conferences. In between, there are several other things at which we shall take a look.

To understand the division of 1844, it is necessary to have some understanding of the position the Methodist Episcopal Church took with regard to slavery. Looking back upon it, it seems obvious to us now that the church should have opposed slavery. This feeling of revulsion toward slavery or even the idea of slavery makes it very difficult to be objective in telling the story of the church and slavery. However, we do not live in those times in which slavery was an entrenched institution and way of life. The magnitude of slavery is born out by the statistics that show there were some 3,953,580 slaves in the slave states in 1860. That posed yet another problem for the whites, many of whom were afraid of what the freeing of those slaves would mean, and rightly so.

At the Christmas Conference of 1784, the infant church ordered every church member to free his or her slaves within twelve months if they were twenty or older. Every younger slave, at least by the time they reached age twenty-five, and every infant born after this rule was in effect, was to be released immediately. What could be clearer? However, when the bishops made their first tour of the south, they found so much opposition and were so fearful the church would be split asunder that within six months the statement on slavery was withdrawn. It was the beginning of compromise.

It should not be thought that Asbury was pro-slavery. He was not. He loved the slave. He loved the slaveholder, too. His position was that the state of their immortal souls was of greater concern than the slaves' freedom from human bondage.

Two laws essentially governed church policy on slavery. First was the General Rule passed in 1789 which forbade "the buying or selling of men, women and children, with an intent to enslave them."[2] It was slave-trading, not slave-holding that was forbidden. Also, it required a two-thirds vote of the General Conference and a majority of the Annual Conferences to change a General Rule. This rule was not amended until 1864. The second was a statement on slavery which appeared in the Discipline. This statement underwent many revisions, but of a minor nature, between 1796 and 1816. After that, little was done until after the Civil War. This statement prohibited slave-holders from holding office in the church and ministers from owning slaves, provided they lived in a state where emancipation was possible. It was not possible in many states. The statement also declared that the church was convinced "of the great evil of slavery." This statement could be changed by majority vote of the General Conference.

Throughout the 1840's and 1850's there were increasing attempts to change the disciplinary statement on slavery to prohibit the holding of slaves. It was not done. Even after the division of the church it was not done. The Methodist Episcopal Church did not favor abolition; however, some of its Conferences did. New England, parts of New York, and some of the western Conferences were for abolition and for abolition now. One result was the withdrawal from the Methodist Episcopal Church in 1842 of La Roy Sunderland and Orange Scott, prominent New England Methodists, to form with others the Wesleyan Methodist Church.

The crisis in the church was reached at the 1844 General Conference in New York. Delegates spent six weeks in arduous and often heated debate. When they left, the church was divided. What precipitated the debate was the fact that James O. Andrew, Bishop from Georgia, had become the owner of slaves. He inherited a young mulatto girl, Kitty, and a young boy from his first wife's estate. Georgia law prohibited emancipation. In addition, his second wife owned several slaves over whom the bishop had no ownership nor control. What do you do with a slave-holding bishop? That was the question with which the delegates had to wrestle.

The decision finally rendered was this: that Bishop Andrew "desist from the exercise of this office so long as this impediment [slavery] remains." On Saturday, June 1, by a vote of 110 to 68, the resolution passed.[3] On Monday, steps were taken to divide the church. It was done.

Now there were constitutional problems involved relating to episcopal authority over against the powers of the General Conference. Frederick A. Norwood has pointed out:

> Let us be clear. Slavery, from start to finish, was the issue over which the church broke in 1844. Neither secular 'revisionists' who would set the whole struggle in terms of economics rather than morality, nor ecclesiastical 'constitutionalists' who would debate the relationship between bishops and the general conference, can evade the inexorable problem of slavery as a moral and . . . theological issue.

Slavery divided the Methodist Episcopal Church.[4]

Before discussing New Jersey Methodists and slavery, a summary review of slavery in New Jersey is in order. There is documentation of slaves in New Jersey as early as 1680. By the time of the Revolution, slaves comprised ten to twelve per cent of the population. In 1786, the New Jersey Legislature prohibited the importation of slaves and recognized the legality of voluntary manumission. In 1804, a Gradual Emancipation Law was passed which said that children born of slaves after July 4, 1804 were to be free after serving the owner of their mother until age twenty-five for males and twenty-one for females.

A law passed in 1846 substituted apprenticeship for bondage, though it is difficult to tell the distinction. As the result of these laws, the number of slaves in the state declined. In 1810, there were 10,851 slaves. Ten years later, still 7,557. By 1860, only eighteen remained who labored as "apprentices" for life. Only with the adoption of the Thirteenth Amendment in 1865 was every vestige of slavery removed from New Jersey.[5]

Throughout this whole period, there was an antislavery impulse in New Jersey led by such early Quakers as John Woolman of Mount Holly and John Cooper of Burlington. They especially helped to keep down the number of slaves in the southern part of the state.

The Underground Railroad was in operation in New Jersey as early as 1810. An Agent was in charge of every Station while Conductors led slaves from one station to the next. There were three main underground routes across

Jersey. The main route went from Camden to Bordentown, then to Princeton and New Brunswick. The Salem Route was the second. It went from Salem to Woodbury, Mount Laurel and Bordentown where it joined the Camden Route. The third was the Greenwich Route which went from Greenwich to Swedesboro, Mount Holly and Burlington where it joined the Camden Route. There were other less traveled routes. Quakers played an important role in this railroad. It is not possible to document Methodist participation. It is estimated that more than 50,000 slaves found their way to freedom by the New Jersey operators of the Underground Railroad.[6]

Springtown in Cumberland County and later Lawnside, and Macedonia near Shrewsbury were havens for runaways who did not wish to go farther north.

How about the New Jersey Methodists? Dr. Robert Williams shows that throughout this period, New Jersey Methodists voted consistently to support the status quo. In 1839 and again in 1840, the Conference voted unanimously against a memorial submitted by the New England Conference to outlaw slaveholding in the church.[7]

At the 1844 General Conference, on the important vote that led to dividing the church, three New Jersey delegates, Winner, Shaw and Porter, voted with the majority. Neal and Sovereign voted no.[8] When it came time to vote for delegates to the 1848 General Conference, in reaction to the voting records of its delegates to the previous General Conference, none of the delegates who voted with the south were returned to General Conference.[9] The Conference was identifying itself with the northern moderates.

New Jersey Methodists were not southern sympathizers nor northern abolitionists. Several times the New Jersey Conference voted on memorials submitted by other northern Conferences appealing to them to take a stronger stand against slavery. Each time they overwhelmingly refused.

One of the voices heard taking a stronger stand against slavery was that of Dr. John McClintock. This prominent clergyman was a member of the New Jersey Conference from 1838 to 1859. He was Professor of Mathematics and Language at Dickinson College, 1836 to 1849, when he was elected Editor of the Quarterly Review, scholarly magazine for Methodist clergy. Later, he served as the first president of Drew Theological Seminary, and with Dr. Strong, edited the *Cyclopedia of Biblical, Theological, and Ecclesiastical Literature.*

While he later became a bit more moderate, Dr. McClintock was not so in his earlier years. He wrote a series of letters to the *Christian Advocate* in 1847. In the March 31 issue, he stated his conviction. "It is the duty of the Christian Church in the United States to direct its influence, as a Church, for the extirpation of American slavery."[10]

Earlier, in 1844, he had written to Stephen Olin at Wesleyan University, Middletown, Connecticut. Writing of the impossibility of compromise with the south, he said:

> The south will go off. The Virginia part of the Baltimore Conference will mostly go with the South: Maryland and Delaware will remain with the North. One good result will follow:

the anti-slavery spirit will firm in Maryland, and perhaps slavery may soon be abolished there. God grant it. If I see any danger of a compromise, I must write and speak against it. I shall burst if I don't. . . . I am more and more disposed to believe, that if the curse of slavery is ever removed from us, it must be by other people than slaveholders: and I do not intend to be backward here-after enlightening the people of these parts on the subject. That 250,000 slaveholders should rule this great empire is a thing not to be endured—and it can't be endured much longer.[11]

We know little of what was said or thought by lay members of the church or preachers outside of official Conference actions. Knowing the tenor of New Jersey Methodists, it is likely they shared their leaders' position. The New Jersey Conference had long been conservative. The prophetic voice has not been the one most readily followed. The woman and man in the pew may have disliked slavery. They probably disliked as much both the radical southern view acceptable to slavery and the northern radical abolitionist. The middle of the road was the more comfortable place to be, although the middle of the road is not always where one ought to be.

Other things were happening in the New Jersey Conference. The spirit of revival was still strong and camp meetings continued. The impression is gained that the New Jersey Methodists were concerned about saving souls, if not the reform of the continent. During the twenty years New Jersey was one Conference, there were 6,897 conversions reported in the Sunday School alone. Church membership increased from 18,260 to 40,021 between 1837 and 1857; the number of Sunday Schools increased from 300 to 458, and scholars rose from 20,714 to 34,045. Missionary collections increased from $1,800 to over $10,000.[12] To accommodate the increasing number of Methodists, two new districts were added in 1841, the Burlington and Rahway. The Newton District was added in 1853.

Education was seen as an important ministry of the Conference. The progress and support of Pennington School was always a concern. The Education Committee in 1841 reported the Seminary "in successful operation." Actually, the Methodist Episcopal Male Seminary started operations in the fall of 1840 with three boys, John Wesley Bunn, Archibald Higgins and Samuel Titus. Howard Bishop, an 1837 graduate of Rutgers was the teacher with Edward Cooke serving as first principal.[13]

The Rev. Dr. Cooke was born in New Hampshire, graduated from Wesleyan University in 1838 and taught two years at Amenia Seminary in New York before coming to Pennington. Later he served as president of the University of Appleton in Wisconsin, Wesleyan Academy, Wilbraham, Massachusetts and Chaflin University. Dr. Cooke seems to have been the right man for the job. On his arrival in the fall of 1840, just before the opening of the first full term, "he found the building still incomplete, 'no furniture, no library, no apparatus, bare and half-finished walls being all that greeted us.'"[14] As the fall term got well under way, the initial three students increased to eleven. By the end of Dr. Cooke's tenure in 1847, there were fifty scholars enrolled.

The school was fortunate in the quality of the men chosen to lead it through its early years. Dr. Cooke was followed as principal by the Rev. Dr. Stephan M. Vail, graduate of Bowdoin College and Union Theological Seminary. He was a pastor in the New York Conference. He served only two years, resigning to accept a position as Professor of Biblical Literature and Hebrew at the Methodist General Biblical Institute, Concord, New Hampshire. This was Methodism's first theological school. It later became Boston University School of Theology.

In his inaugural address, Dr. Vail laid down a principle of Christian education which remains an excellent statement of the aims of a school like Pennington.

> Since our school is a Christian school, our objects are Christian in their character. It is our high privilege to lend our aid to the youth who resort hither from time to time to make them better as well as wiser, more virtuous as well as more knowing, and prepared as well for the life to come as for that which now is.[15]

The Rev. Dr. Jonathan Townley Crane, native of New Jersey and first Conference member to serve as principal of Pennington, was elected in 1849 to head the school. He was thirty years of age and a graduate of Princeton. During Dr. Crane's administration, the school voted to admit female students. A new wing was added, and the first lady students were accepted in the spring of 1853. The name was changed to the Pennington Seminary and Female Collegiate Institute.[16] Dr. Crane's son Stephen, born in 1871 and a Pennington student, earned fame as a novelist. He is best remembered as the author of *The Red Badge of Courage.*

Isaac W. Wiley, M.D., D.D., LL.D., missionary to China, educator and later bishop, was elected the fourth principal of Pennington School and served from 1858 to 1863.[17] He added a theological class for those boys interested in studying for the ministry. Pennington's first gymnasium was also built during his administration in 1862.

The outstanding qualifications of the men leading Pennington School in its beginning years must have added much in giving the fledgling school a name and character much to be desired.

Finances, however, plagued the school throughout the period. One example, a Conference-wide collection ordered by the Conference in 1849 succeeded in bringing in the munificent sum of $274.88. Pennington was founded on what is known as a joint stock principle. The stock holders, thinking to make a profit and finding that no dividends were forthcoming or likely to be, decided to sell the school. They did, to three men from Pennington, for the sum of $7,000, about half of its original cost. At a hastily called meeting, the Conference Education Committee bought it back for the same sum of $7,000. This deal was made between Conference sessions. Conference, when it next met, approved the action of its Education Committee. May 1, 1850, the school became the property of the Conference. It was the New Jersey Conference Seminary of the Methodist Episcopal Church.[18] In its reorganization, the Trustees were composed of an equal number of ministers and laymen, including New Jersey's Governor, George F. Fort of New Egypt. The Rev. James M. Tuttle was appointed Financial Agent of the school in 1851 to try to raise the funds to pay off the debt. Apparently, it did not happen easily.

A detailed report about the school's finances was made to the 1858 Conference by the Education Committee. The report showed the total cost for ground, building and furniture to be $20,939.60. A debt remained of $12,205.27. Conference voted to raise $5,000 that year by an apportionment to every charge.[19] That amount was not realized; however, the majority of the churches of the Conference contributed $2,245.66. That was heartening in that it was the first time the Conference, as a whole, began to really show an interest in a practical way in its school.

Throughout this period, Dickinson College was a concern of the Conference. Financial support was given to it and reports were frequently made. It was one of the decisions made at the time the Conference divided from the Philadelphia Conference to continue the support of Dickinson.

The Conference also gave its patronage to two other schools started by Methodists, both in Bordentown. In 1842, the Rev. William H. Gilder of the Philadelphia Conference founded the Bellevue Female Seminary in Bordentown. It continued only a few years.[20]

Another school was started in Bordentown in 1851. John H. Brakeley, Ph.D., a Methodist local preacher, and his wife, started the Bordentown Female Seminary, chartered in 1853. As a college it was authorized to confer degrees. Dr. Brakeley led this school for twenty-three years. The college continued and had the patronage of the Conference until its doors closed about 1898.[21]

Missions received strong emphasis and support during this period. A strong Missions Committee Report to the 1845 Conference set the tone. Relating it to the great commission of Christ, the committee said "that no evangelical and enlightened minister can be indifferent to its high and holy claims." The committee in its Resolution called on each minister to preach at least once a quarter on the subject of Christian Missions, to establish a monthly Missionary Prayer Meeting, use the "cent a week system" to get every member to support missions, to teach missions in the Sabbath Schools and to receive the regular annual Missionary collection some time during the third quarter of the year.

It was in 1857 that the Conference Minutes listed, by churches and circuits, individual contributions for missions. It might be only twenty-five cents or a few dollars. This practice continued until the early years of the twentieth century. It is a valuable, historical source in the names of persons it mentions, lists of Sunday School classes contributing, and sometimes it is the only way to tell which churches were on a particular circuit.

Here is an example, chosen at random, from the 1859 Minutes.

CHAPEL HILL CIRCUIT — *W. A. Brooks, Pastor*

Wm. Johnson	.50	J. Morford	1.00
Lamb't. Johnson	.50	W. A. Anna	1.00

D. Ayres	.50	M. J. Howard	1.00
M. Swan	.50	Susan C. Brooks	1.00
J. Vanhise	.50	W. M. Brooks	1.00
T. W. Donald	.50	Jacob Swan	2.00
L. Leonard	.50	Mrs. Hield	2.00
S. J. Mount	.50	E. T. Burge	6.00
E. Estill	.50	S. School, Riceville	2.15
J. Skidmore	.50	Riceville Col'n.	3.25
M. Skidmore	.50	Port Monmouth	15.00
Rev. J. Browne	1.00	Harmony	1.78
J. Heding	1.00	Small Sums	2.25
M. Taylor	1.00	Total	$48.93[22]

While the church members gave their penny a week, made their yearly collection and prayed for missions, other Conference clergy were serving on the mission field or otherwise involved in the support of missions.

Charles Pitman's name comes first. This builder and dedicator of churches, indefatigable presiding elder, circuit preacher and camp meeting orator,

REV. CHARLES PITMAN

was elected Corresponding Secretary of the Missionary Society of the Methodist Episcopal Church in 1841. He held this important position by election of the 1844 and 1848 General Conferences until he retired, broken in health, to his home in Trenton in 1849. In this position, he had the general oversight of all Methodist Episcopal mission work within the continental United States.

Pitman's biographer outlines some of his work for 1843. "He traveled six thousand miles, delivered forty-one sermons, thirty missionary addresses, dedicated six churches, and collected ten thousand dollars." As the years progressed, so did his labors, extending to Texas and the west. Also, "his calls to corner-stone laying, dedications, camp meetings and protracted efforts . . . were augmenting rather than diminishing."[23] All this to say nothing of the multitude of his administrative concerns.

This native of Cookstown, New Jersey, was known as a church dedicator. In his later years, Pitman averaged three church dedications a month and sometimes three in one day.

> Among the churches in our conference which he dedicated were Third Street, Camden; Harmony; Lawrenceville; Bordentown; Porchtown; Broad Street, Burlington; Union, Camden; Jacobstown; Pennington; and Cape May Court House. In the Conference Memorials, the Rev. E. H. Stokes comments, there were few churches erected in New Jersey between the years 1825 and 1850 whose walls did not first echo with the gospel from the lips of Charles Pitman.[24]

An interesting story is told of Dr. Pitman's recruitment of a man for missionary service. In 1846, during a round of visits in the cause of missions, he called upon William Roberts, then pastor of the Liberty Street Church in New Brunswick. Roberts was greatly interested in the work. They discussed, among other things, the mission in Oregon. Knowing of the need for a new superintendent, Roberts asked, "Who is to be the superintendent of the Oregon mission?" "You!" was the impromptu answer of Pitman.[25] So it was that this man called the "circuit rider of the far west," received his appointment to the Oregon Mission.

Born in Burlington, New Jersey, in 1812, Roberts had served churches in Paterson, Newark, Jersey City and New Brunswick. He was destined to take Methodism to California, build our first church in San Francisco and supervise the work in the Oregon and California Conference. Once he left New Jersey, he never returned, dying in Dayton, Oregon, August 22, 1888.[26]

What a trip to Oregon! William, his wife Hannah and their two sons, seven year old William, Jr. and five year old John, sailed from New York on November 27, 1846, on the ship *Whiton*. Rounding the tip of South America, they reached California on April 24, 1847, and, per instructions from the Mission Board, surveyed the land. The next day, Roberts preached in the Brown Hotel, San Francisco. In May, a Methodist Class and Sunday School were organized there. It was the first Protestant church of record in California.[27]

It was June 29, 1847, when the Roberts family finally reached their post at Oregon City on the Columbia River. Roberts received help from New Jersey

Rev. William Roberts
Went from N.J. as a missionary to Oregon

in 1852 when J. D. Blain and James B. Hill were transferred to the Oregon and California Mission.

This missionary from New Jersey worked in Oregon, California, Idaho and Utah. He organized the Oregon and California Mission Conference, was agent of the American Bible Society for seven years, presiding elder of the Portland District for six years. Before he died, he established a night school for the Chinese which met six nights a week in Portland.[28]

A minister who came to New Jersey from the mission field was the Rev. Daniel P. Kidder. Daniel Kidder was born in Genesee County, New York, in 1815. Converted in 1833 in Lima, New York, he became a member of the Genesee Conference. Soon after his marriage to Cynthia Harriet Russell of Salisbury, Connecticut, November 9, 1836, the young couple went as missionaries to Rio de Janeiro, Brazil. After the death of his young wife in 1840, leaving him with two children, he returned to the States and joined the New Jersey Conference in 1841.[29] Kidder was a pioneer in preaching in Portuguese. He traveled all over that country and his three volumes on Brazil are of great importance. One, *Reminiscences of Trips and Residence in Brazil,* was translated into Portuguese and published about a century later. It is included in the records of the Brazilian Historical Society.[30]

Kidder later served with distinction as Editor of Sunday School Publications and Tracts, 1844 to 1856. He was also Secretary of the Sunday School Union. He set the Sunday School work of the Methodist Episcopal Church on a firm basis, established Conference Sunday School Unions and became an originator of Sunday School Institutes and Conventions. He taught at Garrett and Drew Seminaries and ended his long career as Corresponding Secretary of the Board of Education of the Methodist Episcopal Church.

Erastus Wentworth was another of New Jersey's leaders in missions in this pre-Civil War time. As a young student at Wesleyan University in 1835, he joined with two other students, B. F. Tefft and Daniel P. Kidder, to issue an appeal to the church to "begin and continue to do something for China."[31] After serving as President of McKendree College, he went to Dickinson College in 1850 as Professor of Natural Science. While at Dickinson he became a member of the New Jersey Conference.

In 1854, the forty-one year old Wentworth, an original sponsor of the China Mission letter, was appointed a missionary to Foo Chow. He served in China for seven years. The mission field seems to have been hard for missionary wives. Dr. Wentworth married Anna M. Lewis of West Chester, Pennsylvania, shortly before leaving for China. Four months after her arrival, Anna Wentworth died, leaving an infant daughter. In 1859, Dr. Wentworth married a missionary teacher, Miss Phebe E. Potter.

Returning to the United States, he transferred his Conference membership to the Troy Conference where he served with distinction. In 1872, he was elected editor of *The Ladies Repository,* a monthly magazine of the Church for women.

A noted missionary couple, who were born in New Jersey and served the church in many places, was the Rev. and Mrs. Dallas D. Lore. Just where Dallas Lore was born is not known. His wife, Rebecca Toy, was a daughter of Isaiah Toy of Palmyra. She was a grand niece of Joseph Toy. Dallas, a member of the Philadelphia Conference, and Rebecca served as missionaries in Buenos Aires, Argentina, from 1847 to 1855. They spent a year in New Mexico and joined the New Jersey Conference for one year, serving in Newark. Dallas Lore was elected Editor of the *Northern Christian Advocate* in 1864. He served in that important post until his death near Auburn, New York, in 1875. He was also one of the founders of Syracuse University. Mrs. Lore, after her husband's death, returned to live in New Jersey where she served as an early leader in the work of the New Jersey Conference Woman's Foreign Missionary Society.[32]

We turn from education and mission concerns to that of assisting the retired preachers, always an interest of every Annual Conference. In the Minutes of 1848 is this statement about the origin and work of the Preachers' Aid Society:

> In common with the whole family of Wesleyan Methodists throughout the world, the preachers and people within the bounds of the New Jersey Conference celebrated the Centenary of Methodism in the year of our Lord one thousand eight hundred and thirty nine. In connection with that celebration, many who had shared largely in the benefits of

the institutions handed down from our fathers, brought forward their thank-offerings of money.... One half of the whole sum collected... was to the support of the Supernumerary and Superannuated Ministers, and the widows and orphans of ministers deceased. Such was the origin of this fund.

When the money so generously contributed came into the possession of the Conference. ... A Society was formed... in 1841, denominated 'The Centenary Fund and Preachers' Aid Society of the New Jersey Annual Conference of the Methodist Episcopal Church.'[33]

The Society was incorporated by an act of the State Legislature in 1842 and has continued to benefit the retired ministers, and the widows and children of deceased ministers ever since.

An effort to provide better support for the retired preachers led in 1854 to the appointment of a Joint Board of Stewards, composed of one layman and one minister from each district. The Joint Board was to estimate the amount needed for the year, apportion it to the churches and circuits and promote its cause within the Conference.

A minister's wife, Joanna Reynolds Hanley, in the memoirs of her husband, the Rev. Joseph J. Hanley, M.D., tells something of what life was like in the parsonage in 1850. The young Joanna, (her husband was twenty-one but she does not tell her age) was from Walnut Grove near Toms River. Converted at a revival meeting in Harmony, she married her preacher on the Freehold Circuit.

Appointed as the Junior Preacher on the Moorestown Circuit in 1850, the young couple went to live in their first parsonage which was at Columbus. Joanna says the salary was small, but the home filled with comforts, and the table provisions were plenty. Choicest flour was left by the hundred weight from farmers, fresh rolls and butter, hams, beef, poultry, mince pies and quilts from members of the church. The Methodists of Columbus saw that their preacher and his wife had plenty to eat. But poor Joanna! Her preacher husband died when he was only thirty years of age.[34] Joanna became one who benefited from the support given ministers' widows.

Doctor J. T. Crane, Principal of Pennington School, in an article in the *Christian Advocate*, November 6, 1851, tells of a trip down the Atlantic Coast and up the Delaware Bay and River. It is of interest for its description of south Jersey churches at that time.

> My route has been from Barnegat, through Manahawkin, West Creek, Tuckerton, Bass River, Batstow, Mays Landing, Tuckahoe, Dennisville, Goshen, Cape May C. H., Cape Island, Port Elizabeth, Millville and Bridgeton. In all these places, as far as I have learned its early history, Methodism was planted at an early period.... The Methodist churches were built generally upon the same plan, and most of those now existing were erected by the fathers. They were usually frame buildings, in size about thirty by forty feet, with a gallery upon three sides, and a little narrow pulpit half way up to the roof. The seats were of the old-fashioned, straight-backed description; and the whole affair, within and without, was generally not painted. The location too was commonly chosen in some quiet, out-of-the-way place, which made the church the first house that greeted the eyes of the traveller— provided he entered the village from the right direction.... I must confess that I was somewhat disappointed by the size and general appearance of the churches.... In justice to the community however, I ought to say that something has been done within a few years,

and that the spirit of improvement is rapidly spreading. . . . The society of Tuckerton have just built their house anew, at an expense of $1000. . . . At Manahawkin the church has been modernized and painted this fall. . . . At West Creek also the house of God has been repaired. Brother Nelson, at Tuckahoe, is collecting funds to modernize the church. . . . At Dennisville there is a 'free church,' but the Methodists have abandoned the partnership plan, and are erecting a new house for themselves. . . . At Cape May Court House the church is of the old stamp. There is sufficient spirit in the society to erect a new house, or repair the old one, could either plan be adopted. . . .

On Cumberland Circuit there are two houses of worship building, one at Fork Bridge [Malaga], and the other at Dividing Creek. The campmeeting held last summer in the place first mentioned, resulted in the conversion of about one hundred souls. . . . In West Bridgeton the new church ediface [Trinity] is progressing as rapidly as the state of funds will permit. The basement is furnished in a very tasteful manner; and if the work is completed as it has been begun, this will be the most beautiful church of our denomination south of Trenton. . . .

The people are plain, warm-hearted, and hospitable. Almost the entire population are Methodists or Methodistic. On the coast, from Barnegat to Cape May, other denominations have scarcely an existence. . . .

Church statistics through the years tell of the number of black members in each society or church, reaching its highest peak of 817 in 1844[35] and declining to only 403 in 1856,[36] the last year in which separate statistics for black and white members were kept. By that time there were black churches at Mt. Hope in Salem, Mt. Zion in Lawnside, Springtown, Mount Zion near Woodbury and Ferry Avenue in Camden. Asbury, Merchantville and Berry's Chapel, Quinton were organized between 1856 and 1860.[37]

Before 1850, presiding elders were using black local preachers to supply the small black societies in New Jersey as well as in Pennsylvania, northern Delaware and New York.[38]

As early as 1844, black members of the Methodist Episcopal Church were petitioning General Conference to allow the bishops to hold annual conferences for traveling preachers of color.[39] Such conferences, however, were not permitted until 1852 and then only for New Jersey and Pennsylvania.[40] Such conferences of Negro local preachers and laymen were held in African Zoar Methodist Episcopal Church, Philadelphia in 1852 and 1855. Annual meetings were held in various churches between 1857 and 1863. The 1861 Conference was held in the Mt. Hope Church in Salem.[41]

The 1857 Conference met at Zoar Church, August 6 and 7. Called by Bishop Levi Scott it represented all of the Districts of the Philadelphia Conference and the Burlington and Bridgeton Districts of the New Jersey Conference. Nineteen black local preachers and six white presiding elders attended. Ten preachers volunteered to devote themselves to work and receive appointments. Among the six appointments was one on the Burlington District and one on the Bridgeton District.[42]

Membership in the New Jersey Conference nearly doubled to about 35,000 in the first twenty years after the Conference had been established. Discussions began to be held about dividing the Conference. Although no official action appears in the published Minutes, the manuscript *Journal* for 1855 shows the following resolution was approved:

> Resolved that a committee of five be appointed by the chair whose duty it shall be to enquire into the propriety and expedience of this conference and should they judge it best to divide, point out the most suitable line of division and report to this conference at its next session.[43]

John K. Shaw, John S. Porter, George F. Brown, Caleb A. Lippincott and Benjamin Weed were the committee entrusted with this important task.

The committee gave its report to the 1856 Conference meeting in Broad Street Church, Newark. The recommendation was to divide the Conference into the New Jersey and East New Jersey Conferences. Debate lasted nearly a day. The decision in favor of division was finally passed by a vote of 81 to 73.

Then came the task of locating the division line. The committee had recommended a line running up the Raritan River and its southwest branch to Quick's Mills near Flemington, then in a direct line to the Delaware River near Milford, leaving Flemington and Milford south of the line. This recommendation was amended to read:

> Commencing on the Raritan Bay, up said Bay and river to New Brunswick thence by turnpike in a direct line to Lambertville on the Delaware River, including Lambertville in the Southern Division.

It was also approved to have the southern conference keep the name New Jersey with the northern to be named Newark, rather than East Jersey Conference.

All this action, of course, had to be referred to the 1856 General Conference meeting in Indianapolis. The General Conference Boundaries Committee concurred with the request to divide the New Jersey Conference. The only debate was in which Conference to put New Brunswick. Several attempts were made to have the report amended, mainly by including New Brunswick in the Newark Conference. It did not happen. The following action is what was approved:

> The New Jersey Conference shall include that part of the State of New Jersey lying south of the following line, namely; Beginning with Raritan Bay and running up said bay and river to New Brunswick, thence along the turnpike road in a direct line to Lambertville on the Delaware River, including the city of New Brunswick and the Lambertville Station.
> The Newark Conference shall include all that part of the State of New Jersey not included in the New Jersey Conference and so much of the States of New York and Pennsylvania as is now included in the Paterson and Newton Districts.[44]

Thus, the two New Jersey Conferences came into being, a division which, while with different names, continues to exist. The unfortunate part of the division was that in this small state, New Jersey Methodism no longer spoke nor acted with one voice. The Newark Conference in time, became part of the New York Area. The New Jersey Conference was linked with Philadelphia. The two seldom met. They did not know and often did not even appreciate each other. It was not until 1964, with the creation of the New Jersey Area under the Episcopal leadership of Bishop Prince A. Taylor, Jr., that some semblance of unity of mission and purpose for New Jersey Methodism was restored. Our story from here on is one of the New Jersey Conference alone.

The New Jersey Conference, before its division, had one more year to go. General Conference gave its consent for the two Conferences to hold their next session together. When they did meet in Green Street Church, Trenton, April 8 to 17, 1857, Bishop Levi Scott, presiding, ruled that "this Conference will remain the New Jersey Conference until the close of the Session." It was not until the appointments were read at the close of the Conference that the two new Conferences began their separate lives.

At the time of division, the Newark Conference had 15,243 members on its four districts of Newark, Paterson, Newton and Rahway. There were 19,466 members in the three New Jersey Conference districts of Trenton, Burlington and Bridgeton.

It must have been with mixed emotions that the members of the 1857 Conference left for their respective Conferences. Gilmore, in his Centennial Sermon, says,

"When they adjourned that session, the Conference ties which had long bound their hearts in closest union, were severed; and each as he departed felt like exclaiming,

> When we asunder part
> It gives us inward pain,
> But we shall still be joined in heart
> And hope to meet again![45]

Chapter 6

THE WAR DECADE

1860-1869

Little by the way of background needs to be said concerning our national life in the 1860's. It was the decade of the bitter sectional strife. Our country was at war with itself. Even families were divided, and brother fought brother. Abraham Lincoln won the presidential election of 1860; but before he could take office, the Confederate States of America was formed. Within six weeks, Fort Sumter was fired upon in Charleston Harbor and the War between the States was on. It was a terribly bloody war in which few communities or families across the nation were unaffected. When the war was over, the Union had been preserved and the slaves set free. Lincoln's assassination, almost as soon as peace was achieved, left the nation ill-prepared to win the peace. The South was a long time recovering.

The story of New Jersey and the Civil War is a strange one. The state supplied 88,305 men to the Union cause, over 10,000 more than had been requested. Most of them were volunteers. Some 6,300 of them lost their lives. The state prospered economically because of the war and was ready for a postwar boom. Lincoln received a tumultuous reception when he crossed New Jersey in February 1861 on the way to his inauguration. After his assassination, April 14, 1865, the state went into deep mourning. Yet, twice New Jersey failed to give Lincoln its popular vote, the only state to do so. From the start of the war, there was strong opposition in the state. "Peace" Democrats and "Copperheads" along with several antiwar papers, including the *Monmouth Democrat* and the *New Brunswick Times,* worked against the peace effort.

The three Constitutional Amendments dealing with blacks were all opposed by the State Legislature. The Thirteenth, which abolished slavery, was not ratified until after it had become law. The Fourteenth, guaranteeing Civil Rights, was opposed by the Democrats who tried to rescind ratification after they regained legislative control. The Fifteenth, which granted suffrage to blacks was not ratified until 1870.

Yet, the area served by the New Jersey Conference did support Lincoln by its vote. How the Methodists voted is, of course, unknown. It will be shown, however, that the Conference in its official actions supported its president during the war and took issue with its elected officials in their opposition to the war and the civil rights legislation. One Methodist layman from Long Branch, William R. Maps, Jr., says, "They refused last year to vote for the Constitutional Amendment abolishing slavery in the United States, but the people have risen in their majesty and rebuked the administration, have changed the vote from the last gubernatorial election 18,000 votes." In other words, the voters of the state put out of office many of those who had refused to sanction an end to slavery.[1]

What was the response of the Methodists of the New Jersey Conference to the Civil War? First, we shall look at the official Conference action, then, at a survey of what clergy and laity said about the issues of those times, and to our response in terms of chaplains and other support groups.

Beginning with the 1862 Conference, a Report on the State of the Country was presented and voted upon. The 1862 report, unanimously adopted, speaks only of patriotism. The rebellion is regarded as treason, "the accomplishment of which would be one of the greatest conceivable calamities to the interests of civilization and Christianity." The first duty is to suppress the rebellion and reestablish the authority of the Constitution. The loyalties of our congregations are hailed with gratitude. Thanks are expressed to the Divine hand for his help. A call is issued for the nation to "humble itself before God."[2]

By 1863, slavery was seen as the villain. For the first time, the New Jersey Conference registered public support for anti-slavery sentiment. The vote on the State of the Country report passed 102 to 1. It contained this resolution:

> Regarding slavery as the prime cause of the war, having rendered those now in rebellion too arrogant to bear the restraints of constitutional and judicial limitations; and as, in the agitations of the times, the character of slavery is a subject of much discussion, we feel called upon to recall the attention of our people to the fact, that the Methodist Epsiscopal Church, viewing it as a great moral wrong, has long maintained on the pages of her book of Discipline, the question: 'What shall be done for the extirpation of the evil of slavery?' And her present recorded testimony in regard to it is, 'That we believe that the buying, selling, or holding of human beings to be used as chattels, is contrary to the laws of God and nature, and inconsistent with the golden rule; and with the rule of our Discipline,' which requires 'all who desire to continue among us, to do no harm, and to avoid evil of every kind.'[3]

The patriotism of the Conference was also shown by unanimous consent to raise the flag of the Union over the church, Broad Street, Burlington, during the Conference sessions.

A State of the Country report was not given in 1864, but a resolution was passed affirming the work of the United States Sanitary Commission on behalf of the sick and wounded soldiers. The flag was again raised over the front of the host church, Commerce Street, now First Church in Bridgeton. During the flag-raising ceremony, the choir sang "We'll Rally Round the Flag, Boys" and "The Star Spangled Banner."

General Conference met in Philadelphia the spring of 1864, the first since the outbreak of the war. A week after it had convened in Old Union Church, the Conference sent a message to President Lincoln in which it said:

> The General Conference . . . takes the earliest opportunity to express to you the assurance of the loyalty of the Church, her earnest devotion to the interests of the country, and her sympathy with you in the great responsibilities of your highest position in this trying hour.[4]

The message also commended the president for "all the acts of government designed to secure freedom to the enslaved."

Lincoln responded:

> Gentlemen, — In response to your address allow me to attest the accuracy of its historical statements, endorse the sentiments it expresses, and thank you in the nation's name for the sure promise it gives.
>
> Nobly sustained as the government has been by all the churches, I would utter nothing which might in the least appear invidious against any. Yet without this it may fairly be said that the Methodist Episcopal Church, not less devoted than the best, is, by its greater numbers, the most important of all. It is no fault in others that the Methodist Church sends more soldiers to the field, more nurses to the hospitals, and more prayers to heaven than any. God bless the Methodist Church! bless all the Churches! and blessed be God! who in this our great trial giveth us the Churches.[5]

General Conference passed resolutions condemning slavery; voted, after thirty years of controversy and debate, to remove the last vestige of slavery from the Discipline and by a vote of 207 to 9 changed the General Rule to forbid slave holding. Every delegate from the New Jersey Conference voted for abolition.[6]

Nicholas Van Sant was a member of the General Conference from the Newark Conference. He was one of four Van Sant brothers from Lower Bank to enter the Methodist ministry in New Jersey, two in each Conference. He wrote:

> In the General Conference of 1864 it fell to my lot to be a member of the Committee on Slavery, and there help by voice and vote to frame the rule by which slaveholding was made an absolute bar to membership in the Methodist Episcopal Church, and afterward to go on record with the enthusiastic, overwhelming majority that adopted the rule in full conference.[7]

General Conference also granted full clergy rights to black ministers and sanctioned black Conferences. The Delaware Conference, which included New Jersey's black congregations, became the first black Conference to be organized.

When the New Jersey Conference next convened in late March of 1865 in Trenton, the war was almost over. Conference concurred by unanimous vote, with General Conference actions in amending the rules on slavery.[8] In the State of the Country report, they expressed their love and honor for their country. They also, in strong words, condemned the State Legislature for refusing to vote for the Thirteenth Amendment to abolish slavery.[9] A year later the voters of New Jersey elected a new Legislature which immediately ratified the Amendment.

Finally, the Methodists of the New Jersey Conference and of the Methodist Episcopal Church ended their years of compromise and middle-of-the-road stance on slavery. At last, they forcefully opposed this great moral evil and travesty of human justice, but only, it must be said, when the country was divided and the war nearly over. The change came, it would seem, not so much because it was the right and Christian thing to do but because it was the patriotic thing to do.

There are available reports of what some of the Methodist clergy and laity of New Jersey were saying about these issues. Already mentioned are the remarks of the layman Maps and the preacher Nicholas Van Sant.

The agony in conscience that some persons felt in giving up their moderate position regarding slavery is shown by the remarks of Rev. A. K. Street. In commenting on the 1860 General Conference at Buffalo of which he was a member, Street says, "The slavery question came up in various forms. I was a conservative on that subject at that time. I feared another division in our church, if not of the nation, a catastrophe we had to meet the next year." Then he says, "My son Frank, after serving in the army for three years, was killed in battle October 8, 1864. *But the country was saved and slavery ended.*"[10]

The Headmasters of Pennington School during the war were ardent supporters of the Union cause. Pennington's historian says that during the Civil War "Dr. Wiley declared from the pulpit and platform and by every other means in his power, that the Union must be preserved, if the whole land had to be deluged with blood to save it.'[11] Wiley was followed in 1863 by Daniel Clark Knowles as president. Dr. Knowles served as Captain in Company D called the "Die-No-Mores," formed largely in Pennington of Colonel Perry's 48th New York Regiment.[12]

Later, Dr. Wiley delivered two lectures in Trenton in 1864 strongly condemning slavery and the South and urging a full prosecution of the war by the government. His lectures were titled, "How We Got In" and "How to Get Out." One example as quoted by Williams:

> Because the world moves, because society grows, because Christianity advances, because the earth, in each cycle it makes, sloughs off a man of sin and hell, and rolls onward toward the brighter day, when heaven and earth in peace shall meet and kiss each other. Why are we in war? Because Christianity has gone so far that the time has come to cry liberty to the bondsman. Slavery, then, we answer, and the recoil of human nature against this system, has been the spirit, the life and the soul of this Rebellion.[13]

Ruliff V. Lawrence, native of Farmingdale and minister of the New Jersey Conference, was a noted preacher of holiness, temperance and patriotism. Speaking at Fairton on July 4, 1866, he said it was the eleventh year he had delivered a Fourth of July address. His biographer calls him "an abolitionist of the old school." "He hated slavery, and flamed against the negro's wrongs." Unfortunately, we cannot chronicle the beginnings of his anti-slavery sentiments. At a July 4 speech at Goshen in 1863, he said:

> It is really more sinful to act a lie than to speak a lie, and our government has been acting a lie for the last eighty-five years. We have said, by the Declaration of Independence, that 'all men are born free and equal, having certain inalienable rights, among which are life, liberty and the pursuit of happiness,' and yet we have been enslaving millions of human beings, depriving them of all liberty and all manhood, buying and selling them as if they were beasts of the field.[14]

Lawrence, at the time, was minister of the Mount Holly Church.

General James Rusling, prominent Methodist layman from New Jersey, for long years a member of State Street Church in Trenton, wrote an article for the *Methodist Quarterly Review* while still serving in the Union Army. General Rusling saw the issues leading to war going beyond slavery. He saw it as a matter of federal authority against states rights. Nonetheless, he writes:

Slavery is only the common platform, the bond of union, the vital cord, which must itself be completely severed before the parts by it united can return to their old condition of peace and loyalty. But it is, after all, only a condition of the rebellion; a necessary condition, we grant, a condition which we would be blind not to see and allow for.[15]

Another Methodist minister who wrote against slavery was the pastor of Camden's Third Street Chruch, the Rev. Joseph B. Dobbins. The Episcopal Bishop, John W. Hopkins of Vermont, had recently defended slavery as in keeping with the Bible. Dobbins' 1863 article was entitled "The Bible Against Slavery; a Vindication of the Sacred Scriptures Against the Charge of Authorizing Slavery, A Reply to Bishop Hopkins."[16]

How did the Methodists of the New Jersey Conference support the war effort? First, of course, was supplying men for the army, most of whom were volunteers. Hundreds of Methodist lads must have fought and many died for their country. We have no way of giving any numbers.

A second way New Jersey Methodists responded for help during the War was in providing chaplains for the Union Armies. William Warren Sweet in *The Methodist Episcopal Church and the Civil War* lists 510 Methodist chaplains. Eleven were from the New Jersey Conference: William T. Abbott, Robert Given, Jacob B. Graw, Charles W. Heisley, Charles R. Hartranfft, Charles E. Hill, Joseph H. James, Frank B. Rose, Thomas Sovereign, William C. Stockton and James White. Chaplains received the pay of a Cavalry Captain.[17]

John C. Lenhart was a well-remembered charter member of the Conference and longtime naval chaplain. He lost his life when his ship, the *Cumberland*, was sunk near Hampton Roads, Virginia, March 8, 1862. The Journalist, William R. Maps, commented two days later: "Heard to-day that the Rebel Meramac has sunk the Cumberland. Mr. Lenhart drowned. Went down with the Cumberland. How sad the effects of war."[18] Chaplain Lenhart had earlier been Mr. Maps' pastor.

Chaplain Frank Rose will serve to illustrate the chaplain's work. Frank Bremwell Rose was born April 5, 1836, in Tuckerton. Three days before his twenty-first birthday, he married Mary Anna King in Philadelphia. They had three sons and two daughters. He was received into the New Jersey Conference on trial in 1861, ordained deacon in 1862 and elder in 1865. After pastorates in Freehold and at St. James in New Brunswick, Frank Rose was commissioned a chaplain in the 14th Regiment Infantry, New Jersey Volunteers, September 1, 1862. He was discharged with his Regiment near Washington, D.C. at the close of the Rebellion, June 18, 1865. Rose later served twenty-eight years as a naval chaplain, attaining the rank of Captain and in retirement, that of Rear Admiral.[19]

A letter from Chaplain Rose is in the files of the Conference Secretary. He wrote this from the Regiment Camp near Petersburg, Virginia, March 12, 1865. He requested the Examining Committee to recommend him for elder's orders. Apparently they did and he made Conference, as he had hoped, for he was ordained elder by Bishop Ames on Sunday, March 26.

Rose writes:

> For two and a half years I have been Chaplain to the 14th N.J.V. during which time I have itinerated thousands of miles & perhaps preached more sermons held more meetings, visited more of sick & wounded, buried more dead & seen more men born anew of the Holy Spirit than has been the privilege of any of my most favored brethren in the Conference.

Later he says:

> Nearly 350 men have found Christ in the 3 Chapels which I have dedicated to His service. The major part of these belonged to my own Regiment. A few have gone back to the service of sin but the great mass have continued to follow the Captain of their Salvation, whilst amid the shock of battle at Locust Grove, Cold Harbor, Petersburg, Monocacy, Spottsylvania, Winchester, Fishers Hill & Cedar Creek, . . . at least one hundred that I claim as spiritual children have endured martyrdom for their Country.[20]

The support of the United States Christian Commission was a third way support was provided for the war effort. The Christian Commission was organized at the New York City Y.M.C.A., November 14, 1861. Its purpose was to help the soldiers in every way it could in hospitals, camps and even on the battlefield. It assisted chaplains, nurses and surgeons. It provided much needed supplies for the soldiers. Between 1862 and 1865, over two and a half million dollars was collected for the work of the Christian Commission. Each year certain ministers of the Conference were appointed Delegates to the Christian Commission.[21] Conference urged the churches to support the Commission's work.

Following, and even during the war, considerable effort was put forth to assist the freed slaves. The Trenton Freedmen's Aid Society was one of about fifteen such societies founded in the north, including the Woman's Relief Association of Philadelphia, to help ex-slaves. Out of these and other similar efforts there was organized in Cincinnati in 1866, the Freedmen's Aid Society of the Methodist Episcopal Church. It was endorsed by the 1868 General Conference and had a long and useful life.[22] Much of its work had to do with the education of the black youth.

The first Vice President of the Freedmen's Aid Society was Major General Clinton B. Fisk. General Fisk later moved east where he and his wife became prominent lay persons in the New Jersey Conference and the Church at large. More will be said about them later.

The next chapter will tell more about the work of the Freedmen's Aid Society. Here let a black educator speak:

> There has never been a group in the Church that went to its task with more zeal, enthusiasm, dedication and determination than the early leaders of the Freedmen's Aid Society. They approached the work and persevered with complete abandon, and with a willingness to suffer ostracism, to vie with incredible difficulties, and to sacrifice all but the joy of dedicated service.[23]

The New Jersey Conference urged in 1866 the support of the Pennsylvania Freedmen's Relief Association. The Conference Freedmen's Aid Society was organized in 1867. Every Church was asked to receive a collection in May or June for education and Christianization of the freedmen.[24]

The war's end found the Methodist Episcopal Church the leading Church in the nation. Her bishops had the ear of the president and his cabinet. With the approval of the Secretary of War, the Church moved into southern, occupied territory and set up churches and Conferences in spite of the presence of the southern Church. Bishop Matthew Simpson preached Abraham Lincoln's funeral in Springfield, Illinois. The war was over. Victory had been won. The slaves were free. The Methodist Church had done its part. There was an air of optimism and triumphalism as the Church prepared to celebrate its Centennial in 1866. One hundred years of Methodist work in America were completed. One hundred years since Barbara Heck challenged Philip Embury "to preach to us or we will all go to hell together."

The General Conference of 1860 appointed a committee to make plans to celebrate the Centenary of American Methodism. Two objectives were proposed: the spiritual improvement of the church and the raising of a large fund for such church enterprises as the committee might designate. The 1864 General Conference enlarged the committee and adopted its recommendation that the Centennial should "commence on the first Tuesday in October, 1866, and continue through the month, at such times and places as may best suit the convenience of the Societies." The primary object was the spiritual improvement of the members. The giving was to come from feelings of gratitude for blessings received.

The raising of funds was for local and connectional needs. The local fund was for whatever local needs a conference, district or church might decide. The connectional fund was called The Centenary Educational Fund, and ten specific educational purposes were laid before the church. To this was added the Sunday School Children's Fund, out of which grew the Children's Day Program and the Student Loan Fund. The goal for the Centenary Educational Fund was two million dollars. The total raised was over $8,700,000. The Children's Fund raised an additional $83,700.[25] Out of this fund our existing church colleges were greatly strengthened and new institutions were founded. Among the new institutions were Drew Theological Seminary in Madison, New Jersey and Centenary College in Hackettstown. An attempt was also made by the Conference to establish a South Jersey Institute in Vineland, comparable to Pennington School. This effort failed. The story of the attempt will be told in Chapter 18.

The Conference celebrated the Centennial with Alexander Gilmore's Centennial Sermon, "What Has God Wrought?" It raised over $30,000 for the Centenary Educational Fund, Dickinson College, Pennington School and the South Jersey Institute. One positive achievement for the Conference was the payment in full of the debt on Pennington School. The school's first president, Dr. Edward Cooke, wrote, "Fortunate Institution! Well done New Jersey Methodists!"[26]

One of the beneficiaries of the Centennial was the Church Extension Society. This fledgling organization was founded by the 1864 General Conference with Samuel Y. Monroe, formerly of the New Jersey Conference, as its first secretary. Upon his untimely death in a train accident, A. J. Kynett was chosen his successor. It was after him that Kynett Church in Beach Haven is named. However, it was the colorful Charles S. McCabe, later bishop, the assistant secretary, who scoured the church to raise funds and made church extension known across Methodism. When the freethinker Robert G. Ingersoll pronounced a funeral over the Christian Church in advance, McCabe wired back that the Methodists were building a church a day and soon hoped to raise it to two. "Two a day" became a rallying cry and inspired Alfred J. Hough to pen a hymn that McCabe sang from coast to coast:

> The infidels, a motley band,
>   In council met and said:
> "The Churches die all through the land,
>   The last will soon be dead. . ."
> When suddenly a message came,
>   It filled them with dismay:
> "All hail the power of Jesus' name!
>   We're building two a day."[27]

The 1866 Conference organized a Conference Church Extension Society with Richard A. Chalker as president. An offering for church extension was to be taken in every church, "wherever practicable" in the months of May or June.[28]

Just prior to the Centennial year, there was a reunion of the Newark and New Jersey Conferences held in Trenton, March 22, 1865. It was a full day's affair of speeches, reminiscences and song. Governor Joel Parker addressed the assembly. The reunion opened in true Methodist fashion by singing Charles Wesley's hymn that I suppose has been sung at every session of the New Jersey Conference and probably most other Methodist Conferences:

> And are we yet alive,
>   And see each other's face?
> Glory and thanks to Jesus give,
>   For his almighty grace.

Alexander Gilmore commented, "Long will memory recall the pleasing associations of that day symbolizing as it did the re-union in Heaven!"[29]

Another reunion occurred in 1866. The New Jersey Conference was meeting in Camden, the Philadelphia in the City of Brotherly Love. At two o'clock on Wednesday, March 21, the New Jersey Conference proceeded in a body to Union Church, Philadelphia, where the two Conferences joined in a Reunion Love Feast.[30]

A spiritual highlight for many in this decade was the opportunity to hear the venerable Peter Cartwright preach while on a visit to New Jersey. Cartwright was a pioneer circuit rider of the old west. Thirteen successive times

Dr. John McClintock
Early Conference Leader and first President of Drew Theological Seminary

he was elected a delegate to General Conference. Twenty years he was a circuit rider and for fifty years a presiding elder. Twice a member of the Illinois State Legislature, probably the only defeat he ever had in his life was when he lost to Abraham Lincoln in 1846 in a contest for a seat in the United States House of Representatives.

An article in the February 9, 1860 *Christian Advocate* describes the visit of this now 75 year old preacher:

> The great Western pioneer, Peter Cartwright, or as they familiarly call him, 'Uncle Peter,' has recently visited us. He lectured at Newark, Trenton, Camden, Haddonfield, Glassborough, and Bridgeton. Many were curious to see and hear him. They have been gratified. For this gratification our New Jersey Methodists are indebted to Brother Graw, pastor of the Haddonfield Church. He lectured at the above named places for the purpose of raising money to aid this church, which is at present somewhat in debt.... How many old Methodists who have heard and read about 'Uncle Peter,' would have died without a sight of the weather-beaten countenance of this worthy veteran if it had not been for a church debt. They ought to have paid liberally for such an opportunity.

Laity concerns were brought to the attention of the Conference in these years as the laymen sought for recognition and a seat in the conferences of Methodism. In 1860, a resolution from the East Genesee Conference proposing lay delegation was discussed. It was rejected by a vote of 72 to 1. The resolution did, however, come before the 1860 General Conference which submitted it to a vote of the male members of the church and declared approval of its introduction into that body when it should be ascertained that the church desired it. The church voted it down two to one. The following vote was tallied in the New Jersey Conference:

	For	Against
Trenton District	278	243
Burlington District	216	272
Camden District	228	206
Bridgeton District	239	253
Total	961	974

Six charges did not vote.

Vote on the Conference floor was 32 for and 76 against.[31] The next vote on lay representation did not come until 1870.[32]

The Trenton, Burlington and Bridgeton Districts, the three Conference Districts formed when New Jersey was divided into two Conferences in 1857, had added to them the Camden District in 1860. The New Brunswick was formed in 1867.

The church's ministry with children was enhanced with the introduction of Children's Day. Its origin can be traced to a New Jersey pastor and a New Jersey Conference church. The Rev. and Mrs. Robert S. Harris came to Merchantville as minister and wife in 1866. He had helped start the church the previous year as an outgrowth of Bethel Church, Camden. Their move to Merchantville was with heavy hearts. Their only son, six years old, had recently died from pneumonia. Rather than let bitterness rule their hearts, the Harrises decided to adopt all children as their own.

Believing that children should have a rightful place in the Christian Church, Mr. Harris planned a Children's Day Service. All the children came bringing flowers, singing, and making recitations. Mr. D. S. Stetson, Superintendent, led the way. Rev. J. B. Dobbins, presiding elder and others also gave addresses. The children gave a special offering for some benevolent purpose. The date was the second Sunday in June, 1866. The idea soon spread and quickly became an accepted day of celebration in the Methodist Episcopal Church and others as well.

When Merchantville's new Trinity Church was built in 1895, a beautiful stained glass window with a reproduction of Plockhorst's "Christ and the Children," in recognition of the origin of Children's Day, was unveiled by Rev. Harris himself.[33]

At the same time as the founding of Children's Day, Methodism was celebrating its Centennial. One part of the Centennial was a special children's offering, the Sunday School Children's Fund. This soon became an annual offering, taken on Children's Day, for the benefit of needy students. This was the start of our present United Methodist Student Loan and Scholarship program.

Children's Day is no longer celebrated in many churches. Even where it is, it is not as it once was. Formerly churches were crowded. Flowers were everywhere. Nervous children were dressed in their finery. It was a happy time. It was one way of pulling the family together. It was a way of showing that "Jesus loves the little children, all the children of the world." Our churches and our world are poorer when we forget and fail to show that truth.

Camp meetings, long prominent in New Jersey Methodism, entered a new era beginning in the 1860's. The days of holding camp meetings at a clearing in the woods or some open and available field began to give way to the establishing of permanent camp meeting sites. The origin of Seaville, Malaga and Ocean Grove can all be traced to the decade of the 1860's. The story of Methodism's Camp Meetings in New Jersey will be told in Chapter 8. Here the story of a Conference Centennial Camp Meeting needs to be told.

Conference Minutes say little except that in 1866 a committee of the four presiding elders and two laymen from each district were asked to hold a Conference Centennial Camp Meeting sometime during the summer at some central point in the Conference. An incomplete article in the August 23, 1866 *Christian Advocate* says that the Camp opened with about 400 tents on the ground. With much preparation still to be done, there was limited opportunity for religious services. Rev. Jacob Graw preached the opening sermon. The four presiding elders took turns presiding. Within a couple of days organization was apparently better and a routine was developed. There was preaching morning, afternoon, and evening with prayer services at other times and at the close of the day. Many Conference preachers took turns exhorting sinners to come to Christ and the Christian to live a holier life. One of the noted preachers from outside the Conference was the Rev. John S. Inskip of New York who later helped found the Holiness Camp Meeting Association and Ocean Grove. From the report, one gathers that many were sanctified, and some were converted.

The Camp Meeting was held near Bethel Church in Hurffville. A member of the church, John D. Turner, donated the use of his woods for the meeting. It was located back of the old Barnsboro Mill, between it and the West Jersey Railroad. The history of Bethel Church says that people gathered in multitudes from New Jersey, Pennsylvania and Delaware and much success crowned the meeting. Water, though, was a problem. People had to get their water from a spring on an adjoining property. To reach the spring they had to walk a plank over a chasm. The owner charged one cent a bucket, bailing the water out for them.[34]

Presiding Elders' reports began to appear regularly in the Conference Minutes about 1867 and in fuller detail about district and local church events in 1869. A look at the 1869 reports help us see what was happening across the Conference.

Much church building was reported in 1869. New churches were built in Long Branch [St. Luke's], Oceanport, Rumson, Kettle Creek [Silverton], Pleasant Plains, Central in Trenton, Centenary Camden, Cedarville, Millville: First, and Watson's Corner. Bordentown and Trinity in Trenton were under construction. Jacksonville, Matawan and Farmingdale were building new parsonages. The Burlington District presiding elder reported four new churches dedicated and four parsonages purchased, but he does not name them.

Revivals, too, were evidenced across the Conference. Three hundred were reported converted at Centenary Long Branch, one hundred at Wall, and one hundred fifteen at Mantua. Other revivals of note were at Salem: First, Allowaystown, and lower Cape May. Presiding Elder Ballard said, "At Port Elizabeth village, during a week's meeting, so strong was the religious influence that all the stores closed for the week, except for an hour each day, when there was no service, and as the tavern could get few customers it followed the example."[35]

Samuel Van Sant, presiding elder on the Burlington District, said, "This district contains an area of about 1500 square miles, has 30 appointments and 50 churches, and extends literally 'from the river to the ends of the earth.' "[36] Not quite, but he had a district that traversed the pine belt and riding through, it probably seemed that way.

The decade of the 1860's began in war and ended in peace. The agony over slavery was over. New Jersey Conference Methodism was ready to move forward. It was a new day. It seemed as though nothing would stop the church's advance.

Chapter 7

A FLOURISHING CHURCH

1870-1899

Late nineteenth century America was a growing country. Between the election of Abraham Lincoln in 1860 and century's end, the nation's population more than doubled to seventy-five million. The Civil War was over, but reconstruction was a stormy and difficult time. The frontier began to disappear. Business and labor expanded with labor unrest becoming a concern. Cities, too, were growing. America's urban population grew from sixteen to thirty-three percent between 1860 and 1899. In 1880, there were only nineteen cities in the country with 100,000 or more people; by the century's end there were thirty-six, led by New York City's three-and-one-half million.

New Jersey, too, was growing. In 1880, the state's population rose for the first time above one million people with more people living in urban than rural areas. In the next thirty years, the population grew to over two-and-one-half million. It was the great age of immigration. In 1880, four of every five persons living in the state had been born here. By 1910, over half the state's citizens were foreign born. While earlier immigrants tended to come from northern Europe, the immigration tide slowly changed to people from southern Europe where language, religion and mores differed. Another facet of New Jersey's life was its popular seashore resorts. Cape May was the first playground. Then Long Branch began to "entertain the nation" and boast of the visits of seven presidents. Atlantic City then followed in popularity. The Methodist-founded Ocean Grove, Ocean City and Asbury Park, were all in full bloom, or soon would be, by the century's end. Our state's resorts have long attracted both the seekers of pleasure and the seekers for God. In all of them, Methodism has sought to bring its witness for Christ.

In this period, the Methodist Church was on the march. Historian Winthrop Hudson calls the period between 1825 and the eve of World War I, "The Methodist age in America."[1] Not only was the Protestant Church the dominant, cultural fact of the nation, the Methodist Church was the predominant ecclesiastical fact. The Methodist Episcopal Church, which grew from 1.5 million in 1875 to 2.5 million in 1900, was the largest single church in the country. Not only did it have ecclesiastical strength but a political influence "perhaps stronger in this period than it ever had before or since."[2] It was presumed in this period by Protestants, as well as Methodists, that America was a Christian nation. Among the principal issues which occupied the thought and energies of Methodists were temperance, political reconstruction and the freedmen question, apart from the lively concern of saving souls.

There were many things happening which the church ultimately had to face. Technological innovations and industrial expansion were rapidly moving across America. Immense fortunes were accumulated, displayed and spent. Mark Twain called it the "Gilded Age." Labor unrest and unionization became a fact of life, and needfully so. One example can be shown. In South Jersey's glass factories, a report of 3,000 glass company pay envelopes in 1899 showed workers had more money deducted than they had earned. Workers had to buy from company stores where prices were ten to fifteen percent higher than non-company stores. Each purchase meant a cut in pay from which there was little escape. Strikes in 1886, 1893 and 1899 failed; but on August 15, 1900, victory was won by the workers.[3] The Church, likewise, had to face changing theological concerns. Darwinism and new forms of Biblical criticism were moving in and they ultimately caused problems across Protestantism. The great moral force which came to fruition in these times was the temperance crusade with Methodists at the forefront.

With this rather sketchy background, we turn to focus upon New Jersey Methodism beginning with relationships to the blacks. Dr. Clement Price, in his study of Afro-Americans in New Jersey calls this period the "quest for racial identity." March 31, 1870, Thomas Mundy Peterson of Perth Amboy became the first black in the nation to vote under the protection of the Fifteenth Amendment. The Amendment's passage also occasioned a huge celebration by blacks in New Brunswick on May 26, 1870. Within a year, the first black juror in New Jersey's history served in West Milford. The most important development in the struggle for legal equality in New Jersey came in 1884 with the passage of the state's Civil Rights Act.[4] The same year, the State Supreme Court decision opening Burlington's white schools to black children outlawed school segregation in the state.[5] All of these gains, however, were impeded as white supremacy began to take over once again.

Robert Williams in his study of the status and role of blacks in New Jersey and the Methodist response summarizes this period.

> The late nineteenth century was a time when some progress was achieved through law and some decline was experienced through prevailing racial prejudices. It was a time the Methodists of New Jersey focused whatever action they took and whatever concern they expressed through the work of the Freedmen's Aid Society. In spite of the prejudice so prevalent in society, it has been suggested that there was a rising tide of optimism in the 1880's, that through education, racial uplift would result and the black would assume a respected place in American society. The education of the freed slave was the one enterprise that New Jersey Methodists seemed willing to assist in the later years of the nineteenth and the early years of the Twentieth century.[6]

The Methodist Episcopal Church's Freedmen's Aid Society, founded in 1866, sought to provide education for Negro youth in the south. By 1868, it had established fifty-nine schools in ten southern states. The Society continued until 1920 when its work was put under the aegis of the Board of Education for Negroes and after 1939 under the church's Board of Education.

The New Jersey Conference supported the Freedmen's Aid Society, but it never supported it well. Its yearly reports to Conference served to lift up the needs of the blacks and tried to sensitize the Methodists' conscience towards the blacks' plight. That it did good cannot be denied, yet, the paucity of the gifts and the number of charges which gave nothing show that the general attitude was one of charity, not service, and a charity that was often ignored. In 1873, the Conference collection amounted to only $293.55. In 1880, the total still did not reach $1,000. Offerings did slowly increase. In 1884 the offering was over $1,400.

A greater concern was evidenced, however, for one institution: Morristown School in Morristown, Tennessee. Morristown Seminary, as it originally was called, was founded in 1881 by Judson S. Hill. Hill was born and raised in Trenton, the son of a pork butcher. His wife was a Trenton girl, Laura Yard. They were members of Central Church. The original building of the school had been built in 1830 as a Baptist Church; then it became a slave market. It took some doing to raise the $250 needed to buy the building. Judson Hill served as the school's president for fifty years, until his death in 1931. In 1888, President Hill influenced Mrs. Clinton Fisk, president of the New Jersey Conference Woman's Home Missionary Society, to have that organization build a home for girls. The project was accepted; and at a cost of $8,000, the New Jersey Industrial Home for Girls was opened in October of 1892 for the teaching of domestic science. The New Jersey home served Morristown for forty years.[7] Southern New Jersey Methodists have continued to support Morristown College throughout its history.

As vital as was the support of blacks, the cause which really captured Methodists attention and energy was temperance. Temperance reform, strong at mid-century, was set back as a result of the relaxation of morals that followed the Civil War and the influx of European immigrants accustomed to habitual use of spirituous liquors. The setback was only temporary, however, for temperance forces. The National Prohibition Party was formed in 1869, the W.C.T.U. with Methodist Frances E. Willard as head began in 1874, and the National Anti-Saloon League was organized in 1895.

General Conference, from 1868 on, moved the Church in the direction of total prohibition. Full time Conference temperance agents were allowed; laws were endorsed to restrict liquor traffic; temperance societies were advocated in all congregations and Sunday Schools; the use of unfermented wine in the Lord's Supper was mandated; and in 1892, a permanent General Conference Committee on Temperance and Prohibition was formed. The Church declared that the 1880 General Conference declaration for "complete legal prohibition" and the 1884 Episcopal Address for "unyielding devotion to the principles of Constitutional Prohibition . . . constitute the platform on which we stand as a denomination, and upon which we will battle until Constitutional Prohibition is secured in every State and Territory of the Union, and finally embodied in the Constitution of the United States."[8] With all of this New Jersey Conference Methodists agreed. It was a crusade over which they lifted their banners.

In 1870, the New Jersey Conference Temperance Society was organized "to oppose the manufacture, and use of, and traffic in all kinds of intoxicating liquors as a beverage, and also to educate the public mind in the principles and demands of the Temperance Reform." Churches were urged to form auxiliary societies. Members subscribed to a pledge "to abstain entirely from the manufacture, sale and use, of all intoxicating liquors as a beverage."[9] In 1875, they urged the churches to use unfermented wine in Holy Communion. The practice of using grape juice at communion started in Vineland. Dr. T. B. Welch, founder of the Welch Grape Juice Company, was asked to be his church's communion steward. He agreed, provided he would be allowed to use the pure juice of unfermented grapes pasteurized in a new method perfected by his company.[10]

Constant reference in Conference sessions was made to liquor bills pending before the State Legislature such as one to prohibit sale to minors, another to allow for local option against the sale of intoxicating beverages, and one to provide temperance hygienic instruction in our public schools.

Jacob Graw, presiding elder of the Camden District, and a strong temperance advocate said, "The question of temperance is becoming more and more prominent in our church work. We are beginning to see that total abstinence and probibition are one and inseparable with our holy Christianity."[11]

The Bridgeton District Superintendent William Walton, in his 1884 report to Conference said, "Sharptown, Quinton, Hancock's Bridge, Roadstown, Fairton, Cedarville, Newport, Port Elizabeth, Harrisonville, Clayton, Leesburg, and in every town in Cape May County where the county court has jurisdiction, there is no legalized rum-selling."[12]

An example of the report of the Conference Temperance Committee, taken at random, in 1886 begins, "The sin of intemperance and the crime of the liquor traffic are the greatest curse and scourge of the land." The report laments "how difficult it is to combine the voting power of even Christian citizens against this gigantic iniquity. . . . We proclaim as our motto the voluntary total abstinence from all intoxicants as the true ground of personal temperance, and complete legal Prohibition of the traffic in intoxicating drinks as the duty of civil governments."[13]

Dr. Aaron Edward Ballard, from 1880 to 1892, was the New Jersey State Temperance agent. In this position it is said he was one of the most active and successful lobbyists in the State Legislature. Dr. Ballard was a strong man for that important job. He had already served thirty-six years in the pastorate, eight of which were as presiding elder. An ardent supporter of Camp Meetings, he was among the founders of both Ocean Grove and Pitman, serving as president of both. For forty-six years he was president of Pitman Grove. Such was the man who led New Jersey in the Temperance concerns.

This post Civil War period was not just a time of crusades; although another kind of crusade for salvation and holiness will be told about in the next chapter, it was also a time for celebrations. New Jersey Methodists joined in celebrating a New Jersey State Methodist Convention in 1870, the Nation's Centennial in 1876, the Centennial of the founding of the Christmas Conference in 1884, and the Fiftieth Anniversary of the New Jersey Conference in 1886.

The New Jersey State Convention met in Taylor Hall, Trenton, September 27 to 29, 1870. It was composed of all traveling ministers of the two Conferences plus a lay delegate from each charge. The Rev. J. S. Porter, D. D. of Hoboken served as president with ten Vice Presidents representing the two Conferences, four secretaries, and a treasurer. Official delegates totaled 191 ministers and 138 laity from 188 charges. It was an attempt to speak to relevant issues concerning the church, both from within the church and from society. After an opening Tuesday afternoon session given to statistics and resources of Methodism in New Jersey, morning, afternoon and evening sessions through Thursday evening each dealt with a major issue or concern. One hour was alloted for each major presentation, then it was opened for prepared and general remarks and discussion.

The sessions dealt with temperance; public schools and appropriation of money to sectarian schools; our educational interests; missions and Sunday School; spiritual life and personal activity along with the developing of our working forces, clergy, lay, male and female; the family; and the press, sectarian and religious.

Statistics showed Methodist membership gaining each decade from 2,374 in 1790 to 58,832 in 1870 while New Jersey's population grew from 184,139 in 1790 to an estimated 940,849 in 1870. The ratio of Methodists to population changed from 1 in 73 to 1 in 16.

The Temperance paper drew perhaps the most response. The Rev. George R. Snyder, delivering the major address said, "The people do not regard alcohol as a public enemy to be opposed, condemned, and extirpated. They do not condemn the licensed traffic, under what are regarded proper restrictions, nor the modest use of mild, palatable beverages."[14] That brought forth near the end of the convention this resolution:

> That in view of the fact that it is a violation of one of our 'general rules' to manufacture, sell, or use intoxicating liquors as a beverage, no person should be allowed to continue as a member in any of our churches, who is guilty of such violation.[15]

It is unfortunate such conventions as these have not been held more frequently. Methodists would have been helped to take decisive stands on issues of major importance.

The Centennial of American Independence was joyfully celebrated in 1876. The center of attraction was an international Centennial Exhibition held in Philadelphia. Bishop Matthew Simpson had the honor of giving the opening prayer on May 11. He praised God for the founders of the Republic and thanked Him for social and national prosperity. Simpson asked that "the new century be better than the past," that, "captial, genius, and labor" be free of antagonism. He prayed for God's benediction on the women of America. He concluded his prayer by asking that "the mission of America, under divine inspiration, [may] be one of affection, brotherhood, and love for all our race! And may the coming centuries be filled with the glory of our Christian civilization."[16]

The plan devised by the Methodist Episcopal Church's Centennial Committee called for all churches to observe the Centenary of Independence with special thanksgiving services between the first Sunday in June and July fourth, to receive a centenary collection for the cause of education, and that each annual conference provide for a memorial discourse.[17]

Rev. C. H. Whitecar preached the Centennial sermon at the New Jersey Conference from Jeremiah 30:18-22. A committee was asked to hold a Centennial Educational Convention in August at Ocean Grove, if possible. Beyond that, we have no other record of activities. Living so near Philadelphia, we can be sure large numbers of New Jersey Methodists took advantage of the opportunity to take part in the Centennial Exhibition. Knowing the patriotism of our people, we can be sure they celebrated with gusto and feeling. We know, too, that because of its location, so close to Philadelphia, Cape May was chosen to host an important Conference of a few select leaders of the Church, north and south, that summer which was destined to be a first step in the eventual reuniting of Methodism. More about that later.

The Christmas Conference Centennial of 1884 was widely celebrated. The 1884 Conference which met in Broadway Church, Camden, celebrated it Thursday afternoon and evening. Rev. Benjamin C. Lippincott and Rev. George K. Morris spoke in the afternoon. Rev. John S. Heisler preached the Centennial Sermon in the evening.[18] The Centennial Committee called for special Centennial meetings throughout the Conference and an Anniversary meeting in every charge. It also asked for a special offering of two dollars per member from each church to be divided forty percent for the Peacher's Aid Society and sixty percent for Pennington School. It is not clear how much was raised from these offerings.

The Methodists of America gathered in Baltimore's Mt. Vernon Place Methodist Episcopal Church for a grand Centennial Conference, December 9-17, 1884. Delegates attended from the Methodist Episcopal, Methodist Episcopal South, African Methodist Episcopal, African Methodist Episcopal Zion, Colored Methodist Episcopal, Primitive Methodist, Methodist Church of Canada and Independent Methodist Churches. Fraternal Delegates attended from the Methodist Protestant and Bible Christian Churches. It was a gala celebration. Morning and afternoon sessions with papers on a wide variety of topics were held in the host church. Evening celebrations were held simultaneously in numerous churches of Baltimore, all on the same subject. Delegates attending from the New Jersey Conference were Rev. J. B. Graw of Camden, Rev. W. W. Moffett of Red Bank and General C. B. Fisk of Sea Bright. Evening addresses on missions were given by Rev. Graw and General Fisk. It was one of the first opportunities for all Methodists, black and white, north and south, across America and from Canada to meet and share together.[19]

Commerce Street Church, Bridgeton, now First Church, was host for the Semi-Centennial Session of the New Jersey Conference, March 11 to 15, 1886, with Bishop John F. Hurst, former president of Drew, presiding. Jefferson Lewis, A. K. Street and G. B. Wight all gave Semi-Centennial Addresses. After fifty years, there were 37,432 church members in the Conference; 293 churches valued at $1,905,752; 121 parsonages valued at $303,850; 324 Sunday Schools with almost 6,000 officers and teachers and 40,493 scholars. Missionary giving totaled $26,881. There were 212 ministers in the Conference including 18 on trial, 31 preachers' widows and 202 local preachers. Only three ministers received salaries of as much as $2,000. Those salaries were paid by State Street Church, Trenton; Centenary and First Churches in Camden. The largest church in membership in the Conference was First Church Bridgeton, pastored by Rev. Willis Reeves, with 700 members. His salary was $1200.[20]

Cape May made Methodist news during the summer of 1876 when this resort city on the Jersey shore hosted a gathering of delegates from the Methodist Episcopal Churches north and south. It was the first time since the church division of 1844 that the two sides officially met to discuss relationships between them and to attempt to resolve differences. It was a most important step in the "long road to unification" which did not occur until 1939. It was important because it laid the groundwork and established the basic principle on which further talks were possible and union could eventually take place. That principle was that both churches were legitimate branches of Episcopal Methodism. One was not father and the other a daughter. One was not the real Methodist Church, the other an illegitimate child. In reality, it confirmed the decision of the 1844 General Conference to divide the Church.

Ten men gathered in Cape May for the August Conference, three clergy and two laymen from each Church. Participating from the Northern Church were Erasmus Q. Fuller of Atlanta, Georgia, Editor of the Methodist Advocate; Judge Enoch L. Francher, Jurist of New York City; John P. Newman, pastor of the Metropolitan Church of Washington, D.C. and later a bishop; Morris D. G. Crawford, Presiding Elder of the New York Conference; and General Clinton B. Fisk of St. Louis, later a distinguished layman of the New Jersey Conference. Southern delegates were Professor Edward H. Myers of Savannah, Georgia; Robert K. Hargrove of Nashville, later a bishop; General Robert B. Vance of Ashville, North Carolina; Thomas M. Finney of St. Louis and David Clopten of Montgomery, Alabama. Crawford and Myers were co-chairmen, Fisk and Finney served as joint secretaries.

The road to Cape May itself was a long one. It began with fraternal visits of Bishops Janes and Simpson to the Southern Church's Council of Bishops. This was followed by fraternal visits to the 1870 and 1874 General Conferences of the Southern Church. The Southern Church responded by appointing fraternal delegates to the Northern Church's 1876 General Conference along with a commission to meet a similar commission from the Northern Church "to remove all obstacles to formal fraternity between the two churches" and "to adjust all existing difficulties."[21] The Methodist Episcopal Church concurred and Cape May was the result.

The Joint Commissioners gathered on August 16 in Congress Hall, but there were still differences to adjust before a formal meeting could take place.

Letters were exchanged between the two groups. When the northerners put in writing:

> Each of the aforesaid Churches is a legitimate Branch of Episcopal Methodism in the United States, and since the organization of the Methodist Episcopal Church, South, was consummated in 1845, by the voluntary exercise of the right of the Southern Annual Conferences, ministers and members to adhere to that Communion, she has been an evangelical Church, reared on scriptual foundations, and her ministers and members, with those of the Methodist Episcopal Church, have constituted one Methodist family.[22] 'You and we together,' as Dr. Pierce remarks, 'make up this Methodism.'

The southerners accepted the invitation to meet the next morning at nine o'clock in Room 168 of Congress Hall.

Rules of Order were adopted and the basis of fraternity, previously stated, that both Churches were legitimate branches of Episcopal Methodism was enacted as "a Declaration and Basis of Fraternity" between the two Churches.

Most of the rest of the sessions involved settling complex property disputes where each Church claimed to be the rightful owner of a church, parsonage or piece of property.

Sixty years elapsed between the 1876 Cape May Conference and the Uniting Conference in Kansas City in 1939. Kenneth Rowe has written, "Although the road between Cape May in 1876 and Kansas City in 1939 was long and rocky, the Spirit of Cape May, together with the Holy Spirit, triumphed in the end."[23]

Nor has Cape May been forgotten. As part of the celebration of the 125th Anniversary of the New Jersey Conference in 1961, a special session was held at Cape May. Bishops representing the former southern and northern churches, along with black Methodism participated in the Cape May Methodist Church. The highlight was the unveiling of a monument, on the grounds of the Cape May Church, commemorating the historic 1876 Conference. The monument was a gift of the laity of the Conference.

Again, in 1976, under the sponsorship of the Conference's Commission on Archives and History, a Centennial Celebration of the Cape May Conference was held on Sunday, September 12, at 3:30 in the afternoon in the Cape May Church with Dr. Kenneth Rowe of Drew as the main speaker. A highlight was the dedication of the Cape May Monument as United Methodist Historic Site Number 44. May the spirit of Cape May live on in the wider ecumenical endeavors of United Methodism.

Other kinds of changes were occuring in Methodism during the later decades of the nineteenth century. The struggle for lay representation in the higher eschalons of the Church began to achieve significant victories. While sought after clergy rights for women were denied, women were successful in claiming their full rights as laity and exhibited trememdous vitality and enthusiasm in developing women's organizations on the local, conference and denominational levels. Youth, too, came into their own in the formation of youth organizations which became tremendously popular and beneficial in the life of the church.

The 1860 plan for admitting lay delegates into the General Conference was defeated. Another proposal was passed by the 1868 General Conference and again referred for ratification to the Annual Conferences and male members of the church. This time the vote was two to one in favor. Two lay delegates from each Conference were allowed in the succeeding General Conferences. The vote across the New Jersey Conference in 1870 was 3,274 yes to 1,630 no.[24] Every District recorded a favorable vote. When it came up to a vote in the Annual Conference, the vote was 66 to 61 in favor, but lacked the necessary three-fourths majority. Next day, Saturday, it was brought up for reconsideration, discussed, then laid over until Monday. The final vote was 80 to 52 in favor, but it still lacked the required majority.[25] The clergy of the New Jersey Conference had a hard time bringing themselves to support lay activities.

Walter Van Sant, in his study of early lay activities in the Conference, shows the following votes taken in the Conference on lay participation. In 1890, the question was on the seating of duly elected women delegates to General Conference. New Jersey voted 43 yes, 118 no. Another vote on the same question in 1891 was defeated 54 to 128. In 1894, the vote was on equal lay and clergy delegates to General Conference. This Conference recorded only 16 yes votes to 121 in the negative.[26] In 1897, another vote on equal representation was defeated 36 to 125. Finally, in 1898, at the urging of the Layman's Convention, Conference voted again on equal representation. This time the vote was in favor, 110 to 65.[27] The 1900 General Conference was made up of an equal number of lay and clergy delegates.

The successful passage of the 1868 General Conference proposal on lay representation led to the holding of the first Lay Electoral Conference in 1872. The meeting was held in Central Church, Trenton, March 1, 1872, at two o'clock in the afternoon for the purpose of electing two delegates and two reserve delegates to General Conference. The honorable Samuel A. Dobbins was elected Chairman, Jesse H. Diverty, Secretary, and William R. Maps, Assistant Secretary. Mr. Dobbins and James Bishop were elected the first lay delegates to General Conference from the New Jersey Conference with T.V.F. Rusling and General James Rusling as alternates.[28]

The Lay Electoral Conference continued to meet every four years to elect delegates to General Conference and pass resolutions of concern to the laity. The 1896 Conference in Central Chruch, Bridgeton, was interesting in that for the first time some of the charges sent women delegates. The men debated whether or not they should be seated. Finally, the chairman ruled that since the roll had already been called and verified, they should be allowed their place. So it was in 1896 that the men allowed the women to be their equal as laity in the life of the Conference.

In 1897, the first Layman's Convention of the Conference was held. This was a new organization. No longer did they meet only every four years to elect delegates to General Conference. Yearly meetings were held at the time and place of the Annual Conference, but still separate from the official Conference sessions attended by clergy only. Sometimes they would meet jointly, but not for the conducting of official business.

Walter Van Sant describes that first Layman's Convention. It met in First Church, Camden, on March 31, 1897. "The attendance was so large that many were standing. General James F. Rusling of Trenton called the Convention to order and led in prayer. General Rusling was made temporary chairman with John S. Turner of Bridgeton as secretary."[29] There were numerous speakers and much support for equal representation of lay and clergy in General Conference. The laity also adopted a resolution in support of President McKinley in the crisis over Cuba and Spain.[30]

The following year, 1898, the Layman's Association of the New Jersey Conference was organized as a permanent organization to meet annually during Conference week. A Constitution was adopted and the following officers elected:

President - General James F. Rusling, Trenton
Secretary - John S. Turner, Bridgeton

Vice Presidents

New Brunswick District - George W. Evans
Trenton District - Gilbert Slack
Camden District - George C. Baker
Bridgeton District - Benjamin Patterson[31]

Meanwhile, women continued their struggle for rights in the Church. The 1888 General Conference refused to seat four duly elected women delegates, including Frances Willard. Finally, the 1896 Conference allowed women to be delegates, but none were seated until 1904.

The struggle for clergy rights for women was much more difficult. Prior to 1880, women had been licensed as local preachers. The 1880 General Conference put an end even to that. This action was precipitated by the request of two graduates of Boston University School of Theology, Anna Oliver and Anna Howard Shaw, for ordination. Not only did the Church deprive them of ordination, but even took away from them their license to preach. They preached anyway, but without official sanction and ordination. Another form of work did open up to women, the sanction of Deaconess work in 1888.

Women were to find new avenues of service, however. Tremont Street Church, Boston, was the place where a group of Methodist women met March 23, 1869, and organized the Woman's Foreign Missionary Society of the Methodist Episcopal Church. Miss Isabella Thoburn, teacher, and Dr. Clara Swain, medical doctor, were the first two missionaries sent to India. Methodist Episcopal women organized a second group, the Woman's Home Missionary Society, June 8, 1880, in Trinity Church, Cincinnati. Their special concern was the southern field and work with freed slaves. Mrs. Lucy Webb Hayes, wife of President Rutherford B. Hayes, was the first president. Jeannette Crippen Fisk of New Jersey, wife of General Clinton B. Fisk, became the third president in 1893. The United Brethren organized their Women's Missionary Association in 1875. The Woman's Missionary Society of the Evangelical Association was formed in 1884. Methodist Protestant women organized their Woman's Foreign Missionary Society in 1879 and in Laurel Hill Church, Bridgeton, in 1893, the Woman's Home Missionary Society of the Methodist Protestant Church came into being. More will be told about these women's groups in Chapter 15, "Women's Role in Southern New Jersey Methodism."

It wasn't easy for the women. The men of the church often gave them a hard time. Early in the twentieth century, a Maria Gibson knelt at a missionary conference of the Methodist Episcopal Church, South, and prayed: " 'Dear Lord, we pray for the men on the Board of Missions. Thou knowest how they have troubled and worried us. They have been hard to bear sometimes, but we thank Thee that they are better than they used to be.' "[32]

These missionary organizations of women across Methodism were soon mirrored with like organizations on the Annual Conference and the local church level. Early Woman's Foreign Missionary Societies in the New Jersey Conference were formed in 1870 in Trenton, Long Branch, and New Brunswick.[33] The Conference Society was organized between then and 1872 when a Mrs. James of Trenton was elected the first New Jersey Conference Corresponding Secretary. She was succeeded by Mrs. John Aber in 1877 and Mrs. Dallas D. Lore in 1883.[34]

March 20, 1885, the Woman's Home Missionary Society of the Conference was formed in New Brunswick with Mrs. General Clinton B. Fisk (that is how they reported her name) as president. Mrs. C. F. Garrison was elected corresponding secretary. Their work at Morristown College has already been told and a fuller story of these two Conference women's missionary agencies will be related later.

Meanwhile, in the local church, women were organizing in other ways. In Philadelphia, in 1868, Annie Turner Wittenmyer led in the organization of the Ladies and Pastors' Christian Union. Their purpose was to do religious work in the homes of people and evangelize the masses in the cities under the supervision of the regular pastorate. In a way, it supplied the need for an order of Deaconesses. It became an official organization of the Church by sanction of the 1872 General Conference.[35]

Women of New Jersey wasted little time in becoming involved. A Conference Ladies and Pastors' Christian Union, with a male president, was organized in 1870. Conference passed this resolution: "That we earnestly recommend the Ladies and Pastors' Christian Union to the favor of our people, and advise the formation of auxiliary societies in our churches, whenever practicable."[36] A Constitution was adopted in 1873. This Union soon gave way to Ladies Aids in the local church with its wider needs replaced by Deaconesses and the Home Missionary Societies.

Youth work, too, had its start in the Conference in the late nineteenth century. The Oxford League was officially organized at the 1884 General Conference by Bishop John H. Vincent, formerly of the New Jersey Conference and the originator of Chautauqua. There were other similar, but less official, youth societies, too. May 14, 1889, in Cleveland, Ohio, representatives of these groups met and formed the Epworth League. A Conference Epworth League was formed the same year, and June 1, 1890 "The Epworth Herald" became the voice of the Epworth League. In the early years, the Conference President was always a minister and not always a young one. The first Conference Epworth League president of which there is a record was Rev. Amos M. North in 1892. He was 57 years of age.[37]

Minutes of the Second Session of the New Jersey Conference Epworth League held at Broadway Church, Camden, February 13 and 14, 1896, are preserved in the Conference Minutes in detail for that year. The Rev. Henry J. Zelley, popular pastor and hymn writer who wrote "Heavenly Sunlight," was president. By that time, each District League was organized and their presidents' names are listed. Also listed is a full roster of delegates, 262 from 111 churches. Reports from each local unit are listed in statistical form.[38]

A complete record of the Bridgeton District Epworth League is in the Conference Archives. It, too, was organized in 1889. It shows five local church Leagues organized that year and twelve more in 1890. Tuckahoe, May 4; Goshen, September 1; South Dennis, September 3; Cedarville, November 19, and Dias Creek, November 20 were all organized in 1889. A fuller story of youth work in the Conference will be told in Chapter 13.

Singling out a few outstanding clergy and lay leaders of this period is not meant to ignore the thousands of other lesser lights who pastored the churches, sat in the pews, built and sustained God's edifices, nurtured the children, led the youth, ministered in all kinds of places, kept the faith and in death went to glory, but leaders are always necessary and are in the vanguard of all that happens. Here a brief word will be said about two lay men, two lay women and two clergy.

General Clinton B. Fisk (1828-1890) has to be one of the leading laymen of all time in the New Jersey Conference. Born in Connecticut, his family moved to Michigan when he was a small boy. Later, he moved to St. Louis. During the Civil War, this ardent abolitionist became a Colonel then Brigadier and later Major General. After the War, he was appointed Assistant Commissioner for the Bureau of Freedmen for Kentucky and Tennessee. In 1866, he left the Freedmen's Bureau and became a railroad Vice President. The Fisks moved to New York in 1877 and in 1879 to their home, Elmwood, in Sea Bright. In 1885, they acquired a cottage in Rumson. He was a founder of Fisk University.

Fisk's biographer says: "No single layman . . . has ever served the Methodist Church in such diverse and responsible positions, and for so long a time as he."[39] He was a member of the Book Committee, Mission Board, Fraternal Delegate to the Methodist Episcopal Church, South, member of the Cape May Conference, Delegate to the 1881 Methodist Ecumenical Council in London, and confidant of the church's bishops. He and Mrs. Fisk, at least

GENERAL CLINTON B. FISK
A leading layman in the N.J. Conference

once, entertained the entire Council of Bishops in their Jersey Shore home. He was also a trustee of Drew and Albion College in Michigan. The 1889 Conference Minutes lists these Conference positions he held: 1st Vice President Historical Society, Trustee of both Pennington Seminary and Dickinson College, Trustee of the Preachers Aid Society and member of the Board of Church Location of the New Brunswick District. Three times, 1880, 1884 and 1888, he was elected lay delegate to General Conference, the only layman from this Conference to serve that often before 1900. General and Mrs. Fisk founded the church in Sea Bright, New Jersey, and it has a memorial window in his memory, much of it paid for by his friends in the Conference.

An ardent prohibitionist, General Fisk joined the Prohibition Party in 1884. Two years later, he was their nominee for Governor of New Jersey and received 19,808 votes. In 1888, the Party named him their nominee for President. General Fisk died in 1890.

General Fisk's wife, the former Jeannette Crippen, was very much his equal. She must have been a gracious hostess for she and her husband entertained frequently. Prominent ministers from New York would be their guests and preach on Sunday in Sea Bright's church. She was the founding president of the Conference Woman's Home Missionary Society. Mrs. Fisk was elected the third president of the Woman's Home Missionary Society of the Methodist Episcopal Church, serving from 1893 to 1908. Previously, she was Secretary of the Bureau for the West Central States. The National Training School for Christian Workers, opened in 1899 in Kansas City, was called the Fisk Bible and Training School in honor of Mrs. Fisk. During her tenure as Conference president, the New Jersey Home at Morristown College was erected, largely under her influence. At the close of one of the denominational Annual Meetings, Mrs. Fisk gave this advice: "When you find a duty facing you, remember these three words: Do it now that you may learn promptness and that your work may be easier." During her tenure the Bancroft-Taylor Rest Home for Deaconesses was established in Ocean Grove.

Another ardent Woman's Home Missionary Society worker demands recognition. Hannah S. C. Garrison, the wife of the Rev. Charles F. Garrison of the New Jersey Conference, was a graduate of the Trenton State Normal School and the Chautauqua Literary and Scientific Circle. She gave much effort to her role as a pastor's wife and to her W.C.T.U. work on the local, county and state levels. Mrs. Garrison became the first Corresponding Secretary of the Woman's Home Missionary Society and succeeded Mrs. Fisk as Conference president in 1895. She still held this position at her death in 1905. It was largely because of the work of Mrs. Garrison that the Society's work was extended throughout the Conference. Mrs. Garrison also founded the New Jersey Conference Sisterhood, now called Wesley Fellowship.

General James Fowler Rusling is the other layman of prominence. Born April 14, 1834, in Washington, Warren County, New Jersey, he served as an officer throughout the Civil War and was named Brigadier General in 1865. A graduate of Pennington Seminary and Dickinson College, be became Professor of Natural Science in Dickinson Seminary, now Lycoming College, Williamsport, Pennsylvania. In 1859, he moved to Trenton and became a member of the New Jersey Bar.

An ardent churchman, he was a charter member and local preacher in Trenton's State Street Church for fifty-nine years. He served as trustee of Dickinson College, and for fifty years of Pennington School, ten of which he was president. For twenty-seven years he was a Manager of the Board of Foreign Missions of the Methodist Episcopal Church. An author and public speaker, he was also active in the Mercer County Sunday School Association, serving a term as the president. General Rusling was elected delegate to the 1896 General Conference and served as the first president of the Layman's Association of the New Jersey Conference. He died in Trenton, April 1, 1914.

The Reverends Jacob B. Graw and George B. Wight are the clergymen of note. Jacob Graw served as delegate to eight consecutive General Conferences from 1872 to 1900, the only clergyman in the Conference to claim that distinction. Throughout his ministry he served a total of eighteen years as presiding elder on all five Districts of the Conference. During the Civil War, he was a Chaplain to the 10th Regiment of New Jersey Volunteers. Jacob Graw was a Dickinson College trustee for twenty-six years and trustee of Pennington School for over thirty. From 1874 to 1880, he was a member of the Book Committee of the denomination and from 1880 until his death a member of the Board of Managers of the Methodist Episcopal Missionary Society and Board of Church Extension. Married to Isabella Stillwell of Staten Island, Jacob Graw's ministry and life closed on February 18, 1901.

Rev. George Bates Wight, native of Massachusetts, was a minister of the Conference, serving with his wife, Virginia Atkinson, from 1866 until his death, June 1, 1916. George Wight's ministry was largely spent as a pastor of local churches. Broadway, Camden; First, Millville; First, Camden; First Church, Trenton; First, Asbury Park; and Union, Camden, all among the largest churches of the Conference, were his successive appointments. He also served two years on the Bridgeton District. His five successive elections to General Conference, 1880 to 1896, make him second among all the pastors of the Conference in the previous century to attain this honor. He left the pastorate in 1905 to serve as the Commissioner of the new State Department of Charities and Corrections. He held this post until his retirement in 1913. Earlier, while pastoring in Mays Landing and Absecon, 1873 to 1876, he also served as Atlantic County Superintendent of Schools. He, too, was a Dickinson and Pennington School trustee, long-time Conference Secretary and preacher and administrator of note.

Since Dr. Crane's trip through South Jersey in 1851 in which he described the churches as plain, frame buildings about thirty by forty feet, often unpainted inside or out, many changes occurred in the churches of the Conference. New churches were built and old ones rebuilt around the Conference. A few of the old ones still remain much as they were—Head of the River, Weymouth, Pleasant Mills, Estellville—perhaps a few others. Largely, the old gave way to the new. The new churches were more commodious, more worshipful, planned for the large audiences who often attended, better lighted for large evening congregations. Even the small country church was improved, painted, looked nice and served the congregation in the name of Christ. The churches built after 1860 had a center pulpit. Some were on the acron plan with pews that fanned out in semicircular fashion from front to back. Many still had balconies for large crowds and some had rooms to one side which could be opened for overflow congregations. Many were two story buildings with an audience or Sunday School room or rooms downstairs and the sanctuary up a flight of stairs, giving little thought to the needs of the handicapped. Some were built largely as preaching houses to handle large congregations. Better attention to Sunday School facilities came later.

Choirs came on the scene. Better music and hymnals with the tunes, not just the words of the hymns were introduced. Churches began using organ music, much to the consternation of some old timers who lamented the passing of the plain old days of old fashioned Methodism. Believe it or not, there were real struggles in many New Jersey churches over introducing organs, padded pews, promiscuous seating, choirs, more "modern" forms of worship and even the latest hymnals. When one church proposed getting the new hymnals with tunes, a dissenting member was heard to remark: "Anybody with common sense ought to know that it will not help the voice to look when you sing upon those things that you call keys and bars, with black and white tadpoles, some with their tails up, and some with their tails down, decorated with black flags and trying to crawl through the fence. It's all the work of the Devil."

Well, it all did not prove to be the devil's work. Methodism prospered in the Garden State. In 1850, only two churches in the Conference could claim 500 members, Burlington with 500 exactly and First Church Trenton with 516. In 1860, only one, First, Bridgeton, and in 1870 only one, First, Trenton. By 1900, there were seventeen, six of which had 700 or more members. The top ten churches in membership in 1900 were:

1.	Camden: Broadway	1190
2.	Millville: First	993
3.	Camden: First	900
4.	Trenton: First	827
5.	Camden: Tabernacle	785
6.	Trenton: Trinity	700
7.	Camden: Union	677
8.	Bridgeton: Central	639
9.	Bridgeton: First	631
10.	Vineland	624[40]

It was a different day. The large city churches were coming into vogue. Broadway Church in Camden was the first Conference Church to top 1,000 in membership. Along with those churches, our Conference had numerous small town and rural churches, always far more small membership churches, but the large church was now a fact. This meant strong preachers were needed to fill these appointments.

Another factor in New Jersey Methodism was the shore church. By 1880, Ocean Grove had 500 members and Asbury Park soon would have that many. St. Paul's Church, Atlantic City, had 761 members by 1910. St. Luke's in Long Branch had 527 members in 1900 and a large building with a new organ. Ocean City soon would top 500. Ocean City and Ocean Grove were attracting the religious-minded who wanted to worship. Other resorts drew the pleasure-minded, but many of them worshipped, too. Keep in mind, the figures quoted indicate church members and tell nothing of the larger numbers attracted to summer preaching services at our shore churches.

At the beginning of this chapter, the moral concerns relating to temperance and race relations which concerned the church were discussed. There were other matters of a moral nature which confronted the Church as well. Camden District Presiding Elder, Milton Relyea, in 1892, told Conference:

> We are unfortunate in our surroundings. Gloucester City, of race track and pool-selling infamy; Lincoln Park and Atlantic City, with open disregard for the Lord's Day, all on my district, have a baneful influence over our people, both young and old. I fear there is a growing indifference and looseness concerning the sanctity of the Sabbath, and also concerning the enormity of these and all other evils.[41]

Milton Relyea blamed most of it on the liquor traffic.

The next year Conference was appalled that the State Legislature legalized race-track gambling and "brought deep disgrace upon our commonwealth and imperiled the virtue and happiness of the people of the State."[42] That afternoon an Indignation Meeting was held in the Conference Church in Mount Holly and Conference pledged to support only those candidates who would vote for repeal. That November in a public referendum, the voters of New Jersey voted against legalizing race track gambling.

Greater concern was shown for more issues as the twentieth century approached. Conference, in 1897, discussed the Lloyd Marriage Bill then before the State Legislature. Delegates did not like some of the bill's provisions that had to do with who could perform the marriage ceremony. Ratification of the Treaty of Arbitration between the United States and Great Britain was urged upon the Senate. Conference wanted the New Jersey Legislature to pass the Pool Room Bill making it illegal for anyone under age eighteen to visit a pool room and no student under twenty-one. It also urged passage of Legislative Bill 162 which would prohibit any person from selling alcoholic beverages in any building within two hundred feet of a church, school or charitable institution, measured at the nearest points between buildings.[43]

While Conference was showing a greater sensitivity to a broader range of social problems, other matters of sometimes a weightier concern seemed to receive little or no attention, like the plight of poor immigrants or the horrible conditions under which many workers, many of whom were church members, had to work. But the day of the social gospel was coming, and there was a sign of some little stirrings in that direction in the conservative Conference of New Jersey Methodism. Presiding Elder Dobbins, in 1890, said, "The labor troubles between glass workers and manufacturers have been serious, and have greatly affected Clayton; Glassboro; First Church, Salem and Broadway, Salem."[44]

Browsing through the Conference Minutes for these years, one is distressed to find that the effort to build a South Jersey Academy in Vineland met with such little success that creditors sold the building and land to recoup their debt. Everything was lost.

Burlington District was dropped in 1877, and the remaining four Districts continued as such for nearly a century. Sabbath desecration was decried in this 1877 report which denounced the running of freight and other trains, pleasure seeking, keeping shops open and other direct and positive violations of God's law. The Creator said, "Remember the Sabbath Day to keep it holy."

Camp Meetings were blooming. The Great Auditorium at Ocean Grove was built. Ocean City, Island Heights and Delanco Camps were started.

Revivals were flourishing at times. In 1880, Samuel VanSant, Elder on the New Brunswick District, reported 250 converted at Toms River, "the influence of which has spread up and down the coast; the whole shore has been in a revival blaze." There were 105 conversions at Silverton, over 100 at Tuckerton, Bayville 90, and Barnegat 80. He spoke of 1,500 conversions on the District. In 1889, George Dobbins on the Bridgeton District tells of the dedication of First Church Salem and says that in the last year there were over 300 souls converted. On the New Brunswick District, "revivals of religion have been frequent all over the District." Reports say 175 were converted at North Long Branch; Bethesda, 120; Hightstown, 91; Keansburg, 70; Cassville Circuit, 80; Port Monmouth, 56; lesser numbers at other churches. On the Trenton District, more than 1300 were converted and added to the Church at special services held in nearly every church on the District.

Vital concerns, amusing incidents and stories of tragedy were often found in reading the Conference Minutes. Every year new churches were built and better parsonages provided for the ministers' families. Dr. Graw, in 1887 said, "The need of the hour is holy living, earnest work, and gospel preaching, under the baptism and power of the Holy Ghost."[45] One is amused by a report like this one in 1885: "On motion of Jefferson Lewis, visitors to literary institutions were directed to inquire if dancing was taught in such schools." On August 3, 1885, a tornado destroyed Tabernacle Church, Camden. They built a new one to seat 1500 people.

Concerns were expressed by the Camden churches for a home for the aged. Success was reported in 1891. A home on York Street was rented and housed eight persons in charge of Mrs. David Baird. A home was to be built near Collingswood on property donated by Mr. E. L. Knight of Philadelphia.[46] Later that year, the "Old People's Methodist Home of Camden County" now at Collingswood, was dedicated on October 22, 1891.[47] This was the start of our present United Methodist Homes of New Jersey.

The Church was also building hospitals to care for the healing of the sick. Support was urged in 1889 for the Methodist Episcopal Hospital in Brooklyn. Later, the Methodist Episcopal Hospital in Philadelphia was opened to patients, April 22, 1892.[48]

Finally, there was rejoicing in 1891 at the good news that the Pennington School debt was all covered. Throughout its history, this school has almost always been in debt.

The Century closed with preparations for a great Twentieth Century Thank-Offering. A goal of twenty million dollars was set for all of the Methodist Episcopal Church. The offering, in full, was to be paid by the first Sunday of January, 1901. Each donor could select the object for his gifts: church debts, church furnishings, Preachers Aid Society, City Missions and Church Extension, special gifts to all our benevolences, Methodist Hospitals in Philadelphia and Brooklyn, Pennington Seminary, Dickinson College or Drew Seminary.

The Methodist Episcopal Church in the New Jersey Conference was alive, well, and looking forward to the new century. In no way could it predict the vast changes which that century would bring in every facet of life. We shall turn to this new century in the history of our Conference, but, first, a look at Camp Meetings.

> Amazing grace! how sweet the sound
> That saved a wretch like me!
> I once was lost, but now am found,
> Was blind, but now I see.[49]

Chapter 8

CAMP MEETINGS IN SOUTHERN NEW JERSEY

Camp meetings and southern New Jersey Methodism seem to go hand in hand. While I have no accurate information before me, I doubt there is any conference in Methodism that has in its midst the continuing legacy of camp meetings that is New Jersey's with Ocean Grove, Ocean City, Malaga, Seaville, Delanco and Pitman. These are all great camp meeting centers that have had a continuous existence since their founding between 1864 and 1898. It is the purpose of this chapter to tell primarily that story of these six enduring camp meetings within the Conference.

Some of the history of the camp meeting in America and Methodism has already been told. Suffice it to say that camp meetings, in some clearing in the woods where folks would gather and pitch their tents for a few days or a week or two, were familiar sights to New Jersey Methodists around the state during the first sixty years of the eighteenth century. It was common practice for larger circuits to hold their summer quarterly meeting in the form of a camp meeting with the presiding elder and other ministers doing the preaching.

The Cape May Circuit Minute Book, which begins with minutes of the June 7, 1834 meeting, has a motion "that the next Quarterly meeting be a Camp Meeting at West Creek on land belonging to Br. John Goff to commence 14th of next Sept."[1] Camp meetings were held in August of 1835 at West Creek, August 1836 on land of Brother Reuben Ludlam, also in 1837.

Farther north was the Freehold Circuit. Available minutes begin with the June 10, 1837 quarterly meeting. At this first session a committee was appointed to confer with a similar committee from the Middletown Circuit to plan for a union camp meeting.[2] The meeting was held at Squankum. In 1838, the camp meeting was held at Green Grove. In 1855, the circuit was reduced to the Farmingdale Circuit, but on August 9, a quarterly meeting was held "at Shark River, on the camp ground."

The diarist, William R. Maps of Long Branch, attended camp meetings most of his life. Here are some samples:

> September 6, 1832, attended camp meeting at Freehold.
> July 29, 1833, Camp meeting began at Freehold.
> September 1, 1852, camp meeting at Squankum.
> August 21, 1859, Went to Port Washington to Camp meeting.

Later he had a tent at Ocean Grove.

By the 1860's, these smaller, circuit camp meetings began to give way to the permanent camp meeting sites we know today. At first, people still camped in tents; but, in time, cottages started to appear and permanent auditoriums for worship were built, although I still remember the sawdust trails at Seaville and Malaga. Ocean Grove still has its tent colony.

Before turning to the story of these enduring camp meetings, the story of the holiness movement must be told. There is a direct connection in all of these camp meetings between the establishing of the camp and the promotion of holiness. An 1865 account of the Seaville Camp Meeting in the *Christian Advocate,* "Cape May on Fire," says, "the great work of the occasion was holiness."[3]

Scriptural holiness has long been an expressed aim of Methodism. John Wesley, at the Methodist Conference of 1765, declared: "Holiness was our object, inward and outward holiness. God . . . thrust us out to raise up a holy people."[4] American Methodists made it their expressed aim, when at the Christmas Conference they said they were going forth to "preach the gospel, reform the Continent and spread Scriptural holiness across the land." In the present *Book of Discipline* of United Methodism are these two paragraphs in our official statement of faith:

> We believe sanctification is the work of God's grace through the Word and the Spirit, by which those who have been born again are cleansed from sin in their thoughts, words, and acts, and are enabled to live in accordance with God's will, and are to strive for holiness without which no one will see the Lord.
> Entire sanctification is a state of perfect love, righteousness and true holiness which every regenerate believer may obtain by being delivered from the power of sin, by loving God with all the heart, soul, mind and strength, and by loving one's neighbor as one's self. Through faith in Jesus Christ this gracious gift may be received in this life both gradually and instantaneously, and should be sought earnestly by every child of God.[5]

This Biblical Methodist doctrine of sancitfication, perfection, perfect love, holiness, as it was variously called, was routinely preached by most Methodist preachers during the first fifty years of American Methodism. In the quarter century before the Civil War, northern Methodist bishops and prominent Methodist ministers began calling for its revival. An early leader was Phoebe Palmer of New York City, wife of a doctor and prominent Methodist, whose "Tuesday night meetings for the promotion of holiness" had among its followers such Methodist leaders as bishops, editors and theological teachers.

The Civil War delayed the advance of holiness ideas; but by the time of the Methodist Centennial of 1866, the new movement was ready to take off. Dr. John C. McClintock, former member of the New Jersey Conference, chairman of the Centennial Committee, and soon to be the first president of Drew, set the stage in a centennial speech. He said the Methodist ministry must hold to this "great central idea of the whole Book of God," even if critics called it fanaticism. "If we keep to that," McClintock said, "the next century is ours. Our work is a moral work, that is to say, the work of making men holy."[6]

Soon, the first National Camp Meeting for Holiness was held and the National Campmeeting Association for the Promotion of Holiness was formed. Though these were interdenominational in character, Methodists were in the forefront and New Jersey in the vanguard. For its first seventy-five years, 1867 to 1942, the Holiness Association was headed by a Methodist, beginning with John S. Inskip of the New York Conference. The first National Camp Meeting was held in Vineland, New Jersey, in a grove of forty acres, July 17 to 26, 1867. In subsequent years there was more than one camp meeting. New Jersey's Pitman Grove was host in 1883, 1884 and 1887. Ocean City hosted the 1885 Camp Meeting.[7]

John Inskip, in his book *Penuel,* dwells at length on the first holiness camp meeting. He credits William B. Osborn of the New Jersey Conference with initiating the proposal.[8] It was attended by approximately one thousand persons, including Bishop Matthew Simpson. Reports were that one hundred to one hundred fifty were converted and more fully sanctified.[9] The holiness crusade, and it was a crusade, was on.

For the next twenty to twenty-five years, the crusade flourished. What the Methodist advocates sought was to make holiness a personal experience of God's grace in the life of the Christian believer. That is a worthy goal to have and a desirable experience to attain.

By the 1890's, the crusade was waning. Radical ideas appeared. Many wanted to go beyond church control. "Come outism" reared its head, and a proliferation of small holiness sects started to appear, some of which, like the Nazarenes, in time became major churches. Holiness has never been so popular since that time. Yet, in its heyday, the holiness movement had the support of most of the bishops of the church.

Nevertheless, it needs to be said, that holiness has never lost its advocates among either preachers or laity in southern New Jersey Methodism. Indeed, it again is not so unfashionable. One example is a major address at a Wesleyan Symposium sponsored in 1984 by Haddonfield Church on "The Wesleyan Doctrine of Scriptural Holiness," given by Dr. Frank B. Stanger, a member of the Southern New Jersey Conference and third president of Asbury Theological Seminary. The point to be made here is that strong leaders of the holiness crusade were found among the clergy of the Conference, all of whom were involved in the founding of these New Jersey Camp Meetings.

William B. Osborn, a leading founder of the first National Camp Meeting for Holiness, was at the time, the pastor at Sharptown. Later he served the church in many places, but always returned to New Jersey. He served in India, Australia and Oregon. He was a member of both the South Carolina and Genesee Conferences. This great camp meeting and holiness preacher also served as a State Temperance Agent and Conference Evangelist. William Osborn is considered the prime mover in the establishment of Ocean Grove.[10]

Rev. Aaron E. Ballard, pastor, presiding elder, State Temperance Agent, participated in the Vineland holiness camp meeting and helped found both Pitman and Oecan Grove. For forty-six years, he served as president of Pitman. He was the third president of Ocean Grove from 1907 to 1919. He died in office at the age of ninety-nine. His death marked the passing of an era.

Rev. George Hughes, another charter member of Ocean Grove, was a pastor, presiding elder, agent of the Freedmen's Aid Society, Secretary of the Pennsylvania Seamen's Aid Society, and a member of the National Camp

Meeting Association. From 1885 to 1897, he was editor of *The Methodist Home Journal* which later became *Guide to Holiness*.

One could mention others, like the Rev. Ruliff V. Lawrence, first Vice President of Ocean Grove and noted holiness preacher. All were strong leaders in the Conference and advocates of camp meetings and holiness. One could repeat for each of these camp meetings in their formative days the praise given to the early Seaville meeting: "the great work of the occasion was holiness."

SEAVILLE

Seaville, called the "mother of our camp meetings,"[11] was organized as the South Jersey Camp Meeting Association of Cape May County, New Jersey in 1863 or 1864.[12] It was an outgrowth of the earlier three day quarterly conference camp meetings of the old Cape May Circuit.

Beginning in 1865, the site of these camp meetings was at the Cape May County Fair Grounds located on Kings Highway near the intersection of the Dennisville-South Seaville Road in South Seaville. The present site was purchased from several land owners in 1875. Camp meeting that year began August 30 and lasted for ten days. The grounds were dedicated September 2.

A reporter for the *Star of the Cape* attended services and gave this report:

> We were one of the throng to step from the train at Seaville Station on Sunday (Sept. 5, 1875) to spend the day at the new camp ground. We found a beautiful grove . . . systematically laid out . . . and quite a large number of cotton tents and comfortable cottages erected, and everything wore a bright and cheerful aspect.
>
> Some three or four thousand persons were assembled at the morning service. . . . A large bell is erected over the stand which rings out the signals for services, and the hours for rising and retiring. An excellent boarding table is kept by Mr. Murphy of Phila. Wells and Corson have the refreshment stand. . . . Nothing but oysters were allowed to be sold by them during the Sabbath, about eleven barrels of which were disposed of. About 130 lots out of about 400, we were told, remain unsold.
>
> At the closing service, as the numerous host passed the stand, giving ministers the parting hand, singing the songs of joy, much feeling was manifested . . . and so reluctant were many to part that not until one o'clock was the last song sung, and the last goodnight uttered.[13]

A prominent Methodist, Judge Jesse A. Diverty of Dennisville, was the first president of the Association at its permanent location, a position he held until his death in 1890. Judge Diverty, a leader in the Laymen's Association of the Conference, was elected a delegate to the 1880 General Conference, and was a Dickinson College trustee. In his home church, he was a class leader for fifty years, Sunday School Superintendent for over forty years, and an ordained local elder.[14]

Holiness preachers regularly preached at Seaville. One frequently reads the names of such speakers as W. B. Osborn, William Taylor, missionary and later bishop, A. E. Ballard, Ruliff Lawrence and others. Ballard had a cottage there.

SEAVILLE CAMP MEETING GROUNDS
South Seaville, N.J.

Women also preached occasionally in those early days. In 1878, a Jane Clark and a Lilly Parker were listed as speakers. The noted Anna Howard Shaw was there in 1892.

Temperance Day early became a regular feature. Often the speaker would be Jacob Graw. In 1886 and again in 1888, General Fisk gave the address. Judge Diverty introduced his friend, General Fisk, in 1886, when Fisk was the Prohibition Party candidate for governor of New Jersey. Diverty led the congregation in singing:

> As voters we will take the risk;
>   There's one more river to cross;
> And stand up square for General Fisk;
>   There's one more river to cross.
>
> There's one more river,———————
>   And that is Prohibition;
> One more river,
>   And that's the river we'll cross.[15]

A schedule of camp services in 1888 included prayer meeting at 6 a.m., family worship in cottages at 7, public prayer meeting at 8, preaching at 10:30 a.m., 2:30 p.m., and 8 p.m. A prayer meeting followed the 8 p.m. service. There were also children's meetings at 1:15 p.m. and a young people's prayer meeting at 6:30.

By the end of the nineteenth century, the W.C.T.U. praticated in the Temperance Day's activities with often the state president or one of the other

114 / WHAT GOD HAS WROUGHT

officers speaking. Epworth League days were also popular at Seaville and local church youth groups competed to see who could win the attendance banner.

As the twentieth century advanced, Seaville's attendance gradually declined. Temperance days were replaced by women's days, Epworth League day by youth camps begun in the late 1930's. Even the youth camps are gone now at Seaville.

Seaville Camp was reincorporated May 9, 1947. "Said corporation shall be known as 'The South Jersey Camp Meeting Association of the Methodist Church.' " One part of the reincorporation states:

> The Camp Meeting Grounds of the corporation shall be used exclusively for the Methodist Church, and all religious meetings held on same shall be under the control and direction of the District Superintendent of the Bridgeton District of the New Jersey Annual Conference of the Methodist Church, or of such other ministers of such Church as the Board of Trustees may from time to time appoint.[16]

Seaville Camp Meeting continues today, over 120 years old, and proudly proclaims, "Seaville and Salvation." The large crowds are not often there. Many of the small cottages are being enlarged and improved to be used for year-round retirement homes. Yet, Camp Meeting still takes place each summer as it did in days of yore on the old Cape May Circuit.

Malaga

Malaga Camp at West Jersey Grove in Vineland, New Jersey, dates from the year 1869. From the early 1860's, camp meetings were held in the vicinity of Malaga. Specific mention is made of a camp at Willow Grove in 1862. In 1869, the first meeting was held on the present site under the direction of Rev. Ezra Lake, one of the founders of Ocean City. Later, it came under the direction of the ministers on the Willow Grove and Gloucester Circuits.

A group of Methodist laymen organized the West Jersey Grove Association on August 2, 1873. A few days later, they purchased for $1,000 twenty acres from Joshua Richman, Sr. of Malaga and named the grove Malaga. The first officers were: President, B. F. Richman; Vice President, J. S. Sanborn; Secretary, A. A. Smith; Treasurer, Hosea Nichols.[17]

Dr. Jacob Graw, who served as president in 1899 and 1900, describes the opening of the first camp in July of 1874:

> The time for the opening was announced and people far and near anxiously awaited the dawning of the day that should make the woods ring with the songs and shouts of the hundreds that would assemble themselves together on the new camp meeting grounds.
> It was a day long to be remembered. Long before the hour for service had arrived hundreds were present. Many preachers were there both from the itinerant and the local ranks. The first camp meeting started off very auspiciously, and a good revival followed.[18]

Dr. Graw also speaks of the Camp Meeting Sunday known as "Big Sunday" when between 10,000 and 15,000 people gathered on the camp ground.

The lighting system was pine knots on each corner and at the feed stand. In the tabernacle there were oil lamps on the platform by the pulpit and by the organ. The pine knots gave a beautiful glow and also helped chase the mosquitoes.

Records for many years are sketchy or non-existent; however, Gail Eisenlohr, in her history of Malaga, says the first real tabernacle of wood construction was built about 1890.[19] Many posts supported a large wooden shingled roof. Arched openings on three sides admitted air and sunshine. Fresh straw or saw dust was placed on the floor each season. Across the front of the building were these quotations:

> I will offer in Thy tabernacle sacrifices of joy.
> Break forth into singing, O Forest.
> Holiness becometh Thine House, O Lord.

Malaga has continued its witness for Christ. Down through the years of the twentieth century the old tabernacle echoed to the prayers, praises, sermons and songs of the faithful.

In 1932, largely under the influence of Dr. Alfonso Dare, the Malaga Assembly program for youth was started. In the 1940's, it was expanded to include junior age children. Every year the Malaga assembly hold several weeks of camping programs for children and youth.

On April 19, 1942, a bad fire struck the camp grounds and destroyed thirty-two cottages. Yet, out of the ashes came progress before unenvisioned. More substantial cottages were built, and people started living in camp the year round. This created the need for street lights and a Chapel where residents of the Grove could worship. The lights came soon, but the Chapel was not built until 1954.

Other improvements to modernize the camp have followed. Girls and boys dormitories have been built, as well as a Preachers' Cottage or Guest House. Still newer, heated dorms appeared. In 1959, a new Tabernacle was built at a cost of $25,000. Bishop Fred Pierce Corson, native of Millville, New Jersey, dedicated it on August 13, 1959.

A Baptist minister, Dr. Norman W. Paullin, staunch friend and supporter of Malaga Camp, was a man of vision who helped guide the Camp into new ventures of faith. A swimming pool was built in the 1950's and then the Norman W. Paullin Memorial Dining Hall, a dream of Dr. Paullin before his death. Dr. Evan C. Pedrick was Malaga's President during these years. As this is written, plans have been approved for the building of a new mulit-purpose building for housing and year round retreats, thus moving Malaga Camp still forward into the modern age.

But it is not new facilities, year round residents, nor modern swimming pools that form the heart of a camp like Malaga. Malaga exists to proclaim the gospel, to invite people to Christ, to witness to that holiness "without which no one can see the Lord." It is not a sawdust trail, nor the newest in modern facilities; it is devotion to Christ and love in people's hearts for all for whom He died. So long as Malaga Camp remembers that, Malaga Camp will live.

Ocean Grove

Ocean Grove, this Christian mecca by the sea shore, is quite a place. It is truly a Methodist Center. Where else can one find a community as large as Ocean Grove with only one church, St. Paul's United Methodist; an Auditorium which seats 8,000 and yet on some Sunday's one cannot get a seat; the massive Hope-Jones organ, one of the largest in the world; two United Methodist Homes; a summer cultural program where the finest performers can be seen, and a religious program which offers world-renowned pulpiteers? In the summer of 1984, when this was written, Bob Hope, Norman Vincent Peale and Oral Roberts were among those scheduled to appear in the Great Auditorium.

Changes come slowly, and painfully at times, and Ocean Grove has changed. When this writer and his family moved to the Ocean Grove area in 1976 and began attending Sunday night services in the Grove, we parked our car outside the Grove and walked to the Auditorium. At that time, no cars could be driven nor parked on the streets of Ocean Grove on a Sunday. Now the chains at the arches are gone. Cars travel in Ocean Grove, as elsewhere, on Sunday.

No one who has ever attended a service in the Great Auditorium and witnessed the presentation of the offering to Clarence Kohlmann's "Ushers March" will ever again think the receiving of an offering is a mundane or unworshipful exprience. To be in attendance at the performance when a 1500 voice choir, at the Annual Choir Festival, sings "The Battle Hymn of the Republic" and the illuminated flag waves, is to have an experience never forgotten.

Rev. William B. Osborn of Farmingdale and others looked for a place along the seashore where "tired ministers could gather for a brief respite away from the din and turmoil of more thickly populated places."[20] It was Osborn who decided Ocean Grove was what he wanted. Others were invited to participate. In July of 1869, several families camped at Ocean Grove a few hundred yards from the sea. The evening of July 31, Mrs. Thornley invited the company to her tent for a prayer meeting, the first religious service in Ocean Grove.

December 22, 1869, at Trinity Church, Trenton, the Ocean Grove Camp Meeting Association was formed. The New Jersey Legislature granted a charter on March 3, 1870. Charter members of the Association included Rev. Elwood H. Stokes, presiding elder of the New Brunswick District, who for the next twenty-seven years served as president of the Ocean Grove Camp Meeting Association; Rev. Ruliff V. Lawrence, host pastor at Trinity Church who was elected Vice President; Rev. George Hughes of Broadway Church, Camden; Rev. William B. Osborn of Farmingdale; Rev. John Inskip of New York, President of the Holiness Association; Rev. John H. Stockton, Conference Evangelist; Rev. Aaron E. Ballard, Bridgeton District presiding elder and a

OCEAN GROVE AUDITORIUM
Showing pavilion and monument of Rev. Elwood Stokes, founding president

future Ocean Grove president, and others. Rev. Osborn was named Superintendent.[21]

The Association set to work. Title to the land was secured from forty-four different owners; lots were laid out and sold, the first one for $86 to James A. Bradley, founder of Asbury Park. Actually, the land is owned by the Camp Meeting Association. Buyers obtain only a ninety-nine year lease. Original blue laws probibited trains from stopping on Sunday within a mile of the Grove, sale of liquor or tobacco, and vehicular traffic on Sunday. The law against the sale of alcoholic beverages is still enforced.

The first camp meetings were held in an octagonal preacher's stand at the head of Ocean Pathway. The congregation sat on rough-hewn pine boards, spread among the trees in a wide circle. The first camp meeting was held July 26 to August 5, 1870. In 1876, the preacher's stand was enlarged, made permanent with a roof and side walls. The first auditorium was dedicated by President Stokes on July 2. The report of the New Brunswick District presiding elder in 1878 said, "At Ocean Grove, Brother Stokes has been quite successful in holding camp meetings for the conversion of sinners, the sanctification of believers and the intensification of sound temperance sentiments."[22]

The present Auditorium, built at a cost of some $50,000, was officially opened by Dr. Stokes on July 1, 1894, and dedicated during the period of August 9 to 12. Dr. Stokes, William Osborn and the other founders of Ocean Grove would be pleased to know that this Great Auditorium still, at times, has overflow congregations. Some of the world's greatest artists have performed from its stage; United States Presidents McKinley, Theodore Roosevelt and William Howard Taft have been speakers; Governors of New Jersey are listed on speakers' rosters, and Ocean Grove Auditorium has been the scene of evangelistic crusades by Gypsy Smith, Billy Sunday in 1916, 1919, and 1928, and Billy Graham. True to the sentiments of its holiness founders, emblazoned across the front of the Auditorium are the words: "Holiness unto the Lord, be ye holy."

The famed Hope-Jones organ, designed by organ-builder Robert Hope-Jones of Elmira, New York, was installed in the Auditorium in 1908. It is a four manual console with an echo chamber in the ceiling. The organ is housed in four concrete chambers, twenty-five feet high with fourteen inch thick walls. Its largest pipe, a low C Diaphone is thirty-two feet in length, twelve feet in perimeter and weighs a ton. This organ is one of the finest and largest in the world.

Other facilities of the Camp Meeting Association are the Janes Memorial Tabernacle, built in 1877; and Thornley Chapel, now used for children's programs, completed in 1889. A former Youth Temple, built in 1879 and enlarged in 1885, was destroyed by fire, and a new one is comtemplated.

Ocean Grove has not only its camp meeting weeks, Sunday morning and evening services from mid June to the Sunday after Labor Day, but Bible Conferences, Choir Festivals, youth and children's programs, daily summer morning Bible Classes and numerous other programs, religious and cultural, to help make Ocean Grove a world-renowned center. One of the most recent outstanding events at Ocean Grove was the World Methodist Camp Meeting held in August of 1984 under the auspices of the World Methodist Council in celebration of the Bicentennial of American Methodism. Ocean Grove is truly the mecca of the sea, a dream of William B. Osborn almost one hundred twenty years ago.

Other chapters will tell the story of Ocean Grove's homes for the elderly, but no account of Ocean Grove would be complete without mention of St. Paul's Church. Need for a year round church was apparent from the start. In 1870, William B. Osborn was appointed pastor of Greenville and Ocean Grove. A year later, Ocean Grove became a separate charge. Services were held in numerous places, including Asbury Park, until 1876 when St. Paul's first building was built just south of the main gate. The present church, on a block given by the Association, was dedicated June 28, 1885. Additions and renovations through the years have made St. Paul's one of the leading churches of the Conference with almost one thousand members.

The story of the Centennial Camp Meeting held in John Turner's woods near Barnsboro in the summer of 1866 was told in Chapter 6. Following that successful camp, Bethel Church, Hurffville, held camp meetings there at least through 1878. As a result of these successful meetings at Barnsboro, the Rev. William A. Perry, then preacher at Glassboro, had the idea of a Conference Camp Meeting ground. During the 1869 camp meeting at Barnsboro, a meeting of interested ministers and laymen was held to consider the idea. Further discussions were held the following year. Conference apparently gave its blessings, and a permanent organization was formed in June of 1871, called the New Jersey Conference Camp Meeting Association. Over two hundred acres of land in Mantua Township were purchased. The name Pitman Grove was given in memory of the famed New Jersey minister and camp meeting preacher, Charles Pitman. The first camp meeting began August 1, 1871 with Rev. William E. Perry as the first president.

The Association was incorporated March 19, 1872 as The New Jersey Conference Camp Meeting Association. The purpose stated is that "of providing and maintaining for the members and friends of the Methodist Episcopal Church, proper, convenient, desirable and permanent camp meeting grounds. . . ."[23] Original trustees were: William E. Perry, the first president; Elwood H. Stokes, president of the Ocean Grove Camp Meeting Association; Jacob B. Graw, second president of Pitman; Henry M. Brown; Samuel E. Post; M. Hays Perry, Rev. Perry's son; Philip Cline; William Walton; James F. Morrell; Garner R. Snyder, noted Conference temperance leader; Isaiah D. King; Joseph B. Dobbins; James M. Cassady; James M. Hoffman; William Fischer and Aaron E. Ballard, who served as camp president from 1874 to 1920 and guided Pitman Grove through the years of its greatest glory. At the time of the founding of Pitman Grove, Dr. Ballard was presiding elder of the Bridgeton District. His position on the District was taken in 1871 by Rev. Perry.

In spite of its name, the New Jersey Conference Camp Meeting Association, the statement of purpose by which the Association was incorporated, and its original Board of Trustees so ably representing the leadership of the Conference, there is no evidence that the New Jersey Conference ever held title to the property nor exercised any supervision over the Camp Meeting. Yet, it remains a Methodist camp for Methodist people.

Pitman was not founded as a town. It was founded as a camp meeting ground. The town grew up around the camp ground and became an incorporated borough in 1905.

Like the other camp meetings in the Conference, Pitman Grove was a popular place to attend camp meetings. It is reported in 1903 that as many as 12,000 people were on the grounds on Sunday. "It was difficult to find places to eat or sleep, or to tie the extra horses."[24]

Some time in the 1870's, board and lodging were listed like this:

Single meals, Dinner, 75 cents; Breakfast or Supper, 50 cents; One Day, $1.25; Three Days or more (per day), $1.00. Lodging (per night), except by special contract, 50 cents. Deduction from these rates to regular ministers one-half, and lodging free at the Association's building.[25]

Camp meetings were usually held over a ten day period. Billy Sunday was probably the best known evangelist to preach at Pitman. He was there Monday afternoon and evening on August 6, 1928.

Music has always been an important feature of Pitman, as at all camp meetings. Professor C. Austin Miles was one of the better known song leaders and hymn writers to appear at Pitman. Miles is best known for his hymn, "In the Garden." In later years, Miles' permanent home was in Pitman.

One of the early reports speaks of Sister Lizzie R. Smith, "whose labors have been so signally blest in leading souls to the experience of conversion and sanctification, has accepted an invitation to be present during the entire meeting and hold special services every day."[26] In 1895 in her honor, the Lizzie Smith Temple was erected. It was there that the children's meetings were held during camp meeting time.

Pitman Grove continues to hold services every summer. The brochure for 1983 announced services every Sunday evening from mid-June to Labor Sunday, sponsored by the Pitman Cluster of United Methodist Churches. The speakers included Bishop C. Dale White and the District Superintendent, Rev. John Ewing. Among the others were two women, Dorothy Worth and Beverly Galucci, a former District Superintendent, the Rev. Hooker D. Davis, and several non-Methodists. The Camp Meeting lasted only five days, July 11 to 15, with the Rev. David Bailey as evening evangelist and Mrs. Dorothy Worth leading the morning Bible Study.

What would Pitman have been without Pitman Grove? What would it be now, though the days of the large crowds are past? What would it be without the United Methodist Church in Pitman? Residents of Pitman began holding religious services informally during the non-camp meeting season as early as 1878. November 10, 1885, the Pitman Methodist Epsicopal Church was constituted with Rev. Charles Berry as the minister. The first church was not built until eleven years later on lots deeded by the Camp Meeting Association. The present church sanctuary was dedicated August 14, 1921. Additions have been made through the years, and the membership of the church has grown. In 1950, it had over 1500 members, the second largest membership in the Conference. In 1983, it still had 1103 members.

Ocean City

Does it all sound familiar? Ocean City was founded by a small group of Methodist clergy as a Christian summer resort founded on the kind of Christian principles that guided Ocean Grove. They reasoned, why not have such a resort in the southern part of the New Jersey Coast? Principal movers were three Methodist ministers, the Lake brothers of Pleasantville, S. Wesley, Ezra B. and James E. They, along with their father Simon Lake, a prosperous farmer and fruit grower who had represented Atlantic County in the State Legislature, and two other clergymen, William H. Burrell and William B. Wood of Philadelphia, were the founders of Ocean City.

September 10, 1879, the Lake brothers and Rev. Burrell sailed over to Peck's Beach, as Ocean City was then called, to inspect the island. Under a cedar tree, they held a conference, opened by prayer for divine guidance and blessing, and Ocean City was born. That tree was on the site of the present tabernacle grounds.[27]

A month later, October 20, 1879, they met at William Wood's home and formed an Association. Simon Wesley Lake was named president. The island was called New Brighton, but soon changed to Ocean City. There was to be a Board of Managers of nine stockholders, three Methodist ministers, three Methodist laymen or ministers, and three others who were not required to be Methodists. Title to the whole island had to be obtained in the name of the Association, which took some doing. Once the title was secured, there were incorporated into all future deeds two principal covenants which were to make Ocean City unique and would assure its Christian character. These two principal covenants were restrictions against commercialism on Sunday and the sale or manufacture of alcoholic beverages.

It was the belief of Ocean City's founders that Ocean City should be a profitable real estate venture as well as a religious resort. They have been proven right.

One of the first things done was to set aside the block between Fifth and Sixth Streets for a tabernacle and to designate certain mid-town lots for a church and a school. The Association governed Ocean City until 1884 when it was incorporated as a borough.[28] Early reports indicate it was as much a desire to build a temperance city, as anything else that led to the founding of Ocean City.

The first annual report of the Association tells us that by 1881 they had sold 508 lots: upon which were erected thirty-five dwellings, one large hotel, ten private stables, two bath houses and three government Life Saving Stations. The report records a newspaper published, the Pleasantville and Ocean City Railroad organized, a steamboat purchased, and a company organized to build a road between Beesley's Point and Ocean City. A Methodist Episcopal Church of twenty-three members was already organized. A camp meeting was held August 6 to 16 with as many as one thousand attending.[29]

By 1883, temperance meetings were being held during camp meeting time. The National Holiness Camp Meeting came to Ocean City in 1885. A report in the 1904 Ocean City *Ledger* advertises an annual holiness camp meeting under the auspices of the Ocean City Holiness Association. It was a ten day camp meeting featuring Bishop Willard F. Mallalieu among others.

In those days, the annual camp meeting included a Bible Conference, Epworth League Convention and Temperance Convention along with special children's services. They even allowed a woman preacher in 1883. The Rev. Anna Oliver of Brooklyn preached on July 23. Anna Oliver was a holiness preacher which is, no doubt, the reason she was invited.[30]

The first permanent place of worship in Ocean City was the Auditorium, a large frame structure erected in the spring of 1881 on the camp ground. Later it was named the Tabernacle and was operated by the Ocean City Tabernacle Association, successor to the original Ocean City Association. The eighty by ninety foot building was badly damaged in the 1944 hurricane, but it was rebuilt. The present modern steel, brick and glass Tabernacle, on the same site, was dedicated by Bishop Fred P. Corson, Sunday, June 23, 1957.

In its first one hundred years, the Association had only five presidents, three of them Lakes and the last two Luffs. S. Wesley Lake served 1880 to 1917, his brother James E. Lake, 1917 to 1930 and W. Elwell Lake, son of the first president, 1930 to 1948. Then a Philadelphia businessman, Ralph G. Luff, served 1948 to 1961 to be succeeded by his son William G. Luff.[31]

For a time after World War II, evening services were held in the air conditioned Strand Theater on the Boardwalk before going back to their Tabernacle home. Noted speakers from around the world are brought to the Tabernacle for two morning and an evening service during the summer months as the Ocean City Tabernacle Association continues to meet the religious needs of all God's people. While gone are the days of the holiness meetings and the temperance services, it is still the stated purpose of the Association:

> First, to encourage and assist all efforts of the city, churches, organizations and individuals in upholding the ideals of the Founders, as well as the general moral standards and character of the community; Second, to provide religious services for summer visitors and strangers, particularly those who have no affiliation with local churches.[32]

The Lake brothers who founded Ocean City were interesting men. They were from an early south Jersey family. Some were inventors of note, one of them inventing one of the first submarines. S. Wesley Lake, first Association president, served a wide range of pastorates across lower Jersey and a term as Trenton District Presiding Elder. Ezra B. became the first pastor at Ocean City. He also was an inventor, obtaining a patent on a shade roller around which a thriving business developed. James E. Lake was a pastor, editor for ten years of the *New Jersey Methodist and Epworth Advocate,* and one of the founders of Atlantic Highlands and National Park, both of which began as Methodist Camp Meeting Centers.[33]

Unlike Ocean Grove, Ocean City is a community of many churches. Oldest, of course, is the St. Peter's United Methodist Church, founded in 1880. The first church was built on the present site in 1890, and the present stone church in 1906. Since 1942, St. Peter's Church has hosted the sessions of the Annual Conference and is looked upon with affection by the many clergy whose ordinations have taken place at its altar. Its membership in 1983 of just under 1500 ranked it third in the Conference. Ocean City has been host to the 1940 and 1956 sessions of the Northeastern Jurisdictional Conference. Ocean City is also home for the Macedonia United Methodist Church, a black church, formerly of the Delaware Conference, which was organized July 15, 1893, under the patronage of leading white Methodists and business men.[34] Another is the African Methodist Episcopal Church which started about 1906.

Ocean City has come a long way since it was visited in 1879 by those four men in a boat.

Delanco

"A Camp Meeting for the promotion of holiness is now in progress at Delanco on the Delaware. Various members of the National Holiness Association are in attendance. The Reverend George Ridout is in charge." This first notice of Delanco Camp appeared in the *Christian Advocate,* July 14, 1898.[35] George Ridout was minister of the Delanco Methodist Episcopal Church.

Delanco Church had held a Grove Meeting in 1897 which resulted in the salvation and santification of many. As a result it became a burden of prayer of many to make this an annual affair. During the winter of 1898, Rev. Ridout; A. C. (Poppy) Ridgeway, owner of a local shoe factory; G. Q. Hammel, a local preacher and Philadelphia merchant; and E. S. Hunter, another merchant, called on M. C. E. Fletcher, a Presbyterian and owner of the grove. After three interviews, he agreed to sell some twenty acres for camp meeting purposes for four thousand dollars.

A series of meetings was held during March and April of 1898 during which the Fletcher Grove Camp Meeting Association was formed. Officers were elected including George W. Ridout as president, a Board of Directors was chosen and plans put forward to begin a permanent camp meeting. The objects of the association were defined as:

> The holding of religious gatherings for the salvation of souls and the promotion of Scriptural holiness according to the doctrines and usages of the M. E. Church, and the buying and selling of such real estate as may be necessary to further the interests of the Association.[36]

The first Camp Meeting was held June 24 to July 5, 1898, in a preaching tent set up for that purpose. It was considered a success in the salvation and santification of souls. In his first annual report, President Ridout said, "We rejoice at the success of our Holiness movement. The Fletcher Grove Camp Meeting Association may be said to be emphatically a holiness movement. We are sure to have the blessing of God in our holy venture."[37]

The first building erected was a boarding house and restaurant, called the Osborne House, in 1902. Plans were then put in motion to build an auditorium which was finished in time for the 1904 camp.

Presiding Elder Alfred Wagg of the Trenton District reported in 1908:

> Fletcher Grove Camp Meeting is the only regular Camp Meeting within the bounds of the Trenton District. This is located at Delanco on the Delaware River and is indeed the creation of our Methodist Church in this place. Here two camp meetings are held annually;

namely, the annual camp meeting from June 21st to July 4th, and the local preachers' camp meeting, from August 31st to September 8th. Some 200 seekers were at the altar and 75 persons were converted.[38]

The Local Preachers' Camp Meeting Holiness Association of the New Jersey Conference was a voluntary fellowship of local preachers within the Conference, and other interested individuals, who united for the saving of souls and the promotion of Scriptural holiness.[39] As early as 1905, they were using Delanco Camp for their annual camp meeting. In 1938, the local preachers reorganized and changed their name to the Delanco Holiness Camp Meeting Association. Doctor Edward S. Sheldon and Dr. Hammell P. Shipps were two, long-time leaders of this Association.

In 1936, a daily camp schedule looked like this:

8:30-9:30 A.M.	Prayer and Testimony
10:30-11:30 A.M.	Young People's Study Hour
1:30 P.M.	Children's Meeting
3:00 P.M.	Preaching
6:00 P.M.	Prayer Groups
7:00 P.M.	Open Air Ring Meeting
7:30 P.M.	Preaching[40]

An interest in youth has always been a part of Delanco Camp. A forward step was taken in 1932 when the Local Preachers' Association invited one hundred fifty youth as its guests to the camp meeting. This became a continuing practice and not until 1942 did they have to pay even a registration fee of one dollar.

After considerable discussion, in 1946 the Fletcher Grove Camp Meeting Association and the Delanco Holiness Camp Meeting Association agreed to merge and become the Delanco Camp Meeting Association.[41] The Reverend Howard Shipps became the first president of the new organization. By 1954, it was decided to discontinue the fall camp and concentrate efforts on one good camp. To that was added a Memorial Day Camp, a one day Ministers' Conference and a week-end Youth Conference over Labor Day.

Growing pains and inadequate facilities were a concern of Delanco Camp in the 1950's and 1960's. Late in 1963, Mr. Charles Shipps made available to the Camp a two hundred eighty-one acre tract of land called Sooy Place near Tabernacle. Finally, at an adjourned meeting of the Board of Directors, July 13, 1964, it was approved 78 to 18 to purchase the Sooy Place property.[42]

Reverend Raymond Hughes describes the first Camp Meeting at Sooy Place:

> In 1965, beset by mosquitoes and limited by facilities, the first encampment was held on the new property. The original building, with renovations, provided dining hall, kitchen, and girl's dormitory space. To this was added the Tabernacle (unscreened), the boy's dormitory and the partially completed Guest Dormitory. The new camp had begun.[43]

Since then, Delanco Camp's facilities have improved in every way. Lovely facilities are provided for youth camps and camp meetings. Horseback riding and swimming in Lake Agape are available. Reverend Hughes makes clear that beyond the new facilities and camp ground, the purpose remains the same as expressed in 1898: "The holding of religious gatherings for the salvation of souls and the promotion of Scriptural holiness according to the doctrines and usages of the M. E. Church."

It was stated earlier in this chapter that there was "a direct connection in all of these camp meetings between the establishment of the camp and the promotion of holiness."[44] This connection has long been forgotten in many of the camps. It remains vitally alive at Delanco, reminding all who would pay heed, that God, through the grace of Christ, calls us all to holiness of heart and life.

OTHER CAMP MEETINGS

This chapter would be incomplete without making mention that other camp meetings were started in the New Jersey Conference. Of these, the most important was Island Heights. Methodist ministers Jacob B. Graw and Samuel Van Sant were principal founders of Island Heights.

On July 1, 1878, the Island Heights Association was formed and Island Heights, formerly known as Dillon's Island, was purchased. In addition to Graw and Van Sant, other prominent ministers involved at Island Heights were A. E. Ballard, George L. Dobbins, George B. Wight and Ananias Lawrence. Many of these men were also involved in other camps. Prominent business men of the area and Philadelphia were also involved.

The first camp meeting was held under the direction of Samuel Van Sant and began August 13, 1878. Large congregations, we are told, attended the services. By 1886, the Association sold all the land, except the camp meeting grounds, to individual lot holders; thus the Association maintained only a nominal existence. At first the Association continued holding the camp meetings; but before 1900, the Island Heights Church, formed in 1880, was in charge. In time, the camp meetings ceased to be held, but even today a yearly meeting is held by the church on the old camp meeting grounds.[45]

Atlantic Highlands began as a Camp Meeting Association in 1880 with the Rev. James E. Lake as president.[46] National Park had a Camp Meeting before 1900. There was also a Wesley Grove Camp Meeting in Groveville from 1912 until it was sold to the Wesleyan Methodists in 1935.[47]

Camp Meetings have played an important role in the life of southern New Jersey Methodism since early in the nineteenth century. The earliest record of one may be the note in the Salem Circuit book dated Pilesgrove, June 18, 19, 1807, "a balance of $3.42 cents put in the hands of John Murphy toward [sic.] to pay for the elements and to help defray the expenses of the Camp Meeting."

Life and Times of Rev. J. B. Graw, D.D.

Rev. Jacob B. Graw, D.D.
Delegate to eight General Conferences
Presiding Elder on all five Districts

Today, they still play an important role. Every year camp meetings are held at Seaville, Malaga, Ocean Grove, Pitman, Ocean City and Delanco. Clergy of the Conference, including district superintendents, serve as officers or are on the Boards of Directors. Methodist laity take active part. Many of our people have summer cottages or permanent homes on the camp grounds. Many retired clergy and laity, too, live or plan to live in retirement at Malaga, Seaville or Delanco. Ocean City and Ocean Grove have long been considered meccas for the retired. On these camp grounds, the fervent gospel is preached, decisions for Christ are called for, and saints are asked to walk more closely with their Lord. "Holiness unto the Lord," it says at Ocean Grove. "Be ye holy." At Delanco, if not at these other camps, the call for holiness is still sounded! Evangelistic Services and Revival Meetings in our churches are not so popular and not nearly so frequently held as they once were. Yet, at south Jersey's camp meetings, the gospel call is still given, and the stirring refrains of old gospel songs are still sung. We live in a modern age, but the old gospel still meets our needs.

> Jesus calls us o'er the tumult
> Of our life's wild, restless sea;
> Day by day his sweet voice soundeth,
> Saying, 'Christian, follow me.'[48]

Camp meetings are an enduring legacy of southern New Jersey Methodism. They are an integral part of the life of our Church. Some even carry the name of the Conference in official title or incorporation. Their charters require certain numbers of Methodist clergy and laity on their Boards. Yet, no one of these camp meetings has ever, at any time, had an official relationship to this Conference. They are not Conference Camps, but our Conference, our churches, and our people are enhanced through their ministry. The life of Southern New Jersey Methodism is permanently in their debt.

Chapter 9

ENTERING A NEW CENTURY

1900-1914

The twentieth century has, without a doubt, seen more changes than the prior twenty centuries put together. Those people who have lived through this century have seen the dawn of the automobile age, the jet age, and the development of the space age with man walking on the moon. They have lived through two world wars and the advent of the atomic age. Many now fear a nuclear holocaust. Transportation, communication, economics, technology, education, family living, nothing has remained the same. The church in 1986 is no more like the church of 1900 than the one room schools of grandfather's time are like the modern computer centers in almost every public school today. Women won the right to vote, gained full clergy rights in the Methodist Church, had a woman, Mrs. Marjorie Matthews, elected bishop in 1980, and saw the first woman Vice Presidential candidate nominated in 1984.

Winthrop Hudson says 1914, the eve of World War I, marks the end of the Methodist age in America. It did not seem so at the time. Even the war was fought with the same optimistic, utopian attitude that had been so characteristically a part of American and American Methodist life. It would be a war to end all wars. It was not. Life and the world were not the same. Winthrop Hudson writes, "By the time World War I was over, it was evident beyond cavil that the churches in general and American Protestantism in particular had entered a new age."[1]

What was there about this period that suggests the end of an age? In politics and national life, President McKinley was shot in 1901 and "Teddy" Roosevelt became the Head of State. Great labor organizations were formed, and there was much labor unrest. Immigration continued at an alarming pace of nearly one million a year between 1901 and 1910, burgeoning the population of our cities. Roman Catholicism really grew. The Panama Canal was built. The birth control movement was launched by Mrs. Margaret Sanger. The N.A.A.C.P., the National Association for the Advancement of Colored People, was started. America was gradually becoming a world power.

In the life of the church, the holiness crusade was spent, but the temperance crusade went on to a shortlived victory. Revivalism's zeal glowed, then waned, and the Social Gospel movement was born. The Federal Council of Churches was established in 1910 with Methodism an important part of it; the ecumenical era had arrived.

At the century's end, New Jersey's historian says, "Probably no part of the Union offered more impregnable defenses to the onslaught of progressivism than did New Jersey. Politically corrupt and boss-ridden, 'home of the trusts' and happy hunting ground of railroad and utility interests, New Jersey seemed fully committed to her role as sponsor and protector of 'the system' against which reformers inveighed."[2] But three successive Republican Governors — Vorhees, Murphy and Fort — followed by the Democratic Governor and future President, Woodrow Wilson, brought New Jersey to the fore as a progressive state, except for women's suffrage which the male voters overwhelmingly rejected in 1915. The state's population increased almost three fourths of a million in the new century's first decade.

Methodism was still on the growing edge, increasing by over two million members between 1900 and 1925. New Jersey Conference membership increased from 50,000 in 1900 to 57,000 in 1914. We need to see how some of these changes, new forces and new ideas were affecting New Jersey Methodism. In this chapter we shall take a look at the new Social Gospel, the continuing temperance crusade and the flickering flames of revivalism. Other important, interesting and significant events will be highlighted as well.

As the twentieth century approached, Methodism prepared to receive a Twentieth Century Thank Offering for the support of its many benevolent programs. A churchwide goal of twenty million dollars was set. The program was eminently successful as the goal was topped by about one million dollars. The New Jersey Conference did well. $247,916 was reported in 1901 and an additional $129,352 in 1902. When the final tabulation was made in 1903, the Conference contributions amounted to $684,809, including a legacy of $10,000 from Colonel Alexander Shaw of Pennington Seminary and another from the estate of Reverend Ezra B. Lake of Ocean City of $85,000.[3]

Triumphant, thankful Methodists moved with anticipation into the new century. It was to be new, indeed. On the horizon lay the social gospel movement. In the beginning "the social gospel . . . may be regarded as American Protestantism's response to the challenge of modern industrial society."[4] It was the challenge of the city and the challenge of the new industrial order which brought into being the social gospel. The social gospel was congenial to some of the newer theological motifs. There was less emphasis on repentence and more on Christian nurture. The new, critical approach to the Bible was accepted, and evolution was seen as a way God was working out his plan in the world. The social gospel held out high hopes for the transformation of society as well as the individual, but it was gospel as well as social. "They may have used the language of the evolutionist and the social scientist, but the word they had for their generation was a word from God, and they fulfilled the function of the prophets in rebuking unrighteousness in high places."[5]

The greatest figure of the social gospel was Dr. Walter Rauschenbusch who moved from the pastorate of a church in the slums of New York City to a professorship at Rochester Theological Seminary. His epoch-making books on the social gospel were published between 1910 and 1917. He based his social gospel ideas around Jesus' teachings about the kingdom of God.

Methodism was slow to adopt the social gospel. Methodism did have a social goal, however unclearly many may have seen it. "Methodists pursued a society unstained by liquor, unstrained by ethnic or religious tension, unscarred by racial pride, and unmarred by class injustice."[6] Walter Rauschenbusch predicted:

> The Methodists are likely to play a very important part in the social awakening of the American churches. . . . They have rarely backed away from a fight when the issue was clearly drawn between Jehovah and Diabolus. . . . Their leaders are fully determined to form their battalions on this new line of battle, and when they march, the ground will shake.[7]

1908 was the epochal year for Methodism and the social gospel. The year previous, five prominent Methodist Episcopal ministers, Frank Mason North, Herbert Welch, later bishop; Elbert R. Zaring, Worth M. Tippy and Harry E. Ward organized the Methodist Federation for Social Service, a voluntary society still in existence, to push the claims of social Christianity within Methodism. The Methodist Episcopal Church was ready to move.

The General Conference of 1908 adopted The Social Creed. It was accepted almost verbatim by the Federal Council of Churches, organized later that year and thus served as the conscience statement of American Protestantism on social issues.

THE SOCIAL CREED

The Methodist Episcopal Church stands—
For Equal rights and complete justice for all men in all stations of life.
For the principle of conciliation and arbitration in industrial dissensions.
For the protection of the workers from dangerous machinery, occupational diseases, injuries, and mortality.
For the abolition of child labor.
For such regulation of the conditions of labor for women as shall safe-guard the physical and moral health of the community.
For the suppression of the "sweating system."
For the gradual and reasonable reduction of the hours of labor to the lowest practical point, with work for all; and for the degree of leisure for all which is the condition of the highest human life.
For a release from employment one day in seven.
For a living wage in every industry.
For the highest wage that each industry can afford, and for the most equitable division of the products of industry that can ultimately be devised.
For the recognition of the Golden Rule and the mind of Christ as the supreme law of society and the sure remedy of all social ills.[8]

The conservative New Jersey Conference was even slower to adopt to the new concerns of the times. Undoubtedly, there were ministers who advocated the social gospel, particularly among the younger, seminary-trained men. However, in official Conference action or reports little can be noted. The first note comes in the State of the Church report for 1911 which says, "The increasing power and influence of the church in political, social and business reformation proves she is the largest factor in the successful solution of perplexing present day problems."[9] That same year a Committee on World Peace and Arbitration was appointed. In 1914, the State of the Church report condemned the new theology of divine imminence, rather than divine incarnation; sin as an unfortunate remnant of man's lower life, instead of a false denial of his higher life; hope for a gradual evolution of humanity from sin, instead of a divine rescue from sin; and the concern with psychology and sociology, rather than what St. Paul called the "power of God unto salvation."[10] This same mood of the Conference is noted in a 1912 memorial sent to General Conference opposing modernism in Methodist Sunday School literature.[11] In 1914, appeared the first of a series of reports that started a crusade against modernist teachings in Sunday School literature and more particularly in the books recommended for the ministerial course of study.[12] The full story of the New Jersey Conference and the modernist controversy, led by Dr. Harold Paul Sloan, will be dealt with in the next chapter. What we see in this period is a reticence on the part of the Conference to adopt the new social gospel, and indeed, a growing opposition to the underlying theology of the movement.

The Methodists of the New Jersey Conference were not opposed to the Social Creed adopted by the church in 1908. What they did oppose was the theology behind the social gospel and the means taken to achieve those ends. The 1914 State of the Church report written by James D. Bills and Harold Paul Sloan says:

> As we face this new age we leave the supreme emphasis where our fathers put it, upon salvation through faith in the person of our atoning Lord. With respect to social service, we view it as the natural self-expression of renewed hearts, it is new only in the sense that present social problems are new.[13]

New Jersey Methodists did not take readily to the social gospel. They did take to the temperance cause. The Methodist Episcopal Church's Committee on Temperance and Prohibition established in 1892, became the Temperance Society in 1904 and in 1912, the Board of Temperance. The Board's headquarters was first in Wichita, Kansas; then it moved to Washington, D.C., in 1916 where, with Clarence True Wilson at its head, it worked closely with the powerful and politically active Anti-Saloon League to bring about prohibition. Dean Walter Muelder of the Boston University School of Theology wrote: "It is easy to forget the multitude of earnest men and women who fought liquor not because it made men happy, but because they knew it made them defeated and unhappy."[14]

While official decisions and reports of Conference Committees and presiding elders are what we have to depend on for Conference action regarding temperance, let us not forget that it was a crusade in which very many Methodists took part. Men joined the Knights of Templar temperance lodge, women the Women's Christian Temperance Union, the famous W.C.T.U., and thousands of Methodists worked in their local communities and voted at the ballot boxes to help bring in the dream of an alcohol-free life.

The Conference Temperance Society continued its work, urging the fight against the liquor interests, trying to secure legislative victories, taking to task law enforcement officials' failure to uphold existing laws, and urging the church forward in its great crusade. Their 1910 report shows continuing victory around the country, while lamenting the problems in New Jersey. There were at that time nine prohibition states and thirty-three others with local option laws. Only Nevada, Pennsylvania and New Jersey were solidly entrenched in the liquor camp.

One way of countering the influence of judges and others who refused to enforce alcoholic beverage and other moral laws was through the formation of Law and Order Leagues. The Camden District presiding elder reports one active in Camden County in 1901.

Presiding Elder Roe of the New Brunswick District reported in 1900:

> It gives me pleasure . . . to report that at some places our brethren have been making aggressive warfare against this curse of all curses. Notably has this been true of Long Branch where public sentiment has been aroused, licenses have been refused and violators of the law have been punished. A Law and Order League has been organized and Brother Shaw is the president. He is ably sustained not only by the pastors of all our churches but by the pastors and by the church generally.[15]

For many years the Rev. Samuel H. Hann was not only the State Temperance Agent, but the New Jersey Law and Order League head.

Victories were frequently announced. The Bridgeton District presiding elder in 1905 reported that Bridgeton, Millville, Vineland and Ocean City had no licensed hotels or saloons. Fifty-one other towns on the District did not license intoxicating drinks.[16] Five years later, the same District reported no ground lost, a Law and Order League established and licenses removed from hotels in Glassboro, Malaga and Franklinville.[17]

The Camden District Superintendent reported success in 1913 in the enforcement of laws in places where no licenses were granted and that a new sheriff in Atlantic County had won indictments against liquor violations. The next year he reported all the saloons of Pleasantville, Linwood and Elwood closed.

Frequently, the Temperance Society appealed for the support of bills pending in the State Legislature. It worked especially hard for local option bills to allow a local community to vote whether it wanted to be "wet" or "dry."

As the first World War neared, the national crusade for prohibition entered its final phase. At the forefront was always the Methodist Episcopal Church. One presiding elder said: "Let it always be understood that whenever a Methodist preacher comes to a town, whether by railroad, trolley, automobile, carriage or horse-back, or on foot, that an enemy to the rum business has arrived."[18]

We have been following the struggle of the blacks for full equality since slavery's end. Of the major types of social problems, the race question received the least attention in the early years of the twentieth century. The social gospel did not seem concerned with this issue at this time. Jim Crow laws and patterns of segregation were everywhere. Clement Price says about New Jersey, "Prior to the great migration of World War I which brought thousands of southern blacks into the state, black communities in many areas were cohesive. The Negro Church, still the paramount institution at the time, stressed Christian respectability. Religious and secular leaders emphasized the work ethic.

Responsibility to family and community seems to have been the central idea among older families."[19]

New Jersey Conference Methodists continued to support Morristown College and the Freedmen's Aid Society. The support was minimal. In 1909, the apportionment for the Conference was $5,500. The total collection in the Conference was only $1,380. The Sunday nearest Lincoln's birthday, which many still remember as Race Relations Sunday, was even then being urged "as a most suitable time to present the cause of the colored race to our people," and receive offerings for the Freedmen's Aid Society.[20] There is not much more that was done.

We have also been following the concerns for women and laymen in the Conference. It is difficult to follow the activities of the laymen. Conference Minutes do not always give the minutes of the lay organization except in the years when General Conference delegates were elected. What became of the 1898 Layman's Association is not known. In 1912, a resolution was passed 62 to 42 to form a "Laymen's Association of the New Jersey Conference." A constitution was adopted and Dr. George H. Franklin of Hightstown was elected president.[21]

Women finally gained a seat in the 1904 General Conference, but it would still be a long time before the New Jersey Conference would send their first woman delegate; in fact, another thirty years would pass.

The ministers' wives of the Conference formed their first association in 1903. At the instigation of Mrs. Charles F. Garrison, a meeting of the wives of the ministers of the Conference was held March 23, 1903, in Asbury Park. At this meeting, the New Jersey Conference Sisterhood was organized. In 1911, one hundred four wives voluntarily formed the Benefit Branch to provide a gift of money to a member at the death of her husband. The first assessment was thirty cents. The first benefit, fifteen dollars and twenty-five cents.

Deaconess work was recognized with the appointment of a Deaconess Board in 1904. Not many reports were given, but in 1906 the Board reported: "Miss Jessie B. Hillman was licensed early last summer and is now rendering efficient service in the State of Ohio, and Miss Sallie B. Heisler, now a student at the Lucy Webb Hayes Training School at Washington, D.C., has been recommended for license by the Quarterly Conference of the Broadway M. E. Church, Camden."[22] These were apparently the first two deaconesses from the Conference. Two years later, Sallie was said to be the only deaconess under the Board's care and was working in Paterson, New Jersey. In 1909, she was commended for having established a Methodist Episcopal Church in Paterson with 21 members and a Sunday School for 104 Italian children.

Deaconess work in Camden was begun in 1913 under the auspices of the Woman's Home Missionary Society. It was the start of the work of the famed Deaconess Home and Community Center today known as the Neighborhood Center. The 1914 Conference Minutes reports: "The Deaconess work, which was begun last year by the Woman's Home Missionary Society, is developing. A house at 273 Kaighn's Avenue, Camden, N. J., has been purchased." During the first year, two sewing classes, a story hour for children, and a mothers' meeting were organized. A Kindergarten and employment bureau were to begin soon. Almost a thousand calls in the homes of the needy were made. Miss Hattie F. Davis was the first superintendent.[23]

In 1897, Ocean Grove became the site of the Bancroft Rest Home for missionaries and deaconesses. In 1914, it was the only such home sponsored by the Woman's Home Missionary Society to stay open all year. That year it served 67 deaconnesses, 15 missionaries, 47 Christian workers, and 218 guests. They were charged only three dollars a week for their board in this lovely home.

The 1904 General Conference approved the formation of Ladies Aid Societies in the local churches, something that had been in effect for several years. The important part of this official approval was that it made the president of the Ladies Aid, if a member of the church, a member of the Quarterly Conference: the first woman so designated.

The boldest step the New Jersey Conference men took in regard to women's rights was the wholehearted endorsement of the right of women to vote in New Jersey in 1915. However, their main reason given was the opposition by the New Jersey Liquor Dealers' Protective Association.

Many people today, when Sunday is given so much to sports, fun, shopping and all sorts of activities, find it hard to believe the concern evidenced in this period over Sunday observance. Our Methodist forbears insisted that Sunday should properly be the Lord's Day. As a matter of fact, no concern received more attention in the New Jersey Conference in the opening years of the twentieth century, apart from temperance, than proper Sunday observance. Today, we may take pride in our liberty, but church after church laments the competition which draws children, youth and adults away from the church.

Hear what the Conference said. In 1902: "We stand determinedly opposed to Senate Bill No. 42, and demand amendments . . . retaining our Sunday laws, jurisdiction of the courts, and no repeal of state law on any of these questions."[24] In 1906, the Camden District presiding elder said: "A strong effort has been made to have our Sabbath laws repealed. Think for a moment of the absurdity of men trying to vote away the commandments of God."[25]

The following year, N. J. Wright of the Bridgeton District said: "South Jersey people may be behind the times in some directions, but are thoroughly up to date on the great moral issues of the day. The Sabbath is religiously observed in most of our communities, though some people have lax ideas on this and kindred questions."[26] In 1908, approval and pledge of support was given to the newly organized New Jersey Sabbath Association, which soon became the Lord's Day Alliance. The Committee on Sabbath Observance the same year said: "We condemn that form of corporate greed and individual selfishness which tramples upon the law of God and the rights of men, by compelling their employees to work upon the Lord's Day."[27] The struggle in New Jersey for Sabbath observance has been a long one.

One of the lengthiest discussions about this history in the Advisory Committee meetings centered around my statement that the period prior to World War I saw the last flames of revivalism in the Conference. The Committee strongly disagreed and wisely, though maybe a bit hesitantly, accepted the wording, flickering flames of revivalism. This contention is not meant to suggest that revival interest died out in the New Jersey Conference. The evangelistic preaching at our camp meetings, the revival services or evangelistic meetings, by whatever name they are called, that are held every year in our Conference churches, particularly in the more southerly part of the Conference, belie that fact.

"Flickering flames of revivalism" is meant to suggest that often a fire may burn bright and seemingly intense as it begins to near its end. It then starts flickering and will soon die out if nothing is done to give it new life. The evidence shows that New Jersey Conference Methodists throughout the nineteenth century and on into the opening years of the twentieth century were a revival people. The church, it was believed, was in the business of saving souls. The presiding elders always reported to Conference on the souls saved or number of conversions on their districts. It was normal for a church yearly, or almost so, to hold revival services, protracted meetings, or extra services to bring people into the Kingdom and revive the hearts of the faithful. Normally, these meetings were conducted by the church's own minister, perhaps assisted by other nearby pastor-friends or local preachers along with the prayers and personal work of the faithful members.

These patterns changed by the end of the first World War. Somehow it became less fashionable to talk about the saving of souls, though we still believed in it. Our District Superintendents less and less spoke of the numbers converted, perhaps because not so many were. Hopefully, Methodists were converted, but we talked, instead, of joining the church. The yearly meeting for presenting the gospel to the lost and reviving the hearts of the faithful was less widely held across the Conference. Professional evangelists were brought in to lead soul-winning efforts, often in mass campaigns. It was like bringing the old camp meeting to the city. At times, these larger services would be held in a tent with a sawdust trail. Take the revival away, however, from the local church, away from the church's own pastor, away from the intimate involvement of the local church's members and soon evangelism is no longer seen so clearly as the local church's predominent concern.

When the Conference had a Focus on Evangelism in 1980 and 1981, training sessions were provided for pastors in which a considerable time was spent defining evangelism. For many church members and local churches, even the word evangelism is an uncomfortable one.

Back in the opening decade of the present century, there were revivals across the Conference. In 1900, two hundred forty conversions were reported in Broadway Church, Camden. The presiding elder said four things were used in that revival: much prayer, faithful preaching, personal entreaty and individual testimony.[28] On the Trenton District, there were twelve hundred conversions reported by the presiding elder, Samuel W. Lake. He said, concerning Pennington: "During the fall term occured one of the most remarkable revivals in the history of the Seminary, resulting in the conversion of a large number of the students."[29]

From 1904 to 1909, the presiding elders report almost yearly revivals. There was a "great revival time on the Bridgeton District" in 1904. One hundred or more were converted at Central and First Bridgeton; Leesburg; and First, Second, Fourth, and Trinity Millville.[30] More of the same occured in 1905. Over sixteen hundred were converted on the Bridgeton District and thirteen hundred on the New Brunswick District. The largest revivals and greatest numbers of conversions were at Bridgeton: First, 300; Ocean City, 150; Whitesville, 125; Ocean Grove, 115; Mount Holly, over 100.

J. Morgan Read of the Camden District said in his 1908 report, "Long may the day be distant when the Methodist Church does not believe in and lay emphasis on revival services."[31] Large revivals were reported in Fourth Church Bridgeton, Newport, Heislerville, South Vineland, Woodbury, State Street in Camden, Broad Street and Trinity in Trenton, and Medford. The 1909 revivals were especially strong on the Camden and Trenton Districts. Williamstown had two hundred fifteen conversions and Medford two hundred. Fifteen hundred alone were reported on the Trenton District.

It has been said that "we can work and pray up a revival, but only God can send it down." There was a lull in revivals until the eve of World War I. While a little outside the years covered in this part of our history, 1915 to 1917 were years of most intensive revival and will be included here to complete the story.

In 1914, Billy Sunday was invited to hold an Evangelistic Campaign in Trenton. The following year he was holding services in Philadelphia during the New Jersey Conference. Conference sent its best wishes and prayers to him, invited him to address the Conference in Atlantic City, and again urged him to come to New Jersey. He declined to visit the Conference.

As a result of the Sunday Campaign in Philadelphia, however, revival swept the New Jersey Conference. George H. Neal on the Bridgeton District said that "for two months revival swept the District. About 2400 saved so far." He said some 30,000 people were converted in Philadelphia and about 8,000 in the New Jersey Conference.[32] Cape May Court House reported 252, Pitman 170, Deerfield and Aldine, 96 converted. Camden District reported 2901 conversions to date. Converts numbered 300 at Williamstown, 250 at Broadway Camden, 174 at Auburn and Center Square, 150 at Linwood. The New Brunswick District Superintendent reported 1500 conversions on his District, centering around Ocean Grove and Toms River. St. Paul's Church, Ocean Grove, had 100 cottage prayer meetings, a continuous twenty-four hour devotional service and over 125 conversions. The great revival on the New Brunswick District was at Toms River. People within twenty miles attended the services with over 275 converted. The Superintendent, James W. Marshall, commented: "Praise God for the real old-fashioned Methodist revival, saving souls, building the church, and defeating the devil!"[33] The Trenton District, too, saw at least 1200 brought into the Kingdom.

These events were prelude to 1916 when Billy Sunday conducted a seven week Crusade in Trenton. There were 16,745 reported converts, 4,350 of whom came to the Methodist Church.[34] Is it any wonder the Trenton District Superintendent said, "Evangelism has been the outstanding feature of the year's work on the Trenton District?"[35] Bridgeton District that year reported the Dr. George Wood Anderson Millville Crusade. Over 4,000 were converted, 2,000 added to the churches of which 1,050 were to the Methodist Churches.[36] Fifty years later, people in Millville still talked about the George Wood Anderson Crusade. New Brunswick District heard Billy Sunday preach with Homer Rodeheaver leading the singing, during Ocean Grove's Camp Meeting. The Camden District had the Stough Union campaign for seven weeks in Atlantic City with grand results. Dr. W. V. Kelley, Editor of the *Methodist Review,* who started his ministry in the New Jersey Conference in 1867, said that in 1916 "The New Jersey Conference led the nation in the number of souls brought to Christ and added to the Church."[37]

Revival fires burned, but not so brightly in 1917. The biggest campaign was the nine week, Camden Interdenominational Revival which started October 9, 1916. Results, however, were given not in terms of conversions, but in cards signed, a total of 4,400. The Methodist Churches received 1,848 and added 506 new members.[38] Bridgeton District had over 1,000 saved.

Never again was there to be another revival like that of 1915 and 1916 in the New Jersey Conference, although many would pray, "Lord, do it again!" Revival flames were flickering. Other important issues, though surely not more important, would rise to the fore. To be sure, there are churches who have continued to maintain their evangelistic aim through all the years, ministers of the Conference that are known to be evangelical in the very best meaning of that term, and numbers of lay people who yearn to recapture the fire of revival. Still, it must be said, 1917 marked not only the drawing to a close of a particular revival time, but also the beginning of the flickering flame of revival in New Jersey Methodism that has never since been fanned into a fervent flame.

Much was happening in the cities in the early 1900's. The Conference's two largest churches in 1915 were in Camden. Broadway had 1104 members and First Church had 1043. Broadway Church that year had 2,071 enrolled in their Sunday School. First Church paid their pastor $3,900, almost double the top Conference salary of $2,000 in 1900. The third largest Conference church was in Camden's suburban town of Collingswood with 975 members. Trenton's Trinity, First and Central Churches all had over 600 members and 450 or more in the Sunday School. Millville and Vineland boasted churches with over 800 members. The resort towns of Atlantic City, Ocean Grove, Asbury Park and Long Branch had large and fast growing memberships. It was a time of large city churches with great pulpits filled with strong preachers. This was true even though the majority of New Jersey Methodists lived in rural communities, and attended small churches. Nor did the small town nature of so much of southern New Jersey Methodism deter the church from ministering in broader ways within the city. Both Camden and Trenton boasted of missionary societies while the Camden Deaconess Home soon built an envious record of Christian service to the poor in the name of the Methodist Episcopal Church.

George L. Dobbins, presiding elder of the Camden District, said in his 1901 report:

> Long before the last General Conference provided for City Evangelization Unions where five or more Churches are found in one city, the Camden City Methodists organized a City Church Extension and Missionary Society, which has already done a splendid work in saving Kaighn Avenue Church . . . and in helping other struggling churches.[39]

In 1908, the Trenton City Church Extension Society was founded. Presiding Elder Alfred Wagg was president with General Rusling as vice president and Rev. George Archer of Clinton Avenue Church as secretary. Dr. Wagg speaks of new work starting at Wilbur and Cadwalader and the possibility of opening an Italian mission.[40]

What other kinds of happenings were taking place during these opening years of this new century? First, new churches were started, and others were built. To take the year 1909 as an example, services were held on the Bridgeton District for the first time at Stone Harbor, Peermont, and Avalon. "It is hoped the new church at Ocean City can be dedicated on July 4th," said the Superintendent. Without naming them, the Camden District Superintendent said eleven new churches had been started in the past ten years. He does name the five new ones dedicated on the District that year: Mantua, June 19, 1908; Chews, November 22, 1908; Thorofare, March 7, 1907; Haddon Heights, September 27, 1908. Audubon's new church "soon will be dedicated," he said.[41] Brigantine Beach had a pastor appointed. A chapel was built there the next year. On the New Brunswick District during the last six years "eight new churches have been built, six new parsonages and a fine library at Englishtown."[42] During the preceding year, Highlands built a new church with assistance from the Church Extension Society, a church was organized at Seaside Park. St. James, New Brunswick, was destroyed by fire. On the Trenton District, Roebling Church was organized February, 1909. Greenwood Avenue Church, Trenton, was built, and Chatsworth bought a former Presbyterian Church in which they had been worshipping.

Conference in 1906 raised the educational qualifications for ministerial candidates seeking admission to the Conference. A full college course and, if possible, a course in a Theological School were now required.[43]

Weather related problems and other deterents were lamented some years. J. L. Roe, presiding elder on the New Brunswick District in 1903, complained of the scarity of fuel and stormy Sabbaths during the fall and winter. John B. Haines followed Rev. Roe in 1904 on the District; but, if anything, times were worse. "The failure of three banks, the absconding of trust funds of a prominent public man in one of our cities, the poor season for our fishermen along the coast, the hard winter, together with the short-crop conditions, has greatly interfered with the Current Expense accounts of our churches and the gifts to our benevolences."[44] Presiding Elder Edmund Hewitt of the Bridgeton District the same year said, "This has been a hard year in some parts of the District. The partial failure of the berry and vegetable crops, the almost complete failure of the oyster supply, the long, cold winter and frequent stormy Sundays."[45] Again it was the New Brunswick District where the effects were felt in 1910. The new Superintendent John Handley said, "The numerous stormy Sundays, the high cost of living, and the severe winter along the shore, have had a detrimental effect on the benevolences, but we hope the statistics will show them in advance of last year."[46]

Pennington School was on the minds of the Conference in these years. In 1903, Thomas O'Hanlon, for thirty-three years president of Pennington, retired. He was Mr. Pennington. During his presidential years, he saw the school through building and curriculum changes, cleared the debt, and started an endowment fund. When he left the buildings and campus were in excellent condition. He is said to have trained over six hundred young men for the Christian, mostly Methodist, ministry. Dr. O'Hanlon for many years led the great Ocean Grove Bible Class that is said to have been the largest in the country. He married Hannah Maps, daughter of William R. Maps of Long Branch. They had eleven children, eight of whom survived him. He died at his Ocean Grove home on September 30, 1912.

The Rev. James W. Marshall, minister of Broadway Church, Camden, succeeded Dr. O'Hanlon as head of Pennington School. While Dr. O'Hanlon was said to have cleared the school's debt, the school was seldom free from debt. Dr. Marshall found about a $50,000 debt when he assumed the presidency of Pennington. Debts have a way of escalating, and this one did. The Forward Fund and other means kept Pennington going. In 1910, a proposal was approved that Pennington once again be a school for boys only.

Besides the local churches and Pennington School, another interest of the Conference was homes for the aged. Early in 1907, at a meeting of the church members of the New Brunswick District, held at St. Paul's Church, Ocean Grove, the Monmouth Methodist Episcopal Home for the Aged of the New Brunswick District was formed. Rev. James W. Marshall, then minister of St. Paul's was elected president of the Board of Trustees. A home at 63 Clark Street, Ocean Grove, was purchased.[47] In 1910, the name was changed to the New Jersey Home for the Aged. In 1914, the Home with Mrs. John H. Parker of Long Branch as president of the Board of Managers was ready to start a campaign for $200,000 to build a new home.

The 1908 General Conference changed the name Presiding Elder to District Superintendent. The conservative New Jersey Conference liked the old name better and requested General Conference in 1912 to restore the old name. It did not and District Superintendents have been with us ever since.

The 1910 Conference was one never forgotten by anyone there. Bishop Henry Spellmeyer of St. Louis opened the first session on Wednesday, March 9, in St. Paul's Church, Atlantic City. The bishop was not feeling his best and saw a doctor just before Conference convened. Yet he presided over each session. Friday evening, he asked to see the doctor again. Saturday morning he asked his friend, Bishop Thomas Neely who was attending Conference, to preside. About forty-five minutes later, the Secretary of the Conference, Melville Snyder, came in and asked for a matter of very high privilege. He announced to the shocked Conference the sudden death of Bishop Spellmeyer. After prayer and the appointment of a committee to take care of all matters relating to the deceased bishop, Conference adjourned until eleven o'clock. A Memorial Service was held in St. Paul's Monday afternoon with Bishop Neely preaching. Honorary pall bearers and a committee were chosen to represent the Conference at the bishop's funeral on March 16 at Centenary Church, Newark, the church he had pastored when elected bishop in 1904.

The 1911 session was held for the first time in Ocean City. It was the seventy-fifth session. Statistics showed 55,261 church members, 61,818 in the Sunday School, 12,944 Epworth League members plus 9,675 more in the Junior League. There were 344 churches valued at $4,373,200 and 218 parsonages worth $798,025. Total church indebtedness was $503,716.[48]

The 1912 General Conference established Episcopal Areas for the first time. Prior to that time, bishops lived in various parts of the country but rotated the Conferences over which they presided. After 1912, bishops have been assigned to an Area with presidential supervision over the Conferences within the Area. Bishop Joseph F. Berry, formerly of Buffalo, New York, was assigned to the Philadelphia Area with responsibilities for the New Jersey, Philadelphia and Wyoming Conferences. Our first resident bishop was an editor, author, ardent foe of the liquor business and staunch supporter of Epworth League work.

Conference was getting into some serious fund raising efforts by 1914. The Pennington Forward Movement was well underway. The Ocean Grove Home for the Aged was seeking $200,000 to build a new home. The Commission on Conference Claimants set 1915 as the year to begin a five year drive for $400,000 to benefit the retired ministers.

As a closing note, the Conference Minutes for 1900 notes the death of Miss Mary Ashton, a local church member. In this day of concern for the handicapped, what Mary Ashton did in 1900 is a fitting close to this chapter filled with so much activity.

> I cannot close this report without a short reference to Miss Mary Ashton, a member of State Street Church, Trenton, who died last August in her mother's summer home at Ocean Grove, N.J. Though deaf and lame she earned and collected for the missionary cause $12,500 in ten years, and for some time has supported six missionaries in China and India. Dr. Parkin, her pastor, has written an account of her life in tract form for the missionary society, which will, I am sure inspire all who read it.[49]

Chapter 10

WORLD WAR I AND THE TURBULENT TWENTIES

1915-1929

War in Europe, triggered by the assassination of Archduke Francis Ferdinand, heir to the throne of Austria-Hungary, increasingly involved the United States. By 1917, we were at war. Strange how feelings can grip a people. The war was almost a holy crusade. It was to be a war to end all wars. How sad that we won the war and lost the peace. The refusal of the United States Senate to ratify the Versailles Peace Treaty and the League of Nations was conclusive proof the progressive period, signalized in Woodrow Wilson, had ended.

While we were winning a war and losing the peace other significant happenings were taking place. The Prohibition Amendment (Eighteenth) went into effect in 1920, and the United States was legally dry. Methodists, among others, rejoiced. We did no better in enforcing that amendment than we did in enforcing peace. The same year, the Nineteenth Amendment (Women's Suffrage) became law and women won the right to vote. Already, Miss Jeanette Rankin of Montana, had become the first woman member of Congress. In 1925, Mrs. Nellie T. Ross of Wyoming became the first woman governor.

Radio broadcasting started in 1920, and Charles Lindbergh flew across the Atlantic in 1927. It was a new era. The turbulent twenties was a decade of changing morals and unbounded prosperity, yet ended in a crash plunging America into its darkest depression, which did not end until once again the world was dark and bloody with war. Dean Muelder describes the revolution in post-World War I morals:

> The on-going moral crisis which every society faces was especially acute in the 'revolt of the younger generation.' New freedoms were asserted in an era that saw the crest of the feminist wave and changing mores of smoking, drinking, petting, and premarital sex relations. The 'revolt of youth' would have come in any case, and indeed had set in at least a decade earlier, but in the context of Prohibition youth took a clue from the oldsters armed with bootleg liquor and flouting the codes of the 'blue noses.' To be sure, the 'revolt of youth' was partly a search for religious meaning. But it was also a flapper-and-flash 'lost generation.' Some of those trails were to disappear in the thirties and forties and to reappear in the fifties with widespread loss of controls involving sex, alcohol, and gambling.[1]

War and peace, temperance and prohibition, industrial concerns and labor unrest, racial problems, and the modernist controversy were some of the important issues which confronted the church in this era. Sydney Ahlstrom describes the twenties as "the crisis of the Protestant establishment:"

> The Protestant churches of America did not lose their historic hegemony during the troubled twenties, but they were made sharply aware that their ancient sway over the na-

tion's moral life was threatened. Even as modern religious ideas steadily advanced or as concern for social issues increased, the churches tended to lose their capacity to shape and inform American opinion. The debacle of Prohibition functioned both as evidence and cause of the churches' loss of authority in a culture where urban values became primary. The decline of the Puritan Sabbath despite strenuous campaigns in its behalf, the emergence of new attitudes toward recreation despite old Puritanic suspicions of play, and the expansion of the amusement industry served meanwhile to weaken the disciplinary aspects of church membership. Modern thought and social change were slowly bringing down the curtains on the 'great century' of American evangelicalism.[2]

New Jersey was a center for America's war effort. By war's end, this state had sixteen military establishments. Forty per cent of all soldiers sent to Europe sailed from Hoboken. About 150,000 New Jerseyans served in the conflict and 3,836 lost their lives. In the fall of 1918, "Spanish" influenza struck the state. At least 300,000 cases were reported in three months. Some 17,000 people died from the flu or its complications. Bootleggers abounded in New Jersey. New Jersey was considered by Prohibition enforcement officials as "one of the hardest spots to handle in the entire country." Industry and population kept expanding. The Garden State by 1926, ranked sixth in the value of manufactured products. Our three million population in 1920, became four million by decade's end[3] even though a new immigration law drastically reduced the number of people coming from abroad. Large numbers of southern blacks, migrating north, increased the black population one hundred thirty-two per cent between 1910 and 1930,[4] and added to racial tensions.

Methodism still grew. The Methodist Episcopal Church membership stood at 4,711,994 in 1925, almost doubling since 1900. The New Jersey Conference had 56,687 members on the rolls in 1915. By 1930 the number grew to 75,124.

War was declared April 6, 1917. The New Jersey Conference ended three weeks previously. Roy L. Lewis was appointed acting Chaplain, United States Navy. A unanimous resolution was passed expressing loyalty to Country and Flag and pledging support of President Wilson in this crisis. Every church was asked to prominently display "the flag of our nation, which we love and for which we would die." Conference rose to sing "America" and Bishop Berry led in prayer.[5]

When Conference next assembled in Atlantic City, March 6, 1918, we had been at war nearly a year. A published honor roll listed seven members of Conference and forty-four sons of preachers serving in the Armed Forces. Richard A. Conover, John Handley, Roy L. Lewis, Alfred C. Oliver, Jr., Sherman G. Pitt, George W. Ridout and Earl C. Senser were chaplains. A Pledge of Patriotism adopted at the opening session included this resolve:

> That we here and now record ourselves confident of the righteousness of our cause, restful concerning the sincerity of our administration and pledge our patriotic cooperation to the President of the United States to remain in this conflict until 'human equality and the inalienable rights of man' shall have universal achievement, and a world-wide brotherhood shall be established, never again to be broken.[6]

Dr. Harold Paul Sloan
Leader of the N.J. Protest against Modernism in the M.E. Church

At Fort Dix, the Board of Home Missions and Church Extension assumed financial responsibility for much of the work on the Wrightstown-Pointville Charge. The Pointville Church Hall was turned into a social center. Throughout the Conference, the patriotic note was sounded. Germany must be defeated. The world must be made safe for democracy.

An interesting story is told how Pennington School solved its coal shortage. There was a wreck on the Philadelphia and Reading Railroad which dumped eight carloads of coal on the school's grounds. It was secured for the school at a greatly reduced price.

The Armistice was signed and the war over when Bishop William A. Shepard convened the 1919 Conference in St. Paul's Church, Ocean Grove. There was subdued rejoicing in the victory.

Names were added to the Honor Roll including two sons of preachers, William A. Eckersley and John H. Read who lost their lives. Also Mark Shepard, son of Bishop Shepard, who died in service. Four more preacher's sons were wounded: Lyman M. Blake, Homer C. Hulse, John W. Magee and

Robert E. Surtees. Chaplain George W. Ridout was also wounded. Albert S. Baner and Norman V. Sargent became Chaplains. In all nine Conference ministers entered the Chaplaincy, fifty-eight sons and one daughter of a preacher saw action. The Lay Association presented to Conference a Service Flag, honoring 2,860 sons and daughters of New Jersey Methodists who served in World War I.

Another war-time disaster struck New Jersey. On October 5, 1918, the T. A. Gillespie shell loading plant at Morgan, near South Amboy, exploded. About one hundred persons died and damage exceeded $25,000,000 in a twenty-five mile redius. South Amboy Church was wrecked. The parsonage fared worse. Reverend James E. Shaw and his wife were shell-shocked. The Red Cross assisted. The Parsonage was repaired. The Church was still able to serve thousands of meals and provide beds in some of its Sunday School rooms.[7]

Who were some of the Conference leaders during these years? Bishop Joseph Berry will have to be singled out. This first resident bishop of the Conference served in that capacity for four quadrennium from 1912 to 1928. During the last two quadrennium, he was the senior active bishop in the Methodist Episcopal Church. His memoir in the Conference *Minutes* of 1931, says he "enriched the preachers of his acquaintance by friendly counsel, timely help and rare sympathy, and . . . proved himself a good minister of Jesus Christ . . . never losing passion for the winning of men to his Divine Lord, preaching the Evangel with appeal and power, 'beseeching men in Christ's stead, be ye reconciled to God.' "[8]

Harold Paul Sloan and Furman A. DeMaris were two leading pastors and District Superintendents throughout this period and the 1930's. Dr. Sloan pastored such significant Conference Churches as Red Bank; Central, Bridgeton; and Haddonfield. He served a term as Superintendent of the Camden District. He authored several books including *Christ of the Ages* and *He Is Risen*. In 1935, he was elected Editor of the New York *Christian Advocate,* a post he held until 1940. He was elected to seven consecutive General Conferences, 1920 to 1940. When he relinquished his editorship, Dr. Sloan transferred to the Philadelphia Conference where he served the Wharton Memorial Methodist Church in Philadelphia until his retirement in 1954. Harold Sloan is best remembered for his leadership of the conservative forces in their fight against moderism in the Methodist Episcopal Church. That story will be more fully told later in this chapter.[9]

Furman A. DeMaris was a slightly older contemporary of Dr. Sloan. He entered the ministry in 1897, serving Eatontown and Tinton Falls. In 1915, he was appointed Superintendent of the Camden District. Then, following a ten year pastorate at Asbury Park, he became Superintendent of the New Brunswick District. He succeeded Dr. Sloan as pastor at Haddonfield in 1933, and served until his retirement in 1942. He died April 15, 1956, in Atlantic City. DeMaris was elected a delegate to the General Conferences of 1916, 1924, 1928 and 1932. He was a reserve delegate in 1920 and one of the delegates to the first Jurisdictional Conference in 1940. He was a popular speaker, much

Harry P. Bennett 1871-1953
Member St. Luke's Church, Long Branch.
Elected to more General Conferences (9) than any other clergy or laity in the Conference.

in demand, whose "sermons and addresses carried a serious, poignant message sprinkled with humor."[10]

A layman of particular influence was Mr. Harry P. Bennett of St. Luke's Church, Long Branch. This sterling Christian holds the record in the New Jersey Conference, among clergy or laity, for being elected to the most General Conferences. His record is nine. He was elected in 1908, 1912, 1916, 1920, 1924, 1932, 1936, 1939 and 1940. In 1928, he was a reserve delegate. That shows the esteem in which he was held by the laity of the Conference. Through all these years, he was active in the lay associations of the Conference, in which he held numerous offices. From his home in Long Branch, he commuted to New York where he served on the staff of *The Christian Advocate*. In his local church he was, among other offices held, for thirty years the Sunday School Superintendent. One of his pastors said, "nothing but his own illness or that of others made his pew empty." His Conference memorial was written by Dr. Frederick Brown Harris, Chaplain of the United States Senate, long-time friend and former pastor, who said of him, "Harry P. Bennett, one of the dearest friends of my life, was a prince among men. He was a great Christian, incapable of meanness, and a devoted churchman, with a consuming zeal for the coming Kingdom."[11]

A second layman with much influence in the Conference was Mr. William E. Massey, son of the Rev. William A. Massey of the New Jersey Conference. Mr. Massey was long an active member of the Conference lay association. For many years he served on the Board of Trustees of Pennington Seminary and was president from 1922 to 1928. He served as a lay delegate to every General Conference during this period, 1916 to 1928. Mr. Massey was a resident of Ocean City, active in First Church, a leading realtor, bank director and business associate of the younger Howard Stainton. It is interesting to speculate that his association with Howard Stainton, may have had some influence on Mr. Stainton's later interest in Pennington School to whom he bequeathed half of his estate. William E. Massey died in 1934.[12]

The New Jersey Conference worked throughout the teen years for the passage of prohibition. This in a state where prohibition laws on the state level were very hard to come by. When Prohibition took effect January 16, 1920, forty-five of the forty-eight states had ratified the Eighteenth Amendment. New Jersey was one of the three who did not vote to ratify. Conference was jubilant when it met in 1920. The Country was now dry. But it was mortified that New Jersey had as Governor, Edward I. Edwards, an avowed wet, who opposed prohibition and promised to make New Jersey "as wet as the Atlantic Ocean." When he left the governor's chair and ran for the United States Senate, which he won in 1922, his slogan was, "Wine, Women, and Song," demanding the repeal of the Eighteenth Amendment.[13]

As the decade progressed, attention was turned to the need to enforce the Eighteenth Amendment. Conference considered it the Christian and the American thing to do.

The Hoover-Smith presidential campaign of 1928, drew the attention of Methodists north and south. Alfred E. Smith, the Democratic candidate, was not only a wet, but also the first Roman Catholic presidential candidate. Dean Muelder says, "Methodists threw their energies into the election of that year and influenced the outcome."[14] Was it religious bigotry against Catholicism or the moral issue of a wet candidate that was the most decisive in turning the Methodists against Smith? Undoubtedly there was some religious bigotry, but Miller in his study of the role of the Protestant churches in the 1928 election says, "When Protestants said they opposed Smith because of his wetness, they meant precisely what they said. Prohibition was not a straw man; it was the factor that more than any other determined the vote of many Americans in the election of 1928."[15] There are no official statements to show how New Jersey Conference Methodists felt. However, one can be fairly certain that New Jersey Methodists voted for Hoover and for these reasons: First, Hoover was dry, Smith was wet. Second, Hoover was a Republican, Smith a Democrat. Third, Hoover was a Protestant, Smith a Roman Catholic. Fourth, the continued prosperity of the country at that time gave little impetus to a change in national leadership. It is my guess that this was the order of importance for most New Jersey Conference Methodists in deciding for whom to vote. The biggest thing, so far as Methodists were concerned, against Al Smith, was his wetness.

Apart from the crusade for temperance and prohibition, and naturally the war, by far the largest issue that concerned the New Jersey Conference and required the greatest amount of time and energy was the "Modernist Controversy" within the Methodist Episcopal Church. The New Jersey Conference took the leading role in this controversy, with Dr. Harold Paul Sloan as its champion.[16] This organized protest against modernism in the church is not to be confused with the modernist-fundamentalist debates. Dr. Sloan was careful to state that "the verbalism, literalism, and premillennialism of the organized fundamentalist movement were never involved in the New Jersey criticisms."[17]

The Modernist Controversy or New Jersey Protest, as it was often called, began in the 1914 Conference with a report of a Committee on Publication. This particularly had to do with Sunday School literature. Beginning in 1917, it focused on the Course of Study, still the principal means by which the majority of ministers entered the Methodist ministry. It led to the formation of the Methodist League for Faith and Life, and culminated in a constitutional victory at the 1932 General Conference in Atlantic City.

The basic concerns were theological. Teachings contrary to historic Christianity and historic Methodism were being introduced into the church. The opponents of modernism sought to uphold the depravity of man, the vicarious atonement of Christ, the deity of our Lord, his virgin birth, and the reality of the resurrection, all of which modernism tended to play down or deny.

The report of the Committee on Publication, of which Dr. Sloan was a member, studied books published by the Methodist Episcopal Publishing House. They were especially critical of certain Sunday School books and the ones to be studied by those preparing for the Methodist ministry.

When the new list of books on the Course of Study was released in the summer of 1916, the New Brunswick District Preachers' Meeting asked Dr. Sloan, pastor of First Church, Red Bank, to review the sixty volumes. In his review, he concluded that the great majority were worthwhile. Ten of the sixty expressed the "new theology." These he criticized, especially Dr. T. G. Soares book, *Social Institutions and Ideals of the Bible.* He was also critical of Dr. Harris Franklin Rall of Garrett Biblical Institute with whom he vigorously debated through the years. The New Brunswick District Preachers' Meeting adopted Dr. Sloan's report. It was submitted to the Annual Conference which adopted it as their position. The report was then sent to the Philadelphia Conference and the Board of Bishops.[18] Dr. Sloan was made chariman of the Conference Course of Study Committee. Other members were John B. Haines, Carlton R. VanHook, Alfred Wagg and Alfonso Dare.

A lengthy report was issued in 1918. The Committee had met with the Board of Bishops in Grand Rapids, Michigan, April 25, 1917, and presented their concerns. As a result, two changes were made in the Course of Study.

Selections from the writings of John Wesley were added and Dr. Soares book was removed. At the instigation of the New Jersey Conference these other Conferences joined in the protest: Philadelphia, Wyoming, Wilmington, North Indiana, Southern California and Baltimore. Conference approved two actions: (1) to present this matter to the 1920 General Conference, and (2) to forward copies of the committee's report to all the other Conferences.[19]

The 1919 Conference formally approved the petition to General Conference, calling on General Conference "to guarantee to the church a ministry thoroughly grounded in the fundamental truths of our holy faith by guarding the Courses of Study against books that promote divergent rationalistic opinions," and asking General Conference to return the responsibility of selecting the Course of Study books to the Board of Bishops.[20] Fifteen members of Conference registered their opposition to the report.

The Committee was busy prior to the 1920 General Conference, communicating to Conferences and elected delegates and speaking before various groups. They reported favorable votes in the following Conferences: Philadelphia, Wilmington, Baltimore, North Indiana, Southern California, Northern New York, Wyoming, Montana, Northern Montana, Columbia River, Puget Sound, Idaho, Pittsburg (Lay Association), Central New York, Wyoming (State), California, Southern German, Northern Swedish, Genesee, Western Norwegian-Danish, Alabama, Savannah, New Jersey Lay Electoral Conference of 1920.[21]

The 1920 General Conference granted the bishops the right to approve and amend the Course of Study books and prescribed that they be in "full and hearty accord with those doctrines and that outline of faith established in the Constitution of the church; and that the Discipline, with some special emphasis upon the Articles of Religion, and the standard sermons of John Wesley . . . shall be included in the conference course."[22] Sloan was roundly praised by the New Jersey Conference at its next session for this victory.

The New Jersey Protest, as it came to be called, continued under Sloan's leadership, though without as much previous involvement of the Annual Conference. The 1924 General Conference extended the victory by allowing any member of the church to examine the list of books being nominated for inclusion in the Course of Study.

February 3, 1925, the Methodist League for Faith and Life was formed in St. Paul's Church, Wilmington, Delaware, by sixteen ministers and laymen including Clarence True Wilson and Harold Paul Sloan. Its purpose was to counter Modernism in the Methodist Church. Dr. Sloan was named president. Sloan also edited the League's monthly Journal, "The Call to Colors," soon changed to "The Essentialist."

Dr. Sloan, in reply to a correspondent in West Virginia, asking why Sloan had not yet read his manuscript, said he was pastor of an 1100 member church, editor of the monthly organ of the League for Faith and Life, carried out its large correspondence and taught in Temple University the chair of Systematic-

Theology. "And you ask me why I haven't yet had time to read your manuscript?"²³

Although Dr. Sloan attended the 1928 General Conference armed with petitions containing ten thousand signatures from five hundred twenty-two churches in forty-one states, charging "flagrant disloyalty to Methodist doctrinal standards in seminaries, pulpits and Sunday School literature," General Conference made clear they had had enough of the controversy.

However, there was one more battle to fight. That was at the 1932 General Conference in Atlantic City. This was over the proposal to remove the Articles of Religion from the Constitution of the Church. The effort failed, though the vote was exceedingly close, 392 to 402. Dr. Sloan and his forces won. To Sloan, this marked the end of the battle.²⁴

Harold Paul Sloan and the New Jersey Protest, succeeded in writing into the law of the church the requirement that books selected for the Course of Study for ministerial candidates must conform to the standards of doctrine established by the Constitution of the Church. They succeeded also in assuring that the Articles of Religion remain a part of the Constitution. That Dr. Sloan was respected for his work and ability, is born out by the fact of his election by the 1936 General Conference, to the prestigious editorship of the New York *Christian Advocate* and by the 1940 General Conference to membership on the Course of Study Committee.

Harold Sloan singles out as being especially helpful; George H. Neal, Harrison Decker and Alfred Wagg, among the clergy of the Conference, and Charles K. Haddon, William E. Massey and Charles M. Kinsley among the laymen. His own Bishop Berry was supportive as were Bishops Leonard, Cook and Quayle.²⁵

While Prohibition and modernism were drawing so much attention, other continuing concerns merit our consideration. Among them is the racial problem. Racial attitudes and tensions heightened in the period following the first World War. Many southern blacks were moving to New Jersey, seeking a better life. They often found work, but in menial and low-paying jobs with limited opportunity for social, political, and economic advancement. Blacks were trying to help themselves and their people through black newspapers, one of which was published in Atlantic City, and organizations like the NAACP.

The New Jersey Conference did speak out on racial matters. Robert Williams notes:

> There can be no question that some individuals in the Conference were sensitive to the real condition of blacks. Some knew that 'the church must discourage racial animosities, arouse moral concern for the slums and maintain a high spiritual tone in attractive houses of worship, and programs of community service.' The Conference recognized that 'the continued migration of the Negro to the Northern cities and industrial centers presents both a problem and an opportunity to perform a ministry of reconciliation.'²⁶ Conference also urged Congress to pass an anti-lynching law.

The 1920's, presented another spectacle in the struggle for racial harmony—the Ku Klux Klan. The KKK's greatest days in New Jersey were in the 1920's. It sought to defend the Constitution, pure womanhood, maintain white supremacy, separation of church and state, and uphold law and order. It was opposed to all aliens, blacks, Jews, immigrants and the Roman Catholic Church. For a while, it was the popular group to join and many Methodists, clergy and laity alike, were members of the hooded society. David M. Chalmers, in his history of the Klan, says it found "a particular haven in the shore towns of Monmouth County and stout champions among the Methodists and other godly folk of New Jersey." "Its truest friends," he writes, "came from the Pillar of Fire Church and the Methodists."[27]

The Klan was welcomed in many Methodist Churches in their full regalia. The *Christian Century* reported eight thousand or more attended a Mother's Day Rally of the Klan in the Ocean Grove Auditorium in 1925. About the same time, some twenty-five thousand participated in a parade down Broadway in Long Branch.

Bishop Berry and others began to take action against Methodist-supporters of the Klan. The bishop made it clear he wanted his preachers to have nothing to do with the Klan. At the 1924 Conference in Central Church, Atlantic City, the *New York Times* reported:

> The Conference was surprised when four candidates who appeared for examination for the Ministry were requested to remove their coats and vests. After complying Bishop Berry asked if they were members of any secret organization or wore emblems of this nature. An emphatic 'no' was the reply. Although no mention of any specific order was made, it was accepted by delegates that the Bishop referred to the Ku Klux Klan.[28]

In the late 1920's, the Klan influence waned. By 1930, it virtually disappeared. Methodists were upset at some of the transformations sweeping American Society. They were too deeply conscious of the Christian ethic to be bamboozled for long by the white-hooded, fear-producing, cross-burning, hate-fostering, prejudice-ridden Klan. Yet the struggle for racial justice on the part of the blacks still had a long way to go.

Women's Rights continued to spark attention. The 1915 Conference supported women's suffrage in New Jersey, but the male voters did not support the Constitutional change. Adoption of the Nineteenth Amendment to the Federal Constitution did give women the right to vote in 1920.

The Methodist Episcopal General Conference of 1924 finally gave limited clergy rights to women. Women were allowed to be ordained, but it would be several more years before this Conference ordained a woman. Along with the continued work of the Woman's Home and Foreign Missionary Societies, District Ladies Aid Societies came into being in the 1920's. The New Brunswick District Superintendent reported that a District Federation of Ladies Aid Societies was organized April 23, 1924, with sixty-seven societies on the District. Mrs. John H. Parker was president.[29]

Having won the right for equal representation in the Church's General Conference, the laymen still were trying to become a part of the Annual Conference. The 1920 Conference voted on a Constitutional change to allow for the election of one lay delegate for every pastoral charge. The New Jersey Conference voted yes—20, no—133.[30] The Lay Conference voted 49 for equal representation to only 8 opposed.[31] In 1921, there was a vote on another proposal passed down from General Conference, the previous one having failed. Conference voted against this 126-0.[32] There seems to have been confusion over the provisions of the proposed Amendment. The Lay Conference complained that inadvertantly omitted was any provision as to the number to be elected. They voted against the proposal 138 to 0. They then voted on an "amended amendment" proposed by the General Conference Laymen's Association. It passed 110 to 14.[33] However, this also failed of passage.

The year 1925, saw yet another vote on the same proposal sent down by General Conference. Again Conference voted 20 yes, 149 no.[34] The laymen did not vote until 1928. They supported the Amendment, 94 to 23.[35] The laymen really had their problems with the Conference. The 1928 General Conference again sent to the Annual Conferences a proposed Amendment allowing for lay representation. Again there was confusion. Delegates voted on the Amendment and corrected Amendment. Conference approved both with only one vote against.[36] Someone must have been campaigning to change some minds. The laity voted down unanimously the Amendment, but approved the amended version by a 97 to 10 vote.[37] Still they had to wait another four years for admission into the Conference.

City Churches remained strong during the 1920's, but felt strongly the influx of foreigners and the problems of the city. Growth was in the suburbs. Of the ten largest churches in the Conference in 1930, only Broadway, Camden, sixth with 1060 members and First Church, Camden, ninth with 993 members were typical city churches. The suburban churches of Pitman, Collingswood and Haddonfield topped the list. The north Jersey Shore churches of Asbury Park: First and Ocean Grove were next, both showing large membership gains.

Alexander Corson, Camden District Superintendent, in his 1923 report, lamented, "Practically in one generation, Camden has been transformed from a residential to an industrial city. . . . This process is accelerated by the coming of the Delaware River Bridge, the fulfillment of a dream of half a century." A bit later he talks of surburbia. "Surrounding Camden, and reaching down for twenty-five miles into the central section of the State there is a rapidly developing surburban and semi-surburban situation. Large numbers of the more substantial and more successful people of Camden are moving to the suburbs, and larger numbers are coming over from Philadelphia."[38] He then writes of starting churches in Brooklawn, Fairview Village, Colonial Manor, Verga and Barrington.

When the Conference's first Social Service Commission organized in 1917, they set up sub-committees on City, Surburban, Seashore and Rural Work. A study of the Conference showed fifty-two per cent of the churches were in rural areas with thirty-two per cent of the total membership of the Conference. Seventy-four per cent were small membership churches with less than two hundred fifty members.[39]

Youth work continued strong with organized Epworth League work in nearly every church on each District. District rallies were attended by large numbers of young people as will be shown in a later chapter. What turned out to be an extremely popular new venture was started in 1921. It was Pennington Institute. This was the first and is the longest lasting summer youth Institute in the Conference. Attendance at the first Institute was two hundred two.[40]

Other opportunities for youth followed. The first Older Boys' Conference was held over the Conference weekend in 1923. Some girls must have come along too, for the report of the Committee on the State of the Church said:

> The Older Boys' Conference, instituted at this session of our Conference, has been a revelation of potential leadership, giving promise that Kingdom tasks will find strong and sanctified hands for years to come. Not in years has this Conference been so stirred as it was on Sunday, when we saw the boys and girls of our homes and churches volunteering their lives for the Christian ministry at home and abroad.[41]

Countless leaders of the church, ministers, missionaries, lay workers and deaconesses, have made such decisions at Older Boys' Conferences, Junior Laymen's Conference and Youth Weekends in the years that followed that first one in 1923. It was at one such Sunday Service in 1949, that this preacher-author made his decision to accept God's call into the Christian ministry.

The Older Boys' Conference became the Junior Laymen's Conference in 1925. Their first president was Lynn H. Corson, later one of the distinguished ministerial members of the Conference.[42]

Work with youth on the college campus was inaugurated in 1923, with the establishment of the Wesley Foundation at Princeton University. It was organized June 16, 1923, at the Princeton Church. James R. Joy, Editor of the *Christian Advocate,* and a member of the Newark Conference, was the first president.[43]

Concern for proper observance of the Sabbath continued. Annual and General Conference alike addressed the issue. The New Jersey Conference was constantly fighting attempts by the State Legislature to water down the Sunday laws.

Chapter Eighteen will tell the story of our Methodist Homes. Suffice it here to say that fire destroyed the first home on February 6, 1916. By the next year, a new one in Ocean Grove was built and was home to fifty residents. Maximum capacity of fifty-two was reached in 1919, and there was a waiting list of fifty. At least by 1923, the custom of receiving an offering for the Home on Mother's Day was inaugurated. By the end of the 1920's, plans were being proposed for a million dollar campaign for the Home.

Revival and social concerns, are they at all compatable? They should be. John Wesley held them both in a remarkable tension. He who was primarily a soul-winner, has known few equals in the compassion he evidenced for a social witness. Convince him of an evil and Wesley fought it — poverty, ignorance, unemployment, poor working conditions, bad housing, gin shops, gambling, slavery, smuggling, inhuman prison conditions, lack of adequate medical facilities, barbarous treatment of those mentally insane or supposed to be, etc. Seldom have others combined Wesley's compassion for the individual and society. Usually if evangelism is in the ascendency, social needs are not. The reverse is also, alas, true. When will we learn to take care of both?

In the last chapter, the story was told of the great revival that swept across the Conference prior to World War I. I called this the "flickering flames of revivalism." Revival did not cease in the New Jersey Conference. The flames just gradually cooled down, to be lit again into a roaring blaze here and there, but nothing like the continuous primary emphasis of the long years before. Conference Minutes tell these stories: A simultaneous Evangelism Campaign on the Camden District in October of 1917 saw half of the churches cooperating. In 1920, some two hundred were attending prayer meeting in Pitman. On the New Brunswick District, the Centenary Evangelism Campaign was in full swing, but only six hundred conversions were reported, less than hoped for. Bridgeton District had a Boys and Girls Revival in November of 1921 with much success. The Superintendent said, "Dividing Creek seems to be getting everybody into the Church." He reported one hundred eight conversions in that small town.

Pitman, Williamstown and Collingswood all had revivals in 1928. One hundred ninety were won to Christ in Pitman, one hundred seventy-eight in Williamstown, including forty-eight Italians. No figures are given on the Collingswood revival, but Dr. Edward S. Sheldon has written an account of that revival. It began that summer when he took twenty-five young people to the Delanco Camp Meeting. It continued in the church at the prayer meeting led by the pastor, Alfonso Dare, on the Wednesday after Labor Day. It caught fire that Sunday night at a farewell service for five young men planning to leave the next morning for Asbury College to begin studying for the ministry. Dr. Sheldon writes: "The fires thus kindled . . . continued from week to week until scores of our young people were converted and scores more, who did not know the joy of a real Christian experience, came into full possession of the blessing."[44] The Epworth League called Rev. Ray N. Johnson, the Texas Boy Preacher, for a week of "Win My Chum" meetings. Nightly, six hundred to nine hundred persons attended the services. The revival went on for weeks with many positive and lasting results.

Dr. Sheldon's closing remarks give a proper perspective to what it really takes to have revival spirit:

> All of this did not 'just happen.' It was the result of spiritual activity among our members which created an atmosphere in which it was easy for the Spirit to operate upon the hearts of people. Souls that were overflowing with the love of God found an outlet for their desire to promote the spiritual life in cottage prayer meetings; men's prayer meetings; all nights of prayer; class meetings with their glowing, stimulating testimonies; all day meetings with inspirational messages and songs; times of agonizing, prevailing prayer; voluntary altar services.
>
> We have been unusually blessed with outstanding spiritual leaders as pastors; noted evangelists have come and made their contribution to the spiritual stream; devoted laymen,

endowed with wonderful qualifications and the spirit of sacrifice; but no men or organization, or organized effort was responsible for the phenomenal missionary passion that has characterized our church through these many years. It was the Holy Spirit operating through numerous human instrumentalities that kept the holy zeal burning upon our Altars.[45]

This was revival. What were some of the emerging social concerns issues that confronted the Conference in these years? How were they dealt with? The first Conference Committee on Social Service was formed in 1915. It made its first report in 1917, Leon K. Willman, Chairman. As already stated, it divided its work into City, Suburban, Seashore and Rural Work.

Through the late teens and into the 1920's, the Social Service Commission sought to sensitize the Conference in areas of social concerns and needs. Ratification and approval of its reports gave at least tacit approval to its aims. How much practical influence it had on the average local church member would be difficult to gauge. It did, however, show that New Jersey Methodists were becoming increasingly aware of society's needs beyond that of temperance and Sunday observance, though these matters were not neglected even in the reports of the Commission.

A review of the yearly Social Service reports for this period reveal an expressed concern in many areas. At first, the Commission repeatedly had to defend its cause and expressed regrets at the discrimination between social service and evangelism. Labor unrest and the rights of workers concerned the Commission. They spoke about child welfare, peace and the "eradication of war," racial and religious intolerance in the days of the KKK, urged support of the New Jersey Council of Churches and proposed the organization of a Rural Fields Committee for the Conference. They lamented that in one community Negro transient workers were being preyed upon by drug peddlers and other criminal agents. They raised the question of the viability of capital punishment. As late as 1929, they declared there still was no minimum age at which a marriage license could be secured in New Jersey and said one was recently given to a girl of eleven.

The Legislature was more often taken to task for what it did not do, or should not have done, but in 1923, the Legislature was commended for passing legislation making mothers and fathers equal guardians of minor children, for raising the age of protection of girls from sixteen to eighteen and securing a fifty-four hour work week for women in stores. The influence of women in the three years since suffrage was credited with making the passage of those bills possible.

One of the main concerns since the reduction of working hours and the close of the saloon was how could the church help to furnish opportunities for wholesome use of leisure time? It was at this time that many churches built social halls or found space in existing buildings for such purposes.

Another chief concern in the 1920's, was work among the foreign-born. There was a lot of comment in the District Superintendents reports of 1920 about foreigners and the need to minister to and help to Americanize them. It was seen as a vital home mission need. Numerous local churches in the city and rural areas responded. In the rural community of Lake, near Newfield, work was instigated among Italian families. A cement block building across the street from the church was purchased called the Lake M. E. Church Annex. The front was a library and class room, the rear a kitchen. In that building were held adult citizenship classes, a sewing and domestic science class, typing and language classes, music class and a Sunday School for twenty-five Italian children.[46] Mrs. Teressa Trimnell was the woman worker employed. Second Church, Millville in 1917, employed a trained nurse to work as a home missionary among the foreign born and a Polish minister to preach occasionally among his countrymen.

Kaighn Avenue Church in Camden in 1921, was ministering to a greater variety of people, said the Superintendent, than were present at Pentecost. Bethany Church, Camden was home to an Armenian Mission. Half of the salary of an Armenian pastor, Avedis S. Darakjian, was paid for from Centenary funds.[47] That same year in Trenton, an Italian worker was employed at Hamilton Avenue Church.

In 1925, Mrs. Mae Nelson was at work at Seabrook Farms outside of Bridgeton. In eleven months, she organized five Sunday Schools for five different nationalities, made 1,800 personal calls, taught 350 Sunday School lessons and distributed 5,800 Sunday School papers, 2,200 cards, 36 Bibles, 61 Gospels, 1,300 magazines, 392 books, 154 Scripture cards and gave 900 garments to persons in need.[48]

One report states that "In the New Jersey Conference an Italian pastor was appointed to an English-speaking congregation in a section nine-tenths Italian. He performed with satisfaction."[49] This was sometime around 1925. In 1929, a group of about fifty Russian Protestants were meeting in Trinity Church, Camden.

New Jersey Conference Methodists were reaching out to others. Our present day work with Spanish-speaking and Korean people is but an extension of work begun earlier among Italian, Armenian, Polish, Russian and other peoples.

The 1920's, was a time of unprecedented prosperity for many in America, prior to the awful Crash. The 1929 Social Service report contained these relevant words: "As preachers, we must from the standpoint of social improvement, as well as from motives of spiritual growth, help our people cultivate a sense of values that will aid them to find compensations and realities in life other than those that may be purchased with money."[50]

Through much of this period and beyond, Conference leadership in the area of social services was provided by Elbert M. Conover, and Richard A. Conover. For four years, Rev. Elbert Conover served the Board of Home Missions and Church Extension of the Methodist Episcopal Church as their Secretary of War Emergency and Reconciliation. Then for the next ten years he was Director of their Bureau of Church Architecture. Richard Conover, served five years as Centenary Evangelist and with the Department of

Evangelism of the Board of Home Missions before returning to the pastorate in 1926.

While main issues predominated, other happenings kept taking place. Some were of great importance, others had human interest. Here are some things which attracted Conference's attention in those years. Finances are always one concern. A $400,000 Endowment Campaign for Conference pensions started in 1915. Total pledges never got above $113,000 and by 1925 only $65,000 had been collected. A Missionary Centenary Fund Campaign across Methodism was started in 1920. Large amounts were pledged, but giving fell far short, curtailing many worthwhile programs that had been started. I found no record of Conference giving, but much of the language work started in the Conference in the 1920's received support from these funds. Money was raised to build a new Deaconness Home in Camden. The cornerstone was laid November 20, 1924 and the Home was dedicated April 30, 1925. The minimum salary for ministers in full connection was set in 1918 at $1,000.

When George Neal, Superintendent of the Bridgeton District, gave his final report after serving his six years, he lamented that none of the District Superintendents had a parsonage provided. They had to rent their own home. Apparently his words were taken seriously. The next year, 1919, the Bridgeton District purchased a home in Millville. Camden District followed suit in 1920. A Trenton home was purchased for the Trenton District in 1922 and by 1926 the New Brunswick District parsonage was purchased in Red Bank. Prior to 1919, the District Superintendent's salary was kind of hit or miss. He collected whatever the churches would give on the rounds of his quarterly conferences. Salary was unequal on the districts, the Camden Superintendent received the most. In 1919, it was put on an apportionment basis, salaries were equalized, and travel expenses, house rents and office expenses included. District ministers, and ministers' wives meetings began about this time also. The Bridgeton District ministers started meeting monthly in 1919. The wives of the ministers of the Bridgeton and New Brunswick Districts both started holding regular meetings in 1923.

New forms of church work, familiar to us today, were started in the 1920's. Family night programs, study classes in the Bible, missions and evangelism are all mentioned in the early 1920's. By the end of the decade churches were holding Daily Vacation Bible Schools and Weekday Religious Education classes. Visitation evangelism was replacing revival meetings in some churches. New things were happening.

Conference meeting in Asbury Park in 1916, held a joint clergy-laity meeting and celebrated the centennial of the death of Bishop Asbury in the city named for him. Churches were requested to take an offering to help in the erection of an Asbury equestrian statue in our nation's capitol.

The flu epidemic hit hard in 1918 and again in 1919. Many churches on the Bridgeton District, and probably elsewhere, were closed from four to six weeks. The much beloved Francis Harvey Green became Headmaster of Pennington in 1921 and brought much distinction to the School.

A new dance was created called the "Wesleyan" dance. Conference in 1921 took strong objection and passed this resolution:

> Whereas, The American National Association of Dancing Masters have created a new dance which they have called the 'Wesleyan,' in order to conciliate, if they can, the Methodists on the dance question,
> Resolved, That the New Jersey Annual Conference view this action of the dancing masters with disdain and hereby register their protest at this most disgraceful attempt to associate the revered name of our founder with the modern dance and its sensuous and shameful heredity. To make an unholy dance after the name of the holy Wesley is nothing short of an outrage on decency and a direct insult to Methodists everywhere;
> Resolved, That we maintain an incessant and unrelenting hostility to the dance institution in every form, regarding it as inimical to purity, destructive to piety, a menace to our church work and a source of unmitigated moral evil wherever permitted and practiced.[51]

That's at least more interesting than some of the dry resolutions we pass today.

World Service became the new format under which churches paid their missionary and benevolent apportionments beginning in 1923.

Port Norris devised a unique way to raise money for their new church in 1926. Their minister, Linwood Miller, tabulated the cost of the automobiles owned by members of the church. He figured they could afford as much for a temple of worship as they could for motor cars. Being the oyster capital of America, oyster beds were loaned to the church, oyster seeds were given, planted and harvested free of charge. After two years this was expected to bring in six thousand dollars a year. This, together with the members' contributions, was expected to soon cancel the indebtedness.[52]

The present Conference Historical Society was formed in 1927, with Alfonso Dare as President. There had been an earlier Society in existence from 1882 to 1913, but the new officers reported they were unable to find anything the previous Society may have collected. In its fifty-nine year history the present Society has had only six presidents: Dr. Alfonzo Dare, Dr. Frank B. Stanger, Rev. David C. Evans, Rev. Robert B. Steelman, Dr. J. Hillman Coffee and Mrs. Lawrence (Penny) Moore.

The 1920's ended with a new bishop at our helm. Bishop Berry, senior active bishop of the church, retired in 1928. His place was taken by Bishop Ernest G. Richardson who served as resident bishop of the Philadelphia Area from 1928 to 1944. The new bishop was born in the West Indies in 1874. A graduate of Dickinson College and Yale University, he was a minister in the New York East Conference. Consecrated bishop in 1920, he served eight years in the Atlanta Area before being assigned to Philadelphia. He was noted as a splendid presiding officer and the best parliamentarian in the church. For several years he served as president of the Anti-Saloon League. Bishop Richardson played an important role in the negotiations leading to Methodist reunification in 1939. This able, scholarly, gentlemanly bishop led our Conference through the depression years and until his retirement in 1944. After retirement he continued to live in Philadelphia until his death in 1947.[53]

Chapter 11

THE METHODIST CHURCH IS BORN

1930-1939

Little background about the 1930's needs to be written. The unbounded prosperity that developed in America in the 1920's was abruptly broken on the day of the Crash, Thursday, October 29, 1929. That day marked the beginning of the longest and most severe depression ever to strike America. Millions of investors lost their savings; banks closed; bankruptcies mounted; debts spiraled; purchases declined; production decreased; workers were laid off; salaries were slashed; farmers could not meet their obligations, and mortgages were foreclosed. In 1930, there were over three million unemployed, by 1933, between twelve and fifteen million were without work. Not until another war did the economy again fully recover.

New Jersey was as affected as anywhere else. Even people with jobs often were not paid. County governments printed script, paper money of little worth that was usually accepted by local merchants. It kept people going in the worst of times. New Jersey's shore resorts suffered extremely. Some never recovered their former glory. The state seemed to stand still. Population gained only 128,841 new people in the entire decade.

Methodism suffered with the rest of the country. The three main branches of Methodism lost 15.4 per cent of their members between 1926 and 1936. Budgets were slashed; salaries were drastically reduced; church indebtedness became oppressive. Churches were forced to close. Benevolent and missionary enterprises were curtailed. An anticipated religious revival did not happen. The American people, shorn of their material wealth, did not turn to God. The Methodist Episcopal bishops, after witnessing the toll brought on by a year's depression, said at the end of 1930, "There is something fundamentally wrong with a social system that, in the midst of plenteous abundance, dooms untold numbers of our people to unbearable poverty and distress through no apparent fault of their own."[1]

The year 1939 dawned full of hope. America was coming out of the terrible depression, slowly, yes, but coming out of it. It was to be the year of Methodist unification. But hope was dashed as dark clouds of war began to hang over Europe and Asia, a war that was to engulf the world. One of the interesting social developments of the 30's for American Methodism was its involvement in pacifism. Robert M. Miller, at the end of his discussion of "Methodism and American Society, 1900-1939," says, "It can . . . be flatly stated that Methodism was more deeply penetrated by pacifism than any other denomination."[2]

The big thing for Methodism in the 30's was unification. After a long separation (1828 for the Methodist Protestants, 1844 for the Church South), on May 10, 1939, in Kansas City, Missouri, the Declaration of Union of the three branches of Methodism was approved. At 8:59 p.m., on that spring night in mid-America, Bishop John M. Moore of the Methodist Episcopal Church, South declared, "The Methodist Church now is! Long live the Methodist Church!" It was, however, a long road to unification and to the brief story of that road and its effect upon New Jersey Methodism we now turn.

It needs to be remembered that the Methodist Protestant Church had objections to bishops, gave their ministers the right to appeal their appointments to the Annual Conference, and insisted on equality of ministerial and lay representation in General and Annual Conferences. The problem of what to do about slavery sectionally divided the Church in 1844. What to do with the black members of the Methodist Episcopal Church in any reunification was the most volatile issue. It was also an issue north and south concerning the authority of the bishops and the General Conference. Personalities enter the picture, of course. Bishop Collins Denny of the Southern Church refused to be a bishop in The Methodist Church. Neither can feelings and attitudes be ignored. Each church had much to give up. All had much to gain.

There were four stages on the road to reunification: Fraternal Relations, Federation, an abortive attempt to unite Episcopal Methodism, and finally Union.

Animosities caused by the Civil War and some rather intransigent attitudes of the Northern Church that it was the only true Methodist Church began to be overcome when Bishops Janes and Simpson visited the Southern Church's Council of Bishops in 1869. Fraternal visits to the Southern Church's 1870 and 1874 General Conferences were reciprocated when the Southern Church sent fraternal delegates to the 1876 Methodist Episcopal General Conference.

The Cape May Conference followed later that same year with its historic declaration that both churches were legitimate branches of Episcopal Methodism. All further obstacles to fraternity were removed. The first Ecumenical Methodist Conference in London in 1881 and the 1884 Methodist Centennial Conference in Baltimore further helped all three Methodist groups to know each other, and fraternal delegates often visited each other's General Conferences.

The period of Federation began in 1894, when the Southern Church created a Commission on the Federation of Methodism. The Northern Church reciprocated with a similar commission two years later. Federation did not mean union, and some were disappointed. Federation meant a working together between the two churches, something that had not happened before, helping to prevent overlapping and a common ministry wherever possible. Federation produced some positive results on the mission field. In this country, Federation produced the 1905 Hymnal, a common hymnal for the Churches North and South, a common catechism, and a common order or worship.

The Methodist Protestants entered the picture in 1908 when a group of Baltimore laymen from both the Methodist Episcopal and the Methodist Protestant Churches discussed union with President Thomas H. Lewis of Western

Maryland College (Methodist Protestant) and Dr. John F. Goucher, founder of the Woman's College in Baltimore (Methodist Episcopal). It was agreed that some move for union would be initiated at the 1908 Methodist Episcopal General Conference. President Lewis played a leading role in these negotiations and in the inclusion of the Southern Church. In addressing the Northern General Conference, Dr. Lewis said: "Our Church is in the South as well as in the North. . . . And when we think of going back home the question will recur insistently and painfully, 'Which home?' . . . Do not force us to separate from each other in order that we may rejoin the family. We want to unite with a united home."[3] Several meetings of the Joint Commission on federation of the two episcopal churches and the Commission of Nine of the Methodist Protestant Church resulted. When it was seen that the real problems were evolving between the Churches North and South, the Methodist Protestants rather quietly withdrew for nearly twenty years until the two larger churches could work out an agreement.

Phase three of unification began in earnest in 1916 when both episcopal churches came out in favor of union and each appointed a Commission on Unification.

The main stumbling block to unification was what to do with the Negro members of the Methodist Episcopal Church, many of whom were in Annual Conferences in the south. Building on a decision tentatively reached by the Joint Commission on Federation at Chattanooga, Tennessee, in 1911, it was agreed that black members should be placed in their own Jurisdictional Conference. Extensive union negotiations went on between 1916 and 1920 when a Constitution was proposed, but not accepted. The Joint Commission went to work again and perfected a second Constitution. There would be one General Conference and two Jurisdictional Conferences, one for the Northern Church and one for the Southern Church. Bishops would be elected at the Jurisdictional Conferences. A Judicial Council would settle Constitutional questions. General Conferences of the two churches in 1924 overwhelmingly voted approval. The northern Annual Conferences likewise approved. The vote at the 1925 session of the New Jersey Conference was 129 for to only 6 against.[4] It passed the southern Conferences by a majority vote, but not by the necessary three fourths and thus was defeated.

There was a necessary pause in negotiations. Then once again the Methodist Protestants quietly suggested to Bishop Herbert Welch of the Northern Church the possibility of all three Churches considering union. Informal discussions were held. The Methodist Protestant and the Methodist Episcopal General Conferences of 1932 approved union negotiation. The Southern Church agreed in 1934, and three subsequent meetings of the Joint Commission on Union were held. In the final plan, formalized at Evanston in 1935, the new church would be "The Methodist Church." It would have one General Conference, five regional Jurisdictions and a sixth to include the Negro Conferences. There would be equal representation of ministers and laity in the General, Jurisdictional and Annual Conferences. A Judicial Council would act as the Supreme Court of Methodism. Episcopacy was to be retained, and the Methodist Protestant Church was to elect two of their ministers as bishops. This plan passed all three General Conferences and the Annual Conferences by large majorities. The New Jersey Conference vote was 205 to 0 by the clergy, and the laymen approved 158 to 1.[5] May 10, 1939, The Methodist Church was born.[6]

To bring unification to pass, the Methodist Protestants agreed to episcopacy, and they, who had no bishops, elected James H. Straughn and John C. Broomfield bishops of the new Church. The two branches of episcopal Methodism had to agree to equal lay representation in the Annual, Jurisdictional and General Conferences. The two groups had come a long way. Methodist Protestants surrendered much of their identity in merging with much larger bodies, but became participants in expanded ministries of all kinds. The Southern Church succeeded in having the Negro Methodists placed in a segregated Jurisdiction. That was a compromise the Northern Church accepted but most blacks did not like. However, the blacks gained full representation in the General Conference and on all Boards and Agencies of the Church. Blacks gave up much, but gained in leadership positions, rights they had never had before. However, it was the presence of the segregated Central Jurisdiction that caused the most pain for the twenty-eight years of The Methodist Church. The Judicial Council, too, was a compromise of sorts, providing a balance between the authority of the bishops and that of the General Conference.

Not all Methodists took to the new Church. In the south, a small denomination, the Southern Methodist Church, grew out of the opposition of some. In New Jersey and elsewhere, a small minority of dissident Methodist Protestants formed the Bible Protestant Church. Yet, nearly everyone accepted the change. At unification the three churches reported the following membership: Methodist Episcopal, 4,684,444; Methodist Episcopal, South, 2,847,351; Methodist Protestant, 197,996.[7]

Unification in New Jersey took place at the 1939 Conference in Ocean City. The final session of the Eastern Conference of the former Methodist Protestant Church met September 27 and 28 in Christ Church, Atlantic City. The New Jersey Conference convened at three o'clock the afternoon of September 28. That evening the Uniting Conference was held. The New Jersey Conference of the former Methodist Episcopal Church merged with those churches of the former Eastern Conference of the Methodist Protestant Church that were within the bounds of the New Jersey Conference. There were twenty former Methodist Protestant Churches with 1,684 members and twenty-one ministers who became a part of the new Conference. Nineteen other churches withdrew to form the Bible Protestant Church. The story of the Methodist Protestants in New Jersey will be told in Chapter 12.

The uniting Conference in New Jersey was a joyous one of celebration. Bishop Richardson, representing the Methodist Episcopal Church, presided. Bishop Straughn represented the Methodist Protestants and Dr. Harry Denman represented the former Methodist Episcopal Church, South. The new

METHODIST UNIFICATION PROCLAIMED
Left to right: Bishop James H. Straughn of the Methodist Protestant Church, Bishop Edwin Holt Hughes of the Methodist Episcopal Church, and Bishop John M. Moore of the Methodist Episcopal Church, South, clasp hands on the stage at the Uniting Conference, 1939.

ministers, lay delegates and churches were made to feel welcome. Former Methodist Protestant ministers like George Ammerman, Bland Detwiler, A. D. Elwell, William C. Howard, Donald T. Phillips, Sr., James S. McGowan, and others became distinguished ministers of the Conference. That they were welcomed is indicated by the fact that Rev. George D. Jones and Mrs. Alice Detwiler, both former Methodist Protestants, were elected to the 1940 Jurisdictional Conference.

"The Methodist Church now is! Long live the Methodist Church!"

We now go back to 1933. The 1932 General Conference wrote into the law of the Church the matter of equal lay representation in the Annual Conference. A review of the struggle for lay representation needs to be made.

As early as the 1820's the "Reformers," so called, were agitating for lay representation. Denied all they strove for, the "Reformers" left and formed the Methodist Protestant Church which, from the start, allowed equal lay representation in the Annual and General Conferences. It was not so in the Methodist Episcopal Church. At first, the appeal was for lay membership in the General Conference. The 1860 Conference accepted the idea of lay representation provided the church desired it. It was rejected two to one. A vote by the male members of the New Jersey Conference showed 961 for and 974 against. Conference disapproved 32 to 76. The 1868 General Conference approved a proposal for two lay delegates from every Conference. This time it was approved two to one. The male members of New Jersey's churches also approved it two to one. It also received a majority vote in the Annual Conference, but not by the required majority. Never-the-less, two laymen from every Conference took their seats in the 1872 General Conference. To elect the lay delegates, a Lay Electoral Conference was held the session before General Conference with each pastoral charge entitled to one lay representative, a male; women were not accepted as delegates to the Lay Electoral Conference in New Jersey until 1896. Samuel A. Dobbins and James Bishop were the first lay delegates to General Conference from the New Jersey Conference in 1872.

The next struggle was for equal clergy and lay representation at General Conference. In 1890, 1894, and 1897, this Conference voted resounding no's. In 1898, at the urging of the Layman's Convention, they did register a positive vote. The 1900 General Conference was made up of an equal number of lay and clergy delegates, but no women. Women were first seated as lay delegates at the 1904 General Conference. The New Jersey Conference did not elect a woman delegate to General Conference until 1936.

The right of equal representation in General Conference won; the Church's laity sought to become part of the Annual Conference. It was on the laymen's agenda for a long time. They got little help from the New Jersey Conference clergy who kept voting no. While seeking this recognition in 1898, a Conference Layman's Association was formed and another in 1912. The second association met regularly to deal with lay concerns at the time of Annual Conference. During General Conference years, the Lay Electoral Conference also met to elect delegates, vote on Constitutional questions, and deal with other matters which would concern the General Conference.

Proposals for lay representation in Annual Conference repeatedly came before General Conference. From 1920 on, each successive Conference approved the proposal, but each time it failed to receive the required vote to become the law of the Church. Usually the New Jersey Conference lay and clergy voted against each other. Finally, in 1932, lay representation was allowed and took place at the 1933 session of the New Jersey Conference.

Lay representation was not, however, a complete victory. That had to wait for Methodist union and 1939. In 1933, Conference began Wednesday, March 8. Laymen did not arrive until Friday. They met in separate sessions, elected their officers and at ten o'clock entered the Conference Church at Asbury Park for the commencement of the two day United Session. Mr. Harry S. Jackson of Asbury Park was president of the Laymen's Conference.[8] A mass Laymen's Rally, held Saturday evening in the Asbury Park Convention Hall, was attended by about two thousand people. Dr. Daniel A. Poling gave an address on "What Price Citizenship."[9] Laymen were finally part of the New Jersey Conference. By 1939, they would be fully a part.

Women had an even harder struggle than men for recognition in the Conference. The list of lay delegates attending the 1933 Conference does show that nineteen were women, eleven of these from New Brunswick District churches. It was 1936 before a woman was elected as a General Conference delegate from New Jersey. It was not until 1939 that the Conference ordained a woman. Both of these was Miss Helen Phillips.

Helen Phillips, now Helen Phillips Neary of Manasquan, is a Trenton native and was a member of St. Paul's Church in our state's capital. Answering God's call to be a Deaconess, she attended the Lucy Webb Hayes National Training School in Washington, D.C. and was consecrated a Methodist Deaconess by Bishop Richardson in 1933. Though she served elsewhere, most of the twenty years she spent as an active deaconess were in Trenton. She was connected with the Widow and Single Women's Homes, Donnelly Hospital and the Florence Crittenton Home for unwed mothers. At various times, she served the St. Paul, Trinity and Central Churches as an assistant pastor.

In 1936, Helen Phillips was elected as the first woman General Conference delegate from the New Jersey Conference. At the age of twenty-six, she may also be the youngest delegate ever elected by the Conference. Three years later, Bishop Richardson ordained Helen as a local deacon. She was the first woman ordained in the New Jersey Conference. In 1943, she received elder's orders. Again, Bishop Richardson ordained her.[10] Miss Phillips was also a member of the 1940 and 1952 Jurisdictional Conferences.

The Methodist Protestants in New Jersey were way ahead of the Episcopal Methodists in their ordination of women. Sunday, October 25, 1908, the Rev. Emma E. Nutter was ordained elder by the New Jersey Conference of the Methodist Protestant Church and appointed to the Peoples' Methodist Protestant Church in Atlantic City. Later, she became the Rev. Mrs. Emma E. Nutter Cairns.[11]

While these significant and long overdue events were transpiring, it was the depression which had the greatest effect upon the churches, communities and people of the New Jersey Conference Area. The difficulties of the times were hard on everyone. Rev. J. B. Kulp of the Bridgeton District described them like this in 1931:

> The year has been one of more than ordinary severity. The unemployment situation has been intense and prolonged. In certain sections of the district many of our people have been only partially employed, and then at a reduced wage. Some members of our Official Boards have been without employment for a large part of the year; business men have met with losses and with baffling conditions, and the closing of banks has added to the difficulty of the situation. Yet, it must be said in all honor to our people, only two churches have reduced their pastor's salaries, and three have been bold and generous enough, in the face of adverse conditions, to advance them.[12]

Problems increased the next year. Many of the funds of the Conference were in the closed Asbury Park and Ocean Grove Bank. Camden District Superintendent, C. I. Fitzgeorge, said, "Unemployment has curtailed the income of the churches and added greatly to the anxieties of the official membership." Especially hard hit were the Camden and Atlantic City areas. "Practically all our churches," he added, "have been active in the social welfare movements of their respective communities. Hundreds of baskets of provisions were distributed during the holy season, and the unfortunate in the membership have been cared for throughout the winter." He signals out for praise the work of Wiley Church, Camden.

> The faithful women of this church have continued the furnishing of daily breakfasts to the undernourished children of the community each school day. Each evening throughout the winter a dinner has been served to sixty or more persons. A three-story brick dwelling was secured and is being used for the housing of men out of employment. Taking note of this activity, the Emergency Relief Administration is now paying the rent for an adjoining corner store and apartment, enabling these whole-hearted folks to care for one hundred men nightly. The store is being used as a salesroom for donated second-hand furniture and clothing.[13]

F. A. DeMaris said, "The Conference year, as far as the New Brunswick District is concerned, may be marked by B. C. and A. D. — before the crash and after the disaster." Thirteen banks and several mortgage companies closed their doors after Christmas.

The situation was no better in 1933. During the previous year, Wiley Mission in Camden served 40,000 meals and housed 27,000 people. Broadway Church in Camden, in cooperation with Campbell Soup Company, fed an average of 1,500 persons a day, seven days a week. In some communities on the New Brunswick District, nine-tenths of the wage earners were out of work. Men once liberal in contributing to their church were now forced to receive aid themselves.

Times were bad, but the Kingdom work went on. There was even much church improvement during these lean years, made possible by the donated labor of men and women out of work and suppliers often willing to sell goods at cost.

Things were somewhat improved by 1934. Yet, churches across Methodism were being threatened with foreclosure for inability to pay their debts. Some five thousand local churches in Methodism were believed affected. Conference authorized a special "Save the Sanctuary" offering to be received on the second Sunday in January. From here on, there was less talk of the hardships of the depression as the nation slowly worked its way to better days and as the church continued to help all it could.

Social Concerns was much in evidence during the 1930's. World peace, movie censorship, Sunday sports and gambling concerned the members of Conference. In 1935, Conference sent a petition to the 1936 General Conference asking for the establishment of a Board or Commission on Social Action for the Methodist Episcopal Church. It also protested the United States' participation in the 1936 Olympics in Hitler's Germany.

Repeal of prohibition shocked and stunned New Jersey's teetotaling Methodists. T. J. J. Wright, in the Conference's first composite District Superintendents' report presented to the United Session in 1934, lamented:

> These have been dark days for the moral forces within and without the Church, and Christian people are facing up to a defiant and destructive element within the social and political life of the nation. Ideals that have called forth great sacrifice and suffering have been swept away as if by a devastating army, and a century and a half of Christian work for social uplift has seemingly come to naught. We seem to be living in a 'Land of Lost Causes.' Once more the abomination of desolation, the vile, corrupting, demoralizing saloon, with all of its vice-breeding, crime-producing, is to be found not only on the corner of the city streets, but dotting our highways and countryside. With conscienceless effrontery and greed it seeks to sabotage the physical, moral, and mental health of the land, and the leaders of the nation seem to delight to have it so. We still believe, and believe with added emphasis, that the only way to control the iniquitous liquor traffic is by making it an outlaw throughout the land.[14]

Racial relations was surprisingly the concern of three resolutions passed in 1936. The first dealt with employing Negroes on the staff of the Church's General Boards. It reminded the Church agencies that "we are an interracial church," and a proportionate number of Negroes should be employed.[15] The second was a resolution of the Social Service Commission deploring discrimination in New Jersey. Churches were urged to learn what was going on and to work with the Negro for constructive action. The third resolution was a memorial to General Conference reflecting upon the proposed plan of union by which the Negro Conferences would be placed in a segregated Jurisdiction. This memorial asked for any Negro Conference that wished, within the bounds of the Northeastern Jurisdiction, to be permitted to transfer from the Central to the Northeastern Jurisdiction.[16]

Civil rights was a continued concern in other years. In 1938, a resolution deplored the denial of freedom of speech, mentioning specific cases in Newark, Jersey City and Hoboken.[17] The following year a resolution was passed and sent to the Middlesex County prosecutor and judge urging no favoritism in the prosecution of nine white men who had broken into the home of a black farm laborer in Cranbury and beat him-and his wife for "no offense other than consenting to be employed as a farm laborer."[18]

Superintendent Leon Chamberlain in 1937 said:

> We boast, not of great achievements, but bow in deep humility because we have done so little in the face of the many things facing the Church, which it alone can do. We have an open Sunday, gambling in many forms, drinking in every form and the voice of the Church is raised against them, but these forms of sin are on the increase. We need to catch the militant spirit of Methodism and make war on these destroyers of our people. Dare we do it? We dare! Then to your knees, Church of John Wesley, and make use of this Aldersgate Year to secure the power of the Holy Spirit.[19]

The New Jersey Conference was host to the 1932 General Conference which met in Atlantic City's Convention Hall. All was not so well as it should have been. The invitation to come to Atlantic City was accepted with the understanding that equal accomodations were to be provided for all, regardless of race. This did not happen. The blacks were treated badly. Black bishops had to use the freight elevator of the hotel that was Conference headquarters. Black delegates were assigned to black hotels. They were not accepted in the beach front hotels. General Conference reacted against this discriminatory treatment of racial minorities by approving an even stronger resolution concerning conditions which must be accepted by cities wishing to host future conferences.[20]

Celebrations in the 1930's must have helped ease the strain of the difficult times. The fiftieth birthday of the founding of the Woman's Home Missionary Society and the nineteen hundredth birthday of Pentecost were celebrated the same day, June 8, 1930. It was also reported that at a January 16 Woman's Home Missionary Society Retreat held at First Church, Camden, five hundred women communed.[21]

In 1934, the Sesquicentennial of Methodism was celebrated in Baltimore. October 10 to 14 were the dates. Sessions were held in the Scottish Rites Temple. It was a joint celebration of the Methodist Episcopal, Methodist Episcopal, South, Methodist Protestant, Primitive Methodist and Free Methodist Churches. The black Methodist Churches were not included on the Joint Commission. Highlights were an opening evening Oratorio, "The Evangel of the New World," written by VanDenman Thompson. A four hundred voice chorus was directed by Earl Evans. The Saturday finale was two performances of a Sesquicentennial Pageant, "The Spreading Flame," written and directed by Harold A. Ehrensperger.[22] American Methodists felt they had much to celebrate. The New Jersey Conference appointed fourteen official delegates to attend the Baltimore celebration.

The Conference Sesquicentennial Committee had Dr. DeMaris prepare a short conference history which was published in the *Minutes,*[23] called for each church to recognize the celebration in some meaningful way, held an Anniversary Service Sunday evening of Conference with Chancellor Joseph M. M. Gray of American University as the speaker, and called on the Conference to move forward in a new evangelistic conquest.[24]

The Conference's own Centennial Year was celebrated in 1936. The actual celebration took place Sunday evening, September 27, on Ocean City's Music Pier. Representatives of the Newark and Philadelphia Conferences brought greetings. The Shekinah Glee Club of Millville, directed by Mr. Arthur Radcliffe, sang. Their music included "Diadem," "Sanctus," "Like As a Hart," a tenor solo, "The Holy City" sung by Mr. Walter Reeves and "The Hallelujah Chorus." Bishop Charles L. Mead of the Kansas City Area, elected to the episcopacy from the Newark Conference, was the preacher. A large, overflow congregation gathered in the Moorlyn Theater to hear Dr. Harold Paul Sloan and the Shekinah Glee Club.[25]

One hundred year statistics showed 79,569 members in 359 congregations. Sunday School membership was 78,523 with 7,574 in the Senior Epworth League, 1,012 in the Intermediate and 4,077 in the Junior. The estimated value of all Church owned land and buildings was $9,498,595 with an indebtedness of $1,015,762. World Service contributions for the year totaled $49,516.[26]

Conference also celebrated in 1938 the one hundredth anniversary of Pennington School and the two hundredth anniversary of Aldersgate.

Financial needs of Pennington School led to a special session of Conference at Pennington on June 23, 1932. It was decided to attempt to raise, by apportionments, $10,000 a year for the next three years to finance the school. The school's trustees were to raise any further balance needed for current expenses.[27] The amount raised evidently fell far short: $1,830 in 1933 and $885 in 1934.

Conference debated changing its time of the annual meeting. Since 1858, it had met in March and before then, in April. The debate was between a June or September meeting. Conference in 1933 voted 180 for September and 77 for June.[28] The 1934 Conference was the first to meet in the fall, assembling in St. Paul's Church, Atlantic City on September 27. In 1939 the recommendation appeared setting aside the November Communion Offering for the work of the Deaconess Home. It is a practice still continued. The year before, 1938, the Camden Methodist Union, predecessor of the Camden Missionary Society, was formed.

Qualifications for the ministry were constantly raised. In 1934, it was adopted that beginning in 1935, the minimum scholastic requirement for admission on trial would be graduation from an accredited college. Beginning with 1940, graduation from an accredited school of theology would also be required.[29] It was amended in 1938, so that a candidate successfully completing the first year's course in an accredited seminary would be eligible for admission on trial and upon graduation from seminary would be eligible for full membership and elder's orders.[30]

Mrs. Jennie S. Parker, for twenty-six years president of the Ocean Grove Home for the Aged passed away at her West Long Branch home in March of 1937. This indefatigable worker labored much in behalf of the home. In 1921, she was severely injured when her automobile was struck by a train in South Carolina. Both her legs were cut off. Though severely handicapped, she continued her work and continued to drive her car until her life "closed to earth to continue in heaven."[31]

The Reverend Thomas S. Brock was a leading minister in the Conference in the 1930's, along with Furman A. DeMaris and Harold Paul Sloan. Thomas Brock was elected to five consecutive General Conferences in 1928, 1932, 1936, 1939 and 1940. Only one other man in this century was elected that often, William R. Guffick. Only two other men, Harold Paul Sloan and Charles Sayre served more. After early pastorates around the Conference, Thomas Brock filled successively the pastorates of Burlington: Broad Street, Vineland, Camden: First, and Atlantic City: St. Paul's. After completing six years as Superintendent of the Trenton District, he transferred to the Florida Conference in 1940. He served numerous positions in the Conference including Trustee of Pennington School and Conference Trustee. From 1928 to 1940, he was a member of the General Board of Pensions and Relief of the Methodist Episcopal Church.[32]

As the 1930's ended, the Great Depression was nearly over. The world, however, was rapidly falling into the more horrible depression of World War II. When that was over, the world, America, New Jersey and the new Methodist Church would not be the same.

Chapter 12

THE METHODIST PROTESTANTS

"Radicals," they were called. "Reformers," they styled themselves. Methodist Protestants is the name by which they were known for over one hundred years. After these "Reformers" were "put down" at the 1828 General Conference of the Methodist Episcopal Church, they formed what they first called "The Associated Methodist Churches." Two years later in 1830, they adopted the name Methodist Protestant Church. This church existed until the three way merger of Methodism in 1939 which brought into being The Methodist Church. At the time of merger, the Methodist Protestants within the bounds of the New Jersey Conference numbered twenty-eight hundred with thirty-six charges and twenty-one effective ministerial members. They were part of the Eastern Conference of the Methodist Protestant Church and merged with the New Jersey Conference of the Methodist Episcopal Church to become the New Jersey Conference of The Methodist Church. The merger date was September 29, 1939.¹

Who were these Methodist Protestants? What caused the division of Methodism in 1828? What helped to reunite them more than a century later? Were they reformers or radicals or both? What basic principles did they espouse? What role did they play within the bounds of our present Conference? Who were some of their leading lights? As we seek to answer such questions, one thing should be clear: southern New Jersey Methodism is richer because of the contributions of the people called Methodist Protestants.

Ethel Wolfe Born, Vice President of the Women's Division of the Board of Global Ministries of the United Methodist Church, and a former Methodist Protestant, says: "We pioneered the way for equal lay and clergy representation in Methodism, including lay participation for women. The ordination of women took place first in the Methodist Protestant Church, and we led the way to church union of the fragmented denomination in 1939!"²

One of their slogans was, "In a country without a king, we should have a church without a bishop!" Yet, carrying out the Plan of Union, their delegates to the Uniting Conference elected two bishops before union was consummated in 1939. For espousing the democratic ideal of having laymen sit in the councils of the church, they were called radicals. They saw written into the constitution of the new church at union the requirement for equal lay and clergy representation in Annual and General Conferences. William C. Pool was expelled by the Baltimore Conference in 1827 for attending a meeting of a "Union Society." Today, the former Methodist Protestants and the former episcopal Methodists belong to The United Methodist Church.

As early as the O'Kelly schism in 1792, some preachers were opposed to what they felt were the autocratic powers of the bishops, particularly in the making of appointments. Accordingly, as early as the 1812 General Conference

Nicholas Snethen introduced a petition calling for presiding elders to be elected. The same petition was introduced in 1816 and again in 1820.

By 1820, the petition had gathered sufficient support to be adopted by a vote of 65 to 25. However, Bishop McKendree and Bishop-elect Soule raised such objections that the rule was suspended until the next General Conference of 1824. In the meantime, it was to be put to a vote in every Annual Conference.

There came to be tied in with this desire for elected presiding elders, thus reducing the bishops appointive power, an expressed desire by some for more lay rights in the church, particularly in District, Annual and General Conferences where the laity had no representation at all. This was promoted as a democratic ideal at a time when democratic idealism was sweeping the country.

Following the 1820 General Conference, William Smith Stockton, a layman from New Jersey, began to publish the *Wesleyan Repository and Religious Intelligencer*. The first issue of this semi-monthly paper was issued from Trenton, New Jersey, April 12, 1821. It was seen as an instrument to promote "Reformers" ideas.

The 1824 General Conference was regarded as significant. The "Reformers" looked for victory. It was denied them by a vote of 63 to 61. The majority of Annual Conferences had not ratified an elected presiding eldership and the action of the preceding General Conference was declared null and void. There was to be no elected presiding eldership and no lay representation.

Though in a minority position, the "Reformers" were still strong. Union societies were organized in many places to debate changes the "Reformers" proposed. The *Wesleyan Repository* was changed to *The Mutual Rights of the Ministers and Members of the Methodist Episcopal Church,* called *Mutual Rights* for short.

Meanwhile, the Baltimore Conference in April of 1827, expelled two of its members, Dennis B. Dorsey and William C. Pool. Dorsey was expelled for circulating *Mutual Rights*. Pool was put out for attending a meeting of a "Union Society" as well as circulating *Mutual Rights*. Their case was appealed to the 1828 General Conference. Before General Conference met there were other expulsions. Eleven local preachers and twenty-two laymen were expelled in trials of doubtful legality for espousing the cause presented in *Mutual Rights*.

At the 1828 General Conference in Pittsburg, the appeals of Dorsey and Pool, though ably argued by Asa Shinn, were denied. So was every petition brought forth by the "Reformers." Following General Conference, there were other expulsions across the church. No longer were the reforming ideas seen to be matters of discussion in the Methodist Episcopal Church.[3]

A general convention of "Reformers" was called for Baltimore. One hundred delegates from eleven states and the District of Columbia met on November 12, 1828. They organized as Associated Methodist Churches. The following month, the first Annual Conference met in historic Whitaker's Chapel, near Enfield, North Carolina. Whitaker's Chapel is now a United Methodist Historical Shrine.

WILLIAM S. STOCKTON
Prominent lay leader from N.J. in the early days of the Methodist Protestants

By 1830, enough societies were established to form fourteen Annual Conferences. Delegates elected by these Conferences met in St. John's Church, Baltimore, November 2 to 23, 1830, and the Methodist Protestant Church was formed. Between 25,000 and 30,000 persons separated from the Methodist Episcopal Church. This new Church had no bishops nor presiding elders. Clergy and laity shared power in Annual and General Conferences. Annual Conferences, either through a stationing committee or by the Conference Presidents, stationed the ministers, but with the minister having the right of appeal to the Conference if his appointment did not please him. Bishop John B. Warman, a former Methodist Protestant, says that having formed this interesting experiment in church government "the heavens did not fall, neither did the millenium arrive."[4]

Bishop Warman further comments, "the Methodist Protestant Church was infused with the spirit of independency. Each congregation was an independent as it could afford to be. The Annual Conference was a loose alliance of local Churches. Yet it held together like a family."[5]

Was this radicalism or reform? Who is to judge now? Certainly, in matters affecting the laity and women, the Methodist Protestants were far ahead of the parent church. It was not until 1872 that laymen were admitted to the Methodist Episcopal General Conference. In fact, it was not until union in 1939 that the laity received equal representation across the entire Church. The

Methodist Episcopal Church did not allow women to receive any kind of ordination until 1924. The Methodist Protestants ordained a woman in 1880.

That separation did come was the fault of both. Lines hardened. Tensions increased. Compromise became almost impossible. The glory is that although it took a long time, reunion did come. In that union, both sides won. The laity have rights exceeding any envisioned by the "Reformers." Even the Methodist Protestants elected bishops prior to union. Now the United Methodist Church has women bishops. Presiding elders are still around, although called by a different name, and still appointed not elected. Ministers have no inherent right of appeal from their appointments by the bishop, but appointments are usually made in a much more democratic manner. Today we call it consultation.

A further judgment by Bishop Warman is significant. "This difficult, rough-textured strand of our heritage (the Strawbridge, O'Kelley, Methodist Protestant, perhaps Good News line of creative discontent that refuses to accept institutional conformity) is not a strand to be rejected and cast out. It is sometimes disruptive, always difficult to live with, but in the challenge and response tremendous energy is created that, harnessed, can move the Church forward."[6]

The purpose of this chapter is not to tell the history of the Methodist Protestant Church but that segment of it within the bounds of the Southern New Jersey Conference. Among the leaders of the new Church were three from New Jersey, the layman-editor, William S. Stockton, his preacher-son Thomas H. Stockton and the eloquent, Quaker-bred Asa Shinn.

William Stockton was born in Burlington in 1785 and died there in 1860, although he was not always a resident of New Jersey. Stockton was the editor who founded the *Wesleyan Repository* in Trenton in 1821 and later published the works of John Wesley. His first wife, Elizabeth S. Hewlings whom he married in 1807, was likewise from Burlington.

Their son, Thomas Hewlings Stockton, was born in Mount Holly, New Jersey, June 4, 1808. In 1826, he became a member of Old St. George's Church in Philadelphia, leaving it in 1829 to become a Methodist Protestant. A year later he entered the ministry. He was an outstanding clergyman. Four times he served as Chaplain of the United States House of Representatives. He compiled the first Methodist Protestant Hymnal in 1837, authored thirteen books, received an honorary D. D. from Gettysburg College and gave the Dedicatory Prayer at Gettysburg National Cemetery.[7]

Asa Shinn was also born in New Jersey in 1781. His exact birthplace is unknown. He was raised a Quaker, converted as a Methodist when eighteen, and became an itinerant preacher at age twenty. Self-taught, he never saw nor knew of a clock until he was past twenty years of age.[8] A very eloquent speaker, he presided over many Conferences and served as president of the Methodist Protestant General Conferences of 1838 and 1842.

As early as 1808, there was in New Jersey a dissenting group of Methodists akin to the later Methodist Protestants. Zenas Conger, who had been an itinerant Methodist preacher, and others became embroiled in a dispute with Samuel Budd who served the Freehold Circuit. The dispute had to do with the proposal to build Old First Church in West Long Branch. Prior to this, the Methodists worshipped in a "Free Church." To take title to property would involve the insertion of the "trust clause" in the deed placing the church to be built under the authority of the Methodist Episcopal Church and its bishops who would appoint the preachers. Conger evidently had it in for Asbury. The dispute spread to other points in the Circuit, and Matthias Barkalow, a local preacher from Wall Township, sided with Conger. The dissident group called themselves the Independent Methodist Church. They were also known as "Congerites."

The Independent Methodists worked in an area between Long Branch, Toms River and Freehold. They had societies or churches in West Long Branch, where they purchased the Free Church; Glendola, where they bought a former Seventh Day Baptist Church; Shark River, Good Luck, Toms River, Freehold and Colts Neck. The greatest number of members taken in at one time was a total of twenty-four at Long Branch between January 1 and April 23, 1809. Records of Matthias Barkalow, 1806 to 1827, show he performed fifty-seven weddings, conducted one hundred four funerals, baptized fifty adults and seven children and took eighty members into the society.[9]

The Independent Methodists seemed to reach their zenith about 1820 and then declined. One writer says, "For some years they continued to worship under the leadership of Matthias Barkalow; but as one has remarked, 'little attention was paid to the children,' and, receiving no young members, the society long since disbanded."[10] Barkalow died in 1827, and that may have been one reason for the demise of the societies. There are several references to the Independent Methodists merging with the Methodist Protestants in 1850. I take it to be so, but cannot document it.[11]

New Jersey is also known to have had Union Societies in the period following 1824. The only one, however, that can be documented at this time is one in English Creek. It was probably organized about 1824. A Union Meeting House was erected on the site of an old family burial ground. The date of its erection is not known, but it was deeded to a Board of Trustees of the Union Methodist Protestant Church in 1856. The Union Society was attended by members of Asbury Methodist Episcopal Church. Out of it was formed Palestine Methodist Protestant Church in Scullville and perhaps Friendship Church in Steelmanville.[12]

William S. Stockton attended the 1828 convention of "Reformers" which organized the Associated Methodist Church. He was also present with his son Thomas H. Stockton at the 1830 Conference which organized the Methodist Protestant Church. In fact, William S. Stockton was elected assistant Secretary of the Conference.

There was, however, a minister from New Jersey, who was present at each of the significant Conferences that established the Methodist Protestant Church and that led to the establishment of the Methodist Protestant's New Jersey Conference. His name was Samuel Budd. Yes, the same man who opposed Zenas Conger and Matthias Barkalow in 1808, who was the preacher on the Freehold

Circuit when Old First Church was built in 1809 and entertained Bishop Asbury on his visit to Old First, Sunday, April 30, 1809. Samuel Budd became a "Reformer" and one of the founding fathers of the Methodist Protestant Church in America and in New Jersey.

Samuel Budd, born on a farm one mile north of Pemberton, was the son of Samuel and Hannah Gill Budd. An ancestor, Rev. Thomas Budd, a Vicar in the Church of England, became a Quaker and died in Ilchester gaol, a martyr of his convictions. Rev. Thomas Budd's four sons were among the founders of Burlington. One returned to the old faith of his father and became a founder of the first Anglican Church in West Jersey. When Samuel Budd's father died in 1796, two of his uncles were appointed his guardians. Since both were active Methodists, the young Samuel became attached to Methodism. In 1802, he was received on trial in the Philadelphia Conference. He located in 1814, resumed preaching in 1818, and located again in 1822. He evidently preached in the Pemberton area and became active in the "Reformers" cause and a preacher in the Methodist Protestant Church. Rev. Budd was said to be a powerful speaker, who could easily be heard for long distances, and a good singer. He and his wife, Elizabeth Ross, were the parents of three sons and two daughters.[13] The name of his wife is perpetuated in Old First Church, West Long Branch, as the name of one of the church's women's circles, the Elizabeth Budd Circle.

The first General Conference of "Reformers" was held November 12 to 22, 1828, in St. John's Church, Liberty Street, Baltimore. St. John's was the first property of the Methodist Protestant Church when title to a former Episcopal Church was obtained. At this Conference, Nicholas Snethen was elected President and William S. Stockton as Secretary. The tentative name, Associated Methodist Church, was adopted; committees were appointed to draft a constitution and form a discipline; Articles of Association were agreed upon, and plans made to meet two years later. The Conference was attended by ninety-three out of one hundred eight chosen delegates from Maryland, Delaware, District of Columbia, Virginia, North Carolina, Ohio, Pennsylvania, Tennessee, Alabama, New York and New Jersey. Present from New Jersey were Rev. Thomas Davis, Rev. Daniel Ireland and Rev. Samuel Budd.[14]

Eleven months later, in accordance with the Articles of Association, the First Annual Conference of the Associated Methodist Churches, East and North of the Chesapeake gathered at ten o'clock in the morning of October 8, 1829, in Philadelphia. An invitation to attend this Conference had gone out to the "Reformers" under the date of July 23, 1829, and was signed by Thomas Dunn, Joseph Cramer and William S. Stockton. Delegates were not listed by states, but recognizable New Jersey names are Rev. Samuel Budd from Pemberton and Rev. Sylvester Hutchinson from Hightstown. Lay Delegates John English and David B. Salter may also have been from New Jersey. William S. Stockton, then living in Philadelphia, was also present and was elected Secretary along with John Q. Wilson of Delaware. Nicholas Snethen attended the Conference and served as President. John Smith from Delaware was elected Conference

President for the first year. This was the first organization of "Reformers" that included New Jersey, along with parts of Pennsylvania, Delaware and the western section of New York state. There were five appointments made for Pennsylvania, two in Delaware, two in New York and six in New Jersey. These were the New Jersey appointments:

Monmouth	George A. Raybold
New Hanover	James Brindle
Barnsboro	William Stephens
Trenton	John S. Christine
Sharptown	Thomas Cheeseman
Missionary in New Jersey	James Chester

Samuel Budd's appointment was to New Castle, Delaware.[15]

The Methodist Protestant Church was formally constituted at the November 2 to 23, 1830, Conference in St. John's Church, Liberty Street, Baltimore. Eighty-two delegates attended from thirteen states and Canada. Forty-nine ministers and thirty-three laymen comprised the list of delegates. George A. Raybold, Samuel Budd and Sylvester Hutchinson represented New Jersey. This Conference constituted the Methodist Protestant Church and approved a Constitution which stated: We are "fully persuaded, that the representative form of church government is the most scriptural, best suited to our condition, and most congenial with our views and feelings as fellow-citizens with the saints, and of the household of God."[16] The Constitution stated that each Conference may determine the mode of stationing the ministers. This was done either by the President of the Conference or a Stationing Committee. But each minister had the right to appeal his appointment during the Conference session. Ministers were to abstain from tobacco and spirituous liquors. It was also recommended that no sermon exceed one hour. Conference boundaries were set. New Jersey, as so often, was divided between the Pennsylvania and the New York Conferences. The New York Conference took in that part of New Jersey north of a line "commencing at the mouth of the Raritan River; thence up said river to New Brunswick, thence by a straight line to the Delaware River opposite Easton."[17] South of that line was in the Pennsylvania Conference.

The first session of the Pennsylvania Conference met in Philadelphia in 1831. Circuits were large; church buildings were few. In the statistical report, Centreville (Centerton) Circuit had one meeting house and eighteen places for worship. Barnsboro Circuit listed eleven places for worship, but no churches. The Monmouth Circuit had two meeting houses and sixteen places for worship.[18]

The appointments were these:

Centreville	Thomas Cheeseman, Supt.
	Thomas Payne, Ass't.
Monmouth and Burlington	Andrew R. Carpenter, Supt.
	Lyttleton S. Cropper, Ass't.
	Sylvester Hutchinson, Taber
	Chadwick, Michael Lecorte,

Glassboro

Conference Missionary

William T. Vanote, Assistants without pay.
Thomas W. Pearson, Supt.
K. S. Cropper, Ass't. without pay
Samuel Budd[19]

An 1892 newspaper gives a brief statement about the New Jersey Conference. Apparently the New Jersey Methodist Protestants withdrew from the Pennsylvania Conference to form their own in 1837 at Centreville, now known as Centerton. Rev. Samuel Budd is mentioned as one of the prominent leaders of the new Conference. The article further states: "After five years of incessant toil and self-denial for the principles of the Methodist Protestant Church, it was thought expedient to unite with the New York Conference."[20] This union was in 1840 when all of New Jersey became part of the New York Conference, but only for a short time. There are no known records available of this early New Jersey Conference.

In 1843, the New Jersey Methodist Protestants petitioned the New York Conference to allow them to form their own conference. The question was debated from one session to another before permission was granted, reluctantly it would seem.

The manuscript minutes of the organizing session of the New Jersey Conference in 1843 have been preserved, eight pages in the back of a book titled *New York Conference, M. P. Church, 1831-1846.* Conference met in Ebenezer Church, Glassboro, April 19 to 24, 1843. It was a small Conference. It included only that part of New Jersey "south of a line running from the mouth of the Raritan River to New Brunswick including New Brunswick and thence to the Delaware River opposite Easton."[21] When Conference convened there were only six official delegates present. Three were clergy: Herman Bruce, William Perkins and Edward S. Schock. Three were lay delegates: Joseph D. Frambes of Egg Harbour Circuit, John C. Sheets of Glassboro and Bridgeport Circuit, and Uriah Brooks of Centerville Circuit. Bruce was elected President. Frambes and Sheets were elected Secretaries.[22] There were other ministers present, but there were problems about their credentials. Samuel Budd, for instance, attended and was accepted as one of the Conference ministers if the New York Conference would transfer him.

There were a total of 839 members in six circuits as follows: New Brunswick, 106; Red Bank, 70; Medford, 90; Egg Harbour, 160; Centerville (Centerton), 90; Glassboro & Bridgeport Circuit, 323.[23]

Although a small Conference, it grew. The New Jersey Conference continued until it merged with the New York and Pennsylvania Conferences to form the Eastern Conference in 1912. In time, the New Jersey Conference embraced most of New Jersey. The 1904 Discipline defines the Conference boundary as including "the State of New Jersey, except that Newark and Elizabeth, until they elect otherwise, shall be in the Maryland District."[24] Apparently they never elected otherwise. They were large churches and evidently wanted to be in a more prestigious Conference. The 1928 Centennial Edition of *The Methodist Protestant* has a picture of the First Methodist Protestant Church of Newark and says, "It is one of the most prominent churches in the Maryland Conference."[25]

The first published Minutes of the N. J. Conference was in 1856. A copy is in the United Methodist Archives. Conference met March 5 to 8 in Newport where Zacchaeus Joslin had built a small church on Landing Road. It was a brotherly Conference. Brothers Albertson and Williams of the Methodist Episcopal Church, Rev. James VanSant, minister of the Newport Methodist Episcopal Church and Rev. Sleeper of the Newport Baptist Church were all given honorary seats in the Conference. There were ten circuits plus the Leesburg Mission. There were 682 full members and 102 on probation. There were 395 Sunday School scholars. The thirteen churches of the Conference were valued at $12,400.[26] Madison College was commended to the patronage of the Conference. A resolution was passed indicating the laity had a right to request a certain minister, but the Conference could grant the request or not as they considered the best interest of the church. Rev. William B. Vanleer was Conference President.

The Methodist Protestants had a division over slavery, too. That division came in 1858, and the New Jersey Conference united with the northern and western Conferences. In 1866, these conferences became the Methodist Church in an abortive attempt to unite with the Free and the Wesleyan Methodists. The Methodist Church was little more than a name for the northern and western Methodist Protestants. Reunion with the southern conference took place in 1877 and the Methodist Protestants were one again.

The earliest record in the Southern New Jersey Conference Archives of the New Jersey Methodist Protestant Conference is the 1892 Minutes. The session that year was held in South Amboy with the Rev. Charles D. Sinkinson, then pastor of Memorial Church, Camden, as Conference President. Appointments had increased to thirty with membership at 3,203.[27]

The churches were these: Glassboro, Fair Haven, Pennsgrove, Bridgeton: First (Laurel Hill), Bridgeton: Second, Camden, Millville (Broad Street), Moorestown, Manasquan, Friendship, Union Valley, Glendola, Lake Como, Clementon including Port Ariel and Watsontown, Barnsboro including Arbutus Hill, Egg Harbor (Scullville) including St. John's Pleasantville, Mt. Pleasant (Pleasantville), New Brooklyn including New Freedom and Cedar Brook, Allenwood, Robertsville, South Amboy, Leesburg, Atlantic City (Christ), Westville, Bridgeport, Osbornville, Centreville (Centerton), Hardingville, Cramer Hill and West Berlin. Bridgeton First was the largest church with 312 members, followed by Manasquan with 219.

The brief historical sketch of the Conference published in 1892 tells us that Rev. Samuel Budd and Ephraim Carlisle were the first delegates elected to General Conference. That must have been the 1846 Conference which met in Baltimore. It also comments on the attitude of the Conference in relation to the questions of the time. "Slavery was denounced in no uncertain terms.

The rum traffic was handled without gloves. Sabbath-desecration was spoken of as ruining both soul and body."[28]

The 1892 Conference temperance report said, "We insist on total abstinence for the individual and the entire suppression of the traffic, requiring all our pastors to use unfermented wine in the Sacrament."[29] That same year, a New Jersey Conference Union of the Christian Endeavor youth organization was formed. There were 20 Christian Endeavor Societies in the Conference with 444 active members, 144 associate members and 34 home members.[30]

An historic event in Methodist Protestant history occured in New Jersey in 1893. First Methodist Protestant Church of Bridgeton, now known as Laurel Hill, hosted the Annual Meeting of the Woman's Foreign Missionary Society. At the conclusion of that meeting, the Woman's Home Missionary Society of the Methodist Protestant Church was organized. Mrs. S. A. Lipscomb was elected the first president. The early work of this Society was in Michigan's Upper Peninsula and the Oklahoma Territory.[31]

The women of the New Jersey Conference had an active Branch of the Woman's Foreign Missionary Society. It was organized in Barnsboro on April 28, 1886 with Mrs. Louisa Stranger as president and Mrs. I. D. Corson, Corresponding Secretary.[32] Auxiliary societies were functioning in many local churches. Japan, where the first Methodist Protestant foreign missionaries were sent, then later China, were the special areas of concern and the prayers of the faithful women of the church.

Christ Church, Atlantic City, the Rev. Charles D. Sinkinson, D.D., pastor, hosted the 1900 General Conference of the Methodist Protestant Church. It was the first and only time New Jersey was host to the General Conference.[33]

The 1911 Conference voted 43 to 9 to merge with the New York and Pennsylvania Conferences to form a larger and stronger Eastern Conference.[34] The Eastern Conference was actually formed in 1911 in Pittston, Pennsylvania, in a merger of the New York and Pennsylvania Conferences. The New Jersey Conference became part of the Eastern Conference in October of 1912 in a meeting at Grace Church, Brooklyn, New York. The Eastern Conference extended from Bridgeton, Millville and Atlantic City, New Jersey to 200 miles north of New York City, west to Daleville, Pittston and Shickshinny, Pennsylvania, and east to include Long Island and southern Connecticut. The new Conference included 38 appointments within the bounds of our present Conference numbering 4,084 members. This was an increase of 881 members since 1892. Christ Church Atlantic City and Trinity Ventnor were the largest with 494 and 284 members respectively, followed by Bridgeton: First (Laurel Hill) and Manasquan with 235 members each. These churches were divided into four Districts: Atlantic City, George Jones, Chairman; Camden, W. D. Stultz, Chairman; Glassboro, A. C. Struthers, Chairman and Manasquan District, N. E. Webb, Chairman.

At the Conference meeting in Shickshinny, Pennsylvania in 1919 there was a merger with the small Congregational Methodist Church. They had eight churches in New Jersey. Billingsport, which elected to join the Methodist Episcopal Church, Runnymeade, South Millville which became Newcombtown; Christ Church, Pleasantville which joined with St. John's; Olive Branch, Pleasantville which was considered too much in debt to handle and three little churches at Milmay, Risley and Dorothy. Newcombtown is the only one which remained a viable church.[35] It was called Millville: Third in the Conference Minutes.

A perusal through the Conference Minutes shows something of the work of the New Jersey Methodist Protestants. They supported the Methodist Ecumenical Councils, now known as the World Methodist Council, and at least two of their members, Thomas B. Appleget and Charles D. Sinkinson were chosen delegates. They had problems about churches in New Jersey that were part of the New York and Maryland Conferences, rather than New Jersey. They supported the Anti-Saloon League and worked for prohibition. Sabbath observance was another concern. In 1917, Carl G. Soderbom, one of their members, was a missionary in Kalgan, China. In 1927 Conference was encouraging ministers and wives to attend the Montrose Ministerial Institute in Montrose, Pennsylvania, under the direction of the Moody Bible Institute of Chicago. It became a popular place for clergy couples and laity to attend.

Plans were well under way in 1927 for the 1928 celebration of the Methodist Protestant Centennial. General Conference called for a $100,000 Centennial Gratitude Gift as a gift to the denomination. Eastern Conference's goal was $7,500. They raised over $10,000 in a show of loyalty to their church. The Eastern Conference celebrated the Centennial at their Conference October 10 to 15 in Trinity Church, Ventnor, and produced for their Conference Minutes a "Centennial Memorial Edition." Rev. Roby F. Day of Inwood, Long Island was Conference President that year. The Women's Foreign and Home Missionary Societies merged that year into what was called the Women's Work of the Methodist Protestant Church. An Eastern Conference Missionary Association for Africa, Asia and South America was organized with Rev. Richard C. Phillips as the first president. Conference was apparently very much alive and well.

Rev. George D. Jones of Ventnor was Conference President in 1932 when it was announced that the Second Eastern Conference Summer School for Young People was held June 27 to July 2 in Fair Haven with 101 registered.[36] Conference that year was supporting four missionaries. J. Wesley Day was their own missionary in China. He was recommended to the China Conference for ordination as elder.[37] The three other missionaries were all serving under independent mission boards. William R. Hurley was in the Amazon Section of South America, Ernest Howard was in the French Congo and William F. Kiessling was in the Belgian Congo. Conference was incorporated that year in Mays Landing.

That brings us to the final session of the Eastern Conference which convened in Christ Church, Atlantic City, September 27, 28, 1939, immediately prior to entering the union of the New Jersey Conference of the new Methodist

Church and the other Conferences in which they were geographically located. The Conference Directory lists 60 ministers, 10 supply pastors and 58 lay delegates who attended this final Conference. Rev. C. S. Kidd of Brooklyn, New York, was Conference President and Chester A. Teates of White Plains, New York was Secretary. Newly elected Bishop James H. Straughn, president of the Methodist Protestant General Conference prior to union, was also present.

Conference organizations included Trustees, T. H. Slater, president; Council of Christian Education, Henry P. Bowen, president; Church Extension Society, Carl E. Oswald, president; Preacher's Aid Society, T. H. Slater, president; Eastern Branch of Women's Work, Mrs. Bland Detwiler, president; Missionary Association, L. F. Moon, president; Ministers' Wives Association, Mrs. C. A. Teates, president. Other committees were on Official Record, Auditing, Stationing, Itinerary and Orders, Ad-Interim Adjustment, and Distribution of the Pension Fund.

Conference Minutes for that year contained a list of 104 deceased ministers, from John H. Smith who died in 1837 to Charles D. Sinkinson who entered his eternal home, February 19, 1939. Richard Brandt was ordained into the ministry.

Conference statistics for 1938-1939 showed 74 appointments, 368 new members added, 402 removed making the current membership 5,375. There were 513 professions, 333 baptisms, 7,920 Sunday School scholars plus 1,069 officers and teachers. Also there were 1,194 members of Christian Endeavor, 1,054 members in local church Missionary Societies and 1,682 members of the Ladies Aid. Total evaluation was slightly more than $1 million across the Conference.

This Conference session was heightened by the presence of a strong minority vehemently opposed to the new merger. The climax of this opposition came on the second afternoon of Conference when the "Great Walkout" occurred.

A request came from the floor asking if the Conference in session was the Eastern Conference of the Methodist Protestant Church or the Eastern Conference of The Methodist Church? President Kidd ruled it was the Eastern Conference of The Methodist Church. Bishop Straughn concurred.

"As soon as this ruling was made, Rev. N. C. Conant [pastor of Calvary Church, Camden], after stating that he was attending the sessions under the call of attending the Eastern Conference of the Methodist Protestant Church, said that he could not continue to sit in a Methodist Conference, and invited all who so desired to withdraw with him, and continue their session at the Scullville Methodist Protestant Church. A group of ten ordained ministers, seven supply ministers, with about sixty other delegates and friends withdrew to Scullville. As they left the Church they sang 'Blessed Assurance,' 'All Hail the Power of Jesus Name' and 'Tis the Old Time Religion.' "[38]

While the dissident members of Conference were making their presence felt, sitting in the back of the church was Rev. Carl McIntyre. He was helping

CHRIST M. P. CHURCH, ATLANTIC CITY

to call the shots. When Rev. Conant led his group in their "Great Walkout," those who remained stood and joined those leaving in song. Eastern Conference was the only Conference which did not ratify the plan of union merging the three branches of Methodism.[39] Members of the Eastern Conference were "radicals" or "reformers," depending on one's point of view, to the end.

The result of the "Great Walkout" was the formation of the Eastern Conference of the Bible Protestant Church. This Church considers itself to be the continuing Eastern Conference of the Methodist Protestant Church and a direct descendent of the original New York Conference organized in 1830.[40]

Nineteen churches withdrew from the Methodist Church: Bridgeton: Second, Camden: Calvary, Haddonfield: Second, Glassboro, Moorestown, Pennsgrove: Mariners Bethel, Westville, Westville Grove, Scullville: Palestine, Steelmanville: Friendship, Manasquan, Osbornville, Robertsville, Hardingville, Point Erial, Allenwood, Glendola, New Freedom and Cedar Brook.

Churches entering the New Jersey Conference from the South Jersey District were Atlantic City: Christ, Ventnor: Trinity, the largest with 177

THE METHODIST PROTESTANTS / 183

members; Barnesboro, Bridgeton: First (Laurel Hill), Friendship Finley, Gibbsboro, Millville: First (Broad Street), Millville: Second (Mt. Pleasant), Millville: Third (Newcombtown), New Brooklyn, Oceanville, Pleasantville: Mt. Pleasant, Pleasantville: St. John's, Somers Point, Vineland (Fourth Street) and Watsontown.

Central District Churches that became part of the New Jersey Conference were Avon, Lake Como which later merged with Spring Lake, South Amboy and Fair Haven.

The effective ministers who were welcomed into the New Jersey Conference were: George E. Ammerman, Charles E. Anderson, Henry P. Bowen, Richard Brandt, Harry J. Bright, H. W. Bland Detwiler, Samuel J. Dorlan, Acquilla D. Elwell, William C. Howard, John S. Huizer, George H. Jackson, George D. Jones, Elwood F. Keller, H. H. McConnell, George H. Naylor, George B. Ogden, Carl E. Oswald, Donald T. Phillips, Sr., Dennis G. Raynor, Steven F. Sliker and James S. McGowan.[41]

The 1940 session of the New Jersey Conference passed a resolution regarding the former Methodist Protestant Churches which were now organized as Bible Protestants. The invitation was extended to any members wishing to remain Methodists to do so. Conference Trustees were authorized to enter any necessary law suits on behalf of the Conference, but otherwise to transfer deeds of title to them.[42]

At the beginning of this chapter, four men from New Jersey who played an important role in the establishment of the Methodist Protestant Church were lifted up. Near the close of the story of the Methodist Protestant legacy in southern New Jersey, three others deserve to be highlighted.

Thomas B. Appleget is one. Born near Hightstown, New Jersey, he graduated from Williams College. Converted at Union Valley Methodist Protestant Church, he entered the New Jersey Conference in 1861. During the Civil War, he served in the Union Army. Enlisting as a private, he rose in rank to that of a Major. As delegate to several General Conferences, he took a leading role in favor of women's rights. He was a delegate to the Second Ecumenical Methodist Conference in Washington, D. C., in 1891, one of two Methodist Protestants to read a paper. He died in 1904.[43] He also served as President of the New Jersey Conference.

Lewis D. Stultz was another leader in New Jersey Methodist Protestant circles. Born near Cranbury in 1848, he moved with his parents to Glassboro when he was twelve. Like Thomas Appleget, Lewis Stultz was converted at Union Valley under his father's preaching. He entered the New Jersey Conference in 1866 and was ordained at Fair Haven in 1868. Famous as a Christian worker and gospel orator, he filled some of the best appointments in the Conference. A long-time Conference Secretary, he also served as Conference President and General Conference delegate. Lewis Stultz died in 1926 after sixty years in the ministry.[44]

Charles D. Sinkinson is the third Conference leader of note. Born in Philadelphia, September 14, 1864, he died in Atlantic City, February 19, 1939.

He was a minister in the Methodist Protestant Church for fifty-three years, forty-two of which he pastored Christ Church in Atlantic City. He helped make Christ Church one of the leading churches of Atlantic City, the New Jersey Conference and the Methodist Protestant Church. Dr. Sinkinson served as President of both the New Jersey and Eastern Conferences and was a delegate to seven successive General Conferences. A member of numerous church boards, he also was one of the Governors of Westminister Theological Seminary. The Methodist Protestant Church sent him as one of their delegates to the Third Ecumenical Methodist Conference in London in 1901 and appointed him fraternal delegate to the Methodist Episcopal General Conference.[45]

The Methodist Protestant tradition is now part of the much larger fellowship of United Methodism. Those churches which came from that background are now a vital part of an enlarged fellowship. Former Methodist Protestants have served in the Episcopacy, like Bishop John B. Warman and in the District Superintendency, like the Rev. Donald T. Phillips, Jr. of this Conference.

Likewise, in all the judicatory levels of United Methodism, the laity, men and women alike, play a role far greater even than that envisioned by the "reformers." United Methodism is more democratic today than it could ever have become in the days of Stockton, Shinn and Samuel Budd.

Whether it was worth the years of separation or not, God only knows. That it should have taken as long as it did for reconciliation to take place was without doubt because of human frailty and pride and not God's desire. That reunion happened at all is surely more because of God's grace and everlasting love than man's achievement.

In the Southern New Jersey Conference of United Methodism, the legacy of Methodist Protestantism is not to be forgotten. As Bishop Warman indicated, this reforming strand of our Methodist Protestant heritage unleases an energy that "if harnessed, can move the Church forward." Forward let us go.

Chapter 13

MINISTERING TO CHILDREN AND YOUTH

Sunday Schools

It would be hard for modern Methodists to conceive of a church not having a ministry to children and youth through the Sunday School. Yet, the Sunday School as we know it is only a little more than two hundred years old. Robert Raikes of Gloucester, England, is given credit for establishing the first Sunday School in Gloucester in 1780. Raikes, a benevolent and Christian newspaper man and Anglican layman, had become concerned about the neglected, illiterate street children of Gloucester. Expressing his thoughts to a young lady friend, a Miss Cook, she said, "Let us teach them to read and take them to church."[1] The result was a school for children on Sunday where they were taught to read, given the rudiments of a basic education and moral instruction. He personally paid four teachers a shilling a week for his Sunday Classes. In November of 1783, Raikes inserted a long personal letter in his *Gloucester Journal* describing the work of the Sunday School. *Gentleman's Magazine* reprinted it in June of 1784, and the Sunday School movement was under way.

John Wesley noted in his *Journal* for July 18, 1784, following a visit to a recently founded Sunday School in Bingley, Yorkshire, "I find these schools springing up wherever I go. Perhaps God may have a deeper end therein than men are aware of. Who knows but some of these schools may become nurseries for Christians?"[2]

Others were establishing schools and doing similar work at this and even earlier times. John Wesley while in Georgia in 1737 taught the catechism to children on Sunday afternoon before the evening service. Wesley always exhorted his preachers to meet with the children. In 1769, Miss Hannah Ball, one of Wesley's workers, gathered children together on Saturday and Sunday in a parish house at Wycombe near London, and taught them the Bible.

Growth in Sunday Schools was slow in America in the beginning. William Elliott, a Methodist, started a school at his plantation home in Accoma County, Virginia, in 1785. Sometime between 1783 and 1786, Francis Asbury started what many regard as the first Sunday School in America opened to the public. It was at Thomas Crenshaw's in Hanover County, Virginia.[3] The earliest books recommended for the instruction of Methodist children in America was John Wesley's *Instructions for Children* and John Dickins' *A Short Scriptural Catechism.*

Much credit in the developing of Sunday Schools and to improved literature and teaching methods must go to two Methodist ministers, both of whom spent time as ministers in the New Jersey Conference. The first was the Rev. Daniel P. Kidder who as a member of the New Jersey Conference was appointed Editor of Sunday School Publications and Tracts in 1844. Later he was Secretary of the Sunday School Union. From 1844 to 1856, he led the Sunday School work in the Methodist Episcopal Church. He is credited with

REV. DANIEL P. KIDDER
Missionary and early leader in Sunday School work for the M.E. Church

setting Methodist Sunday School work on a firm foundation. He also established Conference Sunday School Unions and became an originator of Sunday School Institutes and Conventions.[4]

It was John Heyl Vincent, though, who put the Sunday School in the "big time." John Vincent began his ministry and was ordained in the New Jersey Conference, pastoring churches in North Belleville, Clinton and Irvington between 1853 and 1857 when he transferred to the Rock River Conference. In 1866, he became General Agent for the Methodist Episcopal Sunday School Union and two years later assumed the post as Corresponding Secretary of the Sunday School Union and Tract Society, in which post he edited all the Church's Sunday School publications. It was Vincent, in 1870, who instituted the uniform series of lessons, called Berean Series, for the Church. It soon became the International Lesson Series. The same lesson plan was used throughout the Sunday School from the youngest children to the oldest adults.

Vincent is even better known as the founder of Chautauqua. In 1874, the Chautauqua Sunday School Teachers Assembly, jointly founded by Vincent and Lewis Miller of Akron, Ohio, met for two weeks at Chautauqua, New York. This was the real start of teacher training opportunities for the lay teachers in the Sunday School. Within a few years, the Chautauqua summer courses, home studies and correspondence schools had 100,000 enrolled.[5] Vincent was elected a bishop in 1888.

Josephine L. Baldwin of Newark, New Jersey, started the idea of graded lessons for children. It took twenty years of effort before the International Sunday School Association agreed in 1908 to issue graded as well as the uniform lessons. Two years later they were adopted in the Methodist Episcopal Church.[6]

Through the years, the Sunday School has ministered to children, youth and adults. It is not strictly a children's program; however, it is through the Sunday School that the Church ministers to its children. Blessed indeed is the church that has had some devoted lay people make the Sunday School the object of their attention and have seen it as the avenue of fulfilling their calling by God. How many readers of this book can call immediately to mind some one or more Sunday School teachers whose Christian influences upon their lives have been profound? Sunday Schools are training grounds for faith and life. It is in the Sunday School that our children are challenged to make Christian decisions. In our Sunday Schools, they learn about Christian missions. More people become church members through the Sunday School than any other way.

Sunday School is not the only avenue for ministry to the children, of course. There are our Daily Vacation Bible Schools which have been held in our churches and communities for sixty or more years, weekday sessions in some places, and children's choirs in the majority of our churches. There are church nurseries, nursery schools, day care centers and other means by which the church seeks to reach children for Christ. Yet the main way is through the Sunday School.

Sunday School and the work of Christian Education has always been important in the Southern New Jersey Conference. The Conference has always had a Committee or Board of Education. Statistics mirror the growth and decline of the Sunday School within southern New Jersey.

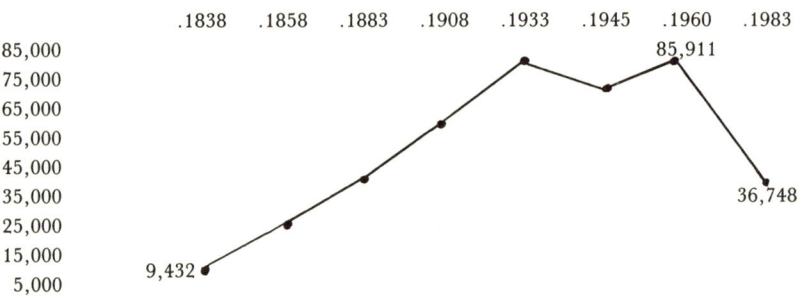

SUNDAY SCHOOL MEMBERSHIP IN THE NEW JERSEY AND SOUTHERN NEW JERSEY CONFERENCE[7]

This chart of Sunday School membership shows a continual increase from 1838 to 1933. Actually membership peaked in 1929 at 82,654, then declined through the 30's until after World War II. There was a rapid increase to the peak year of 85,911 in 1960. Then a precipitous decline occurred and membership is less than it was one hundred years ago. This is not the place to analyze what has happened to our Sunday Schools. The reasons are many. A plea is in order, however, and the urgency of many prayers is to again make our Sunday Schools effective agencies for reaching our girls and boys, youth and adults, but especially our children with the teachings of Christ and the message of the Bible.

Names given to Sunday School classes are interesting. In the Missionary Returns in the 1900 Conference Minutes are listed numerous Sunday School classes. Some use the names of the teachers, or maybe just Class No. 1, etc., and some classes chose names. Wall Sunday School lists these classes: Mites for Heathen, Willing Workers, Workers for Jesus, Little Sunbeams, Buds of Promise, Youthful Gleaners, Missionary Boys, Mission Workers, Willing Helpers, Bible Class. Newfield Sunday School had these names: Crystal Class, Sunshine, Willing Workers, Little Soldiers, Cheerful Givers, Star of Hope, Little Gleaners, Little Dewdrops, Granite Class, King's Daughters.

For many years, Sunday School met in the afternoon. Older members still remember going to Sunday morning church, home for dinner or maybe everyone gathering at Grandmothers, then Sunday School in mid-afternoon for an hour and a half or maybe two hours. Evening was for the Epworth League followed by Sunday Night Service. Sunday was truly the Lord's Day in those days.

Sunday School teachers deserve much credit. Miriam Coffee, in an article on "The Origin of Sunday Schools in England and in America," gives a description of an early nineteenth century Sunday School teacher's assets: "Teachers must not be haughty nor distant, but condescending, and to a proper extent familiar—not irritable nor impatient, but kind and forbearing—not gloomy nor melancholy, but cheerful and pleasant—not partial nor resentful, but administering favors with equal hand, bearing with and forgiving the follies of youth."[8]

The Conference began hiring a full time director of Christian education in the 1940's. Rev. Robert Powell was the first one. He served as Executive Secretary of the Board of Education from 1940 to 1945. He went from that position to teach at Mt. Union College and then to Wesley Theological Seminary. Bob was followed by Rev. Charles A. Sayre who served from 1946 to 1953. Charles returned to the pastorate, serving First Church Asbury Park and Haddonfield. Rev. Clyde Schaff came from the Wyoming Conference to fill the position of Executive Secretary and Director of Youth Work for the Board of Education. Starting in 1953, he moved to the job of Program Counselor from 1968 to his retirement in 1971. The Conference benefited immeasurably from the work of these skilled and dedicated men.

We used to smile at the quantity of "blue" envelopes that used to come from Clyde Schaff's office, but let it be said he worked hard and produced. A summary of his first ten years work is reported in the 1963 Conference Minutes. It shows the increase in Sunday School membership and attendance. It also shows an average annual enrollment in Leadership Schools between 1,000 and 1,500. Christian Witness Missions for youth witnessing to other youth were held in 1953, 1957, 1960 and 1962. Conference Youth Weekend drew 617 youth to Ocean City in 1954. In 1963, 2,196 attended.[9] Conference Center was largely developed under his guidance into a strong summer camping program for children and youth.

The celebration of Children's Day and its inception in Merchantville Church in 1866 has already been told.[10] So largely neglected today, Children's Day can still have meaning when properly and purposefully celebrated. Who can forget Sunday School picnics? They were a long awaited day. As a boy in the 1930's, school buses used to take us from Linwood to Lenape Park in Mays Landing. We would spend the day. Even Dad would come for the afternoon and supper—the one picnic of the year he would attend. There would be swimming, boating, rides, something to eat all the time, roller skating and, of course, a ball game for the older boys and men.

A tragedy occured at one Sunday School picnic excursion in 1870. A ten-car train excursion on Thursday, September 8, took the Sunday Schools of Long Branch, Eatontown and West Long Branch to a picnic at Toms River. A band led the happy excursionists across a sixty-foot long bridge. For some reason, the band stopped as it crossed the bridge, causing the span to be filled with people. Suddenly, the bridge gave way; men, women and children fell into the water. Eight lives were lost, all from St. Luke's Church. It was a somber crowd that awaited the arrival of the train back in Long Branch as word of the tragedy had already reached home.[11]

Epworth League

Youth organizations were started in the 1870's and 1880's. The Church Lyceum began in Philadelphia in 1876 to encourage the reading of Christian literature. John H. Vincent started the Oxford League in 1884 to promote Bible Study, devotional exercises, reading of the Christian Classics and participation in service programs. Other groups appeared around the country such as the Young People's Methodist Alliance started near Chicago in 1883. At Central Methodist Episcopal Church in Cleveland in 1889, representatives of these various youth groups met to try to coordinate their programs. The result was the formation of a single Methodist youth organization called the Epworth League, after the birthplace of Methodism's founder.[12] Methodist Protestant youth belonged to the interdenominational Christian Endeavor, founded in Portland, Maine, in 1881.[13] The Evangelical Church and United Brethren also had their branches of Christian Endeavor. After their 1946 merger it became the Youth Fellowship.[14]

The New Jersey Conference Epworth League was organized in 1889. The first Conference president was Rev. Amos M. North in 1892. In fact, most of the Conference presidents were ministers. Annual sessions of the Conference League would be held in various churches.[15]

The basic unit of the Epworth League was in the local church. Besides the regular League, there might also be an Intermediate and Junior League.

While a youth organization, the League's members might include people we would not call youth today, but I guess were still young in heart. League members made this pledge:

> I will earnestly seek for myself and do all that I can to help others attain, the highest New Testament standard of experience and life. I will refrain from taking such diversions as cannot be used in the name of the Lord Jesus. I will so far as possible, attend the devotional meetings of the Chapter and the worship of the Church and take some active part in them.

Through their "taking part" in the League's work, many a young person was helped, not only to take a more active part in the church, but to develop leadership abilities.

Conference Archives files has a list of the year's program from St. George's Church, Camden, in 1906 and Milltown Church in 1916. Every Sunday's program is listed with the name of the person in charge for the week. Programs for July of 1916 were: "Pulverize the Grog Shop, When? Why? How?" "Open Eyes for Christ on a Vacation Trip," "Do I Honor Christ in My Use of Sunday?" "How Can Our League Make Our Town Better?" and "Is It Easier to Be a Foreign Volunteer than a Home Stand-By?" Scripture selections were given for each topic.

Local youth also had the opportunity to become involved in active District Programs. These Rallies were big times and well attended. In addition there were Mid-Winter Institutes, and after 1920 the Pennington Summer Institute. Thanks to Anne Staats of Woodstown, the Conference Archives has the full record of the Bridgeton District Epworth League from 1889 to 1941. This can serve to illustrate the work of the District Leagues.

October 16 to 18, 1900, the 12th Annual Convention was held in Fourth Church, Bridgeton. A full slate of officers is listed for 1909, 1910.

District Superintendent—N. J. Wright
President—Rev. Henry Bradway, South Dennis
Recording Secretary—Mrs. C. H. Swain, Goshen
Corresponding Secretary—Mrs. Charles Hugg, Millville
Treasurer—J. Thornley Hughes, Millville
Junior Superintendent—Mrs. Richard Wilkinson, Millville
1st Vice President, Spiritual Department—E. A. Chambers, Mauricetown
2nd Vice President, World Evangelism—Miss Abbie Spence, Heislerville
3rd Vice President, Mercy & Help Department—Mrs. Seth Smith, Leesburg
4th Vice President, Literary & Social Department—Miss Clara Wilson, Bridgeton

Epworth League days were celebrated at the various District Camp Meetings and local chapters were urged to attend. Trinity, Bridgeton, hosted on all-day meeting in 1920. Broadway Church, Salem, hosted the 1931 Mid Winter Institute. It was held for six Monday nights, 7:30 to 9:30 starting

January 19. Courses were offered on the Bible, Missions, Methodism, Department Work, Devotions and Recreation.

A typical Saturday rally in 1934 was like this one held in February at Central Church, Bridgeton. It started with a boys' basketball tournament at the Armory at 1:30. Supper was served at the church at 5:30 for thirty cents. Worship started at 7:30. Roll call and collection took a half hour beginning at 8 o'clock and Dr. Harold Paul Sloan spoke at 8:30.

The report of President Charles Robinson in 1941 said the average attendance at the monthly District rallies was over 400. The largest was 861 on February 1 in Central, Bridgeton. Wildwood won the attendance banner.

The Fourth Annual Conference Epworth League Banquet was held at Bradley Beach on Saturday, March 7, 1931. Conference President, Rev. A. C. Brady, presided. Dr. Bruce S. Wright was the speaker. The menu consisted of cream of tomato soup with crackers, roast beef, mashed potatoes, gravy, sweet potatoes, peas and carrots, biscuits, celery hearts and olives, cole slaw, perfection salad, ice cream and cake, mints and nuts, coffee. The program was not given, but one of the songs listed was called, "The Smoke Went Up the Chimney." It was to be sung, with motions, to the tune of "Polly Wolly Doodle."

> You can shove the damper in,
> You can pull the damper out,
>   But the smoke goes up the chimney just the same!
> You can shove the damper in,
> You can pull the damper out,
>   But the smoke goes up . . .!
> Just the same, just the same,
>   But the smoke goes up . . .!
> You can shove, etc.

It was not all serious, as you can see!

The Golden Anniversary of the Epworth League was celebrated May 27, 1939, with a Banquet in First Church, Collingswood. Rev. Henry Ebner, President, presided. Music was by soloist, Mrs. Eda Nickless, a male quartet, a brass quartet and the congregational singing was led by Rev. L. Burdelle Hawk. Dr. Thomas S. Brock spoke on "Methodist Young People's Work Tomorrow."

Methodist Youth Fellowship

Soon after Methodist reunion in 1939, the Epworth League gave way to the Methodist Youth Fellowship. This time an age limit of 23, since reduced to 18, was put on the church's youth program. Many of the same kinds of programs as in the Epworth League, were part of the M.Y.F. In the late 1940's, I remember the well attended sub-District Rallies and the attendance banners. The Camden District in those days had a semi-formal banquet and usually a play. These rallies were well attended into the 1960's. Much has happened since then. There are not many good Cluster, sub-District nor District programs today, and that seems a loss. The Annual Conference Youth Weekend is still a vital success. Local churches still involve their youth in programs of the United Methodist Youth Fellowship. We commend our Christian youth today and twice-commend our youth leaders and counsellors.

CONFERENCE INSTITUTES

PENNINGTON

Institutes and camping programs for young people have played an important role in the life of our Conference since Pennington Institute was started in 1921. Rev. Thomas Brock was chairman of the committee appointed to arrange for the first Epworth League Institute to be held at Pennington School. Rev. and Mrs. Sherman Grant Pitt ("Pa" and "Ma") were the deans from 1921 to 1928. One of the most beloved leaders for many years was Wallace ("Uncle Wally") McKeag. This dedicated layman from Asbury Church, Camden, served as registrar and head of the "work crews" from 1922 to 1960. Beloved by and an inspiration to thousands of young people, "Uncle Wally" passed away in 1963 at the age of 84.

WALLACE "UNCLE WALLY" MCKEAG

Between 1930 and 1932, the Pitt Memorial Fund of $2,500 was raised by contributions from grateful Instituters for a missionary project in India where Malcolm Pitt, son of the first dean, taught. In 1941, the gateway pillars leading to the campus off Delaware Avenue were constructed as a memorial to Mrs. Joseph B. Kulp, wife of the second dean.

In early years, a full schedule was maintained, from Morning Watch at 6:30 to Lights Out at 10:30 p.m. As many as thirty classes were offered from which Instituters chose five and attended five sessions daily. After attending for three years, many received a certificate of accomplishment, having completed a required number of hours of study.

A record high enrollment of 499 was reached in 1943. With faculty and staff, there were 603 attending the two weeks of Institute that summer.

Headmaster, Charles R. Smyth, in welcoming the Fiftieth Anniversary Celebration to Pennington in 1970 said:

> The hundreds of youth whose lives have been blest through one or more summer weeks spent at the old school have fanned out in dedicated Christian service all over the world. There is hardly a church in the Southern New Jersey Annual Conference that does not have among its official family or on its church school staff, adults, who as youth, felt the inspiration of their days at Pennington Institute. Beyond this, pulpits, mission stations and other phases of full time service are staffed with people who made the all important 'life service' decision at Institute.[16]

Pennington Institute Deans

Sherman G. Pitt	1921-28
Joseph B. Kulp	1929-37
A. Corbin Brady	1938-41
Ira S. Pimm	1942-46 (2 weeks)
Everett Palmer	1943-48 (each year)
Charles R. Smyth	1946-49
L. Burdelle Hawk	1950-54
W. Gordon Lowden	1955-59
Robert B. Howe	1960-64
M. Russell Shivers	1965-69
Robert K. Smyth	1970-71
Charles Hankins	1972-73
Ronald Dyson	1974-77
Ronald Dunk	1978-79
Edwin F. Hann, III	1980- [17]

Delanco Camp

Youth work at Delanco Camp began in 1931 when the Rev. Howard Shipps was authorized to invite one hundred young people as free guests of the Fletcher Grove Camp Meeting Association. The following year, the Local Preachers' Camp took the same action. Previously, Dr. Edward Sheldon had brought some youth on his own. As the youth emphasis grew, special classes and programs were introduced by a number of young ministers.

When Delanco Camp moved to its present location at Sooy Place in 1965, its more than 200 acres, including Lake Agape, allowed for further development of the youth program. In 1968, Lois Shropshire began a Junior Camp. That same year, Rev. Kenneth Stevens was in charge of a Junior High Camp. Rev. Gary Turk and Rev. Carlton Bodine, Jr., took over those two groups in 1969 and Rev. Carl Farrell began the Teen Camp. Numerous others have served in various capacities.

Each year about 300 young people attend Delanco Camps, in addition to spring and fall weekend retreats, and enjoy a full program of spiritual development, crafts, recreation and horseback riding.[18]

Malaga Summer Assembly

The first youth Assembly at Malaga Camp was held in the summer of 1932 for Junior High or Intermediate youth as it was called. Fifty-three attended and Dr. Earl T. Hann served as Dean. Later that year, on November 17 in Dr. Alfonso Dare's cottage, a planning meeting was held to form the Malaga Summer Assembly which sponsors the Malaga Institutes. The initial planning group included: Dr. Alfonso Dare, president; John Goorley, vice president; Nelson Hoffman, Sr., secretary; David C. Evans, treasurer; and Lawrence G. Atkinson, John D. Blair, Henry D. Ebner, Earl T. Hann, G. Nelson Moore and Walter Nickless.

The Assembly program consisted only of the Intermediate Assembly in the early years. The assembly for Senior High youth was started in 1944 and a Junior Assembly for children in 1945. All of these Assemblies have continued over a span of several weeks each summer.

Dare Dormitory was the first to be built by the Summer Assembly in 1939 at a cost of $4,500. Through the years there has been much rebuilding and many improvements at Malaga, including a lovely swimming pool, all of which have helped Malaga Camp provide a meaningful program of Christian outdoor education for children and youth.

In 1944, the Assembly instituted an Assembly Scholarship Fund of $100 for two young people planning to attend Asbury College. The first young man to receive a scholarship was Robert J. Beyer, now Treasurer of our Conference.[19]

Seaville

At the instigation of Seaville's president, Dr. T. J. J. Wright, Rev. Franklin T. Buck led Seaville's first Youth Institute in the summer of 1935. About fifty attended. Facilities were quite primitive with outdoor toilets, kerosene lamps and lumpy, straw mattresses. A Model T. bus was borrowed from Pedricktown Church to transport the Instituters to the Sea Isle City beach for swimming, hot dog roasts and camp fire services. This pattern of afternoon and evening programs followed during the next 25 years.

From that initial start, facilities were improved with modern conveniences. A vital camping program resulted. Russell Knight, Camden County Superintendent of Schools; Mrs. Mabel Caldwell, Cape May County educator; Rev. Albert S. Layton; and Rev. and Mrs. Warren Layton were leaders of Seaville Institutes on into the 1950's. At its height, Seaville had as many as 150 Intermediate youth and 75 in the Senior High group. Registration and Board the first ten years of camp was only $8 a week. This was made possible, in part, due to the generosity of many Christian business men who supported and underwrote many Institute expenses.

Rev. Warren S. Layton writes, "Seaville Camp did not keep any records of what happened to the youth in later life. The writer knows of several in full time work for Christ: Robert Crowther, Newton Greiner and A. Keyes Layton, pastors; James Davison, former Conference Lay Leader and Mary Crowther, pastor's wife and nurse."[20]

Seaville no longer has Institutes for children or youth, but during the years it did, they were effective in reaching youth for Christ.

Conference Center

Following World War II, Rev. Franklin T. Buck was instrumental in securing for the Conference at a cost of $2,500 the former C. C. C. Camp S-69 located at Mount Misery in the south Jersey Pine Barrens. The year was 1946. That fall the Conference Center Commission was organized with Rev. Lynn Corson as president and Rev. Ralph Kappler as the first business manager. They had the task of transforming the old Civilian Conservation Corps Camp into a modern Conference Center. A fuller story of Conference Center will be told in Chapter 18. Here we want to relate a bit of the story of the camps for children and youth.

The summer of 1947, Conference Center was put to use. Junior, Intermediate, Youth and Young Adult Institutes were held. Five years later the Conference Center Commission reported 225 attended Boys Camp, 245 Junior Camp, 93 Intermediate Camp and 100 the Family Camp.[21] By 1956, the number increased to 504 Juniors, 421 Junior Highs, 270 Boys Camp, 121 Family Camp and 76 Senior Highs.[22]

The Conference Center Commission and its successor, Committee on Camps and Conferences, has continually improved the facilities at Conference Center, and the summer camping program has grown to include outpost camping and regular camping for children and youth of all ages. Also sponsored are acquatic and craft camps, backpacking hikes, canoe trips and the like. Since 1967, a full-time Director of Camps and Conferences has been employed. The Rev. Ernest O. Kelloway was the first.[23]

A 1963 report shows the number attending all the Conference Summer Camps, Institutes and Assemblies:

Camp	Instituters	Staff	Total
Malaga	677	107	784
Pennington	178	28	206
MYF Assembly	61	11	72
Christian Outreach Fellowship	118	22	140
Seaville	54	9	63
Conference Center	780	164	944
Total	1868	341	2209[24]

Boys Camp

In 1948, Boys Camp was founded and developed by Rev. Daniel Hulitt as an expression of Christian concern for less advantaged boys. Originally, he would bring a group of boys to Conference Center for a week of camping. As the program grew, the need for more space prompted him and his supporters to look for land. A 120 acre camp, situated in the Pine Barrens in Tabernacle Township, was acquired in 1960, and adequate facilities built. Here Rev. Hulitt brought hundreds of boys, most of them from the cities' streets, to enjoy an experience of God, nature and love.

In 1970, Boys Camp was transferred to the Conference and became part of the ministry of Conference Center. It was transferred to the Conference with the understanding that the ministry to less advantaged children would be continued. Through voluntary contributions to the Daniel Hulitt Scholarship Fund, each summer some 300 boys and girls experience the joy of camping in the out-of-doors, and the love of God as it is proclaimed in word and deed.

Since 1970, Boys Camp has been known as Tumethca. Its name is derived from Tabernacle United Methodist Camp.[25]

Girls' Houseparty

A summer mission school for girls was started by the Woman's Society of Christian Service when that organization came into being in 1940. Conference Youth Secretaries of the W.S.C.S. served for many years as dean. Sessions were held at South Seaville Campgrounds, Pennington School and Conference Center.

Girls' Houseparty has had many names. It was called Christian Outreach Fellowship, after the name of an office in the Methodist Youth Fellowship. It is now called Agape Week because it not only lifts up missions but creates an "agape" community for a week. Since 1968, it has been coed and annually meets at Conference Center.[26]

Summer Leadership Training School

The summer Leadership Training School was the Institute attended by the Methodist Protestant youth of the Eastern Conference. Since there was no permanent site, the School was held at various places. The first was held in Roseland, New Jersey, in 1931, with an attendance of sixty. The School in 1932 met in Fair Haven with 110 enrolled. In 1937, 64 youth attended the Conference School at Sea Cliff, Long Island. Dean that year was Rev. H. W. Bland Detwiler, with his wife Alice in charge of the Vesper Hour. Rev. Nelson M. Hoffman, Sr., of the New Jersey Conference was one of the evening speakers.

After unification, the former Methodist Protestant youth participated in all the Conference youth programs.[27]

YOUTH AT CONFERENCE

For over 60 years, youth have participated in the sessions of Annual Conference. The first was in 1923 when an Older Boys' Conference was started. It became the Junior Laymen's Conference in 1925 with Lynn H. Corson as president.[28] The last of the Junior Laymen's Conferences was held in 1948. It was voted that year to have in the future a Youth Weekend at Conference under the auspices of the Methodist Youth Fellowship.[29] This practice has continued, although since Conference moved to June in 1965, the Youth Weekends are no longer held in connection with the sessions of Annual Conference.

I attended my first Conference in 1948 as a Junior Layman from Central Church, Linwood. We assembled in the First Presbyterian Church in Ocean City on Friday evening, stayed in rooming houses, and ate at least some of our meals in the Ocean City Convention Hall. I especially remember a Saturday night banquet and attending the Sunday morning Men's Prayer Breakfast there. Saturday morning we shared in the sessions of Conference when the Youth Fellowship president, Donald Pimm, gave his report. A highlight was the Sunday afternoon Ordination Service on the Music Pier, following which Bishop Corson gave an invitation for those God was calling to full time Christian Service. Many responded. That was an important part of youth weekends at Conference. Our churches have benefitted immeasurably from those youth who made decisions for Christ and first answered the call to full time Christian ministry at the Conferences and Institutes in the Conference.

From the Older Boys Conference in 1923 to the Junior Laymen's Conference to the Methodist Youth Fellowship Weekend in 1949, youth have participated in Annual Conference life. Since 1971, official youth delegates, two from each District, plus other youth officers have attended the full sessions of Conference. Albert V. Lang, presenting the District Superintendents' report in 1972 said:

> We welcome the youth delegates. . . . Their work and ministry deserves our support. And we are proud of them! We have learned not to be upset by long hair and bright colors or informal clothes because we have seen their love for Christ. 'The Jesus People' or 'The Jesus Freaks' are terms used to describe some Christian youth. May God grant the day when this entire Conference will be 'turned on for Jesus!'[30]

During Bishop Corson's time in office, some time about 1956, "Bishop's Crusaders" was started. Everyone answering the call for dedication to Christ's service at the Conference youth rally was enrolled as one of the Bishop's Crusaders and given a small cross to wear as a symbol of this decision. Three hundred thirty became Bishop's Crusaders in 1956 alone. These decisions were not lost nor forgotten. Through the office of the Conference Board of Education, there was a follow up effort to keep in touch with all of the Bishop's Crusaders.

Ministries to Youth in Higher Education

It has already been pointed out that work with youth on the college campus was inaugurated in 1923 with the establishment of the Wesley Foundation at Princeton University.[31] Through the years, this work has continued through Wesley Foundations, Methodist Student Movements, interdenominational ministries like the United Campus Ministries and area-wide programs. Local churches in "college towns" have sought to serve. The church has been concerned with college youth. Sometimes this support has been pitifully small, yet it has not been neglected. Many campuses and many youth have in some way felt this ministry of the church.

The report of the Area Commission on Higher Education and Campus Ministry in 1983, while lamenting the forced reduction in ministry because of a lack of sufficient funds, nevertheless points out that some support is being given for campus ministries on these eleven campuses: Rutgers University, Princeton University, Trenton State College, Rider College, Mercer County Community College, Rockland Community College, Fairleigh Dickinson University in Teaneck, Montclair State College, Rutgers of Newark, New Jersey Institute of Technology, and Essex Community College.[32]

Scholarship and loan help is another important form of ministry to youth in which the New Jersey Conference and its churches have long been involved. In 1866, the Methodist Episcopal Church began offering scholarships and loans to its young people attending college. Offerings of children on Children's Day and others on Student Day have, through the years, provided financial assistance to Methodist youth.

Our own Conference since 1863 has had an Educational Society. Its purpose stated at its inception was "to afford aid to poor and pious young men of good talents, called of God to the work, in procuring an education as preparatory for the Gospel ministry in the Methodist Episcopal Church."[33]

The first loan was for $25.00 in 1864. Every year since, loans and scholarships have been approved and paid, not only to young men, but to young women as well. In its first one hundred years, the Educational Society gave 798 loans to 333 beneficiaries in a total amount of $72,864.50. Since 1951, students in Theological Seminaries who are serving churches in this Conference, have benefited by this scholarship program.

It was in 1948, at the request of the church for full time Christian workers, that the Woman's Society of Christian Service started the Frances Nelson Scholarship Fund. Its purpose is to assist young women planning to go into full time service in the life of the Church, to get a college education. Frances Nelson, in whose memory the Fund was named, was an officer in the District Woman's Society and Conference Sisterhood and the first wife of the Rev. Carlton N. Nelson. Bertha Allgood was one of the guiding lights in establishing this scholarship program. As its long time treasurer, she worked untiringly to set it on a firm financial basis and to help choose the young women who would be achievers in full time Christian work with the financial help they could now receive. This program has helped numerous girls receive their college education and continues to meet the early goals of its founders. More recently, the Bertha Allgood Grant was added to the program in appreciation for the dedicated leadership of one of the Fund's founders. This annual grant is given to a young woman pursuing advanced studies for full time Christian service.

Not wanting to be outdone by the women, the Board of Laity adopted the Kingdom Builders Program to assist young men in pursuing their college careers in search of full time service in the Church. Today, young women as well as young men are eligible for the scholarships offered.

Still more recently, the Ministerial Education Fund makes possible the giving of financial assistance to our young women and men in pursuing their theological education in answer to God's call to ministry in and through the United Methodist Church.

The information available from records tells a story and gives factual data that is so important. Another, equally important part of the story of the church's ministry to youth is the personal side. For more than fifty years, "Chic" and Betty Hawk, now residents of Wesley-By-The-Bay in Ocean City, have been involved in Pennington Institute. Both are still members of the Pennington Institute Commission. I asked them to share some of their memories of Pennington. The reply came the day I was finishing this chapter. "Chic" sent a copy of a two page history he wrote in 1970 for the Institute's Fiftieth Anniversary. I have already used some of this. Betty wrote this:

> Chic first attended in 1923 and I in 1927 . . . so you can imagine the wealth of memories we have. It was here that we each received our call to "full time Christian service"—here we learned to pray—and lead prayer groups—here we developed latent abilities to memorize *lengthy* Biblical play parts, design costumes and scenery—edit the daily newspaper—teach 'Beginners Tennis'—have marvelous fellowship with 'older' statesmen of our Conference who constantly inspired and encouraged us—here we were given many, many opportunities of service which, when we went into the ministry were so very valuable to us—and here, more than any other place, we were able to influence the young people of our churches in making important decisions in their lives—the atmosphere at Institute was conducive and then we had the privilege to follow through when we all returned home—which was always a traumatic experience.[34]

Is it any wonder that we boast of our camps, youth conferences and institutes when their effects have been and still are so apparent in the life of our Conference? Let no one take lightly this ministry to children and youth.

Chapter 14

WAR AND PEACE

1940-1949

Just as Methodism became united in 1939 and struggled through the meaning of that union in united Methodism's first General Conference held in Atlantic City in 1940, the world was becoming tragically disunited in the horrors of World War II. All the efforts for peace were for naught. Every hope that somehow the United States might escape proved hopeless. We were soon at war. This chapter will necessarily deal with the struggles of war times as well as the efforts for peace in which The Methodist Church played a significant role.

But before we deal with the decade of the 1940's, let us take a look at a different phenomenon. New Jersey, and southern New Jersey in particular, has been a breeding place for many popular gospel song writers. Many of these were Methodists. The gospel song has been with us for a long time. The Bible speaks about singing "psalms and hymns and spiritual songs with thankfulness in your hearts to God."[1] Psalms are hymns of divine composition, the words coming from the Bible. Hymns are the stately music of the church and are of human composition. Gospel songs are the more popular and often more easily sung music of Christendom and often have a chorus tacked on to them. Methodists have always delighted in singing gospel songs, and many have been included in our official hymnals.

The modern gospel song, as we know it, is a product of the great camp meeting era described in Chapter 8 and was made extremely popular in the Moody-Sankey era and the years following. It is a period that began after the Civil War. The songs were widely sung at our camp meetings and popularized in the numerous gospel song books that had tremendous sales. We still love to sing many of these gospel songs.[2]

Some of these were written by ministers.

> Come every soul by sin oppressed,
> There's mercy with the Lord,
> And He will surely give you rest
> By trusting in His word.
> Only trust Him, only trust Him,
> Only trust Him now;
> He will save you, He will save you,
> He will save you now.

Rev. John Hart Stockton, for twenty years a minister in the New Jerey Conference, wrote those words. When he retired because of poor health in 1872, he turned to music, publishing and producing two gospel song books. He also wrote "Down at the Cross" and the music to "The Great Physician." Rev. Stockton died in 1877.

Rev. Elwood H. Stokes is best known as the founder and first president of Ocean Grove Camp Meeting. A great preacher in the Conference, when he died in 1897, some 7,000 persons attended his funeral in Ocean Grove's Great Auditorium that is an enduring monument to his ministry. Elwood Stokes also wrote the gospel song with this meaningful refrain:

> Fill me now, Fill me now,
> Jesus, come and fill me now;
> Fill me with Thy hallowed presence,
> Come, O come and fill me now.

Many of us have often sung this chorus:

> Heavenly sunlight, heavenly sunlight,
> Flooding my soul with glory divine:
> Hallelujah, I am rejoicing,
> Singing His praises, Jesus is mine.

Rev. Henry J. Zelley wrote many poems and gospel songs, served as Conference Statistician and Treasurer and pastored numerous churches around the Conference. When he died in 1942, his friend, the Rev. Woodburn J. Sayre, wrote: "Henry J. Zelley walked with God on earth until the day after his eighty-third birthday, and then he continued his walk with God on the other shore."[3] Henry Zelley is best remembered for the chorus of the hymn quoted above.

Rev. William Grum was a great pastor in the churches he served from 1901 until his death in 1931, two days after the Sunday services in his church at Woodlynne. His songs are not so well known today, but were popular for a time. They included "Victory Ahead" and "Elijah's God Still Lives."

Others were lay men and women whose talents set the world singing for Christ. Who has not sung "Higher Ground," "No Not One," "Count Your Blessings," "No Night There," "He Included Me," or heard someone sing "The Last Mile of the Way?" All were written by a Methodist local preacher and insurance agent, Johnson Oatman, Jr., of Lumberton, New Jersey. "No Not One" became so popular that within a year after it was written it could be found in thirty-five different gospel song books. Later it was translated into Chinese and Japanese. Mr. Oatman, who died in 1926, said:

> Let others sing of rights and wrongs,
>   Sing anything that pleases;
> But while they're singing other songs,
>   I'll sing a song for Jesus.[4]

A favorite gospel song of many is:

> I come to the garden alone,
> While the dew is still on the roses,
> And the voice I hear,
> Falling on my ear,
> The Son of God discloses.
> And He walks with me,
> And He talks with me,
> And He tells me I am His own;
> And the joy we share
> As we tarry there,
> None other has ever known.

C. Austin Miles
Wrote "In the Garden" and numerous other gospel songs.

C. Austin Miles of Pitman, New Jersey, wrote that and many other popular gospel songs during his long life. He was a pharmicist, music publisher with the Hall-Mack Company and popular song leader at south Jersey's camp meetings. Among others, Mr. Miles wrote "Dwelling in Beulah Land," "Win Them One By One," "You May Look for Me for I'll Be There," and "Anywhere He Leads Me I Can Safely Go."

Mrs. Frank O. Breck of Vineland was a mother, frail in health, who often had to rest between household tasks. With her children about her, she would sit in a rocking chair on the back porch of her Vineland home and write in a notebook the verses of gospel songs. She penned: "Face to Face," "Hear Ye the Master's Call," "They Are Nailed to the Cross," and "Help Somebody Today."

Another Vineland native who wrote gospel songs was Annie Johnson Flint. Although afflicted with arthritis as a young woman and unable to walk for much of her life, she wrote beautiful songs which have inspired many. It was she who wrote the song that begins and ends like this:

```
God hath not promised              . . . . . . . . . . . .
Skies always blue,                 Help from above,
. . . . . . . . . . . .            Unfailing sympathy,
But God hath promised              Undying love.
```

War and Peace

Still another woman gospel music writer was Lida Shivers Leech of Merchantville. For many years she was choir director of Bethany Methodist Church in Camden. More than 500 of her songs were published. "God's Way Is the Best Way" is one. Another was the favorite hymn of my wife's Grandmother Chance, "Some Day He'll Make It Plain to Me."

Edgar Page Stites was a local preacher from Cape May County. He usually wrote under what he called "the front part of my name," Edgar Page. He wrote that lovely hymn that begins:

> Simply trusting every day,
> Trusting through a stormy way;
> Even when my faith is small,
> Trusting Jesus, that is all.

Another one he wrote was "Beulah Land." Ira Sankey made both of these songs popular and sang "Beulah Land" at Mr. Stites' funeral.

Thomas O. Chisholm of Vineland and C. Harold Lowden of Camden combined their talents, Chisholm writing the words and Lowden the music to the beloved:

> Living for Jesus a life that is true;
> Trying to please Him in all that I do;
> Yielding allegiance glad-hearted and free;
> This is the pathway of blessing for me.
> O Jesus, Lord and Saviour, I give myself to Thee,
> For Thou, in Thy atonement, didst give Thyself for me;
> I own no other Master, my heart shall be Thy throne;
> My life I give, henceforth to live, O Christ, for Thee alone.

Thomas Chisholm, who died at the Methodist Home in Ocean Grove, March 1, 1960, at the age of 93, was a newspaper man, one time preacher, and insurance agent, but above all, a devoted member of First Church, Vineland, and a writer of gospel songs. "O To Be Like Thee" and "Great Is Thy Faithfulness" are two others that are among his better known songs.

Chisholm's friend, C. Harold Lowden, was a musician from a musical family. For years, he was in the music publishing business, eventually owning his own firm. On Sunday, he was organist and choir director at various churches including First and Broadway Methodist in Camden.

The music publisher, Grant Colfax Tullar, was saved from a life of dissipation and an attempted suicide by the grace of God. He promised God that if God would help him to be a man, he would do his best for Him. God did and Grant did. Though living in Summit, New Jersey, he had a summer home in Belmar and spent much time at our camp meetings. He put many of Mrs. Breck's words to music. One night while driving to Bridgeton he thought of the gospel song, "You Ask Me What I Think of Jesus." He, too, passed away in Ocean Grove's Methodist Home.

There are others. Two sons of New Jersey Conference preachers; Richard W. Gilder, born in Bordentown and Carl F. Price, born in New Brunswick, both have hymns in the 1935 Methodist Hymnal. Dr. Carl Price wrote the companion to the 1905 hymnal, "The Music and Hymnody of the Methodist Hymnal." Dr. Eugene M. Coffee of Collingswood, father of Dr. J. Hillman Coffee, editor of this History, wrote a number of gospel songs.

Dr. Charles Albert Tindley, long-time pastor of the famed Tindley Temple in Philadelphia, pastored Franklin Street Methodist Church in Cape May in his early life. He often preached throughout New Jersey and at Annual Conference. This famed, black, Methodist preacher and son of slave parents wrote "Leave It There," "When the Storms of Life Are Raging," and the civil rights song, "We shall Overcome."

Rev. Daniel L. Ridout, Mus. D., served churches in southern New Jersey as a member of the Delaware Conference. A member of the 1964 Hymnal Committee, he arranged the tune "Stand By Me" for Dr. Tindley's hymn "When the Storms of Life Are Raging."

Gospel songs and Christian hymns are still being written by south Jersey Methodists. Esther Duvall Eden, wife of the Rev. Thomas F. Eden, has written numerous songs that have been published by her sister, Ruth Duvall Crawford Porter. While the Edens were at Trinity Church in Bridgeton, their young organist, Blanche Dilks Osborn began to put some of Esther's words to music. One of my favorites they wrote is called "How Wonderful." It begins, "O Lord my God, how wonderful thou art."

It was my privilege for six years to be the pastor of Blanche Osborn and her husband Herb at Trinity Church, Bridgeton. During those years of the 1960's, Blanche was our organist, and Herb was chairman of the Finance Committee. Since then God has given Herb the gift of poetry, and he and his wife collaborate on many gospel songs. They team up now in full-time, musical work for Christ. Scores of our churches have had them and their group "The Osborns Plus" sing in their church, mostly songs of their own composition. They travel now, at times, far from Jersey and their published and recorded songs are reaching across the world. The gospel music of south Jersey is touching people for Christ world wide as it has for over a century.

Our pastors, too, are still writing music. Rev. Harvey Van Sciver, while pastoring in Asbury Park, wrote a Centennial Hymn for his congregation. It was soon published and has thrilled the congregation at the Ocean Grove Choir Festivals and other places where it has been sung.

The psalmist says we are to "Praise the Lord! Sing to the Lord a new song, his praise in the assembly of the faithful!"[5] The gospel song writers of south Jersey have been helping Christians sing praises to their God for over one hundred years. Many of their songs still inspire. Methodism's south Jersey gospel song writers are a vital contribution of southern New Jersey Methodism to the musical life and heritage of world Christendom. This living heritage in gospel music is a product of our conservative, Wesleyan, camp meeting, evangelical, often holiness, tradition. And that at its very best.

> Count your blessings,
> Name them one by one,
> Count your blessings,
> *See what God hath done.*[6]

We leave the gospel song writers for the tragic world of the early 1940's where it took a lot of faith to live one's life. Young men and women went to war. Some never returned. When they did, they found the country and the world a different kind of place. America had at last assumed its role as a leader of the free world. Franklin Roosevelt became the first United States president to seek a third term; and in 1944, he won a fourth. We then changed the Constitution so it could never happen again. The war ended, like all wars, but only after two atomic bombs were unleashed with all their horrors over Japan. It was a new world and we have not yet learned how to deal with it. Forty years have gone by, but the free world and the communist world are still poles apart while the newer third world nations are trying to find their place.

The first General Conference of The Methodist Church met in Atlantic City's Convention Hall, April 24 to May 6, 1940. It was significant in that it was the first General Conference of the new Church. The unifying Conference was not allowed to enact new legislation. Its further significance was that war was raging in Europe. This General Conference did three things of special note. One was to decide on the location of the various Boards and Commissions of the Church. The second was the correlation of Methodist mission work around the world, on a plan proposed by Christendom's missionary statesman, Mr. John R. Mott, a lay delegate from the Newark Conference. Evangeline Booth, daughter of General William Booth of the Salvation Army was the speaker on missions night.

The third matter of significance was the statement on war and peace submitted by the State of the Church Committee chaired by Ernest Fremont Tittle. It was clearly slanted toward the pacifist position which had largely come to be the church's position during the 1930's. Tittle was a staunch spokesman for that point of view. The church agreed to stand by its conscientious objectors. The statement on peace and war read in part: "The Methodist Church, although making no attempt to bind the consciences of its individual members, will not officially endorse, support, or participate in war."[7]

Four years later, General Conference met in the midst of the heat of the conflict raging in the world. Tittle sought to obtain reaffirmation of his position. His committee's majority report was rejected in favor of a minority report emphasizing the responsibility to resist aggression as opposed to pacifism.[8]

Between General Conferences, shortly after America went to war, the Council of Bishops issued a statement which concluded: "We roundly condemn the processes of war even while accepting the awful alternative, not of our making, forced upon us by the selfishness and the perversity of men. From a measure of the guilt of this, none of us is free."[9]

The New Jersey Conference in 1940 was also host to the first session of the Northeastern Jurisdictional Conference. That, too, convened in Atlantic

City's Convention Hall, June 18 to 21, 1940. Since no bishops were to be elected, there was little excitement. Organizational and procedural matters were performed. Considerable discussion centered around "the responsibility of the United States for the present world situation of international anarchy."[10]

In settling into the new church, the New Jersey Conference had to deal with the problem of those former Methodist Protestant Churches that refused to join The Methodist Church. Rather than go to court or insist on any legal rights to property, Conference voted to allow the now named Bible Protestants to go.[11] Conference trustees were authorized to transfer deeds of title to them. Also, the invitation was given to any members wishing to remain Methodists to do so. This problem settled, the new church harmoniously worked together. The New Jersey Conference received over half of the effective and retired ministers from the former Methodist Protestant Eastern Conference.[12] In 1941, the former Methodist Protestant Church of Westville voted to join The Methodist Church and was received.[13]

The 1940 Conference approved a report on "Christ's Church and the Present World Crisis." It was less pacifistic than General Conference. Our utmost support, short of war, was pledged to the people of Great Britain. America was called to be fully prepared to defend itself. It also called for the abolition of war based on a structure of international law.[14] Conference also named Robert R. Powell as the first full-time Executive Secretary of the Board of Education.

Conference had little to say about war in 1941, other than to pray for peace. A Compassion Sunday offering for overseas relief was urged. It would be administered through the new Methodist Committee for Overseas Relief (MCOR). Dr. Edwin Forrest Hann's District Superintendents' Report in 1941 called upon the Church to care for the youth in the five training camps in New Jersey at Lakehurst, Fort Monmouth, Fort Hancock, Fort Dix and Cape May. He said, "Whatever our viewpoint with regard to the war situation . . . our plain and simple duty is to care for these lads as best we can and re-enforce their efforts to go straight when distant from the steadying influences of home."[15]

The United States had been at war ten months when Conference returned to Ocean City to make it their permanent home in 1942 with Bishop G. Bromley Oxnam of the Boston Area presiding. The war was uppermost on everyone's mind. One of the first matters of business was prayers for the chaplains. They were C. W. Bodine, D. A. Earley, F. E. Hand, C. A. Hewitt, N. M. Hoffman, R. L. Lewis, A. C. Oliver, Jr., H. M. Reinard, S. E. Templin, and M. N. Young.[16] Conference showed its patriotism by standing and singing "America." W. R. Raver in the District Superintendents' report lamented the awfulness of war and the wait for the invasion of Europe. Then he asks, "Is the church preparing for that day of Armageddon?"[17]

Other Superintendents spoke of the numbers of Methodist men and women then in their country's service and how churches near camps were trying to help. Central, Christ and St. Paul's in Atlantic City opened service centers for men in uniform. Oceanport Church opened two rooms every night except

Sunday for the service men at Fort Monmouth. Some churches had families invite every service man attending church home for dinner. Local churches kept in constant contact with those in the service. Every church kept a service roll of honor.

More chaplains were listed in 1943: R. A. Anderson, R. C. Laphew, Leon Martorano, W. A. Molyneaux, C. A. Pennington, K. R. Perinchief, W. N. Pike, H. H. Scarborough and S. A. Snedeker. C. R. Nixon was Field Director for the National Red Cross. One chaplain, Francis E. Hand, was reported as losing his life at sea. What it was like in 1943 is captured in District Superintendent Charles D. Whitton's Composite Report to Conference:

> The passing of a year has completely changed our ways of living and our habits. Governmental restrictions have made us ration book conscious. We have had to adjust ourselves to blackouts and air-raid drills. Thousands of our young men and women have departed for service in the armed forces of our Country. Hundreds of our people have been caught up in the shifting populations from communities having no essential war work to centers where defense industries are crying for more. Men have gone first to be followed by the entire families. Now comes the conscription of our very young at the age of 18 years. . . . Many churches have lost the majority of their young people. Some of our churches have lost 20% of their active membership. In addition the uncertainty of tomorrow, the doubts and fears of what it holds; in changing conditions of living and the anxiety attached to it with loved ones in camps, in the air, on the high seas, or in battle areas, have developed a condition which puts the nerve of our people on edge. They are worried. Their hearts are heavy. Some have already had the bitter and dreaded news concerning these loved ones in battle, and many more will have the same experience in the months to come.[18]

When Conference met in September of 1944 the end of war seemed near. There were more chaplains: W. G. Lowden, O. C. T. Peterson and J. D. Merwin.[19] Churches were asked to hold services, union services if possible, on Victory Day.

The following year, Conference mourned the death of President Roosevelt, rejoiced at V E and V J Days and expressed the belief that "one of the greatest achievements of our world history was completed when the world charter was drafted and signed by representatives of fifty nations in San Francisco."[20]

Even as the Church was struggling through the very difficult war times, as peace neared, Methodism was working for peace. In 1943 and early 1944, Methodism's bishops, led by Bishop G. Bromley Oxnam, led the Church on a "Crusade for a New World Order." The main thrust was to develop effective expressions of Methodist will and energy for international collaboration after the end of hostilities. The whole church was involved in study and action designated to support the idea of world government. The result was a tremendous surge of concern and support for a United Nations. No one should underestimate the role played by The Methodist Church in building in this country a level of support which helped make the United Nations a reality.

The 1944 General Conference challenged the Church to a Crusade for Christ. The Church responded. A goal of $25,000,000 was set for the first year of the Quadrennium Crusade for World Relief and Reconstruction. $27,000,000 was raised. It was said by some that this amount was the greatest, single amount raised up to that time in church history. The second year's goal was one million new members. In a little more than a year it was achieved. The third year, goals were set for stewardship, tithing, and full-time dedication to Christian service. There was a large increase in giving and more than twelve thousand persons dedicated themselves to the ministry or other full-time service. The fourth year's goal was for increases in all divisions of the Sunday School. Downward trends were reversed and significant increases achieved.

During this outstanding era of peace, over five hundred new Methodist churches were organized across the United States; mission work was reestablished; educational institutions received financial help; the Crusade Scholarship Fund was started, and goals were reached which have not been equalled nor surpassed since.[21]

The New Jersey Conference entered whole-heartedly into the Crusade for Christ. After District Superintendent Albert L. Baner explained the Crusade in 1944, appropriate committees were appointed. The following year it was announced that the Conference goal of $316,050 for rehabilitation and reconstruction of war-torn work around the world was exceeded by $31,000.[22] Conference registered gains, but did not reach its goal in evangelism in the Crusade's second year. However, there was a net gain for the year of 1818 members received on profession of faith, 4,567 for the year compared to 2,749 for 1945 and a net gain of 961 members received by transfer. The total full members for the year increased by 3,675.[23] The Crusade's third year report showed as much as a 50% gain in attendance for some churches, 2,107 tithers enrolled and 232 youth dedicated for full-time Christian service.[24] The final Crusade thrust was for increases in the Sunday School. The Board of Education reported in 1948 that "after a decade of steady loss in church school enrollment we have gained 8,972 new pupils during the quadrennium. Especially encouraging was the increase of 2,759 in the youth division during the past year."[25]

The 1940's saw the Methodists of the New Jersey Conference struggle through war times, ministering as best they could. They supported the Crusade for a New World Order and rejoiced when the United Nations Charter was ratified. When war ended, hopes for peace were bright. The Crusade for Christ enervated the Church for the next twenty years of forward movement.

In the meantime, Conference expressed its concern over racism in church and society, particularly in the first half of the 1940's. Things must have improved somewhat because the problems which beset General Conference over the treatment of blacks in 1932 did not seem to be present in 1940. Yet, in 1941, Conference passed a Resolution presented by William A. Boyd and Everett W. Palmer on racial discrimination in employment in New Jersey. They complained about employment denied blacks regardless of their qualifications. "Even where employed," the resolution affirms, "there is discrimination against them in pay and advancement."[26]

The following year, a resolution on the Brotherhood of Man presented by Lynn H. Corson commends positive steps already taken, such as the Negroes' better status in defense plants, work in the Migratory Labor Camps and the Negro Army Camp near Westville. Yet, Conference complained, "We find in our own land and state and within the bounds of the New Jersey Conference wide discrimination against other races, particularly the Negroes."[27] It is of interest that later in the same session Dr. D. W. Henry, pastor of Tindley Temple in Philadelphia, addressed the Conference on a planned memorial for Harry Hosier, the first black Methodist preacher in America. The memorial was planned for Gulfside Assembly in Mississippi. An offering of $131 was raised for that purpose.[28]

A 1943 Social Service Commission Report presented by chairman Harry R. Pine said:

> We believe the time has come here in New Jersey when we can no longer ignore the growing racial tensions. Since more than twenty percent of the population of the State is negro, we believe it a part of our task to promote Christian understanding between the white population and the negroes of the State. . . .
>
> We view with concern the growth of antagonism toward other racial and national groups, such as Jewish, Mexican and Japanese. We ask all Christian people to remember these are also our brethren for whom Christ died, entitled to the same privileges we claim for ourselves.[29]

In 1945, Conference commended New Jersey Governor Walter E. Edge and the State Legislature on the passage of a law prohibiting discrimination in employment on the grounds of race, creed, color or national origin. The New Jersey Conference was waking up to its responsibility in the area of racial justice, but there was a long way to go.

New Jersey Conference Methodists were justifiably proud in 1944. Once again they hosted the Northeastern Jurisdictional Conference when it met for its second session in Ocean City, June 7 to 11, 1944. Two of the four bishops elected were sons of the New Jersey Conference, Fred Pierce Corson and W. Earl Ledden.

Bishop Corson was a native of Millville, New Jersey, where he graduated from high school and was a member of Trinity Church. After graduating from Dickinson College, Phi Beta Kappa, and Drew University, he joined the New York East Conference of the Methodist Episcopal Church. From 1920 to 1934, he pastored churches in New York and Connecticut and served as a District Superintendent. He was elected the twentieth president of Dickinson College in 1934 and served in that capacity until his election to the episcopacy.

His record of twenty-four years of service as bishop would be hard to surpass. He served as trustee of seven schools, colleges and seminaries of the Church. He was a frequent lecturer. From 1948 to 1960, he was president of the Methodist General Board of Education. He was president of the Council of Bishops, 1952-1953 and elected president of the World Methodist Council in 1961.

A world traveler, he made seven trips around the world besides visits to such places as China, Japan, Korea, Formosa, South America and Germany, all in the interest of the Church.

The bishop was a popular preacher, author of numerous books, leader of youth, and world ecumenist. Part of his long responsibility as bishop of the Philadelphia Area was Puerto Rico, a place dear to his heart.

It was Bishop Corson's privilege to lead his home Conference, New Jersey, from his election in 1944 until the Conference became part of the New Jersey Area in 1964. Upon his retirement in 1968, he was accorded the status of "honorary member" of the Southern New Jersey Conference.

In 1922, Miss Frances Blount Beaman of Charlotte, North Carolina, became the wife of Fred P. Corson. Their one son is Hampton Payne Corson, M.D. Bishop Corson passed away in 1985.[30]

Bishop W. Earl Ledden was the senior bishop in the United Methodist Church when he died in 1984. Glassboro was his home town and Glassboro Church his home church. He graduated from Pennington School with a major in organ music. He also was a graduate of Dickinson College and Drew Theological Seminary.

Earl Ledden began his ministry in his home Conference of New Jersey and served pastorates for fifteen years in Rumson, Belmar, State Street and Broadway, Camden. During his pastorate from 1920 to 1925, Broadway Church was one of the largest churches of the Conference. He moved to Buffalo, New York in 1926, Providence, Rhode Island in 1930, and to Trinity Church, Albany, New York, in the Troy Conference in 1938, from which pastorate he was elected a bishop.

As bishop, he served the Syracuse Area from 1944 until his retirement in 1960. He served as president of the Council of Bishops, 1956-1957, president of the New York State Council of Churches, and numerous positions in the church, including a term as vice president of the Commission on Worship.

Bishop Ledden was widely recognized as an accomplished musician and an authority on church music. After his retirement, he taught at Wesley Theological Seminary in the field of Ritual and Church Music.

Bishop Ledden was married twice. He married Lida Iszard in 1913, following her death he married Henrietta Gibson in 1964. His second marriage was performed in the Chapel of Christ Church, Methodist, New York City by Bishop Herbert Welch, then one hundred and one years of age. He was the father of two sons and a daughter. He, too, was an honorary member of the Southern New Jersey Conference. Bishop Ledden died, October 20, 1984.[31]

Four other men with ties to the New Jersey Conference have been elected bishops. Mention has already been made of Bishop Levi Scott, charter member of the Conference;[32] Bishop Isaac W. Wiley, one-time principal of Pennington School;[33] and Bishop John H. Vincent, founder of Chautauqua.[34]

Bishop Wiley began his career as a medical missionary to China in 1850. Upon his return to the United States he joined the New Jersey Conference and pastored Halsey Street Church in Newark. He became a Charter Member of the Newark Conference in 1857. From 1858 to 1864, he served as Principal of Pennington School. Elected bishop in 1872, he died November 22, 1884, in Foochow, China, while on a trip to the mission field.[35]

John H. Vincent, elected bishop in 1888, was assigned first to Buffalo, New York, then to Topeka, Kansas. Prior to his retirement in 1904, he served a Quadrennium in Zurich, Switzerland, in charge of all Methodist work there.

Bishop Everett W. Palmer is the other bishop related to the New Jersey Conference. Born in Menomonie, Wisconsin in 1906, he started his ministry in the Dakota Conference. Transferring to New Jersey in 1934, he was ordained both Deacon and Elder in the New Jersey Conference. He served the Silverton Circuit in 1933, Highland Park from 1934 to 1941, Centenary Tabernacle, Camden, 1942 to 1945 and First Methodist Asbury Park, 1946 until his transfer to First Church, Glendale, California, in 1951.

Everett Palmer was elected bishop in 1960 by the Western Jurisdiction and assigned to the newly created Seattle Area. He died, while still an active bishop, of an apparent heart attack in Palm Springs, California, January 5, 1971. He was married to Florence Ruth Wales. They had three daughters, Joanne, Elizabeth and Ruth.[36]

An important event in New Jersey political history which must be mentioned was the adoption of a new State Constitution in 1947. The 1844 Constitution was considered to be the most wordy and outmoded in the nation. The new Constitution, which the voters overwhelmingly approved, created a strong governorship giving the governor, for the first time, the right to succeed himself for two four-year terms. It increased the terms of State Senator from three to four years and Assemblymen from one to two years. The court system of the State was needfully streamlined and strengthened.

Most importantly, the 1947 Constitution outlawed discrimination on the basis of race, color, sex, religion and national origin. The previous Constitution outlawed it only on the basis of religion. The effect was immediate. Several municipalities had to take immediate steps to end school segregation. The New Jersey National Guard had to accept blacks for the first time in integrated units. It is said, this "document made New Jersey the first state to outlaw segregation constitutionally."[37]

One of the delegates to the State Constitutional Convention was Judge Francis A. Stanger of Cedarville. Judge Stanger was the Conference Lay Leader.

We have been following throughout this history the struggle for women and lay rights in the Church. The next chapter will deal in depth with the role of women in Southern New Jersey Methodism. Here, let me simply point out that 1940 saw the emergence of the new and unified structure for women in The Methodist Church. The Ladies Aid, and Woman's Home and Foreign Missionary Societies were replaced by the W.S.C.S., Woman's Society of Christian Service. Mrs. A. Corbin Brady of Woodbury was the first Conference President.

Meanwhile, the new Conference Board of Lay Activities had its inception at the 1939 uniting Conference. Judge Francis A. Stanger was elected the first Conference Lay Leader, a position he held until 1948.[38]

FRANCIS A. STANGER, JR.
First N.J. Conference Lay Leader

Conference moved ahead on many fronts in the second half of the decade of the 40's. The first front was ministerial pensions. At a special session of Conference, held in Mount Holly on November 28, 1945, the following proposals were adopted:

1. All compulsory membership in the Preachers Aid Society be discontinued.
2. All Penalties for failure to pay 1% dues revoked for all prior years.
3. Each pastor to pay 2% of cash salary, one half to go to the Permanent Fund and one half for distribution.
4. A 17½% assessment be placed on cash salary for Conference Claimants, 12½% for distribution and 5% to the Permanent Endowment Fund.[39] In 1946 this was rescinded. Assessment was put at 12½% and a special Endowment Campaign was to be held to raise $300,000.[40] Conference annuity rate at this time was $22 per service year. Total pledges for the Endowment Campaign was $275,000.

Secondly, Conference in 1946 authorized the purchase of the Conference Center, a former C.C.C. Camp No. S-69. Funds from the sale of the Point-

WAR AND PEACE / 213

ville Church and parsonage were made available.[41] Conference now had its own camping center which has proven of inestimable value in the years which followed. Dr. Franklin T. Buck was the chief instigator of this significant project. The cost of the original twenty-seven acres was only $2,500. It was quite a buy!

Thirdly, a forward step in the ecumenical movement in New Jersey was announced as having occured February 3, 1945. On that date, the former Council of Churches and the New Jersey Council of Religious Education combined to form the New Jersey Council of Churches. Fifteen church bodies, including The Methodist Church, with a combined membership of almost 600,000 made up the Council's membership. That was 95% of all Protestant Church members in the state.[42]

Fourthly, evangelism was not forgotten. The decade ended with Bishop Corson leading the Philadelphia Area in the "Philadelphia Area Evangelistic Advance." One hundred thirty-seven charges in the Conference participated. Visiting preachers from across the country held preaching services in each church, conducted training classes for lay workers, while teams of lay people went out on visitation evangelism. In that one week, 7,833 visits were made, 1,931 souls confessed Christ and joined the church on profession of faith while 3,143 were received as new members by transfer. I, personally, will not forget some of the experiences I had that week as a young man just called into the ministry, in seeing persons of all ages brought to Christ. Some were neighbors I had never before seen in church. Seeds were sown that later resulted in fruit for the Master. The climax of the Advance was a mass rally at Philadelphia's Convention Hall on Sunday afternoon, December 4, 1949, when an estimated 33,000 gathered in and around the Hall. Nearly 8,000 decisions were recorded at that service alone.[43]

Fifth, a new day arrived in the history of New Jersey's ministry to the elderly. On Saturday, August 23, 1947, Bishop Corson laid the cornerstone of the new $1,032,000 Methodist Home in Ocean Grove.[44] The new home began receiving guests on November 29, 1949, with a capacity of 230 to 235.[45]

Sixth, a period began in the life of the churches of the Conference in which there was considerable building and rebuilding. It is doubtful if there was any church in the Conference that did not embark on a new building or rebuilding program between 1945 and 1965. In the last three years of the decade, 1947, 1948 and 1949, a total of $1,914,064 was spent by Conference churches for buildings and improvements. The District Superintendents reported in 1948 that new churches were built or under construction at Ballard in Asbury Park and Highlands, replacing churches lost by fire. New Churches were also built in Somers Point and Cumberland. A new parsonage was ready for the Camden District in Haddon Heights. Delanco, Mt. Ephraim, Haddon Heights and Neptune City churches also built parsonages. Social and recreational centers were built at Buddtown, Friendship-Landisville and St. Paul's Pennsgrove. A Church School building and recreation center was completed at Belmar. Asbury Church in Long Branch rebuilt its church walls. Central Church, Bridgeton, remedied several structural defects and redecorated the whole church. New organs were installed in Pennington, First Church: Millville, Avalon, Williamstown, West Creek, Spring Lake and Central Church: Point Pleasant. This touches only on the major work underway or completed.[46]

Seventh, the field of Social Concerns was not forgotten. The Social Service Commission in 1946 was changed to the Commission on World Peace and Social Justice. Rev. Paul M. Corson was the first chairman. There was still a Board of Temperance with Judge S. Rusling Leap of Woodstown as president. A strong program of temperance education and a reiteration of Methodism's stand on total abstinence was approved in 1947.[47] A 1948 report of the Commission on World Peace and Social Justice dealt with "The Church and State" and declared:

1. That no public funds should be used for the direct or indirect support of non-public schools.
2. That no impediment should be allowed to the sale or distribution of the Scriptures.
3. That no persons be discriminated against by law because of their religious views.
4. That no preferment or privilege should be accorded by the State to any religious body.[48]

Quite a change in Conference leadership was experienced in the 40's. In 1940, Thomas S. Brock and Harold Paul Sloan were elected to their fifth and seventh General Conferences respectively. Then both transferred, Brock going to the Florida and Sloan to the Philadelphia Conferences. The ministerial delegation to General Conference in 1944 were all new men. They were District Superintendents Baner, Brady and W. R. Raver, and Ocean City's pastor, Dr. B. F. Allgood. Between 1940 and 1956, no General Conference ministerial delegate went more than once except Dr. Allgood. He went in 1944 and 1948. Seventeen different men were elected. No one assumed a position as a Conference leader, such as was evidenced before and since. Perhaps this sharing of leadership among many was a good thing. We also had a new bishop. There was evident vitality in the Conference. These were days of advance, forward movement and much growth.

Among the laity, one name especially must be singled out from among the many who contributed much. This layman's name is Frank C. Propert. At his death, December 28, 1955, his pastor at Haddonfield, Rev. Lynn H. Corson, called him "one of New Jersey Conference Methodism's most active and consecrated laymen."[49] He was an esteemed lawyer who spent most of his life in the Camden area. He was a member of State Street Church, Camden, and later Haddonfield Church. As a Conference layman, he was elected to six consecutive General Conferences from 1936 to 1952. Only one other layman, Harry P. Bennett, ever served more often than he. He was vice president of the New Jersey Conference Laymen's Association from 1932 to 1939 and Camden District Lay Leader until 1942. He was a trustee of Ocean Grove and Pitman Camp Meetings, a member of the Board and, for a time, president of the Pennington School trustees. In the general Church, he served on the Board of Missions and was vice president of the Board of Publications. This esteemed layman contributed much to his Church.[50]

At the end of the 1940's, New Jersey Methodism exhibited life and vitality it had not shown in a long time. The revival of the 50's had already begun. There would be some glorious years ahead; but before we tell the story of The Methodist Church from 1950 to 1967, the story of the women's role in Southern New Jersey Methodism needs to be told.

Chapter 15

WOMEN'S ROLE IN SOUTHERN NEW JERSEY METHODISM

Women keep making news in ministry in United Methodism. During the summer of 1984 while this history was being written, our Church elected two new women bishops. Marjorie S. Matthews, in 1980, was the first woman elected bishop in the Church. July 1984, two more joined the ranks. Leontine T. C. Kelly, the first black woman bishop was elected by the Western Jurisdiction and assigned to the San Francisco Area. The North Central Jurisdiction elected Judith Craig as the third woman bishop, assigning her to the Michigan Area. Not very many years ago, the prospect of having a woman bishop would have seemed like a distant, if not impossible, goal. The struggle for women's rights in the Church was a long and difficult one. To that story, we must now turn.

In this chapter we shall review the historical background, already partly traced, of women's struggle to gain full laity, as well as clergy rights, in Methodism. We shall take a brief look at the history of local units of women in ministry. Then we shall focus on the women's missionary societies, Conference agencies of women in ministry, Deaconesses, women ministers and close with a look at some significant personalities.

By way of background, two things must be remembered. First, the struggle for women's rights in Methodism parallels that in other churches and the nation. Women served in Methodism's General Conference and could vote on all issues relevant to the life of the Church before they could vote in most states and national elections. Women were seeking their place in society at the same time they were seeking it in the church.

Second, women have always had a place in ministry in Methodism, even though some doors were closed to them. One need think only of Susanna Wesley, preaching in her Epworth kitchen and advising her son John or consider Barbara Heck counted as a founder of Methodism in the United States and Canada. John Wesley used women in ministry and allowed them to exhort. Although he never formally gave them permission to preach, some did. Women in American Methodism have served as class leaders, local preachers, evangelists, missionaries, clergy wives, and Sunday School teachers. A real study needs to be made of the role of clergy wives in American Methodism. Many times they accompanied their husbands on preaching tours around the circuit. When they stayed at home, one can easily picture them sharing their faith as did Susanna in her Epworth kitchen. Some of those described as "Susanna's American daughters" would be Catherine Garrettson, wife of Rev. Freeborn Garrettson; Phoebe Palmer, woman evangelist and mother of the holiness movement; and Maggie Newton VanCott, licensed as a local preacher in New York in 1869.

Previous chapters have told part of the story of women's rights in Methodism. Here it needs to be summarized and brought up to date. Prior to 1880, women had been licensed as local preachers. Whether or not any had been in New Jersey, I do not know. The 1880 General Conference, at which there were lay delegates as well as clergy, took away even that right and did not return it until 1920. This action was precipitated by the request of two graduates of Boston University School of Theology, Anna Howard Shaw and Anna Oliver, for ordination. Not only did the Church deprive them of ordination, but even took away their license to preach. They preached anyway, but without official sanction and ordination. Anna Howard Shaw left the Methodist Episcopal Church and became a Methodist Protestant minister.

In 1888, four women, including Frances Willard, were elected by their Conferences as delegates to General Conference. General Conference refused to seat them. Their reason, in this case when the Discipline says laymen it means lay men in a literal not in a general sense. It was not until 1904 that women were given full laity rights and admitted as delegates to the Methodist Episcopal General Conference. Not until 1920 did they gain that right in the Methodist Episcopal Church, South.

The New Jersey Conference was no more sure than the general Church that women should be accorded equal lay status with men. In the two votes recorded on the seating of women delegates to General Conference, in 1890 and 1891, the women's cause was soundly defeated.[1] Some churches sent a woman as delegate to the 1896 New Jersey Lay Electoral Conference. That was a first, and their seating was hotly debated. Finally, the chairman ruled that since they were elected by their local church and since the role of delegates had already been called and verified, they should be allowed their places.

These victories won and rights recognized did not mean the end of the battle. For some years now, there has been a requirement that the general boards and agencies of the Church have at least one third lay women as members as well as one third lay men and one third clergy. As late as the 1984 General Conference, the ruling was passed that every local church Board of Trustees, the bastion of male supremacy in some churches, must have at least three women members.

The first woman delegate to General Conference elected by the New Jersey Conference was Miss Helen Phillips in 1936. None were elected to the 1939 Uniting Conference, but Mrs. George Yard was elected in 1940 and thereafter at least one woman has represented the New Jersey and Southern New Jersey Conference at every General Conference.

Gaining the right to preach was a more lengthy struggle. The Methodist Protestants were way ahead of the rest of the family in ordaining women. The New York Conference of the Methodist Protestant Church ordained Anna Howard Shaw in 1880. While the Methodist Protestant General Conference never officially sanctioned women clergy, it effectually left the matter in the hands of the Annual Conferences, that were much more independent than those in the Methodist Episcopal Church. At any rate, since 1892, the Methodist

Protestants had no bar to women serving as General Conference delegates or receiving clergy ordination if approved by the Annual Conference. Rev. Thomas B. Appleget of New Jersey was the leading Methodist Protestant spokesman for women's rights. The New Jersey Conference of the Methodist Protestant Church ordained Rev. Emma E. Nutter as an Elder on October 25, 1908. She was the first Methodist woman ordained in New Jersey.[2]

Emma Nutter, who became Mrs. Cairns, came to Atlantic City in 1902 to conduct evangelistic services in the People's Methodist Protestant Church. A year later she became the church's pastor. She pastored People's Church until 1919 when it merged with Trinity, now Ventnor: Trinity Church. For twenty-four years she served as the Executive Secretary of the Social Service Bureau in Atlantic City. She went to be with her Lord on October 27, 1955.[3]

The Evangelical United Brethren gave a varied response to the ordination and licensing of women to preach. A United Brethren quarterly conference in 1849 gave a license to preach to Charity Opheral. The 1851 United Brethren General Conference recognized Lydia Sexton as a "pulpit speaker." In 1894, the celebrated Sarah Ann Dickey was ordained by the Miami Conference. From 1873 until her death in 1904, Sarah Dickey taught at Mount Hermon School in Clinton, Mississippi, a school she had founded for black children. She was one of the first ordained women in the United Brethren Church.[4]

The Evangelical Church, on the other hand, did not ordain women. At merger in 1946, the United Brethren gave up their right to ordain women until the 1968 merger which created the United Methodist Church.

Things were not so easy for women who wanted to preach in the Methodist Episcopal Church as in the Methodist Protestant or United Brethren. Apparently, Maggie (Margaret) VanCott of New York was the first Methodist woman to get a license to preach. The year was 1869, and she maintained a vigorous ministry for thirty years.

When women could no longer be licensed to preach after 1880, they had to wait forty years until 1920 to have that right restored. In 1924, women were given limited clergy rights. They could be licensed to preach and be ordained as local deacons and elders, but they could not join the ranks of itinerant ministers and become members of the Conference.

The listing of local preachers in the Conference *Minutes* so often gives only the first initials so that it is impossible to identify who might be women. The 1921 *Minutes*, however, the first after licensing a woman was permissable, does list a Mrs. Parmelia Powell of Woodbury as a local preacher.[5]

The first woman's ordination in the New Jersey Conference took place in 1939 when Deaconess Helen Phillips was ordained Deacon by Bishop Richardson who also ordained her an Elder in 1943.[6]

Full clergy rights were not granted to Methodist women until 1956 when all the final bars were removed after two days of General Conference debate. Eighty-seven years after Maggie VanCott received her license to preach and seventy-six years after Anna Shaw and Anna Oliver were denied ordination, The Methodist Church gave full clergy right to its women. Since 1956, women

MRS. BESSIE LARKIN
of Collingswood, one of the first licensed woman local preachers (1922)
and evangelists in the Conference.

have advanced in ministry. In 1983, there were 1,456 United Methodist women serving churches in the United States. That same year, there were 1,282 women elders or probationary members.[7] There were seventeen women clergy, full or probationary members, in the Southern New Jersey Conference in 1983. That same year, Sandra Murphy became the first clergy woman elected to Jurisdictional Conference by this Conference which also elected Lanie Price as a clergy reserve delegate.

Gladys Showack, in 1974, was the first woman probationary member of the Southern New Jersey Conference. The following year, Margaret Abrams, Lynn M. Cheney, Carolyn J. Montgomery and Ellen Wirta were all received and ordained Deacons. In 1977, Margaret Abrams, Lynn Cheney Hardy and Carolyn Montgomery were ordained Elders and became the first full women clergy members of the Southern New Jersey Conference.[8]

Following this survery of women's struggle for full lay and clergy rights within Methodism, let us turn for a brief look at organized units of women in the local church. An early organization was the Ladies and Pastors' Christian Union established by Annie Turner Wittenmeyer of Philadelphia in 1868. Its purpose was to do religious work in the homes of people and evangelize the masses in the city. All was to be done under the supervision of the pastor.

A Conference Union, with a male president, was formed in 1870 with auxiliary societies in some of the churches.[9]

The Ladies and Pastors' Christian Union soon gave way to the Ladies Aid for local church work while the home missionary societies and deaconesses took care of its wider concerns. Ladies Aids just kind of grew in Methodist Churches and received no kind of official notice nor sanction. Their first mention was in the 1904 *Discipline*. In most churches they were formed long before that. Ladies Aid Societies were strictly local units. Traditionally, they raised money for numerous church projects and usually took care of furnishing the parsonage. They also served the important function of a social outlet for women who spent most of their time in the home.

Dan B. Brummitt, one of the editors of the *Christian Advocate,* praised the Ladies Aid as "an organization that never suspends, dies, nor takes a leave of absence. It is many things in one: a pastoral reinforcement, a financial treasure chest, a woman's exchange, a recreation center, a cookery school, a neddlework guild, a relief society, a school of salesmanship, a clearing house for domestic and church problems, a prayer meeting — each in turn plays many parts."[10]

The story of the Ladies Aid in one church will serve to illustrate them all. A predecessor group called the United Earnest Workers was organized in 1881 with thirty-six men and seventy-seven women signing in as charter members. The men were required to pay fifty cents dues, the ladies only twenty-five cents. All of the offices were held by women. Their first project was an oyster and clam supper to raise funds for a new organ. In 1885, they voted to become a Ladies Aid. Men could still belong, but only women served as leaders. They always celebrated Decoration Day, held an August fair and a fall Harvest Home as their main money-making functions. For some time, nearly every meeting was a "sociable" of some kind where they usually raised a little funds. They held badge sociables, a bean bag sociable, lunch box sociable, mush and milk sociable, fishing pond sociable, a husking bee, talking machine entertainment, a calico carnival and an Old Maid's Convention.[11] They had fun, raised lots of money, worked hard, supported their church, aided their pastor, and developed leadership qualities.

At the same time as the Ladies Aid was functioning in the local church, most churches had units of one or the other or both of the mission societies, Woman's Foreign and Home Missionary Societies. These groups studied about missions. The money they raised went through the Conference Society to the parent Society to support missions at home and on the foreign field. Sometimes these three groups worked harmoniously together; sometimes they did not. Is it not often a topic of discussion how much of our money should be spent locally and how much should be "given away?" Although these three units of Ladies Aid and mission societies have been merged into one local woman's unit in the church since 1939, this writer knows of churches in the Conference that still have Ladies Aids and others which still have mission societies.

Methodist merger in 1939 changed the pattern of organized units of women's work in the local church. The Woman's Home and Foreign Missionary Societies and the Ladies Aid gave way to the new W.S.C.S., Woman's Society of Christian Service, which existed in the local church and on the District, Annual Conference, Jurisdictional and General Church level. It was not always easy to bring these groups together in a local church, but it was done with remarkable alacrity and produced results that were amazing.

The Methodist-Evangelical United Brethren merger in 1968, which produced the United Methodist Church, merged each church's women's groups into the Women's Society of Christian Service and continued the Wesleyan Service Guild for employed women. Careful study and preparation led in 1972 to the United Methodist Women whose purpose is to be "a community of women whose purpose is to know God and to experience freedom as whole persons through Jesus Christ; to develop a creative, supportive fellowship, and to expand concepts of mission through participation in the global ministries of the church." Our women are remarkably successful and their support of missions never seems to waver. It is also true in every church of which I have been a part that our women are equally adept in assisting the maintenance and ministry of their church.

Between 1869 and 1893, when Methodist and Evangelical United Brethren women were struggling for full lay and clergy rights, eight founding societies which now constitute the United Methodist Women were formed. These helped, according to Rosemary Skinner Keller, in "creating a sphere for women in the church."[12] Mrs. Keller says, "At the same time the General Conferences were constricting women's role . . . women of prominence and capability recognized that opportunities had to be developed for leadership and service of their sex in the church. They consciously created a sphere for their sex by founding women's organizations of service to the church and maintaining their authority within the carefully carved out domain."[13]

The first of these eight founding societies was the Woman's Foreign Missionary Society of the Methodist Episcopal Church, organized March 23, 1869, in Tremont Street Church, Boston. Within a year, Isabelle Thoburn and Dr. Clara Swain were in India.[14] Eleven years later, in 1880, the Woman's Home Missionary Society of the Methodist Episcopal Church was formed in Cincinnati. Mrs. Lucy Webb Hayes was the first president. Much of their work was in the south with freed slaves. Five years later, Lucy Rider Meyers founded the Chicago Training School for women missionaries and soon after started the Deaconess Order.[15]

The Methodist Protestant women organized their Foreign Missionary Society, February 14, 1879, in Pittsburg and set out to minister in Japan and later in China.[16] At a meeting of this Society in Laurel Hill Church, Bridgeton, in 1893, the Woman's Home Missionary Society was formed with Mrs. S. A. Lipscomb as president. Early work of this Society was in Michigan's Upper Peninsula and the Oklahoma Territory.[17] These two Societies merged in 1928 to form the Woman's Work of the Methodist Protestant Church.

Meanwhile, women of the Evangelical and United Brethren Churches were forming their Societies. The Women's Missionary Association of the United Brethren Church was founded in 1875 and in 1884 the Woman's Missionary Society of the Evangelical Association was started. Upon the Evangelical and United Brethren merger, the Women's Society of World Service came into being in 1948.[18]

The other two of the eight founding societies were the Woman's Foreign Missionary Society of the Methodist Episcopal Church, South begun in 1878 and their Woman's Home Missionary Society founded in 1890.[19]

Our purpose here is to tell something about the work of these missionary societies within the life of the New Jersey Conference. A year after the organization of the Woman's Foreign Missionary Society in 1869, the New York Branch covering the states of New York and New Jersey was formed March 10, 1870.[20] The same year, local societies were started in Trenton, Long Branch and New Brunswick.[21] Some time between then and 1872 when a Mrs. James of Trenton was elected New Jersey Conference Corresponding Secretary, the Conference Society was organized.[22] It is not easy to give a full account of the work of these missionary societies. Their records are not available. Conference *Minutes* give only a report of a committee of ministers. About all they advocate is for local churches to be responsive to the missionary societies' fine work. It is not until 1896 that a listing of their officers is even given. In the Woman's Foreign Missionary Society, it was the Corresponding Secretary who was the chief officer. Mrs. James was succeeded by Mrs. John Aber in 1877 and Mrs. Dallas Lore in 1883.[23] Mrs. Lore, a former missionary in Buenos Aires, held this position for many years. Her daughter Julia was a medical missionary.

One of Mrs. Lore's responsibilities as Conference Secretary was to arrange itineraries for visiting missionaries. In a letter she explains something of what was involved.

> I came from Vineland yesterday and on the way took six railroad trains, three hacks, and two stage carriages, besides a family carriage—a varied experience, but a successful day's work, arranging for Miss Cushman in Camden, Burlington, Bordentown, and Pemberton.[24]

The first listing of Conference Officers in the 1896 Conference *Minutes* give these names:

Conference Secretaries	- Mrs. D. D. Lore, Summit
	- Mrs. Kennard Chandler, Ocean Grove
Conference Treasurer	- Miss Sue S. Chase, Trenton
District Secretaries	- Mrs. E. A. Margerum, Bridgeton
	- Mrs. A. M. Hartranft, Camden
	- Mrs. M. J. Sparks, Trenton
	- Mrs. E. S. Parsons, New Brunswick[25]

The last Conference Secretary was Mrs. William B. Williams of Margate. Mrs. Williams and her husband had served many years as missionaries in Liberia.

Some of the missionaries supported by the Woman's Foreign Missionary Society who went from New Jersey are Eleanor LeHuray from Asbury Park who went to Buenos Aires, Argentina, in 1884; Dr. Mary E. Carleton from Asbury Park who went to China in 1887; Sylvia R. Harrington from Collingswood who went to Wonju, Korea, in 1918; and Lena Ware of Atco who was assigned to Rome in 1923.[26] Another missionary was Lucilla H. Green Cheney, daughter of Rev. & Mrs. Enoch Green, who went to India as a medical missionary in 1876 and died there of cholera in 1878.[27]

One advent evening late in 1984, there was placed in my hands as Conference Historian six volumes of records comprising the work of the Bridgeton District Woman's Foreign Missionary Society from its inception in 1888 until its last meeting was held in 1940. Its value is inestimable because it is the only primary record available at this time, beyond the local church, of the work of either of the women's missionary societies within the Conference. Some remarks are in order.

The first District Convention was held November 16, 1888, in Vineland. Mrs. Keighley of Vineland was elected president. Vineland, Broadway Salem, First Millville, Cedarville and First Bridgeton were the five auxiliaries then in existence. A resolution adopted at this first meeting expresses the work these women wanted to do.

> We, the ladies of the Woman's Foreign Missionary Society, resolve that in the future we will do better work, be more earnest, more prayerful in this cause of helping our Heathen Sisters, by sending the Gospel to them.

Thereafter, annual spring meetings were held in various churches of the District and beginning in 1914, fall meetings as well. Still later, yearly young people's rallies and banquets were held.

At the 1919 annual meeting led by Mrs. Charles Hugg of Millville, the historian gave a report on each auxiliary. The District had twenty-two local auxiliaries representing nearly 800 members. India, China and Korea were the main fields of interest, but work was also supported in South America and elsewhere.

Annual meetings always included a missionary worker. A joint meeting with the District Woman's Home Missionary Society was held in Port Norris in 1933. May 6, 1937, First Church in Ocean City hosted the Fifteith Annual Spring Meeting in which Mrs. Paul Miller of India was the principal speaker.

The last meeting was held April 17, 1940 in Vineland when Mrs. Walter B. Williams, Conference president, spoke on "Our Unfinished Task." An India missionary, Miss Vida Graham also spoke.

A fall meeting at Fourth Church Bridgeton in 1919 ended with this challenge being given:

> The women of the nineteenth century were staunch workers, but we women of the twentieth century have a greater task before us and we must keep our faces toward the One who said, "If I be lifted up, I will draw all men unto me."

> Let us then be up and doing,
> With a heart for any fate,
> Still achieving, still pursuing
> Learn to labor and to wait.

In this spirit our women worked for missions.[28]

The New Jersey Conference Woman's Home Missionary Society was organized in New Brunswick, March 20, 1885, with Mrs. General Clinton B. Fisk as president, Mrs. C. F. Garrison, corresponding secretary, and officers for each District. In its first report, the Society had sixty members, eighty-two subscribers to *Woman's Home Missions,* and one hundred forty mite boxes in circulation. "The Society since its organization has sent over $100 for the general treasury. Allow me to prospect that the little one will become a thousand."[29] Mrs. Fisk and Mrs. Garrison were the leaders of this Society for the first twenty years.[30]

The New Jersey Conference Woman's Home Missionary Society was involved in several significant projects. One was the New Jersey Industrial Home for Girls at Morristown College in Tennessee which opened in 1892.[31] Another was the support of the Hilah Seward Home in Sinuk, Alaska. Women of the New Jersey Conference gave a boat, the *New Jersey,* for this work. The boat with all aboard was later lost at sea.[32] A third project, closer home, was the establishing of the Deaconess Home, now the Neighborhood Center, in Camden. This project was started in 1913.[33]

The New Jersey Society was also involved in various programs at Ocean Grove. As early as 1886, the New Jersey, Philadelphia, and Newark Conference Societies inaugurated an Anniversary Day at Ocean Grove which became an annual feature of the Camp Meeting Program. In 1894, the first National Deaconess gathering was held in Ocean Grove. This, too, became an annual event. In 1896, a rest home for deaconessess and women missionaries was opened in Ocean Grove. This home later became the Bancroft-Taylor Home.[34]

The first listing of Conference Officers in 1896 shows these names:

President - Mrs. C. B. Fisk, New York
Corresponding Secretary - Mrs. C. F. Garrison, Cranbury
Treasurer - Mrs. S. J. Turner, Camden
Secretary of Supplies - Mrs. G. M. P. Wells, Trenton
District Secretaries - Miss Eva Smith, Bridgeton
　　　　　　　　　　Mrs. S. H. Thompson, Camden
　　　　　　　　　　Mrs. Crowell Marsh, Trenton
　　　　　　　　　　Mrs. A. J. Whittier, New Brunswick[35]

The Fiftieth Anniversary was held on June 8, 1930. The report states that the New Jersey Conference Woman's Home Missionary Society had 7,816 members, who raised yearly over $31,000.[36] Mrs. George W. Yard was the last Conference Society president.

The Methodist Protestants in New Jersey had an active Woman's Foreign Missionary Society. It was organized April 28, 1886, in Barnsboro with Mrs.

Louisa Stanger as president. Early meetings were held in Glassboro, Millville, Bridgeton, Westville, Leesburg, Camden and Moorestown. Support was given for mission work in Japan.[37]

After the merging of the Methodist Protestant Conferences into the new Eastern Conference, this women's work became the Eastern Branch. In 1920, there were twenty-five local auxiliaries with 680 members and a yearly budget of $2,000.[38] Mrs. H. W. B. Detwiler was the last president of what was then called The Women's Work of the Methodist Protestant Church for the Eastern Conference at the time of merger in 1939.

In order to merge the various women's organizations, missionary and Ladies Aid of both the Methodist Episcopal and Methodist Protestant Churches, into the new Woman's Society of Christian Service in 1940, Provisional Committees were set up in each Annual Conference. The New Jersey Conference Committee consisted of Mrs. Bland Detwiler, Chairman, representing the Methodist Protestant Church and three from the Methodist Episcopal Church: Mrs. Walter Williams, of the Woman's Foreign Missionary Society, Mrs. George Yard from the Home Missionary Society and Mrs. Lois Briggs, representing the Ladies Aid. This committee met with a called Conference Meeting of women from all the Districts in First Church, Camden, March 29, 1940. Bishop Richardson presided, and the following slate of officers was nominated and elected to lead the New Jersey Conference Woman's Society:

President	Mrs. A. C. Brady
Vice President	Mrs. H. W. B. Detwiler
Recording Secretary	Mrs. B. F. Allgood
Corresponding Secretary	Mrs. H. D. Ebner
Treasurer	Mrs. A. M. Jennings
Missionary Education	Mrs. C. T. Clarke
Service	Mrs. R. T. Hand
Social Relations and Local Church Activities	Mrs. John B. Cole
Assistant	Mrs. P. C. Greenley
Wesleyan Service Guild	Mrs. Reba Ebner
Student Work	Mrs. W. H. Matthews, Jr.
Young People's Work	Mrs. I. S. Pimm
Junior Work	Mrs. H. J. Smith
Literature and Publications	Mrs. George Whitfield
Supplies	Mrs. B. H. Decker
Status of Women	Mrs. A. W. Nash, Jr.
Missionary Personnel	Mrs. Walter Nickless, Jr.
Spiritual Life	Mrs. A. R. Mandeville
Thank Offering	Mrs. Donald Phillips
Gift Boxes	Mrs. F. B. Stanger

Climaxing all the ground work in the Conference was the Charter Meeting, held in Centenary-Tabernacle Church, Camden, on October 15, 1940. Too much gratitude cannot be expressed toward the first officers who laid the foundation for all that was to come. Important, too, were the first presidents of the four Districts:

Bridgeton	- Mrs. Miller H. Gravenstine
Camden	- Mrs. Raymond B. Ingersoll
New Brunswick	- Mrs. Loretta Higginson
Trenton	- Mrs. Lawrenson Correll[39]

Anniversary Meetings such as the tenth, fifteenth and twentieth were of tremendous impact. Annual fall meetings on the Ocean City Music Pier attracted as many as 2,000 women. For one such gathering, Mrs. Detwiler and Mrs. Pimm produced a drama, *To the End of the Earth.*

In 1969, the first anniversary of the merger with the Evangelical United Brethren women was celebrated, and the name was changed to the Women's Society of Christian Service. In 1972, this organization became the United Methodist Women. At the same 1969 meeting, the women presented *The Calico Girls,* celebrating the founding of the Woman's Foreign Missionary Society in 1869. It was during this time that some women chose to wear calico dresses in order to save their money and contribute it for the mission work to which they were devoted. In 1984, history repeated itself as two buses and a van transported Southern New Jersey women to Boston to a Jurisdictional meeting which again recalled those early women of Methodism who sent the first missionaries to India. A "Calico Parade" was held.

September 23, 1984, yet another nostalgic gathering of some 1100 women and men filled the Ocean City Music Pier for a two hour program, "A Centennial Tapestry." The committee, chaired by Connie Shivers, worked for over a year. The program was an outstanding success. It began with the singing of the chorus of the Centennial song written by Penny Moore which begins, "We're going to march right into the future while praising God for the past." The program depicted monologues of "women from our past," the beginning of the Woman's Society of Christian Service presented in pageantry, music of the former Delaware Conference women and their story, and "women and youth in mission" in dialogue and music. As the program neared its close, Korean and Spanish women flanked the stage and recited the United Methodist Women's purpose in their native languages. The entire audience sang the Centennial song as sixteen women from nearby churches marched and carried banners representing the work of United Methodist Women.

Summer Schools and retreats have played a large part in the growth and development of the individual woman as well as local church units in understanding the work and fostering missions. This Conference has often been asked to host significant Jurisdiction, National and World Federation meetings. Christ Church, Atlantic City, entertained the World Federation Tea in 1944. Ocean Grove's North End Hotel was the center for the Jurisdiction's Summer School from 1942 to 1954. Atlantic City hosted the Assembly of Methodist Women in 1962. The Conference was also hostess to Ecumenical National Conversation Groups in 1963.

Women of the Conference have served well beyond the Conference level. Alice Detwiler, the first vice president for the Northeastern Jurisdiction, for eight years wrote "The Program Page" for *The Methodist Woman*. Others serving on the Jurisdictional level have been Ethel Pimm, Fay Smith, Bert Marker, Marguerite Gardner, Elizabeth Brogden and Marjorie Lentz. Mrs. Detwiler and Mrs. Pimm served on the General Board of Missions. Miss Ruth Flaherty was president of the Northeastern Jurisdictional Deaconess Association. Elizabeth Brogden was a member of the General Council on Finance and Administration. Gertrude Klein and June McCullough have also served on General Church Agencies.

Mrs. Marker, "Bert" as she is known to her many friends, while serving as Jurisdictional Secretary of Supply Work in 1958, founded "Interchurch Medical Assistance," which is now located in New Windsor, Maryland. Through this project, medical supplies, donated by pharmaceutical companies, are shipped to hospitals and medical centers around the world. In 1983 alone, seven million dollars worth of supplies were shipped, of which $320,000 went to United Methodist Hospitals and Clinics. This activity indeed exemplifies women serving women in the name of Christ in the Conference and beyond.

There is so much more that could be said about the Conference Woman's Society and United Methodist Women. Every one of the twelve Conference Presidents from Bessie Brady in 1940 to Margaret Howell in 1986 have contributed so very much. Their experienced and trusted leadership has endeared them to the Conference. They have led the women of the Conference to accomplish many exciting and challenging goals. They have held high the banner of missions and challenged all church women to support United Methodist missions generously and sacrificially.

A year's activities, selected at random, will serve to illustrate our women at work in the Conference. 1966 is the year chosen. The material is culled from the scrapbook of the Woman's Society historian.

The twenty-sixth annual spring meeting was held on Wednesday, May 4, 1966, at Broad Street Church, Burlington with Conference President, Mrs Albert Stretch, Jr., presiding. The theme was "Each . . . Called . . . Challenged . . . Committed." Dr. J. Edward Carothers, Associate General Secretary of the Board of National Missions spoke, in the morning. At the afternoon session, Mrs. Arville Gilmore, Northeastern Jurisdictional Woman's President consecrated the officers, including new president, Mrs. Carlton Nelson of Pemberton.

Outgoing president, Mrs. Stretch, in a note in the May *Relay* said, "My heart is full to overflowing as I bid farewell to each of you. You have endeared yourselves to this president in so many ways." The new president, Mrs. Nelson in the same *Relay* challenged every Woman's Society member to "Grow in understanding and spiritual power. Increase in our knowledge of needs around us. Share in the witness, and service of the church."

It was reported that over five hundred women participated in the two January "Day Apart" services led by Mrs. Philip Worth of Collingswood and held in the Pitman and Ocean Grove Churches. It was also announced that a large delegation from New Jersey would attend the Seventh Woman's Society of Christian Service General Assembly in May in Portland, Oregon.

District presidents elected in 1966 were: Bridgeton, Mrs. Benjamin Rainear; Camden, Mrs. Morris W. Brewin; New Brunswick, Mrs. Edward Fieldler; Trenton, Mrs. William T. Adams.

In the Haddonfield Church on June 3, the Sisterhood Chorus gave a concert, "With a Voice of Singing." Mrs. Robert Allin directed and Mrs. Fred Bowen accompanied the Chorus in a benefit performance for the Frances Nelson Scholarship Fund.

Mrs. H. W. Bland Detwiler served as Dean of the Summer School of Missions held July 11 to 15 at Pennington School. The theme was "Christian Being and Doing." It was to be a coed school.

The merger with the Delaware Conference Churches brought twenty-two new societies into the Conference Woman's Society. Total Conference membership was 17,313 with a new high in pledges for the year of $83,150, a 25% increase in mission giving for the quadrennium.

The twenty-sixth Anniversary Meeting was held on Ocean City's Music Pier, Friday, September 16 with the theme, "Christian Being and Doing." The new president, Mrs. Carlton Nelson, presided. Dr. John Johannaber, Executive Secretary for Missionary Personnel of the Board of Missions spoke in the morning. Deaconness Hazel Horner of the Community Center in Camden was the afternoon speaker. Missionary Coaching Conferences for workers with children and youth were announced for September in Manasquan Church and at the Conference Office in Cherry Hill.

Dr. John A. Stroman was spiritual leader for the third annual Spiritual Retreat held October 13 and 14 at Conference Center.

Thus were our Conference women involved in 1966.

Methodist ministers' wives are surely a group of their own. For many, it is a calling as true as that to the Christian ministry itself. With what devotion and love they labor with their husbands serving Christ, His Church and the people of God. Mrs. Charles F. Garrison, Hannah was her name, did many things in the Conference. It was she who organized the ministers' wives of the Conference into the Sisterhood. The organizational meeting was held March 23, 1903, in First Church, Asbury Park. Subsequently, District Preachers Wives' meetings began in the 1920's. The Sisterhood in 1911 organized the Benefit Branch. For a small assessment, a gift of money is provided the member upon the death of her husband. The initial assessment was thirty cents. The first benefit was $15.25. Reflecting the fact that ministers' spouses may be men as well as women, the Sisterhood changed its name in 1976 to the Wesley Fellowship whose purpose it is "to bring together the membership in mutual Christian fellowship and concern."[40] Mrs. Walter (Leona) Quigg is the current president.

The Methodist deaconess was inspired by deaconesses in Germany in the late 1800's and came into being because of the needs of the city. Mrs. Lucy Rider Meyer of Chicago started the Deaconess movement in the summer of

1887 when she and seven other Methodist women canvassed Chicago's tenements seeking to find how they could help. From her Chicago Training School for women missionaries, Mrs. Meyer trained young women to help. When the 1888 General Conference sanctioned the idea, Methodist deaconnesses became a reality.[41] The heyday for the Methodist deaconess was from 1888 to about 1910. From farm, small town and city, she came, received training and served Christ and people in the city. Here is an example of what one Deaconess saw:

> A Bohemian family was found in two rooms, one a mere shed of an old frame building. The father had been sick for five months with rheumatism. A dead child was lying in the back room. A tiny baby, lacking clothes, was tied up in a pillow. Their destitution was shocking. They lacked clothes, bedding, bread, everything.[42]

Chapter nine relates the story of the beginning of Deaconess work in the New Jersey Conference[43] with the appointment of the first Board consisting of five men and four women. Miss Jessie B. Hillman, who served in Ohio, and Miss Sallie B. Heisler, whose work was in Paterson and Newark, New Jersey, were the first two deaconnesses from the New Jersey Conference.

The Woman's Home Missionary Society started deaconess work in Camden in 1913, the beginning of the famed Deaconess Home and Community Center. Calls in the homes of the needy were always a vital part of the deaconess work.

The Bancroft-Taylor Rest Home in Ocean Grove, in operation since 1897 and winterized in 1901, provided a place where countless deaconesses and home missionaries could find rest. Many finished their days there.

We do not have a complete record of deaconesses from this Conference, but here are some that we do have. Alma Wolverton from Lambertville, worked in Baltimore among other places. Dorothy Woolverton Hamm from Greenwood Avenue Church in Trenton did most of her work in Brooklyn. She is an ordained local deacon.[44] Lucy V. Ellison served eight years in her own Conference at Camden and Gloucester from 1918 to 1925. Rebecca A. Robertson of Camden served as a deaconess for forty-five years in Bayonne, Jersey City, Paterson and Newark prior to her death in 1945. Kathryn Newcomb from Leesburg served from 1949 until her death in 1980. She served first at the National College in Kansas City and after 1965 at Scarritt College in Nashville, Tennessee.[45]

Margaret Brown in Dayton, Ohio; Audrey Frank in Philadelphia, and Miriam Parsell in New York are active deaconesses from this Conference.[46]

Helen Phillips Neary will serve as an example of a deaconess at work. For twenty-three years, starting in 1930, Helen served as a deaconess. After two years in settlement work in Wilmington, Delaware, she spent the next twenty-one years in Trenton. She served as pastor-assistant at three Trenton churches: St. Paul, Trinity and Central. For six years she directed the Trenton District Missionary Society and served as interim pastor in Trenton's Clinton Avenue Church. She was connected with three Trenton institutions: the

Widow and Single Women's Homes, Donnelly Hospital and the Florence Crittenton Home for unwed mothers. She visited inmates in the Mercer County Jail and preached, baptized, married and administered Holy Communion as an ordained elder in many churches. Her friends called her "a lady circuit rider" because she traveled widely by public conveyance, first as a deaconess and then as a lady minister.[47]

Women ministers, as Conference members with full clergy rights, first came into the Southern New Jersey Conference in 1974, eighteen years after full clergy rights were granted to women. Gladys Showack in 1974 and Margaret Abrams, Lynn Cheney, Carolyn Montgomery and Ellen Wirta in 1975 were the first to receive probationary status and be ordained deacons. Margaret Abrams, Lynn Cheney and Carolyn Montgomery became the first women full Conference members and elders in 1977. Let us take a look at these women clergy.

Gladys Showack served Embury Church, Collingswood in 1975 but the next year she was discontinued. Margaret Abrams served at Wesley Church, Pleasantville and Bethel, Somers Point; Billingsport and Repaupo; Hammonton and Batsto. Lynn Cheney served Magnolia and Glendale; Westville: First and Victoria. Carolyn J. Montgomery pastored West Creek and Warren Grove, attended school for three years, and since 1980 has been a Chaplain in the Pennsylvania State Institution, an appointment in Extension Ministries. Ellen Wirta did not serve a church during her one year as a probationary member of the Conference.[48]

The seventeen women clergy in 1983 were pastors of local churches and served in extension ministries. They were serving on Conference Boards and Agencies and made their presence known beyond the Conference in election as Jurisdictional Conference delegates. Women clergy are taking their place as Conference ministers. There are problems, however. Clergy couples are not always easy to place in appointments. Open itineracy is a goal, not a reality. Sex as well as race brings out prejudicial feelings. It is, however, a safe prediction that women clergy will be seen more often in Southern New Jersey Conference churches, in positions of greater leadership roles, and some day not far off in the District Superintendency. Churches, too, will be more eager for a woman clergy to occupy their pulpits as their gifts and graces in Christian ministry become better known.

In this chapter, as well as in previous ones, some significant women personalities have been singled out: Mrs. General C. B. (Jeannette) Fisk, Mrs. Charles F. (Hannah) Garrison, Helen Phillips Neary, Rev. Emma E. Nutter Cairns, Mrs. Dallas D. (Rebecca) Lore and others.

There are more who must be mentioned. Hazel Mary Horner was a deaconess for twenty-four years. She served in Wilmington, Delaware; Philadelphia; and in the U. S. Navy as a WAVE. Her last service was as Executive Director of the Camden Neighborhood Center. She served four years as president of the Northeastern Jurisdictional Deaconess and Home Missionary Association and eight years on the General Board of Higher Education. Her

MRS. CLINTON (JEANNETTE) FISK
Woman's Home Missionary Society Leader

courageous enthusiasm and abundant joy served her well in her many duties and service in the local church as well.

Alice Shattuck Detwiler has been involved in every aspect of women's work in the Conference since 1939. Serving as the last president of Women's Work in the Methodist Protestant Eastern Conference, she chaired the committee which organized the Conference Woman's Society of Christian Service, served as the first Vice President of the New Jersey Conference Woman's Society and was also the first Vice President for the Northeastern Jurisdiction's Woman's Society. Alice was a member of the General Board of Missions. An astute teacher and writer, she has spoken and taught in every Conference in the Northeastern Jurisdiction and beyond. She wrote a regular column for five years in the *Methodist Protestant Recorder* and for eight years in *The Methodist Woman*. She has contributed much to this history as a member of the Advisory Committee.

Coming to the Southern New Jersey Conference from the former Central Jurisdiction was Matilda Saxton Winn, for many years a staff person with the Woman's Division of the Board of Global Ministries. She was active in women's work in the Little Rock, Central West and Delaware Conferences before coming to Southern New Jersey. She was awarded a certificate of appreciation in 1978 from the Board of Global Ministries for ten years of unselfish service and distinguished commitment in community development and full time Christian vocation. She has visited seven African countries, India and the Middle East in the interest of missions. A signal honor was to be selected to serve on the Lay Committee that compiled and presented the first laity message to the 1980 General Conference.[49]

Time and space do not permit us to tell at length of others. Each of the Conference Woman's Society and United Methodist Women presidents has contributed much, each in her own unique way. We salute them here: Bessie Brady, Anne Ebner, Ethel Janke, Evelyn Schalick, Christine Marple, Marguerite Gardner, Mabel Stretch, Dorothy Nelson, Elizabeth Brogden, June McCullough, Betty Ricards and Margaret Howell.[50]

A challenge presented in one of the Woman Society's Anniversary Celebrations seems an appropriate way to close this chapter on women in mission. "Our Christian witness can be the dynamic for changing life. It can bring the message of the Gospel into every part of life. It does not turn things upside down, but does turn the world right side up. With all the past as foundation for the future, may we, through Jesus Christ our Lord, today, become effective women in taking the message to the ends of the earth."[51]

CENTENNIAL SONG

There's a story we would tell you
As we celebrate our birth,
The United Methodist Women
Is the greatest group on earth.

CHORUS

We're going to march right into the future
While praising God for the past;
United Methodist Women's work we know
Is going to last and last and last.
Though we've been working for 100 years
From early morning till setting sun,
With all the plans and programs we have underway
It seems that we have only begun.

VERSES

1. We have sent out missionaries
   Here at home and foreign shore,
   We have built our hospitals and homes
   And still have need for more;
   So with missions needing our help,
   And with hungry children yet,
   While minorities cry to be heard
   Priorities we've set.

2. Many still have never heard God's Word
   For prayer there is great need
   So we've learned to be supporitve
   And to teach in word and deed;
   Working through our local units
   We can listen and take note
   Of the issues facing each of us
   For which we have a vote.

3. Now as long as women are abused,
   As long as folks are poor;
   And as long as the illiterate
   Are knocking at our door,
   With our women needing equal rights,
   And shelters to be run;
   And with prison reform started
   Then our task has just begun.

4. Looking back we are rejoicing
   For the work that has been done,
   And we praise God for accomplishments
   We number one by one;
   Every day brings a new challenge,
   So we look to God on high
   To fulfill our Purpose daily
   As we lift our battle cry.

   —Penny Moore, 1/26/84[52]

Chapter 16

THE METHODIST CHURCH

1950-1967

I began my ministry in 1954. Those of the younger generation will find it hard to appreciate what a wonderful time that was to start in ministry. It was a very upbeat time in America and for the Church. Writing of this time, Sydney Ahlstrom says, "Consciously and subconsciously with and without government stimuli, the patriotism of this 'nation with the soul of a church' was aroused. Being a church member and speaking favorably of religion became a means of affirming the 'American way of life.' "[1]

The 50's began with McCarthyism in full swing. Senator Joseph R. McCarthy of Wisconsin sought to root out the "Commies" from every facet of American life, including the church. In time that was seen as a sign of ugly anti-Americanism. Peace failed again in 1950 with the advent of the Korean War. Then followed the eight years of the Eisenhower presidency, a time of peace, prosperity, a vast, growing suburbia and an unprecedented post-war revival of religion. In 1940, 49% of the American population were related to the church. The percentage climbed to 55% in 1950 and 69% by 1969.[2] This was accompanied by a distinct increase in church attendance and a remarkable surge in church building construction. In 1960 alone, a total of $1,016,000,000 was spent by America's churches on new construction.[3] The Methodist Church in this one decade alone added almost one million new members. There were 9,910,741[4] members reported for The Methodist Church in 1960. That figure increased to 10,304,184[5] in 1965.

Other kinds of things were happening in the 1950's which permanently changed the shape of America's life. In 1954, the Supreme Court passed its momentous decision outlawing segregation in the nation's schools. This decision helped spawn the Civil Rights Movement under the Rev. Martin Luther King, Jr. which probably reached its peak that day in 1963 when he stood on the steps of the Lincoln Memorial and gave, before a vast throng, his famous "I Have a Dream" speech. It was a dream that "We will be free one day:"

> This will be the day when all God's children will be able to sing with new meaning, 'let freedom ring'. . . .
> When we allow freedom to ring—when we let it ring from every city and every hamlet, from every state and every city, we will be able to speed up that day when all of God's children, black men and white men, Jews and Gentiles, Protestants and Catholics, will be able to join hands and sing in the words of the old Negro Spiritual, 'Free at last, Free at last, Great God a-mighty, We are free at last.'[6]

The Space Age also began in that era when the Soviet Union launched the first, man-made satelite, Sputnik I on October 4, 1957. The next year, the United States entered the space race by putting Explorer I and Vanguard I into orbit.

The 1960's are often described as "the turbulent sixties." This decade closed with the racial riots in America's cities and the trauma of the Vietnam War. America became a different nation as the revival of religion of the 1950's sputtered out. The 60's began with the presidency of John Fitzgerald Kennedy, the first Roman Catholic president in our country's history. His tragic assassination, November 22, 1963, stunned America. It brought to the presidency Lyndon B. Johnson, a Texan. His Great Society program and War on Poverty focused the nation's attention to the needy in our midst. The Vietnam War he escalated in 1965 with the ordered bombing of North Vietnam triggered unparalleled hostility to a very unpopular war and caused the pot of turbulence in our midst to seethe.

Another Supreme Court decision in 1963 shocked the religious community. The Court declared Bible reading and religious ceremonies unconstitutional in the country's public schools. In response, the 1963 session of the New Jersey Conference passed a resolution regretting such a ruling which it called "contrary to our American traditions and the will of the vast majority of the people."[7]

The end of the segregated Central Jurisdiction in The Methodist Church and the merger with the Evangelical United Brethren Church into the United Methodist Church as well as other happenings of the late 1960's will be told elsewhere.

New Jersey was a growing state during these years. Population increased by more than one million during the 1950's. The growth was mainly in suburbia while the cities decayed. "The urban crisis," declared District Superintendent Ernest W. Lee in the 1962 Superintendents' report, "is the greatest challenge facing this state and our Protestantism."[8] This same report showed the population increase during the 1950's in the ten counties served by the Conference was 487,000. Meanwhile, membership in The Methodist Church grew 12.7% from 94,395 in 1950 to 106,385 in 1960.[9] The completion of the Garden State Parkway in 1957 from the New York state line to Cape May greatly aided the growth of the shore areas. Monmouth and later Ocean Counties grew substantially.

With all of this as background, we need to look more closely at the revival of the 1950's. New Jersey Methodism was growing. In 1945, our churches reported 74,283 members. The figure grew to 94,395 in 1950, topped the 100,000 mark for the first time in 1957 and reached its peak at 113,608 in 1966. This was an increase of just under 40,000 in those twenty-one years. Contrast this with a membership decrease of 26,285 in the seventeen years that followed.[10] Sunday School membership shows the same trends. In 1950, there were 62,388 Sunday School students in our churches. That was an increase over the previous year, but still less than in 1945. By 1960, however, Sunday School membership had increased by 23,523 to a peak of 85,911. Since that time, Sunday School membership has declined almost every year, to a disturbingly low figure in 1983 of only 36,748.

In a further comparison between 1940 and 1967, a study of the churches shows that in 1940 there were 34 churches with a membership over 500, nine of which had over 1,000, topped by Pitman's 1,482. This number increased in 1967 to 56 churches with plus 500 members including fourteen with more than 1,000, led by Haddonfield's 2,062. Camden and Atlantic City were the cities most strongly affected by the urban decline. In 1940, it would have been hard to predict that by 1967 four of Atlantic City's churches, Central, Christ, First and St. Paul, would be merged into one, Calvary Church with only 371 members. Nor could Camden's demise have been thought possible. In 1940, Centenary Tabernacle Church was the seventh largest in the Conference with 1,059 members. It had only 228 in 1967. The other churches suffered a similar fate.

Suburbia was the center of growth. Cherry Hill's St. Andrew's Church was started in 1954. Thirteen years later, it ranked number eleven in the Conference with 1,269 members. Willingboro, begun in 1958, had 838 members by 1967. Another new church, East Brunswick, in four years grew to a membership of 610. Two other churches showing remarkable growth between 1940 and 1967 due to significant population increases in their parishes were Oakhurst, from 470 to 1,437, and Linwood, from 345 to 1,092.

Another sign of the vitality and growth of New Jersey Methodism during this period is the amount of new buildings and modernization which went on all across the Conference in churches of all sizes. New churches and parsonages

St. Andrew's Church, Cherry Hill
First of the post-World War II Churches to be organized in the N.J. Conference. Present Sanctuary erected in 1966.

were built; some were relocated. There were few churches that did not improve their facilities for Christian education or build church school buildings. On the Camden District alone in the 1950's these congregations built new sanctuaries: Audubon, Brooklawn, Camden: Asbury and Fairview Village, Haddonfield, Northfield, Paulsboro: Billingsport, Stratford, Woodbury: Colonial Manor and Woodland.[11] To attempt any recitation of the names of churches which added to or remodeled their facilities or built new ones would be redundant. Let the record show, however, that from 1950 through 1969, a total of $25,382,422 was spent on buildings and improvements by the churches of the Conference, an average of close to one and one half million dollars a year, and this was well before today's inflationary prices. The top years were 1957 and 1958 when over five million dollars was spent. That is a remarkable record of achievement on the part of the churches and sacrificial giving on the part of the members.

In a previous chapter, something of the kind of churches Methodists built was told. The new building following World War II reflected changed thinking in style, worship and Sunday School practice. A liturgical renewal was taking place. More preachers wore clerical collars and vestments. The pulpit-centered church gave way to the divided chancel and altar-centered sanctuary. This change took place even in churches not designed for it. Electronic organs made it possible for more churches to have organ music, but fortunately or unfortunately, depending on one's point of view, electronic organs even replaced pipe organs. All of these changes did not come about easily, even for such a seemingly simple thing like placing candles on the communion table. No one style of architecture predominated as each church built to suit its congregation's tastes or maybe, sometimes, its architect's whims.

Church School buildings made it possible for many churches to offer the kind of Christian education not possible before. Classes were properly graded, adequate facilities were offered, and training opportunities were provided for teachers. The unfortunate thing today is that our facilities are often underutilized for the purpose for which they were built. Yet, imaginative congregations are finding other ways to use the space not needed for Sunday School classes. Sometimes they are used for weekday activities, instead of only Sunday morning classes.

This growth in members and the accompanying building progams did not just happen. One must, of course, be aware of the divine initiative in all cases of church growth. No matter what our programs are or are not, God moves in mysterious ways, His wonders to perform. It is evident that God was bringing people into His Church during those days of the revival of religion in the 1950's and early 1960's. The tragedy is that many were not sufficiently grounded in the faith to stay when the way became hard. We need to pray that God will yet again cause His Church to overflow with those truly seeking Him.

The Church did, however, use some means through which God's Spirit might move on the human heart. The Philadelphia Area Evangelistic Advance in the fall of 1949 has already been mentioned. Through it, over 5,000 new members were received into New Jersey Conference Churches. A vital part of that Advance was visitation evangelism in which nearly 8,000 interviews were held as lay people witnessed to other lay people about Jesus Christ and His Church. Those programs of visitation evangelism continued to function prayerfully and faithfully in numerous churches across the Conference either regularly or at least intermittently with positive results.

One part of the Quadrennial Program adopted by the 1952 Conference called for a two and one half per cent net increase in church members each year in every church for a ten per cent gross increase. As part of this emphasis, a Spiritual Life Mission was set for February 28 to March 7, 1954, in the New Jersey Conference and later in Philadelphia. Visiting ministers helped. It began with a mass rally in Trenton with Bishop Corson preaching. Fervent preaching combined with effective, friendly visits in local churches attracted 27,760 to services during the week. A total of 705 new members were received as a result, 9,159 committed themselves to attend church regularly, and a proportionate number pledged to observe the holy habits of our faith.[12]

Christian Witness Missions were effective for the youth. Albert S. Layton, reporting in 1955 for the Bridgeton District, told how 816 youth conducted 2,957 interviews with other youth which resulted in 559 making professions of faith in Christ and 1,494 new M.Y.F. members.[13]

Operation Victory took place in October, 1958, in the three Conferences of the Philadelphia Area. Two hundred sixteen Conference Churches participated. Again, there was preaching and visitation evangelism. A total of over 30,000 participated either in the preaching services or were visited in the evangelism calls. The result was 2,300 new members received, slightly over half on profession of faith. Operation Victory was followed in 1959 and 1960 with District evangelistic programs in which preachers from one District helped out in another.[14]

Another evangelism program found the Church reaching out to others in the fall of 1962. It was called "The Methodist Challenge — Put Christ First." A report in the December *Methodist Relay* reveals that the Methodist Challenge for Christ was not over, but just beginning. In this local church evangelism program, visitation evangelism was again the primary tool. Of the first 9,000 plus calls, nearly 2,000 new commitments or transfers were reported. The *Relay* said,

> The challenge is *still* before us and always will be. The challenge is not only to reach the unreached, to activate the inactives, to enrich the lives of the saints, but to PUT CHRIST FIRST, not as a slogan to a campaign, but as continuing expression of deep-rooted faith. CHRIST IS FIRST — always, it is the privilege of every church and Christian to KEEP HIM THERE![15]

So be it.

A final note on the revival of religion and growth of the Church during this period is the five new churches which were started: Erlton, now St. Andrew's, Cherry Hill; St. Paul's, Willingboro; Aldersgate Church in East

Brunswick; Old Orchards and Middletown. These five churches had a combined membership in 1983 of 2,689.

St. Andrew's Church was started as an outreach of Haddonfield Church and its associate minister, the Rev. Edward B. Cheney in 1954. The first meetings were held in the Cheneys' parsonage. Worship Services and Sunday School Classes began in March of 1955. On May 1, one hundred sixty-seven charter members formed the nucleus of the new church. Today, it is a church of over 700 members.[16]

St. Paul's Church, Willingboro, was started in 1958. In the area of the former Charleston Church in Willingboro Township, a new Levittown was developed. Later, the name was changed back to Willingboro. About four acres of ground were given to The Methodist Church for the development of a church. Charleston Church was closed and razed. A new church, St. Paul's, was built in 1959 in its place. The Rev. Walter Quigg was the first pastor. Willingboro Church now has over 700 members.[17]

In 1963, Milltown Church became the mother of a new church in East Brunswick. It was named Aldersgate Methodist Church because the year of 1963 was the 250th Anniversary of John Wesley's Aldersgate experience. Aldersgate Church was officially chartered on September 8, 1963, with 301 members. That Conference, the Rev. Charles Wilcock left Milltown to become the first full time minister of East Brunswick.[18]

Middletown and Old Orchards were both started during the 1965-1966 Conference year. Lawrence G. Atkinson in the 1966 District Superintendents' report said, "Two new churches were established in our Conference this year. One at Old Orchards, Cherry Hill and one at Middletown, with 110 and 80 charter members respectively."[19] Actually, 1965 was the year both churches began. Middletown was started through the ministry of Red Bank Church and its associate minister, the Rev. Wayne Conrad. Old Orchards was started in that section of Cherry Hill Township at the Conference Building. The Rev. Robert R. Marshall was the first pastor.

In this period of church growth, the Conference, too, set its sights high and several, significant, new developments and ministries took place between 1950 and 1967. First was a series of Quadrennial Programs. What was simply called "The Quadrennial Program" was instituted in 1952. There were six goals:

1. Evangelism, a 2½% net increase each year in every church for a 10% gross increase. [The actual increase totaled only a little more than 3%.]

2. Youth and Education, develop a strong youth program and increase facilities for summer programs.

3. Ministry, recruit 30 full time and 20 supply pastors and increase the Pastor's Pension Endowment Fund. [The fund was increased somewhat and the annuity rate was doubled from $21 in 1952 to $42 in 1954.]

4. Lay Activities, seek the best lay leaders for Lay Leader and Methodist Men in every Charge.

5. Institutions, make the church aware of responsibility to our institutions — Pennington School, Drew University and the Methodist Hospital in Philadelphia.

6. Church Extension, make a Conference-wide survey to show places where new churches and better facilities are needed. The financial goal was $500,000 or ½ cent per day per member.[20]

The financial goal was only about half met, but much good was accomplished. Conference Center, Pastor's Pensions, Good Will Industries, stewardship and evangelism within the Conference, Drew Seminary, Pennington School, Ocean Grove Home, Methodist Hospital, Collingswood Home, Church Extension across Methodism, Puerto Rico and many local churches in their building programs[21] were all helped by the Quadrennial Program.

This program gave way in 1956 to the "New Jersey Conference Program for the Quadrennium." Its purpose was to strengthen local churches, strengthen Methodist Schools of Higher Learning and meet a goal of one dollar per member per year for church extension.[22] The emphasis was placed on church extension. Again, only about half of the goal was met, but about $168,000 was received, ten per cent of which went to Puerto Rico. Twenty-four churches in the Conference received help with their building programs.[23]

The third program was a multi-faceted program which had a large goal with far-reaching consequences. It was called "Methodist Dollars for Christ," MDFC. Announced at the fall 1959 Conference, it was set for the 1960-1964 Quadrennium. The goal was for $2,100,000, to be allocated for these programs:

1. $375,000 - Church Extension
2. 250,000 - Urban Work
3. 225,000 - Conference Center
4. 100,000 - Wesley Foundation
5. 300,000 - Pennington School
6. 100,000 - Institutions
7. 250,000 - Higher Education
8. 300,000 - Pension Endowment
9. 75,000 - To build a Conference Office
10. 125,000 - Promotion of Program[24]

This ambitious program was truly successful. A total of $2,245,000[25] was subscribed. When the final report was given in 1968, as monies kept trickling in, the total raised was $1,845,228.[26] Something of the accomplishment of MDFC is gathered from this report of District Superintendent William R. Guffick in 1963:

> This campaign has wrought wonders. . . . Through the funds contributed . . . we have: built an attractive dining hall at the Conference Center; constructed a new Conference Office building at Old Orchard; aided churches to erect educational buildings and several sanctuaries. These dollars have made possible a new dining hall at Pennington School and laid the foundation for a new gymnasium. Drew University and Wesley Theological Seminary . . . , Lycoming and Wesley Colleges have been aided. A scholarship has been provided for a young man at Dickinson College.
>
> In addition, we support our share of Wesley Foundation work, ministering to the underprivileged in Trenton, Camden and Atlantic City. We have added to the pension funds of retired ministers and widows. What shall I say more?[27]

Methodist Dollars for Christ gave way in 1964 to the "Future Is Now" program of the Conference. This developed from the report of a Future Needs Survey Committee and sought to raise annually the sum of $182,500 for Conference Advance Specials for urban ministries, church extension, Conference Center, Pennington School, Morristown College and Methodist Hospital. Each church was given a Fair Share Asking.[28] At the final tabulation, a total of $308,280.46 was given for the Future Is Now program.[29]

The establishing of a Conference Office was a significant, forward step in 1950. The office was set up in the Centenary Tabernacle Church, Camden. Miss Dorothy Wolcott was hired as the first office manager at a salary of $2,100. The office remained at Centenary Tabernacle Church until the present office building on Route 70 in Cherry Hill was built in 1963 from funds raised by Methodist Dollars for Christ. December 18, 1963, the old offices in Centenary Tabernacle Church were closed. Goodwill Industries moved the staff and furnishings into the new building which has served the Conference well for the past twenty years. Not only has it served as an office for Conference staff, it has housed a resource center, for a time the Conference historical library and archives, the Old Orchards Church until its present facilities were built next door, and as a central meeting place for numerous Conference boards and agencies.

An earlier chapter told of language work conducted in several places of the Conference in the 1920's. This effort was short-lived. However, in 1955, Spanish work began in the Conference among the Puerto Rican people living in Camden. James Luis Rodriguez, a university student from Puerto Rico, was brought to the states to continue his studies and work among his people. The work began in February, 1955, and used facilities of Broadway Methodist Church in Camden. Mr. Rodriguez conducted Sunday School classes, held services Sunday and Thursday nights and taught an English Class.[30] Much has been done through the years since in working with the Spanish speaking people throughout the Conference. The story will be told more fully in the next chapter.

The *Methodist Relay* began dispensing the news of the New Jersey Conference, February 1956. Originally the voice of the New Jersey Conference, it became an Area-wide paper ten years later with the December, 1965, January, 1966 issue. In the opening Editorial in 1956, Editor Edward S. Zelley, Jr., gave three reasons for the existence of the *Relay*. "It exists," he said, "to report news, inspire the individual and as a spur to action on behalf of the Kingdom of God."[31] In the thirty years that have followed, the *United Methodist Relay*, its current name, continues to convey news, provide inspiration and spur the church to action.

Edward S. Zelley, Jr., Robert J. Beyer, James White, Howard Remaly and Robin A. VanCleef have been the paper's editors through the years. All have performed well a task that is not easy and is heaped upon other duties and numerous responsibilities. Of all who have served so faithfully on the *Relay* staff, Dr. Robert J. Beyer deserves the highest accolades. For seventeen and

First issue of Methodist Relay

a half years, from January of 1959 until his appointment as Northeast District Superintendent in June of 1976, "Bob" Beyer edited the *Methodist Relay*. He made it a paper of value, first for the Conference, then for the Area.

Methodists are great people for celebrating. There always seems to be some significant anniversary to celebrate. The 250th Anniversary of Aldersgate was celebrated in 1963. Methodists everywhere were challenged to seek in Christ to have their hearts "strangely warmed" as did John Wesley in those days of yore.

The New Jersey Conference had its own celebration in 1961. We were one hundred twenty-five years old as a Conference. At the 125th Conference session in Ocean City, September 20 to 24, 1961, significant celebrative events took place under the sponsorship of the Anniversary Committee chaired by the Rev. F. Elwood Perkins, Jr. *The Methodist Trail in New Jersey,* edited by Dr. Frank B. Stanger and associate editor Dr. J. Hillman Coffee, provided the Conference with its first published history, comprised primarily of a capsule history of every local church in the Conference. The two hundred ninety-five page, hard bound volume sold for three dollars a copy. Copy one, volume one was presented to Bishop Corson.

THE METHODIST CHURCH / 243

On Saturday afternoon of Conference, a pilgrimage was made to Cape May. There, in the First Methodist Church, a special session of Conference met in commemoration of the historic 1876 Cape May Conference.[32] Present, besides Bishop Corson, were Bishops Ivan Lee Holt, Edgar A. Love and Nolan B. Harmon. Following Bishop Holt's address, Bishop Corson unveiled the commemorative monument on the grounds of Cape May Church, marking the historic Cape May Conference. The monument was a gift of the laity of the Conference and was presented by Mr. Herbert J. Schoellkopf, Conference Lay Leader.

That afternoon, to the youth on the Music Pier and in two evening performances, Ruth Parsons Strahan's Anniversary Pageant, "The Singing Years," was performed. Some of the scenes were taped for later showing on TV channel six.[33]

At the age of 125, the New Jersey Conference had 107,251 members, with an average Sunday morning attendance of 41,007. Sunday School attendance averaged 46,879. The W.S.C.S. had over 18,000 members, and weekly M.Y.F. meetings drew more than 5,200 youth to our churches. The total valuation of all church buildings, equipment, and land topped $45,000,000.[34]

That celebration over, 1966 brought one of Methodism's Bicentennial observances, the celebration of the 200th Anniversary of Methodist preaching in America. Many attended the Bicentennial celebration in Baltimore that spring which featured celebrative events, historical papers, tours, and an address by President Lyndon B. Johnson.[35]

Prior to the Baltimore celebration, New Jersey Area Methodists, including members of the Christian Methodist Episcopal, African Methodist Episcopal and African Methodist Episcopal Zion Churches, joined in an outstanding worship experience in the Princeton University Chapel in celebration of the Bicentennial. Bishop Prince Albert Taylor, Jr., host bishop and president of the Council of Bishops, presided at the April 17 service. Speaking was Dr. Walker Lee, president of the British Methodist Conference. It is said to have been the first time the president of the British Conference and the president of the American Methodist Council of Bishops ever united in a single service in the United States.[36]

The Bicentennial was celebrated during Conference with an historical address by Dr. Frank B. Stanger, president of Asbury Theological Seminary and a distinguished Conference member. He spoke on "Landmarks That Are Luminous."[37]

From Quadrennial programs which challenged churches and individuals, to the establishing of a Conference Office, initiating a Spanish ministry, developing the *Relay* and celebrating our heritage, must be added the reaching out into what was called "unconventional evangelism." Under the leadership of the Executive Director of Evangelism, Rev. James W. Robinson, the Conference, through its Board of Evangelism, designed programs to reach persons far beyond the walls of the church. These special efforts were especially seen on fairgrounds, in state forests and on the beach and boardwalk of Ocean City. No one will ever know who was reached as Christ's presence was made known to thousands of youth as they flocked to Ocean City's boardwalk, to countless campers at early Sunday morning "come as you are" services in our state forests and parks, and to numerous persons and carnival hands milling around the "Methodist Tent" on the midway of a county fair.[38]

I remember being with Dr. David Randolph, then of Drew University, who with two seminarians spent the week of Cumberland County's fair on the midway at our tent, witnessing for Christ. The carnival workers got to know he was there and appreciated his presence. He stopped his talk one night I was there to speak to an obviously upset young couple. When they left, he told me that the young man was the knife thrower in the carnival act. His attention had been momentarily diverted as he was throwing the knife at "his girl." It knicked her, and frightened them both. Knowing Dr. Randolph was there, they came seeking his help and a word from the Lord.

A momentous event for all of Methodism in New Jersey occurred at the Jurisdictional Conference at Syracuse University in the summer of 1964. Bishop Prince Albert Taylor, Jr., who had been Bishop of Liberia serving in the Central Jurisdiction, was transferred to the Northeastern Jurisdiction as part of the plan to phase out the Central Jurisdiction by 1968. The Jurisdictional Conference changed the Area's boundaries, something it is frequently doing or attempting to do. The New Jersey Area was created in a linking of the two New Jersey Conferences. The Newark Conference lost its Staten Island Churches to New York, and both Conferences' names were changed, effective July 1, 1965, to the Southern and Northern New Jersey Conferences. Bishop Taylor, residing and having his office in Princeton, became the first resident bishop of the New Jersey Area.

Bishop Taylor thus became the fourth resident bishop to lead our Conference following Bishops Berry, Richardson and Corson. All had long tenures. Bishop Taylor and his wife Annie Belle were our spiritual guides for twelve years. They were, of course, the first episcopal couple to reside permanently in New Jersey.[39] Bishop Taylor was also the first black bishop to be appointed in Methodism to lead an essentially white Area. His ministry was received as a brother in Christ, which he was. He served in a difficult time for ministry, but he led us well. His pastoral spirit toward his ministers and churches will long be remembered. His effective leadership in the troublesome days of the civil rights movement and the dark nights of racial unrest in the cities of our state were respected by those far beyond the realm of the church.

Bishop Taylor is a native of Hennessey, Oklahoma. He is a graduate of several schools including Gammon Theological Seminary, Union Theological Seminary and New York University. He was ordained in the North Carolina Conference and served pastorates there. He taught at Bennett and Clark Colleges and Gammon Seminary. From 1948 to 1956, he was editor of the *Central Christian Advocate*. From that post, the Central Jurisdiction elected him to the episcopacy in 1956. His two assignments as bishop were to Liberia and New Jersey. He has served as trustee of numerous institutions and as a member and officer in many responsible positions. These include a term as president of the Board of Directors of Religion in American Life and as a member of Governor Richard Hughes' Select Commission on Civil Disorder. His wife, the former Annie Belle Thaxton, is herself a teacher and active church leader. The Taylor's have one daughter, Isabella.[40] Soon after his arrival in New Jersey, Bishop Taylor presided over his first New Jersey Conference convening in Ocean City, September 16, 1964. This was the last fall conference.

Following closely upon Bishop Taylor's arrival in New Jersey was the dissolution of the black Delaware Conference and the reception of its churches and ministers in the contiguous conferences in which they were located. The Delaware Conference's final session was held April 27 and 28, 1965, in Tindley Temple Methodist Church, Philadelphia. At that time, twenty-four churches were transferred to the Southern New Jersey Conference along with eighteen ministers including one probationer and two retired plus one retired supply preacher and eight ministers' widows.[41] Their transfer was made effective May 13, 1965, and they were welcomed into the New Jersey Conference[42] on the evening of June 9. The welcoming speech was given by District Superintendent Paul A. Friedrich. Hooker D. Davis responded. The official motion was:

BISHOP PRINCE A. TAYLOR, JR.
(1964-1976)

Be it resolved, that we extend a hearty welcome to our brethren, both lay and clergy, from the former Delaware Conference Churches within the bounds of the New Jersey Conference, and express our deepest desire to enter into full Christian fellowship with them and they with us.[43]

The motion was adopted by everyone standing and singing "Blest Be the Tie That Binds."

Bishop Taylor spoke of the very moving experience of the evening. It was. It was a new day for southern New Jersey Methodism and The Methodist Church. The full story will be told in the next chapter.

Part of the excitement of these times within the Conference was a period of new and emerging leadership. No one nor two nor small group of leaders dominated the Conference as had happened at times in the past. It helped produce a vitality not always present nor apparent. No full accounting of these leaders can nor should be given here, for most are still living, and some are still bearing the mantle of leadership and making their mark. Future historians may be able to note with greater accuracy the contributions these leaders have made. A simple listing of their names here, with a brief notation about some, will show who some of our leaders were by virtue of the office they held or their election to General Conference.

Our District Superintendents were Benjamin F. Allgood, who left the Superintendency in 1951 to serve with the Board of National Missions; Ira S. Pimm, who became Headmaster of Pennington School; Herbert J. Smith, one of our elder statesmen; W. Neal Raver; Franklin T. Buck, who later served many years as Executive Secretary of the Board of Missions and Conference Program Counsellor; William R. Guffick, who returned for a second term as Superintendent and was twice minister of Ocean City Church. Dr. Guffick served as a member of five successive General Conferences, 1956 to 1970. No one else, clergy nor lay, was elected to more than two.

Other Superintendents were Albert S. Layton; B. Harrison Decker; Nelson M. Hoffman, who entered the Church Triumphant while serving on the Camden District, May 16, 1960. Then there was F. Elwood Perkins, Jr.; Charles R. Smyth, who served one year and then was elected Headmaster of Pennington; Marvin R. Guice; Ernest W. Lee, who was Superintendent twice on three Districts and also served as Conference Treasurer and Program Counsellor. George R. Propert, Robert E. Acheson, Lawrence G. Atkinson and Paul A. Friedrich were the Superintendents as this period ended.

Two pastors, both of Haddonfield Church, showed their leadership in elections to General Conference. After serving as Jurisdictional Conference delegate in 1952, Lynn H. Corson was elected to the 1956 and 1960 General Conferences before transferring to the Pacific Northwest Conference in 1961. In 1964, while pastoring at First Church Asbury Park, Charles A. Sayre was elected to what was to be the first of seven successive General Conferences he was to attend, the others as Haddonfield's pastor.

Dr. Hammell P. Shipps, Herbert J. Schoellkopf and Robert J. Mumford were the effective Conference Lay Leaders during this period. From 1948 to

1980, Dr. Shipps won election to three General Conferences and to three additional Jurisdictions, showing the esteem in which the Conference laity held this distinguished physician and Christian layman from Delanco Church.

Each of the Conference Woman's Society presidents likewise made her presence felt in the total conference life. All, except Mrs. Janke, who served in this period of the 1950's and 1960's were delegates to General Conference. These presidents were Mrs. O. C. F. (Ethel) Janke, Mrs. W. Orvyl (Evelyn) Schalick, Mrs. George (Christine) Marple, Mrs. E. Emerson (Marguerite) Gardiner, Mrs. Albert (Mabel) Stretch and Mrs. Carlton (Dorothy) Nelson.

Another layman of note was Mr. Howard Stainton of Ocean City. He was a Jurisdictional Conference delegate in 1952, 1960 and 1964 and went to both the General and Jurisdictional Conferences in 1956. This generous, Christian businessman, at his death, left the bulk of his large estate to Pennington School which named its new classroom-office complex the Howard S. Stainton Building.

We single out certain ones among many for mention because of the special quality of the leadership they gave to the Conference or the distinctive office of service to which they were called in the church. This, however, in no wise means to ignore the mark of the faithful pastors in churches large or small, the many who served in Conference positions of all kinds, the faithful lay people of all ages whose faithful attendance, sacrificial giving and loyal service have helped make the church what it is. Would that every name could be written down in a book like this. Glory to God! They are written in the "Lamb's Book of Life."

Numerous kinds of Social Concerns resolutions were passed by Conference vote in these years as Conference sought to speak its concerned, Christian voice on the issues of the day. Thirteen resolutions were adopted on recommendation of the Commission on World Peace and Social Justice in 1951, dealing with such diverse issues as gambling, corruption, McCarthyism's "big lie," communism, disarmament and the Bill of Human Rights. Two years later, the same committee's resolutions supported international control of nuclear bombs, opposed universal military training, communism and fascism. Resolutions supported civil rights, migrant work, and the elimination of the Negro Conference in New Jersey.

The 1957 Conference addressed resolutions to the State Legislature petitioning it to pass a "Sunday Closing Bill," "Grace Before Meals in Public School Bill," and a "Bill to Limit Harness Racing." The District Superintendents urged a renewed concern on the teaching of total abstinence from beverage alcohol.

Gambling was still a concern of the Board of Christian Social Concerns in 1966, but so was drugs in a resolution on LSD. Mental health, traffic safety and fair housing were also brought before the Conference. Strong resolutions were also passed against extremist groups, meaning especially a resurgence of the KKK, on social concerns in Atlantic City and regarding Vietnam and America's escalating involvement.

In browsing through the Conference *Minutes* for these years, one is amazed at the many things which concerned Conference, its churches, people and ministry besides all that has been mentioned. A munitions explosion in 1950 shattered South Amboy and caused extensive damage to our two churches there.

The new Ocean Grove Home, Francis Asbury Manor, which opened November 29, 1949, was dedicated debt free by Bishop Corson, September 8, 1951. In 1962, it was reported that new Homes were being built at Branchville and Ocean City as expansion helped the church serve more of its senior citizens, yet failed to make much of a dent in the long waiting time for admission of most applicants.

The Conference Historical Society entered into a relationship with the Philadelphia Conference in 1951 whereby Old St. George's Church became the first, official depository for the historical records of the Conference. Since then, the depository was moved to a room in the Conference Office, then to a room in Pennington School's Meckler Library, and in 1983, to much enlarged quarters on the first floor of the Bishop's Building on the campus of Pennington School. There, our Historical Library and growing collection of Conference archival material are kept and made available to researchers. One very important part of the Archives is a large collection of church records of all kinds from many of the former churches of the Conference.

Two, long-time servants of the Conference, Rev. Henry L. Bradway and Rev. Edward M. Munyan, retired in 1952. Long a member of the Conference Secretary's Staff, Henry Bradway was a Journalist from 1925 to 1947 and Conference Secretary from 1948 to 1952. Edward M. Munyan served the Conference as its Treasurer from 1937 until his retirement. The 1952 *Minutes* was dedicated in their honor.[44] Elected to fill their positions were Rev. Robert B. Howe, Secretary, and Rev. John B. Kirby, Sr., Treasurer.

Conference met in special session May 2, 1953, in Centenary Tabernacle Church, Camden. The future of Pennington School was at stake. In a series of ten recommendations, Conference affirmed support of Pennington, that it should be continued, that the plant be put in A-1 condition, that the program and curriculum be improved and all grades below seven be eliminated.[45]

Clyde Schaff transferred to the New Jersey Conference and began his fifteen year tenure as Executive Secretary of the Conference Board of Education in 1953.

A relief offering for Korea was requested in 1954 and another the next year to help in flood relief in the Poconos resulting from the devastation caused by Hurricane Hazel. Conference met in 1961 for its 125th session in the aftermath of Hurricane Esther. A severe, March 1962 storm along the coast left many churches and communities in need and resulted in an offering for help in the Philadelphia and Wyoming Conferences as well as in the New Jersey Conference churches.

New Jersey was host Conference to the 1956 Jurisdictional Conference in Ocean City. The 1962 Assembly of Methodist Women was held in Atlantic City's Convention Hall.

Dr. Charles R. Smyth was elected Pennington's Headmaster in 1958, succeeding Ira Pimm. In 1959, the Rev. Eric W. Baker, President of the British Methodist Conference, attended the New Jersey Conference and presided over some sessions. It was "the first time a presiding officer of British Methodism had presided over a Methodist Annual Conference in the United States."[46]

Floods and fire have both destroyed church property in the Conference. In 1963, a forest fire in the pine lands caused much damage to Conference Center, but from the ashes, rose something even better. The 1963 Conference was the last over which native-son Bishop Corson presided.

Conference sessions were moved to June in 1965. We were the last conference in Methodism to move from the fall. July 1 of that year we had a new name, Southern New Jersey Conference.

The ninth Annual Missions Banquet was held in the Holly House, Pennsauken, in 1966. These gatherings which drew hundreds in the 1960's brought much inspiration for mission work.

Recommended Parsonage Standards were adopted in 1966 for the first time. They have since been revised. These standards should be adhered to by every church and parsonage family. They should also be responsibly enforced by the Conference.

As this period ended in 1967, significant changes were in the offering. Conference membership declined that year by 695. That started a decline which has seen us lose ground every year since through 1984, the last figures available at the time of this writing. Structurally Conference voted in 1968 to move to six districts, all but one with a new name. The church would become The United Methodist Church in 1968 with the union of The Methodist and Evangelical United Brethren Churches. Difficult times were also coming. The increasing involvement in Vietnam and the long, hot, violent summers in our cities would shake our country and our state and turn many against any kind of establishment, including the church. Yet, those days, too, would pass and The United Methodist Church in the Southern New Jersey Conference would be at work in ministry in the name of Jesus Christ. We can still say, look at "What God has wrought!"

Chapter 17

OUR ETHNIC CHURCHES

As the Southern New Jersey Conference celebrates its sesquicentennial in 1986, the United Methodist Church is in the second quadrennium of its missional priority emphasis on the Ethnic Minority Local Church. It is the Black, Spanish and Korean Churches which constitute the ethnic minority local churches of this Conference. The history of the Spanish and Korean Churches are of recent origin. The black presence is a long one. To the story of our ethnic churches we now turn.

Black Churches

> We welcome most cordially the members, ministerial and lay, of the former Delaware Conference, who have recently transferred into the Southern New Jersey Conference. The Saviour has said, 'There shall be one fold, and one shepherd' (John 10:16). The coming of these brethren into the family of our Conference will bring to us new warmth of fellowship, increased joy of song, and a widening scope of the Kingdom of God, at a time most significant in the story of our Church and Nation.[1]

These words of greeting by Superintendent Robert E. Acheson welcomed the black churches, ministers and congregations of the former Delaware Conference, into the Southern New Jersey Conference. No longer were there to be white conferences and black conferences. There was one Conference for all Methodist people.

Not all black Methodists belong to the United Methodist Church. There are three, great, black Methodist Churches: the A.M.E. (African Methodist Episcopal), A.M.E.Z. (African Methodist Episcopal, Zion) and the C.M.E. (Christian Methodist Episcopal). Each of these denominations has churches within the bounds of the Southern New Jersey Conference, yet, large numbers of black Methodists remained part of the parent body of Methodism, namely, the Methodist Episcopal Church. Some of this story has already been told, but must be summarized here for purposes of continuity.

Black Methodists were part of the New Jersey Conference from its origin until the Delaware Conference was formed as the first black conference in Methodism in 1864. Separate statistics were kept of white and colored members until 1856. These figures show that at the first session of the New Jersey Conference in 1837, there were 502 colored members. Well over half were in the West Jersey District which comprised Burlington County and those counties to the south.[2] When the last, separate statistics were recorded in 1856, there were 402 colored members.[3]

In 1852, 1855 and annually between 1857 and 1863, a series of conferences of the Colored Local Preachers of the Philadelphia and New Jersey Conferences were held. Bishop Levi Scott usually presided. The session which began August 1, 1861, was held in Mt. Hope Church, Salem, New Jersey. Records of the

MT. HOPE CHURCH, SALEM
Oldest black congregation in SNJ Conference
and Site of 1861 Colored Local Preachers Conference

1857 Conference show that two appointments were made in the New Jersey Conference, one on the Burlington District and one on the Bridgeton District.[4]

Joshua Licorish lists these churches in New Jersey as having been organized prior to the formation of the Delaware Conference in 1864:

    1801   Mt. Hope, Salem.
    1827   Mt. Zion, Lawnside.
    1856   Ferry Avenue, Camden.
    1857   Asbury, Merchantville.
    1859   Berry's Chapel, Quinton.[5]

The formation of the Delaware and other black Conferences provided for the ordination and conference membership of black preachers, serving under presiding elders of their own kind. It gave leadership and status to black Methodists. Other than as missionary bishops, it took until 1920 before Negro bishops were allowed to be elected, but blacks from 1868 on sat as full members of the Methodist Episcopal General Conference. The Delaware Conference has a great history that needs to be told fully.

The Delaware Conference was organized by Bishop Edmund S. Janes, July 29, 1864, at John Wesley Chapel, predecessor of Tindley Temple, in Philadelphia. Rev. Wilmore S. Elsey was elected Conference Secretary. The Conference boundaries included Delaware, the eastern shore of Maryland and Virginia, eastern Pennsylvania, New Jersey, and the region to the north. The Conference was made up of "the colored preachers who had been traveling within the bounds of the Philadelphia and New Jersey Conferences."[6]

There were eleven charter members: Isaac Henson (16),[7] James Davis (15), Harrison Smith (12), Isaiah Brighton (10), John Manluff (10), Samuel Dale (8), Frost Pollett (7), Wilmore Elsey (6), Jehu Pierce (5), Nathan Young (4), and Joshua Brinkley (3). Ten others were admitted on trial. A Conference Missionary Society with Frost Pollett as president was organized.[8]

Altogether, the new conference reported a total membership of 4,871 with 34 churches valued at $38,000. There were also 21 Sunday Schools with 151 officers and teachers and 841 scholars.[9] In one year, there was an increase of 1,633 members.[10]

The appointments listed for New Jersey, all in the Delaware River District with Isaac Henson as presiding elder, were these:

```
Camden - Robert Robinson  - 4 Churches - 220 members
Salem   - Harrison Smith  - 2 Churches - 95 members
Springtown -              - 2 Churches - 46 members
Goshen and Cold Spring    - 2 Churches - 32 members[11]
```

An example of the growth of black Methodism in New Jersey can be seen by a perusal of the *Minutes*. In 1875, Salem, Goshen, Bridgeton and Mount Zion in Lawnside were the appointments on the Philadelphia District with 475 members. By 1900, there were 965 members reported for New Jersey. The appointments were to Atlantic City, Bridgeton, Bridgeton Circuit, Burlington, Camden, Cape May, Delair, Merchantville, Mount Holly, Magnolia, Salem and Salem Circuit. In 1925, there were two churches in Atlantic City, Asbury and Hamilton Memorial. Grenlock and Rhodes were added. Churches are also listed for Ocean City, Pleasantville, Swainton and Woodbury. In 1940 this was the record.

Church	Members	Sunday School	No. Schools
Atlantic City: Asbury	921	289	
Atlantic City: Hamilton	138	145	
Bridgeton	146	130	
Camden	242	86	
Cape May-Swainton	119	69	2
Delair	36	147	
Fordville	158	165	
Grenlock and Rhodes	63	36	2

Church	Members	Sunday School	No. Schools
Lawnside	273	198	
Merchantville	148	143	
Mt. Holly	47	49	
Ocean City	32	20	
Pleasantville	101	122	
Port Norris	10	65	
Quinton-Springtown	111	120	2
Salem	159	188	
Woodbury	101	75	
Totals	2805	2047	6

Several sessions of the Delaware Conference were held in New Jersey churches, five hosted by Asbury Church in Atlantic City. They were in 1901, 1915, 1922, 1927 and 1937. Others in New Jersey were held at Mt. Hope Church, Salem, in 1871, Ferry Avenue Church, Camden in 1907 and Franklin Street Church, Cape May in 1918.[12]

Dr. William C. Jason, Jr., prominent layman and historian of the Delaware Conference, in an article "The History and Contribution of the Delaware Conference," said:

> As men and money go, size of membership, outstanding scholarship, large donations, the Delaware Conference was not great. But for stirring up those for whom no one cared; teaching Christ as the doctor to salvation, decency, and dignity; living on little; moving up in qualifications generation by generation, affording opportunity to the willing and able; remaining loyal to the main stream of Methodism through good and evil days, the Delaware Conference was very great. Its record is void of shame. Wrong in principle, it was right in practice, for aside from baptizing and burying the dead of a confused and troubled people, it ever pointed them individually and collectively to the more excellent way of faith wedded to works. Many of us have believed and followed.[13]

Two of the outstanding ministers of the Delaware Conference in its one hundred one year history were Noah W. Moore, Jr. and Charles Albert Tindley. Born in Newark, New Jersey, Noah W. Moore, Jr., was elected bishop in 1960. The only other Delaware Conference member to be elected bishop was Alexander P. Camphor, elected a missionary bishop in 1916. Bishop Moore pastored several churches, including Zoar Church and Tindley Temple, Philadelphia, before his election to the episcopacy. In the Central Jurisdiction, Bishop Moore administered the Louisiana, Texas and West Texas Conferences. After 1968, he was bishop of the Nebraska Area. Upon his retirement, Bishop and Mrs. Moore moved to Atlantic City.[14] He is recognized as an honorary member of the Southern New Jersey Conference.

Charles Albert Tindley, eminent pastor, pulpiteer and gospel song writer, pastored Tindley Temple Church, Philadelphia from 1902 until his death in 1933. In 1902, the church had four hundred members. At his death, the membership was more than seven thousand. It was one of the largest Methodist churches in the world. At one time, as a young man, Charles Tindley was sex-

REV. C. ALBERT TINDLEY
Noted Delaware Conference preacher and gospel song writer,
began his ministry in Franklin Street Church, Cape May

ton of the church he later pastored. Tindley's first appointment as a preacher was to Franklin Street Church, Cape May, New Jersey, 1885 and 1886. In 1888, he was appointed as a missionary in New Jersey to canvass the area for more black Methodists. His hymn "Stand By Me" is in the United Methodist Hymnal.[15]

The last session of the Delaware Conference was held in Tindley Temple Methodist Church, Philadelphia, April 27 and 28, 1965. At that time, the following churches were transferred to the Southern New Jersey Conference.

CHURCH	MINISTER
BRIDGETON DISTRICT	
Bridgeton: John Wesley	Howard E. Anderson
Cape May: Franklin Street	Adolphus A. Berry
Swainton: John Wesley	Adolphus A. Berry
Fordville: St. John	William M. Tasco
Port Norris: John Wesley	John E. Bishop
Quinton: Haven	Gilbert A. Sherman
Salem: Mt. Hope	Cyrus W. Derrickson

OUR ETHNIC CHURCHES / 255

Camden District

Atlantic City: Asbury	George H. McMurray
Atlantic City: Hamilton Memorial	Charles E. Kiah
Camden: Eighth Street	Charles I. Young, A.S.[16]
Camden: Ferry Avenue	Clarence W. Bagwell
Westmont: Rhodes Temple	Clarence W. Bagwell
Lawnside: Mt. Zion	O'Connell Milbourne
Pleasantville: Asbury	Charles P. Spencer
Ocean City: Macedonia	Charles P. Spencer
Woodbury: Mt. Zion	Stephen G. Fullman, A.S.
Jericho: Wesley	Stephen G. Fullman
Blackwood: Solomon Wesley	Stephen G. Fullman

New Brunswick District

Spring Lake: St. John's	Howard S. Franklin, P.T.S.P.[17]

Trenton District

Burlington: St. Mary's	Horace J. Fisher, A.S.
Delair: St. Matthew's	George E. Geddis
Merchantville: Asbury	Charles W. S. Cannon
Mt. Holly: St. Paul's	Walter L. Gray
Trenton: Asbury	Frederick D. Arnold[18]

In addition, Wesley Church at Springtown near Greenwich in Cumberland County was transferred as an abandoned Church. In 1967, it was sold for five hundred dollars to St. John's Baptist Church with the proceeds going to Haven Church.[19]

Besides those ministers noted above, Rev. Hooker D. Davis was transferred as Executive Secretary of Urban Work with the Southern New Jersey Conference Board of Missions. Cyrus W. Perry and Lucius E. Jordan were transferred as retired ministers. Rev. Leslie W. Cottrane transferred as a retired supply pastor.

Also transferred to Southern New Jersey were these eight ministers' widows: Mrs. Douglas M. (Isabelle) Collins, Mrs. Elmer W. (Dorothy) Dean, Mrs. James M. (Josie) Dickerson, Mrs. W. J. (Mary) Helm, Mrs. Paul C. (Dorothy) Jackson, Mrs. Francis C. (Lillie) Laws, Mrs. William R. (Ella) Price and Mrs. Fred R. (Martha) Richardson.[20]

What has happened in the years since the merger of the Delaware Conference and the disolution of the segregated Central Jurisdiction? Much, of course. For one thing, the quota system, plus intentionality, has placed blacks as well as other ethnics, in leadership roles across the denomination. Blacks have been appointed to key leadership roles they did not have before. Second, the fear of some that blacks could not achieve status in certain sections of the Church, has been at last partially alleviated with the election of Bishop Ernest W. Newman by the Southeastern Jurisdiction in 1984. He was the first black bishop elected by that Jurisdiction. Third, the Episcopal elections of 1984 brought five new blacks, including the first black woman bishop, a Hispanic and an Asian into United Methodism's highest office. There are now thirteen ethnic minority persons serving as bishops. "There are now more ethnic minority individuals in top leadership positions in the United Methodist Church than in any other predominantly White Protestant body."[21] Woodie W. White, formerly head of the General Commission on Religion and Race, was one of those elected bishop. He said, "The denomination now has more Blacks in leadership positions than it would have if the former racially segregated Central Jurisdiction had continued to elect its own Black Leaders."[22] Fourth, the Ethnic Minority Local Church missional priority of the last two quadrennium has necessarily and purposely focused the attention of the Church upon the needs and opportunities of black and other ethnic minority local churches. The goal of complete open itineracy has not been realized, yet, great strides have been made. One day we shall be one.

In the Southern New Jersey Conference, competent blacks have assumed leadership roles. At the first election of General and Jurisdictional Conference delegates after 1965, the Rev. Hooker D. Davis headed the list of clergy delegates elected to the Jurisdictional Conference. This was 1968. In 1972 and 1980 he was elected to General Conference, and in 1976 both he and Rev. Ernest Lyght were elected to the Jurisdictional Conference. Laymen William A. Kirk and Elwood Davis were elected Jurisdictional Conference delegates twice, William Kirk in 1972 and 1980 and Elwood Davis in 1972 and 1976. Alice Moore was also a Jurisdictional Conference delegate in 1976. Two blacks have also been reserve Jurisdictional Conference delegates, Mrs. Sudie Nichols in 1976 and Mr. Carl Still in 1980. One can also look at the officers and members of Conference Boards and Agencies and see the role blacks have assumed in their new Conference. Hooker Davis was also appointed the first black Superintendent in the Conference in 1969. He headed the Southwest District for six years.

Yet, black Methodists, like the rest, have suffered from the malaise that has affected the Church since the late 1960's. The need for renewal, revival, growth is evident everywhere. There has been a decline in membership of about five hundred in the black churches between 1965 and 1983, and there are fewer of them. Most of the decline is in the Atlantic City churches. The largest black churches in the Conference in 1983 were Trenton: Cadwalader-Asbury with 319 members, Lawnside with 292, Asbury in Atlantic City with 260 and Asbury, Merchantville with 259.

Black pastoral leadership in the Conference has declined. A 1982 report of the Board of Ordained Ministry revealed only seven black churches staffed by full time pastors. At that time the Southern New Jersey Conference had only five black elders, two probationary members and two full time local pastors. In addition, there were four part time local pastors, a student pastor and a retired pastor serving as a supply.[23] The goal that was established was for a total of "10 full/probationary black members of the Conference by December 1984."[24] Intentional means of recruitment were established. This goal was not reached, but progress was encouraging. Likewise, the goal of open itineracy is not yet realized, though important strides have been made.

Through the more than twenty black churches of the Conference, their ministers, and those serving in and belonging to integrated churches, the black presence is keenly and meaningfully felt in the life of the Southern New Jersey Conference.

Spanish Ministries

Chapter 16 told of the beginning of Spanish work in the New Jersey Conference in 1955. Through the efforts of Nelson M. Hoffman, Conference Missionary Secretary, James Luis Rodriquez was recruited in Puerto Rico. While continuing his studies in this country, he instituted a work among the Puerto Rican people of Camden. Broadway Church became the center for this early Spanish work. Sunday School classes, evening worship services, English classes and summer camps for children were all part of the ministry emphasized.[25]

A year later, the Board of Missions reported the success of the work in Camden. Mr. Antonio Valentin, a member of First Church, Vineland, started a work there. A Spanish service in Harrisonville Church for summer migrant workers was held. For many years the migrant ministry, often under the aegis of the New Jersey Council of Churches, was an important ministry. The Trenton District Missionary Society was exploring the possibility of starting a Spanish ministry there.[26]

For many years, especially during the episcopal leadership of Bishop Corson whose work embraced Puerto Rico, the island of Puerto Rico was seen as an important mission work of the Conference. In 1958, every church was asked to assume a World Service Advance Special for Puerto Rico. It seemed natural to some, therefore, that a Spanish ministry be developed in New Jersey among those emigrating from Puerto Rico. In time, Cuban, Haitian and other Spanish speaking peoples came to live here.

By 1957, the work in Trenton was under way in Central Church under the leadership of Rev. Agripino Perez.[27] Work in Camden languished a while after Rev. Rodriquez left. It was revived in 1961 with the arrival of Rev. Jorge Leyva,[28] a member of the Cuban Conference. He served very effectively in work centered at Camden's Broadway Church until he transferred to the Rio Grande Conference in 1966. The Camden Methodist Missionary Society purchased a parsonage for the Leyva's at 627 Clinton Street.

Three Spanish ministers, all Conference members, were ministering in our Conference in 1965. Jorge Leyva was in Camden. Julio Gomez started his long ministry in Trenton which he is still carrying out in 1984. Julio transferred from the Cuban Conference which he had joined in 1958. The third minister to come in 1965 was Rev. Francisco F. Sanfiel. He started the Spanish mission in Keyport in 1965 before moving to Camden in 1973 and transferring to Florida in 1974.

Rev. Emerson W. Rubio arrived in 1967 from Spain where he and his family had fled from Cuba. A member of the Cuban Conference, he transferred to the Southern New Jersey Conference in 1968 and began his long pastorate to the Spanish people of the Lakewood Area.

District Superintendent Paul A. Friedrich in his 1967 Composite Report says: "We will have five Spanish speaking ministers in this Conference next year, a most commendable effort and one which has received national recognition. The work in Camden, Trenton, Atlantic City, Keyport, Long Branch, Bradley Beach and Lakewood is effective as a witness of the church and for the church."[29] The five men were Julio Gomez in Trenton, Francisco Sanfiel in Keyport, Eugene Madeira and Ramon Martinez in Camden and Emerson Rubio in Lakewood. The work in the Long Branch-Asbury Park area began and has continued as a joint ministry with the Presbyterian Church.

Perfecto Romero joined our Conference in 1969 and was the Spanish minister in Bradley Beach until he transferred to the Ohio Conference in 1973.

The Spanish ministry in the Conference, by the mid 1970's, settled down into four main areas: Camden, Trenton, Keyport and Lakewood. Work has also continued with the Presbyterians in the greater Asbury Park-Long Branch area. A real problem in the latter place has been to find a suitable location for ministry in the area of the greatest concentration of Spanish people. For a while, Central Church in Bridgeton hosted a Spanish ministry with some support from the Conference.

Spanish ministry has moved slowly, but under qualified and dedicated leadership. There is a great mobility among these people. Large numbers of them are unskilled laborers; therefore, they are on the bottom end of the economic ladder and most apt to suffer unemployment in bad times. Yet, the work has progressed. In 1980, the first Spanish church was organized in the Conference: El Buen in Camden with Ezequiel Gonzalez as pastor. Two years later, El Redentor Church in Camden was the second to be organized with Jeremias Rojas as minister. This church resulted from a merger of the Fairview Church with the Fairview Spanish Congregation. These two Spanish churches were combined in 1983 as the Spanish Parish under the pastoral leadership of Jeremias Rojas. In 1983, the twenty year ministry in Trenton of Julio Gomez was rewarded with the organizing of the Trenton Spanish Church. The Keyport Spanish mission became El Mesias Church at the 1985 Conference session with Rev. Ezequiel E. Gonzalez as pastor. The Lakewood ministry is served by Emerson Rubio.[30]

A Hispanic Ministries Study Committee report adopted by the 1983 Conference set some significant goals for Hispanic ministries in the Conference by 1986. These call for the developing of two additional Hispanic ministries; an increase to six full or probationary Hispanic clergy members; the identification of three Hispanic candidates for Diaconal Ministry; and a plan for the training of Hispanic Lay Speakers.[31] These are modest goals, but their fulfillment can have far-reaching consequences in extending the gospel to the Hispanic people and in incorporating us all in the oneness that is God's Kingdom.

Hispanic ministry in United Methodism reached a long-sought height in July, 1984, when the Western Jurisdictional Conference, on the fourteenth ballot, elected United Methodism's first Hispanic bishop. Bishop Elias G.

Galvan, a Mexican-American, won that honor. He had been a council director in the Pacific and Southwest Conference.[32]

The Southern New Jersey Conference has a thirty year history of Spanish or Hispanic work. It seems the day is near for it to take its rightful place as a recognized part of Southern New Jersey United Methodism.

KOREAN CHURCHES

The year 1977 brought to this Conference the first of four new congregations of a people and language few knew were here in any sizeable numbers. These are Asiatic-Americans from the Republic of South Korea. Large numbers have settled throughout the Southern New Jersey Conference area. Most tend to be of the professional class. They are well educated, highly trained, skilled and a most dedicated people. Their stewardship and level of involvement in their church is truly amazing. In four successive years, four Korean United Methodist congregations were organized in the Southern New Jersey Conference. Their history is so new that it is more nearly current events than history. Only a few, bare facts can be told. Yet, in these emerging, new congregations of Korean United Methodists, we rejoice with wonder and say, "look at 'what God has wrought!' "

It was at the 1977 Conference that we were introduced to the first Korean congregation and met the first Korean members of Conference. At this Conference, the Korean United Methodist Church of New Brunswick received the Certificate of Organization. Rev. Sung Eun Park was received from the Korean Methodist Church. Jong Keun You was the first Korean lay member of Conference.[33] Rev. Park served this congregation until 1981. He retired in 1982 Following Rev. Park, In Hwan Kim, a full time lay pastor, has served this congregation which meets in the First United Methodist Church of New Brunswick. In 1983, they reported 121 members.

Almost as soon as Conference adjourned in 1977, Northeast District Superintendent, Robert J. Beyer, with the co-operation of the Northern Cluster of Churches, set in motion the plans which resulted in the formation of the Korean United Methodist Church of Monmouth County. This church was officially received as an organized United Methodist Church by Bishop White at the 1978 Conference. The Certificate of Organization was presented to Rev. Dong-Chan Chang and the Lay Member, Mrs. On Kyong Rhee.[34] Pastor Chang served this growing congregation until his appointment in 1984 as Professor in the Methodist Theological Seminary, Seoul, Korea. He was followed as pastor by Rev. Sun Ryang Kim. This church in 1983 reported 129 members. They have been worshipping in the First United Methodist Church of Red Bank.

The First Korean United Methodist Church of Cherry Hill, meeting in the Conference Office Building, was welcomed in 1979.[35] Rev. Ik Soo Park was their founding pastor. He came to this Conference from the Korean East Conference. In 1983, they reported a membership of 107. They meet now in the Old Orchards United Methodist Church.

The fourth Korean Church received its Certificate of Organization in 1980. Organized as the Korean United Methodist Church of South Jersey, they worshipped in the First United Methodist Church of Mays Landing. Bishop White presented the organization certificate to their pastor, Rev. Ik Soo Park and two laymen, Dr. Yhop Y. Lee and Dr. Zae Uh Shim.[36] Rev. Hoon K. Lee then assumed the duties as pastor. This congregation reported 66 members in 1983. A year later they moved to Pleasantville.

Altogether these four, growing congregations had a combined membership of 423 in 1983. At least one of them has plans for building its own church.

OTHER ETHNIC WORK

The vagaries of immigration have brought many kinds of people to the Garden State. To some of them, it has been our privilege to minister in the name of Jesus Christ in days past. Chapter 10 tells briefly the story of some of this language work done by churches of the Conference in the 1920's and early 1930's. In the rural community of Lake, in Trenton and other places, there was work with Italians. Polish speaking people were ministered to in Millville. There was an Armenian and Russian ministry going on in Camden. Kaighn Avenue Church in Camden was ministering, said the Superintendent, "to a greater variety of people than were present at Pentecost." That was in 1921. Sunday Schools for five different nationalities were going on at the same time at Seabrook Farms near Bridgeton.[37]

It has been a kaleidoscope of people to whom the Methodists of Southern New Jersey have sought to minister in the past sixty-five years. It has truly been a "rainbow coalition" of nationalities and races. In recent times, churches of the Conference have sponsored refugee families from Vietnam, Cambodia, Afghanistan and Central American countries. A few years back, it was Hungarian refugees, and a bit earlier, people from war-torn areas of Europe. But that has been part of the dream of America. Our country is seen as a place of refuge, hope and a better life for huddled masses of all kinds "yearning to breathe free." That is the symbol for which the Statue of Liberty stands in New York's harbor. Christians understand the meaning of freedom in a deeper sense, too, as expressed by St. Paul: "For freedom Christ has set us free; stand fast therefore, and do not submit again to a yoke of slavery."[38]

In recent years, this Conference has not only ministered to those of ethnic minority peoples, but we have received ministries from them. Ethnic minority clergy have come to be our pastors, and not only to those of their own race or nationality. Sydney Sadio came to New Jersey from the Methodist Church in the Caribbean and the Americas in 1977 and has served Highland Park and Hightstown. In 1984, Reverend Sadio was elected a delegate to the Jurisdictional Conference. Dr. George T. Wang of the Singapore Conference also joined the Southern New Jersey Conference in 1977. He has served as an associate minister at Pitman and as the minister of Central Church in Bridgeton. In 1983, he was appointed Superintendent of the Southeast District, only the second ethnic minority Superintendent in our Conference's history.

As the Conference looks ahead to the last decade of the twentieth century and beyond, it is hoped that such programs as the Ethnic Minority Local Church Priority and the plans for the recruitment and training of ethnic minority pastoral leadership, will enhance not only the ministry of ethnic churches but also that of the entire Conference. We all have much to offer each other. We need to glory in our common heritage as United Methodists as well as in the separate traditions and backgrounds from which we come. We need to accept what each has to offer: male, female; black, white, Hispanic, Asian; Spanish, Korean, Chinese or English language. Where the gifts of leadership match the talents and skills of a person, there she or he ought to serve. The goals of inclusiveness and open itineracy must become more than mere statements of idealistic dreams. They must become a reality in our common life. This is not a utopian hope. It is an injunction of the Bible in which we all believe. "In Christ Jesus you are all sons [and daughters] of God, through faith. . . . There is neither Jew nor Greek, there is neither slave nor free, there is neither male nor female; for you are all one in Christ Jesus."[39]

Chapter 18

INSTITUTIONS OF THE CHURCH

This chapter will try to draw together some of the history of the Conference Institutions: Pennington School, the ill-fated South Jersey Institute in Vineland, the United Methodist Homes, including the former Bancroft-Taylor Home, the Deaconess Home in Camden, now called the Neighborhood Center, and the Conference Center, including the former Boys Camp, now known as Tumethca. Some of it has already been told; much has not. A lot more ought to be said about each of these institutions. Will someone rise to the challenge and do the work necessary to tell the full story of our Conference Institutions?

Pennington School

Pennington School was founded as a direct result of an action taken at the first session of the New Jersey Conference in 1837 when the presiding elders were appointed "a Committee to receive proposals for the Establishment of two Seminaries of Learning within the bounds of the New Jersey Conference." It was intended that one be a male and the other a female academy. The 1838 Conference decided that the "Jersey locality offering the largest subscription for the school would receive it." Rev. John Knox Shaw, Pennington's pastor, secured the most subscriptions, about $5,000, and the 1839 Conference voted to put its school in Pennington.[1]

Within a month of the close of the 1839 Conference, the cornerstone of Pennington School was laid with Bishops Hedding and Waugh in attendance. The school was incorporated, and work on its construction continued in earnest. Members of the first Board of Trustees were Absalom Blatchly, M.D. of Pennington, President; Henry P. Welling, M.D., Secretary; Joseph Bunn, Treasurer; Henry Higgins, Rosewell Howe, Joshua Bunn and Major Benjamin Van Cleve.[2] Augustine Van Kirk was the architect in the building of "Old Main."

While 1838 is considered the year of the school's founding, it was in October 1840 that Pennington Seminary, called the "Methodist Episcopal Male Seminary," formally opened with Howard Bishop as teacher, Rev. Edward Cooke, D.D., as Principal and three students: John Wesley Bunn, Archibald Higgins and Samuel Titus.[3] To Dr. Cooke must go the credit for launching the school. When he arrived, there were but three students; the building was incomplete, "no furniture, no library, no apparatus, bare and half-finished walls being all that greeted us." By the end of the first term, there were eleven students. When he left Pennington in 1847, there were fifty.

The Rev. Dr. Stephen M. Vail of the New York Conference was elected in the spring of 1847 to succeed Dr. Cooke as the school's principal. He stayed only two years, but left his mark at Pennington.[4]

When Dr. Vail resigned in July of 1849, the third principal to be elected was Dr. J. Townley Crane, graduate of Princeton and member of the New Jersey Conference. Much happened during his administration. Pennington was founded on a joint stock principal. The stock holders, apparently expecting to make a profit and finding that no dividends were likely to be paid, sold the school to three men from Pennington for $7,000, about half of its original cost. Conference, however, bought it back for the same sum. May 1, 1850, the school became the property of the Conference. In its reorganization, the Trustees were to be composed of an equal number of ministers and laymen, and included New Jersey's Governor, George F. Fort.[5] Lack of finances continued to plague the school. Attempts to raise funds from the Conference met with feeble success. Facing a debt of $12,205.27 in 1858, Conference voted to raise $5,000 by apportionment of the churches. Only about one half was actually paid, but Conference, as a whole, for the first time really began to back its school.

In 1853, the school's name was changed to Pennington Seminary and Female Collegiate Institute. A new wing was added to the school. The first female students were accepted in the spring of 1853.

Isaac W. Wiley, missionary to China, educator and later bishop, became the fourth principal of Pennington in 1858. He added a theology class for those students interested in the ministry and saw to the building of Pennington's first gymnasium in 1862. Dr. Wiley left the school in 1863 to return to the pastorate. He was elected Editor of *The Ladies Repository* in 1864 and bishop in 1872.[6]

Dr. Daniel Clark Knowles, a graduate of Pennington and of Wesleyan University, became the School's fifth principal, serving from 1863 to 1867. During his first three years, eighty-two students joined Pennington Church, and twelve others joined elsewhere. For the first time in its history, it was announced in 1866 that Pennington was free of debt. Dr. Cooke, the first principal wrote, "Fortunate Institution! Well done N. J. Methodists."[7] That accomplishment was short-lived. The trustees bought additional land and enlarged the facilities. By 1877, the debt reached $40,195.21.[8]

Kenneth Anderson, in describing life at the school before the Civil War says that in 1840, the cost of board was $100 per annum including room rent, furniture, fuel, washing, care of clothing and lights. Tuition was $20 per annum for common English branches, $30 for higher English, mathematics and modern languages.[9]

Charles P. Whitecar of the Class of 1845, in reminiscing about life at Pennington said, "Nor must I fail to make mention of Uncle Noah and Aunty Tindall. . . . They were the confectioners per excellence of the town. Aunty baked the sweetest ginger-bread and most luscious pies, and over her counter, in exchange therefor, passed all the loose change we had."[10]

When Dr. Knowles resigned in 1867, his place was taken by Dr. Thomas O'Hanlon. Except for a four year period, 1872 to 1876, when Rev. Joseph A. Dilks was principal, Dr. O'Hanlon served as Pennington's head until 1902, a total of thirty-one years. He saw the school through many building and curriculum changes, started an endowment and worked on the debt problem.

Pennington School
Photo taken 1946

In 1877, Dr. O'Hanlon ran the school as president on a "Lease Arrangement." He paid $2,150 per year to lease the school. This was taken to help liquidate the debt. On the 50th Anniversary of the opening of the school in 1890, a concerted effort was made to eliminate the debt. The Trustees, largely through Dr. O'Hanlon's efforts, raised $20,000. Churches of the Conference contributed $13,716.43 and the debt was cancelled.[11] The need for improvements, however, soon had the school in debt once more. Conference, in 1901, near the end of Dr. O'Hanlon's presidency, reported the cost of new buildings at $70,000. Upon his retirement, there was a debt of about $50,000, but the campus and buildings were in good condition. The Shaw Memorial Chapel was dedicated in 1903 in memory of the founding pastor, Rev. John Knox Shaw.[12] It is said that Dr. O'Hanlon trained over six hundred young men for the Christian ministry.

Historian Anderson, in a chapter titled "Did You Ever Set the Bell A-Ringing Wildly?" writes about student life in the 1880's and 1890's. One of the important features of student life was the semi-secret literary societies, the Alpha-Omega, Philomathean and Calligogian. Football and baseball began to be played during this period with Pennington usually having strong teams. Dr. Edwin Forrest Hann of the Class of '97 reminisced about some of the well-known graduates during his four years at Pennington. They included Adna Leonard, bishop of the Methodist Episcopal Church; Eugene Grace, head of the Bethlehem Steel Corporation; Charles Morris, missionary to Korea; Miriam Lee Early, head of the Dramatic Department of Swarthmore College and Dr. Damon Phieffer, internationally known surgeon and Chief of Staff at Lankenau Hospital. Dr. Hann himself was a distinguished minister in the New Jersey Conference.[13]

Following Dr. O'Hanlon's long term as president, three different men held office between 1903 and 1910. Rev. James W. Marshall, D.D., left the pastorate of Broadway Church, Camden, to take charge of Pennington in the fall of 1903. Pennington then had one hundred sixteen boarding students and fifty-one day students. An estimated 15,000 students had attended Pennington since its founding, 1,200 of whom entered the Methodist ministry.[14] Ill health forced Dr. Marshall's retirement October 31, 1904.

Dr. Marshall's replacement was Rev. Frank Moore. This distinguished pastor of the New Jersey Conference served one year as Dean before being elevated to the presidency. In three years, the school's enrollment increased from 82 to 245. He received a salary of $2,500 plus the privilege of the Seminary table. During one of his years, the Pennington football team outscored its opposition 199 to 0. Dr. Moore resigned in 1909 when he was appointed by Governor Franklin Fort as Superintendent of the State Reformatory at Rahway, a position he held until his retirement in 1938.

Dr. J. Morgan Read, another distinguished New Jersey Conference minister and District Superintendent, was inaugurated as the tenth president of Pennington, October 13, 1909. Poor health forced his retirement after only one year of service. Pennington became a boys only school in 1910, while Centenary Institute in Hackettstown became a girls school.[15]

Dr. J. B. Haines served as acting president of Pennington until the election of Dr. Frank MacDaniel of the Newark Conference in December of 1910. Dr. MacDaniel was the first to be called Headmaster. It was a period of extreme financial stress. There was talk of closing the school, but the institution of a "Forward Movement Fund" in 1913 raised over $100,000 in subscriptions in six months and the school took on new life. A new gymnasium with a swimming pool was started in 1911. An Infirmary was built in 1915. During the first World War, compulsory military training was instituted for the boys.[16] During Dr. MacDaniel's term, he had such distinguished members of the Board of Trustees as ex-Governor John F. Fort and Mrs. Thomas A. Edison.

Dr. MacDaniel resigned in 1920 and Dr. Francis Harvey Green, aged 60, was elected the twelfth Headmaster to begin in 1921. He served as the esteemed head of Pennington School for the next twenty-two years. His was the second longest tenure as Pennington's Headmaster. In 1921, boarding students paid $700 to $800 a year, day students $150.[17] Dr. Green was highly acclaimed as a speaker, after-dinner wit and preacher. He was a literary man who brought many fine scholars to the school. His affection for his boys was one of his strong elements. Two of Pennington's graduates of the 1930's went on to stardom in athletics. Nick Basca, Class of 1935, played for the Philadelphia Eagles before his death in World War II. Frank Hayes of the Class of 1933 was a major league catcher for twelve years with the Philadelphia A's, St. Louis Browns and Cleveland Indians.[18]

Hard times hit Pennington during the Depression of the 1930's. Conference held a special session at the school June 23, 1932, to discuss the financial situation. It was decided that Conference would endeavor to raise $10,000 a year for the next three years for the school. The Trustees were to raise the balance needed for current expenses.[19] John A. Sparks died Janaury 1934, leaving a large estate to Pennington, to which Mrs. Sparks left additional sums. The value of their endowment, May 1959, was $1,700,743.[20] The financial future of Pennington seemed assured as the school celebrated its Centennial, November 5-7, 1938.

At the age of eighty-two, Dr. Francis Harvey Green retired as Headmaster in 1943. His place was taken by Dr. Joseph Wentworth Seay who served two years. Nineteen Pennington graduates lost their lives in World War II, including Bishop Adna Leonard who died in a plane crash while on a preaching mission.[21] When Dr. Seay resigned, December 1945, Dr. Green was called back to serve as Acting Headmaster until another could be secured.

The fourteenth Headmaster assumed office in May of 1946. He was Rev. J. Rolland Crompton, who had been District Superintendent of the Wilkes Barre District in the Wyoming Conference. Dr. Crompton served for nearly five years before resigning February 1951, to become Headmaster of a school in Tilton, New Hamspshire. In the mid 1940's, Pennington accepted students as low as the second grade. By 1950, second and third grades were dropped.

Soon the sixth grade was the lowest accepted.[22] When Rev. Crompton assumed office, the school had 173 boarding and 65 day students. At the end of 1948, one of Pennington's institutions, Joseph "Pop" Martin, resigned as the school baker after sixty years service.

A New Jersey Conference minister, Dr. Ira S. Pimm, was elected the fifteenth Headmaster to succeed Rev. Crompton. This former Trenton District Superintendent began at once to put Pennington in top condition. A Survey Committee chaired by Charles R. Smyth brought its report to a special session of the Annual Conference in Centenary Tabernacle Church, Camden, May 2, 1953. Conference affirmed its support of the school and that it be continued. The physical plant was to be put in A-1 condition, the program and curriculum were to be improved, and all grades below seven were to be eliminated.[23]

Dr. Charles R. Smyth, Bridgeton District Superintendent and the first alumnus since Dr. Frank Moore in 1903, was elected Pennington's Headmaster in 1958. For the next twelve years he untiringly worked for his school, rejuvenating it in every way. Major rebuilding during the Smyth era included a new dining room and kitchen in 1961, new gymnasium and swimming pool in 1964, and a new dormitory with faculty quarters built in 1968.[24] Coach Harold Pone retired as Coach and School Athletic Director in 1969. His teams had far exceeded one hundred victories each in football, basketball and baseball.[25]

Conference support continued in a substantial way for Pennington. Methodist Dollars for Christ, begun in 1960, contributed $300,000 to Pennington.[26] The Future Is Now Conference campaign, authorized in 1964, brought another $25,000 to the school.[27]

April 25, 1963, the 125th Anniversary was celebrated with a Convocation on "Religion In Education." It was marked as a special session of the New Jersey Conference. Bishop Corson and Bishop Paul N. Garber, President of the General Board of Education of The Methodist Church, delivered the major addresses. During the Convocation, Bishops Corson and Garber officiated at the ground-breaking for the new gymnasium and student center.[28]

August 1, 1970, Dr. Smyth retired. His place was taken by a former missionary to India, Vice President for Academic Affairs of West Virginia Wesleyan College and son of a New Jersey Conference parsonage, Dr. Nelson M. Hoffman, Jr. He served from 1970 to 1978, during a most difficult time for schools like Pennington. Admissions declined, cut backs had to be made as well as significant changes, but once more Pennington weathered the storm. Again the school became co-educational. The Meckler Library was built with a room given to the Conference to house its Historical Library and Archives. Dr. Hoffman resigned at the close of the 1978 school year to assume the presidency of Midway College in Midway, Kentucky.

Dr. G. Donald Miller is the current Headmaster (1985). He assumed his duties August 1, 1978, after five years as Headmaster of The Valley School in Flint, Michigan. Much has happened to change the face of Pennington

School, to make it more prominent in the eyes of the church and to enhance its character as an educational institution.

It all began the night of January 16, 1980, when a spectacular fire completely destroyed O'Hanlon Hall with its eighteen classrooms, science labs, three faculty apartments and the lovely Shaw Memorial Chapel. Fortunately, no lives were lost, and only minor injuries were suffered by two Pennington firemen. Five days later classes resumed, meeting in the library, gymnasium and facilities in the Pennington United Methodist Church.[29]

Out of that tragedy has come the new $2.2 million Stainton Hall, an up-to-date administrative and classroom building which was ready for occupancy in the fall of 1981. It was named for long-time trustee and school benefactor, Mr. Howard Stainton of Ocean City. Out of the ashes came the glory. A year later a new dormitory for eighty-four students and with four faculty apartments was built.

The Bishop's Building is the last to be built to house the office of the resident bishop of the New Jersey Area. Bishop C. Dale White moved into his new office in 1983, thus making Pennington School the center from which the activities of the New Jersey Area permeate. The ground floor of the Bishop's Building houses the Historical Library, Archives and Memorabilia of the Southern New Jersey Conference moved from much smaller quarters in the Meckler Library. At their June 1984 sessions, the two New Jersey Conferences voted approval of a proposal presented by the Area Committee on the Episcopacy to build an episcopal residence on land provided by Pennington School. Bishop and Mrs. Neil Irons moved into their new home in 1985.

Thus the Southern New Jersey Conference's Pennington School continues its service to the Conference and to its youth. During the 1983-84 academic year, the school had 322 students, 229 boys and 93 girls of whom 153 were boarding students. The student-faculty ratio is about nine to one with the average class size numbering twelve students. Pennington is essentially a college preparatory school and nearly all of its graduates go on to advanced education. Pennington is the Southern New Jersey Conference's one institution of learning. Its history has been remarkable. Its future look bright.

South Jersey Institute

Not many people today know that at the close of the Civil War, the New Jersey Conference voted to sponsor a second school in the southern part of the state. As an outgrowth of the 1866 celebration of the Centennial of the beginnings of Methodism in America, there were numerous colleges and theological centers started like Drew University in Madison and Centenary College in Hackettstown, New Jersey. The 1866 Conference concurred with the report of its Centennial Committee that a seminary of learning be founded in the southern part of the state.

Ministers and laymen of the Bridgeton and Camden Districts met in Grosscup's Hall, Bridgeton on February 7, 1867. Offers of land and money to build a school were received from Bridgeton, Ewanville, Salem, Woodstown, Williamstown, Vineland, Glassboro and Fislerville (Clayton). This report was presented to Conference which appointed a Committee on the Seminary in South Jersey.[30]

By 1868, Vineland was chosen as the site. The City gave twenty acres of ground and guaranteed contributions of $15,000 from the citizens of Vineland. Plans were drawn to build a $47,000 building, the cost to include furnishings. Conference elected a twelve member Board of Trustees. Bishop Matthew Simpson laid the cornerstone on Wednesday, November 18, 1868[31] and construction began. By 1870, the building was nearly completed, but the Trustees had exhausted their funds. The Vineland citizens contributed their share and were fearful Conference would back down. Conference continued to voice its approval and urge churches and individuals to contribute. An effort in 1873 to raise funds by apportionment, brought in only $7,000 in conditional subscriptions, just a little cash and the plan was called a failure. It was. Only thirty-seven of the one hundred sixty-eight Conference Charges paid anything. After that, it was too late. The 1875 Conference reported that during the year the Seminary building was "advertised and sold for taxes."[32] A noble prospect. An ignominious ending. The abortive South Jersey Institute in Vineland was one of the Conference's most abject failures.

However, it should be said that the building did not go for nought. In 1884, it was purchased by the Fathers of Mercy and became, for a time, the College of the Sacred Heart and the Diocesan Seminary. It, too, closed for good in 1894. At one time, it did have a student body of three hundred boys. The State of New Jersey then purchased the property. June 1, 1899, it was reopened as the New Jersey Memorial Home for Disabled Soldiers, Sailors, Marines and their Wives and Widows.[33] Known locally as the Vineland Soldiers' Home, the building begun as the South Jersey Institute of the New Jersey Conference of the Methodist Episcopal Church, continues to serve America's veterans.

United Methodist Homes

> The United Methodist Homes of New Jersey is a non-profit organization, related to the Northern and Southern New Jersey Annual Conferences of The United Methodist Church. Its mission is to serve the physical, mental and spiritual needs of persons of age 65 or older, residing in the New Jersey Area of The United Methodist Church, without regard to race, color, creed or national origin. This mission is to be carried out within its financial resources by providing residential and health-care facilities, outreach services to those who are not residents of our facilities, and consultation and resource information to others serving the elderly.[34]

Operating under the above mission statement, with assets of nearly $20,000,000, having over 500 full and part time employees, the United Methodist Homes of New Jersey serves over 800 residents in its eight units: Collingswood Manor, Collingswood; Epworth Manor and Francis Asbury

Manor, Ocean Grove; Methodist Manor, Branchville; Wesley Manor, Wesley Homestead and Wesley-by-the-Bay, Ocean City; and Pitman Manor in Pitman. How did it all happen?

It started in Camden. At the 1889 Conference, a committee was appointed to consider a Conference "Home for the indigent aged members of our Church."[35] The committee reported back the next year that it seemed impractical, but the churches of Camden "have inaugurated a movement in this direction."[36] February 3, 1890, "The Home for the Aged and Infirm of the Methodist Episcopal Church of the County of Camden, N.J." was incorporated. Mr. William T. Bailey of Centenary Church, Camden made available a home at 531 York Street, Camden and nine ladies became residents of the home.[37] Later that year, Mr. E. C. Knight of Collingswood donated the lot on Haddon Avenue where Collingswood Manor now stands. July 9, 1891, the cornerstone of the building was laid by Bishop Cyrus Foss.[38] The home was dedicated October 22, 1891.[39] Additions to the home were made in 1910, 1938 when men were first admitted, and 1959 when a wing was added for an infirmary and rooms for couples.[40] In 1904, the District Superintendent said, "Forty-two persons in Collingswood Home."[41] Today the capacity has about doubled.

Mrs. David (Christianna) Baird was the founding president of the Board of Managers who did so much to get the Home started. Her untimely death in 1897 was keenly felt, but her place was taken by her daughter, Mrs. Mary Baird Fox, who served for the next twenty-six years.[42]

Until 1971, Collingswood Home was under the care of the Methodist Churches of Camden County. In that year, it became part of the Methodist Homes of New Jersey.[43] At the time it was established in 1890, it was thought "to be the seventh Methodist home for the aged in the United States."[44]

From 1890 in Camden County, we move to 1907 in Monmouth County. That year, reports the Conference *Minutes*, the "Monmouth Methodist Episcopal Home for the Aged" was established, trustees elected and property purchased at 63 Clark Avenue in Ocean Grove.[45] Bishop Luther B. Wilson officially dedicated the Home, July 24, 1907.[46] An adjacent building called "The Annex" was purchased in 1910 and twenty residents could be cared for. The Homes name was changed in 1911 to The Methodist Home for the Aged of The New Brunswick District. Although affiliation was established in 1916 with both the Newark and New Jersey Conferences, it was not until 1939 that the corporate name was changed to the Methodist Home for the Aged of New Jersey, now the United Methodist Homes of New Jersey.[47]

In 1910, Mrs. John H. (Jennie) Parker of West Long Branch became chairperson of the Board of Managers, a position she held until 1936. She was an indefatigable worker and spokesperson for the Home.[48]

Fire destroyed the Home on February 1, 1916. All the residents were safely evacuated and places found for them. Rebuilding began almost at once and a new and larger building was completed for $21,000 by Christmas. A new wing in 1919 and two annexes in 1922 brought the Home's capacity to 92 residents.[49]

UNITED METHODIST HOMES

Wesley Manor, Ocean City

Wesley Homestead, Ocean City

Epworth Manor, Ocean Grove

Francis Asbury Manor, Ocean Grove

Pitman Manor, Pitman

Wesley-by-the-Bay, Ocean City

Collingswood Manor, Collingswood

Methodist Manor, Branchville

Large waiting lists demanded a solution. Ground at 70 Stockton Avenue was purchased and in 1937, a fund raising program was begun. World War II delayed building plans and escalated the costs. November 29, 1949, the present Francis Asbury Manor with a capacity of more than 200 was officially opened.[50]

Since 1960, expansion has been the keystone of the plans of the United Methodist Homes. Dr. Friedrich wrote in 1977, "The United Methodist Homes of New Jersey has grown from a single home serving six residents in Ocean Grove, to an agency operating seven homes for approximately 840 residents." Since then Wesley-by-the-Bay apartments in Ocean City has been completed and even more residents are cared for.

The first expansion was northward to Branchville. November 29, 1961,[51] the first residents began entering Methodist Manor, the only Home within the bounds of the Northern New Jersey Conference.

Further expansion has been to the south of Ocean Grove. Groundbreaking for Wesley Manor with its main Manor and fifteen two unit cottages occurred September 21, 1961 with Bishop Corson presiding. Occupancy began on August 12, 1963.[52] The ground on which Wesley Manor is built was donated by Mr. Howard Stainton.

The former Bancroft-Taylor Rest Home for women missionaries and deaconesses in Ocean Grove was purchased by the Homes from the Women's Division of the Board of Missions of the United Methodist Church for $100,000 in 1970. Half of the purchase price was a gift from St. Paul's Church in Ocean Grove.[53] The home was renamed Epworth Manor after the English town where John and Charles Wesley were born.

Two more homes were added in 1971. July 1, 1971, Collingswood Manor became part of the United Methodist Homes family. October 1, 1971, Wesley Homestead in Ocean City became the sixth unit of New Jersey's United Methodist Homes.[54] Originally constructed in 1927 as the Hanscom Hotel, it was purchased in 1967 by a group of United Methodists of the Philadelphia Area who operated it as a year round residence for senior citizens calling it The Homestead. When it became part of the United Methodist Homes family, it was renamed Wesley Homestead.

Pitman became the site of the newest Home addition in 1974. Securing the property of the former Robinson Memorial Nursing Home, and obtaining the assets of the William E. Straub Estate that had been left in trust with the Pitman National Bank for the purpose of erecting a home for the elderly in Pitman, Pitman Manor became a reality. Groundbreaking, May 3, 1972, was led by Bishop Prince A. Taylor, Jr. and Dr. Arthur S. Fleming, United States Commissioner on Aging and a prominent United Methodist layman. Following Consecration Services on Mother's Day 1974, the first of the Manor's residents began arriving that August.[55]

By the late 1970's, it became necessary to do something about replacing Wesley Manor's cottages in Ocean City. Poor drainage and sometimes flooded conditions led to the decision to close them as soon as other arrangements could be made. Land was secured a few blocks south of Wesley Manor on Bay Avenue and by the fall of 1983, Wesley-by-the-Bay, a two story apartment complex opened, making facilities available for many more couples and also for handicapped persons.

Nor is this to be the end of expansion projects. Additional facilities and growth is planned. Since 1977, the Homes has owned the Case Farm in Andover Township, and plans are being developed for its use. The United Methodist Homes plans to serve even more of New Jersey's elderly. Mr. Jack L. Taylor is current (1984) Executive Director.

United Methodists of the Conference today and in the past support the Homes in many ways. Some will recall the days of Harvest Home Sundays when local church altars would be filled with all sorts of canned and home grown produce for the Homes to use. That has given way to monetary gifts, but the same needs are served. Mother's Day Offerings, Fellowship Fund gifts, volunteer programs, active Auxiliaries in each of the Homes, all serve to show the church cares for its institution called the United Methodist Homes and the senior citizens whose residency there adds life to their years.

BANCROFT-TAYLOR HOME

Bancroft-Taylor Rest Home was never a Conference Institution until it became Epworth Manor in 1970. Yet its location in Ocean Grove, the support it received from many within the Conference, particulary the women and the Woman's Home Missionary Society, demands some recognition be accorded it. For seventy-four years, women missionaries and deaconesses on furlough, vacation, and in retirement found a place to rest and live in this lovely mecca by the sea shore.

In 1896, the Woman's Home Missionary Society rented a home in Ocean Grove where missionaries and deaconesses could rest during their summer vacations. The following year, Mrs. George O. Robinson and her sister Miss Henrietta Bancroft, who owned two lots and two cottages in Ocean Grove, offered generous terms and a $1,000 gift. The Society purchased their cottages at 72-74 Cookman Avenue.[56] Thus came into being the Bancroft Rest Home. By 1901, it was winterized and soon missionaries and deaconesses were living there year round. When Mrs. Martha A. Taylor, a member of the first Board of Managers, died in 1917, members of her family paid off all the indebtedness and the home was renamed the Bancroft-Taylor Rest Home. In 1921, Sunset Cottage next door was purchased for nursing facilities and the entire home enlarged in 1923.

Then disaster. February 11, 1926, fire completely destroyed the Bancroft-Taylor Rest Home. All lives were spared for which God was praised. Eleven months and one day later a new home was ready for use, dedicated by Bishop William Anderson, in March of 1927.[57] A health care annex was added in 1957.

As the number of women living at Bancroft-Taylor declined to twenty-three in 1969, the Women's Division voted to merge Bancroft-Taylor with the

Brooks Howell Home in Ashville, North Carolina. This led to Bancroft-Taylor being sold to the United Methodist Homes. Some of the retired missionaries and deaconesses living there elected to stay. One of the women from New Jersey who had much to do with the Home for a long period, was Mrs. Richard Stout of Asbury Park. Mrs. Stout served as Bureau Secretary of Rest Homes and was one of those who helped to rebuild it after the fire.[58]

Many residents of the Home were single women. Few if any family members survived them. The Woman's Home Missionary Society and its successor organizations own two large plots in area cemeteries where these people can be buried. Several years ago, a 90 year old lady wrote me from a church in Georgia. Years before, a missionary by the name of Susan M. Lewis had started a Sunday School in her church. They had just opened a new library and named it in memory of Susan M. Lewis. The writer was asking if I could tell her what happened to Miss Lewis. I replied that I really did not know, but I kept her letter for a long time. One morning I threw it in the trash. That evening, my family and I were out for a drive and found our way into Mount Prospect Cemetery near Asbury Park. What a surprise to find a large marker that said Woman's Home Missionary Society of the M. E. Church. Beside it were buried fifty-one women missionaries between 1921 and 1969, including Susan M. Lewis. I went home, retrieved the letter from the trash can and sent a reply. She was gone, but not forgotten.

Neighborhood Center

"The role of the Methodist Deaconess Community Center is to be a witness to the love of God, as revealed through Jesus Christ and its power in the daily lives of individuals."[59] This is how the role of the Deaconess Home, now known as Neighborhood Center, was conceived in 1967. Since 1913, Methodism has been at work in a special way in the City of Camden.

The New Jersey Conference Woman's Home Missionary Society in 1913 saw a need, responded to it and its ministry through over seventy years has been multiplied many times over. The Camden District Superintendent, Rev. S. M. Nichols, in his 1913 report to Conference said:

> The Woman's Home Missionary Society of our Conference, recognizing the need of the deaconess' work, have organized a board of managers, and will open a deaconess home in a few days. We prophesy great success for this new department, and congratulate this society on the purpose and plan for this work, and assure them the support of the pastors and churches.[60]

This home was at 271 Kaighn Avenue. Deaconesses Curtis and Davis were the first to arrive in Camden. Miss Hattie F. Davis was in charge. That first year nearly one thousand calls in the homes of the needy were made, sewing classes were started, a mothers meeting and childrens' story hour were conducted. An employment bureau and a kindergarten were planned.[61] Those deaconesses knew how to work.

NEIGHBORHOOD CENTER, CAMDEN
former Deaconess Home

Quarters were soon outgrown. In 1921, the Kaighn mansion at 278 Kaighn Avenue was purchased and used for a short time. By 1923, a $100,000 building plan was underway. The Kaighn home was torn down and November 26, 1924, the cornerstone of the new Deaconess Home was laid.[62] The present home was dedicated April 30, 1925.[63] Additional expansion has taken place through the years. Adjoining land for an outdoor area was purchased in 1958. A Craft

Building was erected in 1964. The Broadway Center in Broadway Church opened in 1971.

The Neighborhood Center is far more than a building or even a program. It is people helping people in the name of Christ. A 1967 report said twenty-three Deaconesses, over three hundred staff persons and thousands and thousands of volunteers have witnessed through the Center since 1913. Many more have served since. In that one year, almost four thousand personal contacts were made through the Center. During the winter over six hundred were enrolled in fifty-three weekly groups. Several hundred children and youth participated in the summer program.

The 71st Annual Report issued in 1984, showed the opening of a new Thrift Shop, a Government Equivolency Diploma Program, over 500 children enrolled in a summer program at five sites, a soup kitchen that served more than 70,000 meals in 1983, emergency services of food, clothing and counselling are provided. There are Bible classes, recreation, music, after school programs and family events. In a city of great need, the church is there to minister.

Mrs. Elizabeth Ann Rogers is the current (1984) Executive Director of the Neighborhood Center, Inc. The Center is an urban outreach mission of the Conference and a part of the National Division of the United Methodist Board of Global Ministries. In many and numerous ways, the churches of the Conference support their Center. Through United Methodist Women gifts, Sunday School class support, communion offerings, responses to special appeals, gifts of clothing, food and Christmas gifts, all help to support "our mission" to bring the joy of the Lord to Camden.

Conference Center

Franklin Buck was instrumental in purchasing the site of the Conference Center at Mount Misery. It was done in the name of the South Jersey Camp Meeting Association. The 1946 Conference voted to use funds obtained from the sale of the Pointville Church to the United States Government to purchase the grounds at a cost of $2,500. Former C.C.C. Camp (Civilian Conservation Corps Camp) S-69 in the Pine Barrens became our Conference Center. The original key to the old camp was presented by Dr. Buck to the Conference Archives. Rev. Lynn Corson was elected president of the Conference Center Commission with Rev. Ralph Kappler designated the business manager. What a difficult task the Commission had to prepare the old grounds to make them suitable for a Conference summer camping experince. It was done, however, and Junior, Intermediate, Youth and Young Adult Institutes were held there the summer of 1947.

In order to provide direction for future development, Professor Brad Sears of Syracuse University was hired to survey the needs and facilities and make recommendations. His plan was presented in 1949 and accepted as the basis of camp development. This was augmented by the work of the Conference Center Evaluation Committee whose report Conference adopted in 1950.

$10,000 was to be spent in putting existing buildings in top condition, Conference was to pay current debts of $3,000, rebuild the dam for $2,000, allocate $3,500 to the Conference Center Commission and make available $2,000 as a revolving fund account for operating expenses. This began the serious improvements at the Camp. By 1952, 663 youth used the summer camp, a figure which increased to almost 1,400 by 1956.[64]

The physical features of the Center improved as its program and use increased. The first half of the 1950's, with Rev. Lawrence G. Atkinson as Commission head, were years of growth and development. Camp sites were developed, sewerage work was tackled and a large Assembly Hall built. The late 1950's brought the winterizing of buildings for year round camping use and a second Sears Plan in 1959 which was followed by a third in 1969. The 1960's were major years of building a camp to meet the Conference needs for year around as well as summer programs. A forest fire in April of 1963, burned one wing and leveled the Infirmary, Recreation Hall, shop and storage rooms.[65] The fire only spurred more improvements. During these years, while Rev. Ernest O. Kelloway was the guiding light of the Center, the Glassboro State College's South Jersey Conservation and Environmental Science Center came to use the Center's facilities from September to June. A lot of these improvements were made possible through some $200,000 raised by the Methodist Dollars for Christ programs and some $10,000 more in the Future is Now campaign, both of which were in the 1960's.

Conference Center has continued to serve the needs of the Conference through the years. Summer camping experiences are augmented by group retreats and conferences of all kinds, by local church groups, as well as various Conference agencies. Reservations have to be made well in advance.

Much of the forward work at Conference Center is due to the dedicated leadership of the full time Executive Directors employed since 1967, along with the leadership and members of the Conference Center Commission, called the Committee on Camps and Conferences since 1964. Rev. Ernest O. Kelloway was the first full-time Executive Director hired in 1967. He was followed by Mr. Neil Alexander in 1975, Rev. Carlton J. Curtin in 1979, Rev. Roy W. Quist in 1983 and Rev. Eugene M. Westley in 1985.

A new study of Conference Center and its future, including the possibility of a name change was authorized by the 1984 Conference at the request of the Committee on Camps and Conferences.

TUMETHCA

TUMETHCA, Tabernacle United Methodist Camp, joined the Conference Center family in 1970. TUMETHCA grew out of an idea in the heart of the Rev. Daniel Hulitt to provide a camping experience in God's out of doors for underprivileged boys from our cities. He started Boys Camp in 1948, by bringing a group of boys to Conference Center for a week's camping experience. As the program grew, more space was needed. In 1960, a 120 acre camp in

Volleyball game at Tumethca

Tabernacle Township was acquired and adequate facilities provided. Here hundreds of boys from our cities streets learned about God, nature, and love.

Conference acquired Boys Camp in 1970 with the understanding that its unique ministry of helping underprivileged children would continue.[66] It has, largely through voluntary contributions to the "Daniel Hulitt Scholarship Fund." Through these camperships provided, each summer some 300 girls and boys experience the enrichment of spending a week in God's beautiful out-of-doors. Daniel Hulitt's dream continues to be nurtured.

TUMETHCA too, provides more than a few weeks of summer ministry, although that may be its chief function. Year round facilities are available there also and it is increasingly used as part of the Conference Center facilities.

Pennington School, the United Methodist Homes, Neighborhood Center and the Conference Center Camps are our Southern New Jersey Conference Institutions. There are, however, others which bear mention. Chapter 8 has dealt with our Camp Meetings. These are not institutions belonging to the Conference, but they are an institution within the Conference receiving the support and energetic backing of many persons within the Conference — Seaville, Ocean Grove, Malaga, Pitman, Ocean City and Delanco.

The Methodist Hospital in Philadelphia, opened in 1892, has always enjoyed the patronage and support of Conference churches. The Camden Center of Goodwill Industries has been an institution supported by Conference churches and Conference action. Rev. David Bailey's Ranch Hope for Boys in Alloway, New Jersey, is a more recent institution founded by one of our popular pastors designed to help troubled boys. It has come to be recognized as a Conference Advance Special, but even before, drew the support of numerous churches and individuals from our churches.

These institutions can all be conceived as an extended arm of the church. Reaching out in the name of Christ they help the young and the old, the sick and the lame, the troubled and the deprived. Their purpose is to prolong life and make it better, to educate the mind and quicken the spirit, help the needy and save the lost.

Part of the genius of United Methodism is its connectionalism. Few of our churches could do any of this alone. Together we reach out in Christ's name through these institutions to touch lives that could not otherwise be reached. Let none of us fail to help.

Chapter 19

THE UNITED METHODIST CHURCH

1968-1986

This chapter brings us to the end of a history. This historian finds it much easier to write about the past, than to be historical about the present. The closer to one's own day it is, the more difficult it is to be objective historically. A bit of time must elapse before any kind of real objective analysis is possible. One can chronicle events, and that is what part of this chapter will be, but who knows yet which events will prove to be of the most enduring significance?

These have been strange years. The late 1960's witnessed a revolt against authority — in state and in church. The long Vietnam War caused much protest and anti-American feelings. It precipitated the long hot summers of racial unrest in our cities. Radicalism of all kinds was on the ascendency. Hippies, yippies and Jesus freaks abounded. The sexual revolution and drug culture blossomed. Perhaps the bottom was reached when, in 1974, Richard Nixon became the first American President to be forced to resign.

Then came 1976. America was 200 years old. It was a great birthday celebration. We began to feel good about ourselves again. We beat the Russians in ice hockey at Lake Placid. Then we suffered through the long ordeal of the Iranian hostage crisis, thanking God when they were free. Many were startled to find "born-again Christian" Jimmy Carter in the White House, but Ronald Reagan beat him badly four years later. We learned about the energy crisis and bid goodby to low cost gas and oil prices. Inflation startled us. Hunger shocked us. Such have been these days.

We began this period with a new name, United Methodists. Names like John Wesley, Francis Asbury, Philip William Otterbein, Jacob Albright and Martin Boehm took on new significance depending on our background. We have watched rather numbly as church membership has declined year after year and wonder what has happened to our evangelical passion. As we have watched the erosion of morality, we have yearned for the days of pietistic religion.

Yet these have also been days of celebration for us. Evangelical United Brethren and Methodists celebrated becoming one in 1968. The next year we celebrated the 200th Anniversary of the arrival of Wesley's first preachers in America — Richard Boardman and Joseph Pilmore. An Asbury Bicentennial was celebrated in 1971. We joined with all Americans in the 1976 Bicentennial. The year 1984, was our own Bicentennial, the 200th birthday of the Christmas Conference that organized the Methodist Episcopal Church in America. Such were these days.

April 23, 1968, in Dallas, Texas, The United Methodist Church was born. It was a merger of the 738,000 member Evangelical United Brethren Church with the 10,289,000 member Methodist Church. These two churches of kindred background, theology, polity and practice, one of German-speaking background, the other of English-speaking, were now one. Who were the Evangelical United Brethren?

Three key men are important in their roles as founders. The first is Philip William Otterbein,[1] born in Germany in 1726. He came to America as a young German Reformed minister in 1752, serving in Lancaster and York, Pennsylvania before moving to Baltimore in 1774 to pastor the church which bears his name and in which he served until his death in 1813. He was a man of a warm, evangelical spirit who became an intimate friend of Francis Asbury, and at the latter's request, participated in his ordination at the 1784 Christmas Conference.

The second important figure was Martin Boehm.[2] He was a Mennonite from Lancaster County, Pennsylvania, where he was born in 1725. Thus he was but a year older than Otterbein. Boehm was a farmer upon whom the lot fell to be a preacher. He recoiled against this idea, not believing himself to be worthy or of sufficient faith. Then one day, while plowing his field, he came under intense conviction, surrendered his heart to Christ and experienced the personal assurance of sins forgiven. Martin Boehm and Asbury likewise were intimate friends. It was Martin's son Henry who was Asbury's long-time traveling companion and aide.

Boehm and Otterbein met at a meeting in Long's Barn, Lancaster County, Pennsylvania, where Martin Boehm preached. It was Whitsuntide, probably in 1767. At the end of Boehm's sermon, Otterbein embraced him warmly and said, "Wir sind Brüder!" ("We are Brethren!")[3] This can be taken as the root beginning of the United Brethren in Christ. It was not then a church, but a movement of real spiritual import.

Yearly meetings of these kindred souls began to be held. Two early ones were at Pipe Creek in 1774 and 1776. A bit later, larger Conferences were held in 1789 and 1791. George Adam Geeting, John Neidig and Christian Newcomer became significant leaders among the United Brethren. At a meeting held September 25, 1800 at Peter Kemp's home near Frederick, Maryland, a more formal organization took place at which both Otterbein and Boehm were chosen as bishops. It must, however, be qualified to say that the term bishop was not used until 1813, nor were the United Brethren in Christ called a Church until 1815. By that time, both Otterbein (1813) and Boehm (1812) were in glory. So we have the United Brethren strand of the Evangelical United Brethren Church.

The third figure, representing the Evangelical strand of heritage, was Jacob Albright. Frederick Norwood says, "Jacob Albright, at first, was all there was of the Albright Movement. The beginnings of the Evangelical Association are concentrated in his personal career."[4] He was born in 1759 and was from the German Lutheran Church. Living on a farm in Lancaster County, Pennsylvania, he suffered the shock of the death of at least three of his children from an epidemic of dysentery in 1790. The next year he was converted, joined a

Methodist Class, received an Exhorter's license and began preaching to his German neighbors in 1796. By 1800, he had organized three classes plus a large number of constituents. In 1803, he brought together a group of his helpers for a two day meeting at which Albright was ordained a minister. This marks the beginning of the Evangelical Association. Regular Conferences were held starting in 1807. After Albright's death in 1808, George Miller, John Walter and especially John Dreisbach carried on the work. The official formation of the Church, called the Evangelical Association, occured at Martin Dreisbach's home in Union County, Pennsylvania in 1816.

By 1816, all the founding fathers had passed away — Philip William Otterbein, Martin Boehm, Jacob Albright, and Francis Asbury.

It is not possible here to give the history of these two churches. Both had their schisms. Among the United Brethren, it happened in 1889 over the issues of Constitutional change, secret societies, laity at the General Conference and especially a new Confession of Faith. Bishop Milton Wright, father of the famous Wright brothers, led a group who withdrew to form The United Brethren Church (Old Constitution). In 1979, this independent Church had a few more than 25,000 members.[5]

A chart may help show the background of the Evangelical United Brethren Church.

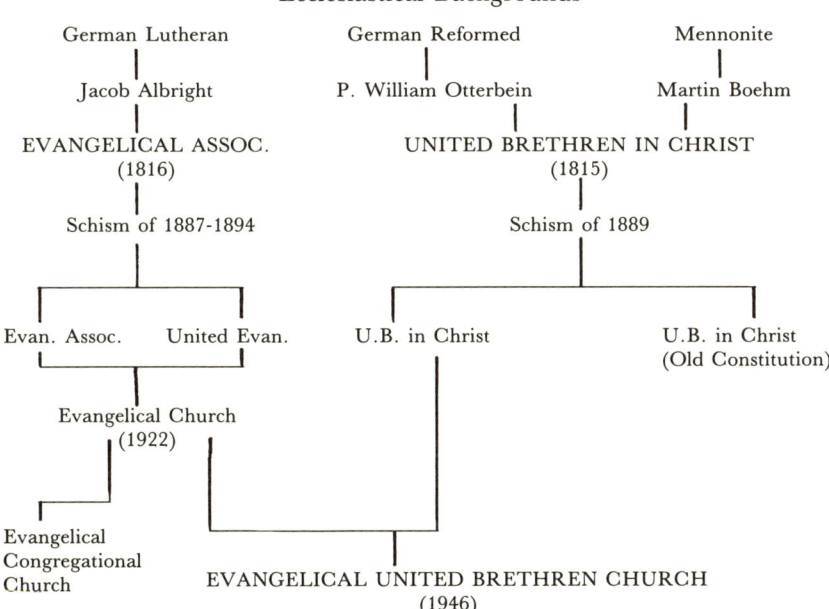

The Evangelical schism occured during the years 1887 to 1894. There were numerous issues which caused division including geographical sectionalism and whether to use the German or English language. The minority, centered around Philadelphia and Naperville, Illinois, were organized as the United Evangelical Church. The majority, centered around Indianapolis and more favorable toward the newer immigrants, continued as the Evangelical Association. Happily, this division came to an end in 1922, except for a group of former members of the Eastern Pennsylvania Conference of the United Evangelical Church. About 20,000 of their members left and formed The Evangelical Congregational Church.

Both Churches were in the main stream of American Protestant Christianity, active in interchurch movements, concerned about current social problems and ready to meet the challenges of the new day. Merger talks between the two, which began in 1926 and more earnestly in 1934, bore fruit. In the First United Brethren Church of Johnstown, Pennsylvania, November 16, 1946, the Evangelical United Brethren Church was formed.[6]

The Evangelical United Brethren Church and The Methodist Church merged in 1968 to form The United Methodist Church. This merger affected the Southern New Jersey Conference a little. There were three churches of the former Evangelical Church within the bounds of the Conference: Zion Evangelical in Clarksboro, the oldest of the three; Church of the Master in Howell Township north of Lakewood, and the Church of the Good Shepherd in Willingboro.[8] The last two were organized after 1946. The three Evangelical United Brethren ministers who joined this Conference were: Paul A. DeHoff of Church of the Master, who was later transferred to First Church, Millville; Donald R. Repsher of Church of the Good Shepherd, who withdrew in 1971; and Keith B. Wise of Zion Evangelical Church, who later became a United Methodist missionary in Alaska. Their transfers became effective December 31, 1968.[9] However, there is more to tell about the Evangelical United Brethren work within southern New Jersey.

It was the Evangelical Association which did missionary work in New Jersey in the latter part of the nineteenth century. The *Journal* of Bishop John Seybert for the year 1852, records a New Jersey Circuit on the Philadelphia District of the Eastern Pennsylvania Conference. C. Gingrich and H. Major were the preachers.[10] Although Bishop Seybert preached frequently in Philadelphia, his *Journal* does not record any preaching in New Jersey.

The next record appears in the *Minutes* of the Eastern Pennsylvania Conference for the year 1859.[11] There it was reported that J. Frey, a missionary, began work in the German language in the cities of Camden and Glassboro. Work followed in Berkley (Mt. Royal), Woodbury, Bridgeton, Richwood, Aura and Paulsboro. This work was initiated from the Ninth Street Church in Philadelphia. Small Classes were formed which served as a circuit for several years. Out of this early German work, four Churches were formed. The first was in Glassboro, originating in missionary work dating back to 1859. The Camden Church was organized in 1874 and a building erected in 1878. This

EVANGELICAL UNITED METHODIST CHURCH, CLARKSBORO
Organized in 1880 as Zion Evangelical Church
Oldest former Evangelical United Brethren Church in the SNJ Conference

congregation disbanded in 1911. The Clarksboro congregation, long known as Zion Church, was organized in 1880 by the Rev. Charles Philipbar of Glassboro. It came about when Mr. John Nolte, who became a charter member of Zion Church, attended a funeral at Glassboro and invited Rev. Philipbar to preach to the German speaking people around Clarksboro. He accepted. Prayer meetings were conducted in peoples homes. In March of 1879, he began holding worship services in the Berkley Baptist Church. A congregation was organized and incorporated, March 24, 1880, as Zion Church of the Evangelical Association.[12]

A fourth congregation was organized in Trenton in 1880. They worshipped in St. John's Church on South Broad Street in the capitol city until the church was discontinued in 1916.

The only work which endured as a result of the labors of these German Evangelical Association missionaries was the one at Clarksboro. There were twenty-nine charter members of Zion Church, including John Nolte and his wife who invited Rev. Philipbar to preach at Clarksboro. Three days after the church was incorporated, a lot was purchased on what is now Cohawkin Road, and a building committee appointed. The cornerstone was laid April 24, 1880 and the church, built at a cost of $2,400, was dedicated by Bishop Thomas Bowman in September. Rev. A. S. Stelz was the first pastor assigned to the new church. From 1880 until 1902, Clarksboro and Glassboro were served by the same pastor. He lived in Clarksboro and held afternoon services in Glassboro. In 1902, the Glassboro congregation moved to Aura.

Clarksboro Church continued to grow and enlarge its facilities. Then on Palm Sunday, April 2, 1944, scarcely an hour after the close of the morning service, fire completely destroyed the church. Rebuilding began almost immediately and a new church was dedicated June 9, 1946. An enlarged Sanctuary and new Educational Building were built in 1963. In 1968, because the Methodist Church in Clarksboro was also named Zion, this church chose the name Evangelical United Methodist Church, to denote its mission and as a reminder of its heritage.[13]

A prominent layman in the Clarksboro Church the years following World War II was Mr. Ulysses S. Estilow, Jr. He was a delegate to several Evangelical United Brethren General Conferences, the Uniting Conference in Dallas and represented The United Methodist Church at the July, 1968, World Council of Churches meeting in Uppsala, Sweden. Mr. Estilow was also the first former Evangelical United Brethren to represent the Southern New Jersey Conference as an elected lay delegate to the 1972 Jurisdictional Conference and the first lay alternate to the General Conference.

The Church of the Good Shepherd in Willingboro was formed in 1959 by the Northeastern Conference when Levitt and Sons offered to give them a lot to establish a church in Levittown, as Willingboro was then called. Rev. R. J. C. Pottieger was the founding minister. The church was dedicated November 27, 1960.

In 1961, the Northeastern Conference, with funds available from the sale of a discontinued church in Newark, secured property in Howell Township. Rev. Leonard S. Buxton was assigned as the organizing pastor. Services began on April 30, 1962, and the congregation was organized as the Church of the Master in 1964.[14]

At the time of merger these three churches had a combined membership of 576. In 1983, their membership stands at 531. The heritage of the Evangelical United Brethren Church is an enriching one in the life of United Methodism. It is a part now of the total heritage of the Southern New Jersey Conference.

Unlike the 1950's and early 60's, the period now under review has been a period of numerical decline in church and church school. The figures are startling. Church membership in the Conference peaked in 1966 at 113,608. Decline, while steady, was not overly large through 1971. The following six years saw a net loss of 14,881 members, dropping the membership to 93,702. A loss of 4,558 members in 1972 alone was recorded. Membership in 1983 stood at 87,323. Losses are much smaller, but an upswing has not yet been seen. A decline of only 137 in 1983 brings hope that brighter days will soon dawn.

Church School statistics are even more alarming, as has already been pointed out. A peak membership of 85,911 was reached in 1960. In 1983, there were only 36,748 church school members, a loss of 49,163. There seems to be a leveling off. In 1981, the loss was only 115, while average attendance increased by 15 a Sunday. There was actually a 39 member increase in 1982, but 1983 brought another drop of 221.

We have been looking at the top membership churches in the Conference and noting the changes through the years. Those ranking in the top ten in 1983, had a combined membership of 17,121, 2,517 less than the top ten total in 1967. St. John's Church, Hazlet, led all Conference Churches with 2,262 members, followed by Haddonfield's 1,808. Ocean City, Toms River: First, Collingswood: First, Woodbury, Red Bank, Moorestown, Hamilton Township: St. Mark's and Vineland followed in order. Pitman, Turnersville and Linwood were the other three churches to top the 1,000 membership figure. Toms River: First, Moorestown and St. Mark's are new to the list.

It is difficult to draw any general conclusions from this study of the top churches. There are no startling changes over these sixteen years. St. John's gained 800 new members, some others lost between 400 and 600. Is there a danger of their continued decline? Others remained relatively stable, probably sharing only in the general membership loss. More study needs to be made to show why growing churches grow. Also, a question not yet determined is whether there is an optimum membership beyond which any but the exceptional church is likely to grow. Also evident, is the continued decline of the city church, even in cities of lesser population than a Camden, Trenton or Atlantic City. Asbury Park, Long Branch, Millville, Burlington and Bridgeton are such examples.

The turmoil with which this period began can not be forgotten. The Vietnam War, longest our Country ever fought, with its sad conclusion, strained at every fibre of American life. It seemed to threaten our soul. Add to that the tragic assassinations of President John F. Kennedy, Martin Luther King, Jr., and Robert Kennedy and it is little wonder the late 1960's were a time of turmoil.

Violence erupted in our cities' streets, fanned by long-simmering racial hostilities, the general unrest of the times and growing lack of respect for law and authority. Newark and Plainfield are in north Jersey. Camden, Atlantic City, Asbury Park and Bridgeton are in southern Jersey. Some riot areas looked like war zones. Years later, in some places, there were still large vacant areas where once there had been homes and stores.

At the 1968 Conference, the Board of Christian Social Concerns responded to the times in a series of resolutions dealing with the possession of firearms, the propagation of violence, civil rights commissions, inter-racial relations and integration. The Board stated:

> It is a sad commentary on the temper of the white power structure of our state and nation to realize that it took the assassination of Dr. Martin Luther King, Jr. with its resulting riots to move the establishment to reverse its action on the Fire Arms Bill and to get out of committee and passed in the House, a Civil Rights Bill that appeared to be doomed to die in committee.[15]

A major "Address on Reconciliation" by Charles A. Sayre at the 1968 Conference, zeroed in on the problems and needs in our society, particularly as it had to do with New Jersey. He pleaded with the Church and each Christian to become agents of reconciliation. Dr. Sayre said, "We are marking a transition from an emphasis on pietistic religion to a new world oriented sense of the mission of the church. And certainly for us from South Jersey this transition is painful."[16]

As we moved into the decade of the 1970's, we were aware that we were living in a changing world. Hooker Davis, in the 1971 District Superintendents' report, said the 50's were hectic — the 60's difficult — the 70's started out as being revolutionary. "But they were saying that 4000 years ago." He said:

> We have made it possible for men to . . . walk on the moon, but we haven't learned to walk on earth as men of Peace and Goodwill. . . . We have squandered the wealth of the earth in producing sophisticated instruments of death and destruction, yet knowing that such cannot be reconciled with the mind of God and the Spirit of Christ. . . . Despite the fertility of the earth, poverty abounds. The seeds of love are not being planted, or else they fall upon stony ground; and the lessons of brotherhood go unheeded. . . . Each of us must ask ourselves the basic questions — 'Am I a part of the problem or am I part of the solution?'[17]

The major response by the United Methodists was the Fund for Reconciliation. The Conference goal was $225,000 to be raised over a four year period. Fifty per cent was to remain in the Conference, the other half went to the general church for use wherever needed. The 1969 Conference reported pledges of $201,000, initial receipts of over $65,000 and 13 grants totaling $17,350. By the 1971 Conference over $180,000 had been raised. The Committee reported eight day care centers assisted. Project Equality, Open House Ministries, Ecumenical Housing Projects, Project Uplift, day camps, cooperative ventures in Atlantic City, Camden, Bridgeton and Trenton were among the many projects helped. The Committee concluded: "The financial emphasis . . . is being phased out. The need is ever present. . . ."[18]

Special celebrations were highlights of these times. The first occured in 1969 with the Pilmore-Boardman Bicentennial Celebration. This marked the 200th Anniversary of the landing at Gloucester Point, New Jersey of John Wesley's first missionaries to America, October 21, 1769.[19] This Bicentennial was marked by a Banquet at the Holly House in Pennsauken on Friday, October 24. Dr. Frederick E. Maser, editor of Pilmore's *Journal* made the official presentation of the first published edition. Dr. Frank B. Stanger gave the address on "A Giant Leap for Methodism," and Ruth Parsons Strahan presented a dramatic review, "Appointment to America." The next afternoon at Gloucester Point, Bishop Prince A. Taylor, Jr. gave an address on "The New Wilderness" following the dedication of a commemorative monument given by the New Jersey Area Boards of the Laity. Numerous persons attended the celebration from across the New Jersey Area and the Eastern Pennsylvania Conference. The Northeastern Jurisdictional Commission on Archives and History made the celebration the focal point of their annual meeting.[20]

Two years later, in 1971, a Francis Asbury Bicentennial Celebration was marked. It commemorated the 200th Anniversary of his coming to America. The Commission on Archives and History asked every church to have an observance sometime between October 24 and November 14. The Commission sponsored a special observance on Saturday, November 13 which included a walking tour of historic Burlington, dedication of an historical Asbury plaque and an address, "Asbury and American Methodism" by Bishop Taylor.[21] Numerous local churches held Asbury celebrations including the United Methodists of Asbury Park who dedicated a monument in the town park across from First Church in memory of Asbury, after whom the town was named.

By 1976, America was back on track with the celebration of its own Bicentennial. Every local congregation was asked to make Sunday, July 4, 1976, a very special day. Numerous resources were made available. United Methodists, always patriotic, found many ways to call America back to its spiritual heritage, to remind the people that we are "one Nation under God." Perhaps most significant were the many prayer vigils held in local churches around the Conference, as well as across the land.

Our own United Methodist Bicentennial came in 1984. In the year in which this is being written, we have learned anew of our heritage. Lovely Lane and the Christmas Conference of 1784 are again familiar to our people. Study Classes, films, intergenerational Church School experiences, tours, pan-Methodist celebrations, bulletin inserts and one-liners, historical displays, cluster events, sermon series, musical programs and much more have informed our people and challenged them to experience grace and freedom anew in their lives today. Some seven hundred Southern New Jersey Conference United Methodists took part in a bus pilgrimage to the Bicentennial Celebration at the General Conference in Baltimore. Still more saw Lynette Bennett Danskin's performance of Susanna Wesley at our own June Conference session. American Methodism is 200 years young in 1984, and still proclaims grace and freedom. Methodists love to celebrate.

We celebrated the arrival of a new bishop and his wife in 1976. Bishop C. Dale White and his wife Gwen, native Iowans, came to the New Jersey Area from Rhode Island. Having been a Board of Christian Social Concerns staff person in Washington, D.C., then a pastor and District Superintendent in New England, Bishop White began his episcopal career as New Jersey's bishop. Soon after his arrival, a series of airplane rides across the state showed him the lay of the land. Then followed days when every church in the Area received a brief visit from its bishop and his wife as they sought to get to know the people and churches of the Garden State.

For eight years, Dale White was our bishop. A friendly, compassionate man, Bishop White sought to sensitize New Jersey Methodists in dealing with the poor, hungry and powerless of the world. His personal Christian diplomacy during the days of the Iranian hostage crisis, including a Christmas visit to that mid-Eastern country, was an embodiment of that concern. He was a good Bishop and a good leader. His wife, Gwen, brought her unique talents and

BISHOP C. DALE WHITE
(1976-1984)

gifts to share in ministry. She became a most beloved first-lady of the Area, widely in demand as a speaker and retreat leader. At the 1984 Jurisdictional Conference, Bishop White was assigned to the New York Area.

Structural changes were many during these years. With the creation of The United Methodist Church, we learned what a Council on Ministries was and discovered its unique benefits as a program-initiating agency. The Official Board gave way to the Administrative Board and in some of our smaller churches, the Administrative Council. Annual Conference began to use Forums in 1968 to discuss much of the business of the Conference. In a few years, we gave them up. The Conference Program Council was formed in 1969 and Program Counselors became part of the Conference Staff. By 1976, the Program Council became the Council on Ministries and Program Counselors were called Council Directors. We streamlined our Conference organizations at that time and Clusters came into being. A few Clusters were found to be effective in ministry and have continued. Most, however, are no more. Fall Charge Conferences began in 1978.

In the first change in Districts since 1877, Conference moved, in 1968, to a six District alignment. Gone were the names Bridgeton, New Brunswick and Trenton; only Camden remained and now that is gone. Somehow, it is supposed to mean more to name districts by points of the compass than by names hallowed by tradition. At any rate, we now had the Camden Metropolitan, Central, Northeast, Northwest, Southeast and Southwest Districts. That didn't last very long. We restructured again in 1982, following a report of a Task Force on Administrative Costs presented at a special session of Conference in Haddonfield Church. District lines were rearranged and the Camden Metropolitan District disappeared. At the close of the 1982 Conference, we were left with five realigned Districts. Jurisdictional Conference threatened even more radical realignment in 1980 and again in 1984. The Jurisdictional Conference Boundary Committee both times called for the two Conferences of the New Jersey Area to be merged into one Conference. It was approved once in 1984, then later reconsidered, and we were left alone. What the future will offer in that regard, no one knows.

Pensions, too, has been a major concern of the Southern New Jersey Conference since we became a United Methodist Church. Finding a way to adequately take care of the retired ministers, wives, widows and dependent children, while at the same time meeting our unfunded liability, has been the major crux of the problem. In 1970, Conference took a major forward step by entering the Reserve Pension Fund of The United Methodist Church. In 1976, a $2,000,000 Pension Fund Campaign was voted. It sought to deal with the unfunded liability and the inadequate annuity rate in a time of unprecendented inflation. The final goal was set for $2,500,000 for the campaign to start January 1, 1978. The campaign was successful. A total of $3,299,159 was subscribed.[22] The total amount received as reported to the 1982 Conference was $2,717,034.[23] It fell short of what was accepted, but exceeded the goal.

General Conference of 1980 embarked the Church on a new Ministerial Pension Plan. It went into effect January 1, 1982 and eliminates all future unfunded liability. Each church sends its monthly check directly to the General Board of Pensions. It goes into each minister's personal account. In addition, each minister's own three percent or more contribution goes into another personal account to be either added at retirement as an additional pension annuity or made available to the retiree in a lump sum payment.

Conference still has to deal with the previous unfunded pension liability and the annuity rate for all pension liability prior to 1982. Conference has come a long way. The annuity rate that did not reach $100 until 1977 was set at $168 per past service year for 1985.

These then were the major concerns of Conference in these years under study: merger with the Evangelical United Brethren, numerical decline, the turmoil of the late 1960's and early '70's, special celebrations, the arrival of a new bishop, structural changes and pensions.

That wasn't all of course. Leisure ministries continued to be effective in the early days of the United Methodist Church. Conference sessions changed in 1970 from their Wednesday to Sunday format to a Monday to Thursday schedule. Project Equality was initiated by the Conference September 30, 1969, and the Pastoral Counseling Service for ministers and their families started in 1970.

Associate Members of Conference were first elected in 1971. This was a special relationship available for full time Lay Pastors who lacked only the necessary educational qualifications for full Conference membership. Because so little has been said about the yeomen work of our lay preachers, full and part time, the list of this Conference's first class of Associate members is given:

George Bewley	Edgar Schopp
Bertrand Carter	Fred R. Sharp
Ralph Davis	Archie Shull
Joel Duncan	George Starsmeare
Harold Dunn	William Stockton
Horace Estelow	James Thompson
Louis Kickasola	Moro Tussey
Walter I. Little	William Waters
William McCullough	Samuel Way
Thomas Panico	Thomas B. Wright[24]
Walter Sawn	

Conference in 1971, opposed the lowering of the drinking age to eighteen. Ten years later, New Jersey raised it back to twenty-one. The Board of Christian Social Concerns emphasized three priority concerns in 1971: (1) White racism and black revolution in New Jersey, (2) Patterns of economic exploitation in New Jersey, (3) Environmental pollution in New Jersey.[25]

Ronald Beppler became the first lay person elected Conference Secretary when he replaced the Rev. Robert Howe in 1972.

The report of a Study Committee on Ministerial Compensation was approved in 1972. It was a far-reaching report, raising the level of minimum salaries and establishing travel allowances. It called for ministerial evaluation, established guidelines for continuing education and vacation time. An important part, which was not implemented to any extent, was the recommendation that within four years Cooperative Ministries should be in wide-spread use throughout the Conference. This was coupled with the recommendation of a minimum pastoral work load of 400 members. Failure to move in these directions continues to cause the Conference problems.[26]

Conference in 1972, also adopted an Archival Policy which is still in effect. Quite simply, it names the Commission on Archives and History as the custodian of the official records of all the Boards, Commissions, Committees and Agencies of the Conference, of the records of the general officers of the Conference and of the records of all closed and abandoned churches.[27] Where this has been implemented, it has brought valuable records into the Conference Archives. The failures of implementation and the non-availability of significant records through the years makes the writing of this history more difficult.

Key 73 was on the agenda in 1973, the Women's Society of Christian Service became the United Methodist Women and an Historical Society sponsored United Methodist Heritage Tour, November 5 to 13, led 194 pilgrims on a visit to Methodist sites in England.

Key 73 was a significant interdenominational evangelistic outreach which saw the church in many communities reach out in new and imaginative ways in witness for Christ, often in concert with churches of other denominations. The Church was really being the Church.

A poem at the end of the Key 73 Task Force Report sums up what was attempted.

> If all the sleeping folks will wake up,
> And all the lukewarm folks will fire up,
> And all the dishonest folks will confess up,
> And all the disgruntled folks will sweeten up,
> And all the discouraged folks will cheer up,
> And all the depressed folks will look up,
> And all the estranged folks will make up,
> And all the gossipers will shut up,
> And all the dry bones will shake up,
> And all the true soldiers will stand up,
> And all the church members will pray up —
> And the Saviour for all is lifted up —
> THEN
> You can have the world's greatest renewal.[28]

Casino—No Dice won out against widespread casino gambling in New Jersey at the November, 1974 general election. The election of 1975, however, brought gambling to Atlantic City.

The 1976 Conference was Bishop Taylor's last. He and Mrs. Taylor retired that summer to their home in Princeton. At his farewell, Bishop Taylor presented these eight points as fundamental convictions he has held across the years:

1. God has not given up His dominion over the world.
2. Life without intrinsic values is built on a shaky foundation.
3. Positions and possessions are of relative value only.
4. What happens in you is far more important than what happens to you.
5. Life that is not nurtured by faith withers.
6. Mere adjustment to conditions and circumstances is a dangerous venture.
7. There are no simple problems or simple solutions. In every problem we find a web of relationships which must be taken into account.
8. By grace we are saved. None is so good as to earn it, none so bad as to be denied it.[29]

"The energy crisis is real in our Churches,"[30] said Superintendent C. Wesley Crossley in the 1977 Superintendents' Report. It was indeed and required several years of adjustments and learning ways of energy conservation.

World hunger began to receive special emphasis by 1978 and we learned much about hunger and related problems following the Bishop's and Mission Team's visit to Afghanistan, Pakistan, India, Bangladesh and the Middle East.

Four retired bishops: Fred Pierce Corson, W. Earl Ledden, Noah W. Moore, Jr., and Prince A. Taylor, Jr. were granted honorary membership in the Conference in 1979.[31]

Sunday afternoon Evangelism Rallies at St. Peter's United Methodist and St. Augustine Roman Catholic Churches in Ocean City opened the 1981 Conference sessions. Bishop Kenneth Goodson preached.

The 1984 Conference not only celebrated the Bicentennial of American Methodism, but marked the close of Bishop White's eight years as episcopal leader of the New Jersey Area. Bishop and Mrs. White were bid a fond farewell. Later in June, an official testimonial was tendered them.

It is August 29, 1984, as these words are being written and this history is being brought to a close. September 1 will find the Southern New Jersey Conference and the New Jersey Area under the leadership of a new bishop. He is Bishop Neil L. Irons. Bishop Irons will lead us into our Sesquicentennial celebration and beyond. A native of West Virginia, Bishop Irons is a graduate of Davis and Elkins College, United Theological Seminary and Vanderbilt University. He began his ministry in 1958, in the Evangelical United Brethren Church. In his last position, he was the Romney District Superintendent in the West Virginia Conference. Married to the former Inez Rossey, the Irons have two children, Andy and Anne.

Having begun this chapter with the story of our Evangelical United Brethren heritage, it is fitting to close it with a welcome to Bishop Neil Irons, a product of that heritage. As United Methodists we move onward. One hundred fifty years and more of our history is behind us. My, "What God Has Wrought!"

Chapter 20

LOOKING BACK - LOOKING AHEAD

One hundred fifty years of Conference history are past. It was over two hundred years ago that organized Methodism appeared in New Jersey. In reflecting on this past one can only say with wonder, this is "what God has wrought."

The beginnings were humble enough. The silver-tongued George Whitefield calling men to repentance helped to prepare the way. Laymen, witnessing to their faith in Christ, initially sowed the seed. Captain Thomas Webb organized classes in Burlington, New Mills, Trenton and maybe elsewhere. John Early at Bethel and Squire Murphy in Hazlet were early local leaders of Methodism. Then came the preachers, led by the indominable Francis Asbury. The work advanced. The harvest began.

Ignoring the Revolution, Benjamin Abbott, on his own, went on a 1778 preaching tour and introduced Methodism where it had never been before. New Jersey's unique contribution to early American Methodism boldly preached Christ and called Christians to a life of holiness. Then followed, in 1780, the appointed circuit riders. William Gill, John James and Richard Garrettson were the advanced guard of Methodism's evangelical cavalry. Asbury was always their leader. By century's end these indefatigable laborers for the Lord had taken Methodism to all parts of the state and meeting houses were built to the glory of God.

The first decades of the nineteenth century saw continual advance. Classes grew into societies and from society to church. Circuits grew, became smaller but more numerous and the first stationed churches appeared. Circuit riders, working with devoted laymen like James Sterling, the Murphys, Blackmans and Swains, led the way. Methodism had a message of free grace and salvation to offer to all. The doctrine of assurance was preached and Christians were called to a life of holiness and love. Quarterly meetings were enthusiastic times of celebration, gospel preaching and sacramental services. Camp meetings sprang up on every circuit and were immensely popular. Bishop Asbury died in 1816. It was the end of an era. Charles Pitman became New Jersey Methodism's favorite preacher who was at his best on the camp grounds or dedicating a church.

The New Jersey Conference was born in 1836 and held its first session in 1837 in Newark's Halsey Street Church. Methodism in New Jersey had come of age. For twenty years New Jersey was one Conference, then became two. South and north seldom met after that until New Jersey became one Area in 1964.

Church divisions of 1828 and 1844 were weathered as the church continued its advance. We built a school at Pennington. Missionaries left New Jersey for Oregon, South America and China. New Jersey Methodists struggled

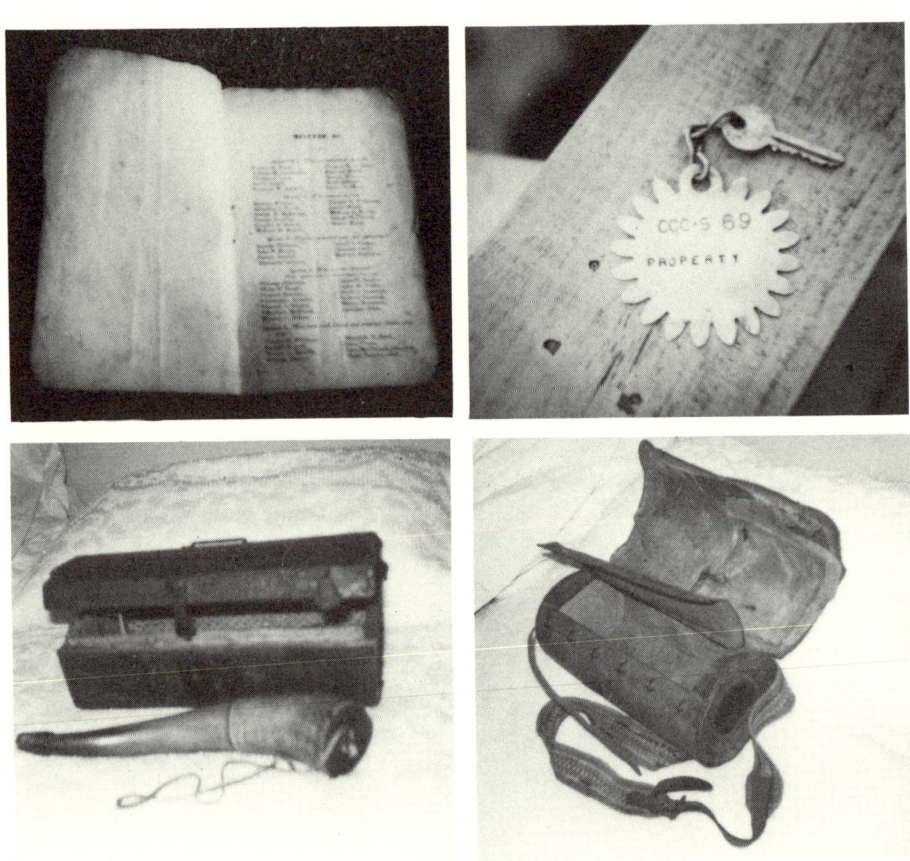

MEMORABILIA FROM SNJ CONFERENCE ARCHIVES
Clockwise: 1838 *Minutes,* Original Conference Center key,
Saddlebag, Preacher's powder horn and trunk.

with the slavery question. They preached and worked for revival. Sunday Schools became more important and many churches were built.

When the Civil War came, southern New Jersey Methodists proved to be intensely patriotic. They were union men in a state that never voted for Lincoln. It suddenly became right to oppose slavery and work for its eradication. The first Children's Day was celebrated in Merchantville Church while a Centennial Camp Meeting helped celebrate one hundred years of American Methodism.

The last three decades of the nineteenth century were the time of greatest glory for Methodism. The country was growing and so was the state. Our cities and seashore resorts came into their own. This was the "Methodist Age in

America." The Methodist Episcopal Church was the dominant ecclesiastical force in America. New Jersey Methodists showed themselves to be a revival people. They were willing to be deeply involved in temperance reform. Cape May, New Jersey, hosted the 1876 Conference between southern and northern Methodists that chartered a course which ultimately led to reunion. We found it hard to accede to lay and women's rights, yet in spite of our votes saw laity enter the General Conference. Women were not as fortunate, but these were the years of the founding of the great women missionary societies, wholeheartedly supported by the women of New Jersey.

The closing decades of the nineteenth century also witnessed the birth of southern New Jersey's great camp meetings. All were, in part, an outgrowth of the holiness crusade. The first National Holiness Camp Meeting was held in Vineland. Camp meetings at South Seaville, Malaga, Ocean Grove, Pitman, Ocean City and Delanco were all started between 1863 and 1898. It is doubtful that any Conference has the camp meeting legacy that is ours.

The twentieth century brought many changes to the Church. The last great revival swept the Conference on the eve of World War I. New Jersey Methodists rejoiced at the victory of prohibition, and worked hard to enforce it in a state that wanted to be "wet." This was the time of the social gospel, but this Conference was slow to adapt to it. We opted instead to support Harold Paul Sloan's protest against modernism in the church. This was the period when women won the right to be licensed to preach and receive ordination as local deacons and elders. We did not hurry to comply. Work among the foreign born in some of our cities and rural areas was a portent of our future ethnic ministries.

Methodist union was the big news of the 1930's. We learned anew about the history of the Methodist Protestants in this state and welcomed the larger fellowship brought to us by our brothers and sisters in Christ. In the 1930's we struggled through the depression. We also elected the first woman delegate from the New Jersey Conference to General Conference in 1936. Soon after she became the first woman ordained by this Conference.

War and peace were the concerns of the 1940's. After the war we moved forward with the Philadelphia Area Evangelistic Advance that introduced visitation evangelism to our churches. Conference Center was purchased and the Ocean Grove Home for the Aged was built.

The period between 1945 and 1966 was one of much advance. Church membership increased 40,000 in those years. Sunday School membership grew 23,500 in the 1950's alone. An average of 1.5 million dollars a year was spent on buildings and improvements by New Jersey Conference churches in the 1950's and 1960's. These years saw many quadrennium programs like Methodist Dollars For Christ. Spanish work was started, the *Relay* was born, unconventional evangelism began to be practiced on the beach, in camp grounds and on the fair grounds' midway. This period ended with the Conference part of the New Jersey Area, led by Bishop Prince A. Taylor, Jr. Former Delaware Conference Churches joined us in New Jersey in 1965. As whites and blacks we faced a turbulent period as we became the Southern New Jersey Conference.

Decline has been a permanent feature of the Conference since 1966. In spite of celebrations and the merger with the Evangelical United Brethren Church, every year since 1966 church membership has decreased. Sunday School decline has been even more dramatic. We changed our Conference structure, added two districts than took one away, welcomed new bishops, raised a lot of money for worthy causes, but still declined. Yet, this is God's Church. The work is His. If we are faithful we will again see what God will do.

John Wesley wrote a tract in 1786 and called it "Thoughts Upon Methodism." He said:

> I am not afraid that the people called Methodists should ever cease to exist either in Europe or America. But I am afraid, lest they should only exist as a dead sect, having the form of religion without the power. And this undoubtedly will be the case, unless they first hold fast both the doctrine, spirit, and discipline with which they first set out.[1]

Is that our problem today? In an age of theological pluralism, have we forsaken our doctrine? Concerned as we should be about spiritual growth, have we lost the spirit? Living in a time of relativity and "anything goes" philosophy, where is the discipline?

Is it possible that lessons from the past can help us chart the future and bring us out of the spiritual malaise of the present? It is possible. Let our Wesleyan heritage be our guide.

The needs of today seem obvious. We need a spiritual revival to bring people to Christ. We need a moral reformation to lift our ethical standards. We need a crusade for social justice and righteousness that will effectively call the Church to decisively stand for what is right.

This is our heritage. John Wesley was the leader of the evangelical revival. He not only preached a message of personal salvation by the grace of God, but urged Christians to step out by faith to the higher ground of holiness of heart and life. Nor was Wesley content to be only an evangelist. He was a social gospel advocate long before anyone knew of that term. He fought to right societies wrongs and led the people called Methodists to minister to the total needs of all people.

This too, was the expressed aim of American Methodism. Our fathers in the faith left the Christmas Conference determined to "preach the gospel, reform the continent and spread Scriptural holiness across the land."

If New Jersey United Methodism is to move forward once again, we need to know our roots. We must have a strong faith in Christ for today. We, of necessity, must have a vision for the future of a world being won for Christ.

This, then, is our history: the one hundred fifty year history of a Conference. The history of a people of God called United Methodists. It is the story of what God has been doing with us, through us, and yes, at times in spite of us. We do not know the future, but we know the future is God's. Because the future is God's, we believe that United Methodism in southern New Jersey will continue to exist and to exist as a living sect. If that is so, future historians, in writing even of our day, will be able to say this is "What God Has Wrought!"

ABBREVIATIONS

Anniv.	Anniversary
Eastern Conf.	Eastern Conference
Enc. World Meth.	*Encyclopedia of World Methodism.*
EUB	Evangelical United Brethren Church
HAM	Bucke, Emory S. (ed.), *History of American Methodism.*
Hist. Trail	*The Historical Trail*
ME	Methodist Episcopal Church
MP	Methodist Protestant Church
Meth. Trail	Stanger, Frank Bateman (ed.), *The Methodist Trail in New Jersey.*
Minutes	*Minutes,* N. J. Conference, ME Church. *Minutes,* N. J. Conference, The Methodist Church. *Minutes,* SNJ Conference, The Methodist Church. *Minutes,* SNJ Conference, UM Church. Identified by date.
SNJ	Southern New Jersey Conference.
UM	United Methodist Church
UMW	United Methodist Women
WSCS	Woman's (Women's) Society of Christian Service

NOTES

Chapter 1 METHODIST ORIGINS

1. Amos 4:11.
2. Frank Baker in "The Wesleys in Georgia," in *From Wesley to Asbury* shows that it was in Georgia that Wesley came to realize that a personal assurance of salvation was needed for a fruitful ministry. Baker says the following methods later used by Wesley were first experimented with in Georgia: class meetings, use of lay leaders in parish work, appointment of women as "deaconesses," use of extempore prayer, itinerant preaching, preaching in the open air, early morning services before the start of the working day, and the use of hymns. p. 13.
3. A significant chapter on "The Great Awakening" is in Winthrop S. Hudson, *Religion in America,* chapter 3, pp. 59-82.
4. Piles Grove was near Sharptown, Salem County.
5. Cohansie is an old name for the Bridgeton area. This Service, however, was in nearby Greenwich, Cumberland County at the Presbyterian Church built in 1735.
6. George Whitefield's *Journals*. The Banner of Truth Trust, 1965, pp. 495, 496.
7. See Gaustad, *Historical Atlas of Religion in America,* 1962, p. 4.
8. For the priority of Strawbridge see Baker, "The Lay Pioneers of American Methodism," in *From Wesley to Asbury,* 33-40 and Frederick E. Maser, *Robert Strawbridge, First American Methodist Circuit Rider*.
9. Quoted in Maser, Ibid., 47.
10. Baker, 41.
11. Methodist Magazine, 1826, pp. 438, 9.
12. Baker, "Captain Thomas Webb, Consolidator," *From Wesley to Asbury,* 63.
13. Original source material on Webb is hard to find. Several recent studies of note are: Baker, Ibid.; Baker, "Captain Thomas Webb, Pioneer of American Methodism," in *Religion and Life,* Summer 1965; Bates, "Captain Thomas Webb;" Moss, "Thomas Webb, A Founder of American Methodism;" Steelman, "Captain Thomas Webb, Founder of Methodism in New Jersey," in *The Historical Trail,* 1976.
14. See article by that title in *The Historical Trail,* 1968 by Lloyd E. Griscom. Also Griscom, "Early American Methodism: The Unique Career of a Pioneer," *The Historical Trail,* 1984.
15. See article by his descendant Charles Earley, "John Early: Pioneer Methodist in New Jersey," in *The Historical Trail,* 1963, pp. 5-7.
16. Asbury, *The Journal and Letters of Francis Asbury,* II, 53.
17. Harry F. Green, "Historic Gloucester Point," in *The Historical Trail,* 1969, pp. 33-36.
18. Noted in Nehemiah Curnock, *The Journal of John Wesley,* V, 330n.
19. J. B. Wakely, "One Hundred Years: A Centennial Discourse," *The Methodist Home Journal,* 1870, 4.
20. Steelman, "The Rev. Richard Boardman," *The Historical Trail,* 1969, pp. 38-49.
21. Quoted in J. Hillman Coffee, "The Reverend Joseph Pilmore, D. D.," Ibid., 53.
22. See *The Journal of Joseph Pilmore*. Pilmore-Boardman Bicentennial Issue of *The Historical Trail,* 1969. Frank B. Stanger, *The Life and Ministry of the Rev. Joseph Pilmore, D. D.* (Thesis) Temple University, 1942.
23. Asbury, *Journal,* I, 4.
24. Transcript of the *Diary of Reverend Thomas Rankin*. Original in possession of Garrett Biblical Institute Library. See also, Albea Godbold, "Francis Asbury and His Difficulties With John Wesley and Thomas Rankin," *Methodist History,* April 1965, 3-19.

Chapter 2 THE EARLY YEARS

1. Richard P. McCormick, *New Jersey from Colony to State 1609-1789,* 137.
2. Ibid., 152.
3. Benjamin Abbott, *Experience and Gospel Labors,* 1836, p. 18.

4. John King and William Waters were appointed to New Jersey in 1773. They do not seem to have preached here and Philip Gatch took their place.

5. The maiden name of Mary Abbott is not given by any of Abbott's biographers. It is given in Ralph Ege, *Pioneers of Old Hopewell,* pages 256-259. Mary was the daughter of William and Catron (Catherine) Snook of Hopewell, N.J. In his will dated 1760 he identifies one of his five daughters as "Mary Abbott." His widow Catron in her will dated 1763 further identifies Mary as the wife of Benjamin Abbott.

6. Abel Stevens, *A Compendious History of American Methodism,* 1868, p. 211.

7. Abbott's autobiography gives very few dates. Historians differ as to the date of this tour. From all evidence I can gather I date it in 1778.

8. Abbott, 66.

9. Ibid., 70.

10. Ibid., 212. Besides his autobiography, the best sources for Abbott are: Howard F. Shipps, *The Forgotten Apostle of Methodism,* unpub. STD Thesis, Temple University School of Theology, 1955.

Shipps, "War Time Evangelism, A Chapter in the Life of Benjamin Abbott," *The Historical Trail,* 1978, pp. 3-6.

Joseph Henry Bennett, *Preaching Stations of Benjamin Abbott in the Jerseys,* unpublished manuscript, no date. Copy in author's files.

11. 169, 170.

12. John Lednum, *A History of the Rise of Methodism in America,* 295, 296.

13. For a discussion of what Wesley did relative to the new church in America see Frank Baker, *John Wesley and the Church of England,* chapters 14 and 15.

14. Asbury, Letters, III, 38, 39.

15. Quoted in Warren T. Smith, "The Christmas Conference," in *Methodist History,* July 1968, 11.

16. For the Christmas Conference see Ibid., Norman W. Spellman, "The Christmas Conference" in *History of American Methodism,* Vol. I, 213-232. Thomas Ware, "The Christmas Conference," in *Methodist Magazine and Quarterly Review,* January 1832, pp. 96-104.

17. Ware, Ibid.

18. *Extracts* of the Journals of the Late Rev. Thomas Coke, L. L. D. Dublin: The Methodist Book Room, 1816, 53, 54.

19. Ibid., 188.

20. The Address and the President's Reply are printed in Asbury, III, pp. 70-72. The story of this visit is told in *History of American Methodism,* I, 247-251.

21. Asbury, I, 597, 598.

22. Coke, *Extracts,* 136.

23. Asbury, I, 651.

24. Phoebus, 46, 47. See also Vernon Hampton, ed., *Newark Conference Centennial History,* 55.

25. Phoebus, 70, 71.

26. Quoted in Phoebus, 78, 79.

27. Hazel B. Simpson, Compiler, *History of Bethel M. E. Church,* 35ff.

28. Ibid., 60-62.

29. Most of this information comes from Frank B. Stanger, ed., *The Methodist Trail in New Jersey,* 1961.

30. C.f. Newark Conference History.

Chapter 3 CIRCUITS - CIRCUIT RIDERS - CLASS LEADERS

1. Jamison, 1964, 76.

2. For an account of "The Methodist Way," see Barclay, *History of Methodist Missions,* II, chapter 4, 338-342.

3. For an account of Learner Blackman, see Robert B. Steelman, "Learner Blackman," *Methodist History,* April 1967, pp. 3-17.

4. For an account of the three families, see Robert B. Steelman, *Beginning of Methodism in Southernmost Jersey,* unpub. Master Thesis, Temple Univ., 1962, pp. 69-78.

5. John Atkinson, *Memorials of Methodism in New Jersey,* pp. 152-164.
6. Quoted in Barclay, II, 305.
7. Thomas Ware, *Sketches of the Life and Travels of Rev. Thomas Ware,* 1839, 57.
8. Romans 8:16. (RSV).
9. *Extracts of Letters Containing Some Account of the Work of God Since the Year 1800,* 1805, 91, 92.
10. Quoted in Barclay, II, 315.
11. Ibid., 427n.
12. Ibid., 429.
13. Ibid.
14. W. Lomax Childress, *The Circuit Rider.*
15. See Asbury's *Journal* for 1809. Steelman, "Bishop Francis Asbury," *The Historical Trail,* 1971. Bennett & Steelman, "Along the Asbury Trail," unpublished slide lecture, 1966.
16. Alexander Gilmore, *Centenary Memorial Sermon,* "What Has God Wrought," delivered before the New Jersey Annual Conference, March 26, 1866.
17. Roy H. Short, "Camp Meeting Movement," *Encyclopedia of World Methodism,* I, 382-384.
18. Gilmore, 23, 24.
19. Norwood, *The Story of Methodism,* 1974, 127.

Chapter 4 A NEW CONFERENCE IS BORN

1. *Journal of Rev. Learner Blackman,* January 27, 1813. Original is in the Archives of the Mississippi Conference. Microfilm copies in SNJ Conference Archives and United Methodist Archives.
2. Ibid., September 29, 1812.
3. *Philadelphia Conference Journals* (1800-1836), 531. Quoted in John Hillman Coffee, *The New Jersey Conference 1836-1861,* unpublished Thesis, pp. 29, 30. A handwritten copy of the *Journal* of the Philadelphia Conference for the above years is in the Archives of the SNJ Conference.
4. *Journals of the General Conference,* 1836, 472. Quoted in Coffee, Ibid., 31, 32.
5. Barclay, *History of Methodist Missions,* I, 205.
6. The Minutes of the 1st session of the N. J. Conference were not published. They are contained in a large Journal, handwritten by the Conference Secretary. For the first time in the 1983 *Historical Trail* they were published as transcribed and edited by Robert B. Steelman, pp. 3-26. The information and quotes about the 1837 Conference were taken from the printed account.
7. *New Jersey Conference Memorial,* 1865, 61.
8. Ibid., 240.
9. George A. Raybold authored, *Fatal Feud, Paul Perryman, Annals of Methodism, Reminiscences of Methodism in West Jersey, Revival Scenes,* and *Incidents of Itinerary.*
10. Much of the material in the preceding pages is from Robert B. Steelman, "Charter Members of the New Jersey Conference of the Methodist Episcopal Church," *The Historical Trail,* 1980, 15-19. A list of presiding elders is in the *New Jersey Conference Minutes,* 1911, 172. General Conference Delegates are listed in the 1928 Conference Minutes, 690.
11. Coffee, op. cit., 59.
12. Robert John Williams, *A Century of Compromise:* New Jersey Methodists on the Status and Role of Blacks in the Church and Society, 69.
13. Ibid., 82 ff.
14. Ibid., 67.
15. Ibid., 88-90.
16. Gilmore, *Centenary Memorial Sermon,* 26.
17. Ibid., 26, 27.
18. Conference Secretary's Files, Conference Archives, 1839.
19. Ibid., 1841.
20. *Minutes,* 1838, pp. 15, 16.

Chapter 5 THE PRE-CIVIL WAR ERA

1. HAM, II, 207.
2. *The Doctrines and Discipline of the Methodist Episcopal Church,* 1798, 133.
3. HAM, II, 57, 59.
4. For general information on the M.E. Church and slavery, the various decisions made and the division of the Church see HAM, II, Chapter 14. Frederick A. Norwood, *The Story of American Methodism,* Chapter 17. Williams, pp. 112-134. Donald G. Mathews, *Slavery and Methodism,* pp. 293-303.
5. See Clement Alexander Price, *Freedom Not Far Distant,* A Documentary History of Afro-Americans in New Jersey.
6. See "The Underground Railroad in New Jersey," pamphlet published by the W.P.A., 1939-1941.
7. Williams, 117.
8. Ibid., 126.
9. Ibid., 133, 134.
10. *Christian Advocate,* March 31, 1847. Taken from Abel Stevens "Scrapbook on Slavery and the M.E. Church," Book B. Drew University Archives.
11. Letter from Carlisle, Pa., October 31, 1844. In the manuscript collection, Drew University.
12. Statistics from Gilmore, 31.
13. Kenneth Anderson, Manuscript History of Pennington School, 1838-1970, Chapter 4, p. 1. A copy of the rough draft of the manuscript is in the office of the Alumni Director of the School. The completed manuscript was destroyed in the Pennington fire.
14. Ibid., 2.
15. Ibid., 4.
16. Ibid., 11.
17. Ibid., 11, 12.
18. Ibid., 10. N. J. Conference *Minutes,* 1851, p. 21.
19. *Minutes,* 1858, pp. 12, 13. 1859 *Minutes,* pp. 27-39.
20. *Minutes,* 1843, 11. *Meth. Trail,* pp. 30, 31.
21. *Meth. Trail,* 31.
22. *Minutes,* 1859, 36.
23. Caleb A. Malmsbury, *The Life, Labors and Sermons of Rev. Charles Pitman, D. D.,* 129, 130.
24. William J. Kingston, "Charles Pitman: New Jersey Apostle," Part III, *The Historical Trail,* 1974, 21.
25. Malmsbury, 147.
26. Union List of Ministers of the New Jersey Conference.
27. Elizabeth M. Smith, "William Roberts: Circuit Rider of the Far West," *Methodist History,* January, 1982, p. 62.
28. Ibid., 73.
29. G. E. Strobridge, *Biography of the Rev. Daniel Parish Kidder,* 10, 65, 76, 87, 129.
30. See article on Kidder in Nolan B. Harmon, ed., *The Encyclopedia of World Methodism,* I, 1331.
31. Barclay, III, 135.
32. See Simpson, *Cyclopaedia of Methodism,* 540. *Enc. World Meth.,* II, 1452. Correspondence and files in the author's possession. Information on Rebecca Lore from Lloyd E. Griscom.
33. *Minutes,* 1848, 12.
34. Mrs. Joanna P. R. Hanly, *Memoirs of the late Rev. Joseph J. Hanly, M. D. of the New Jersey Conference,* 197, 198.
35. *Minutes,* 9.
36. *Minutes,* 6.
37. Joshua E. Licorish, "Delaware Conference," *Enc. of World Methodism,* I, 652. *Historical Trail,* 1967, 1968. Williams, 74, 75.

38. William C. Jason, Jr., "The Delaware Annual Conference of the Methodist Church, 1864-1965," *Methodist History,* July 1966, 30.
39. Secretary's Files, 1844, SNJ Conference Archives.
40. Reginald F. Hildebrand, "Methodist Episcopal Policy on the Ordination of Black Ministers, 1784-1864," *Methodist History,* April 1982, 134.
41. Licorish, Ibid.
42. Francis H. Tees, *Methodist Origins,* 137.
43. *Manuscript Journal,* 1849-1868, 147.
44. The above recorded actions are outlined in and quoted from Coffee, *The New Jersey Conference,* pp. 40-44.
45. John Fawcett, "Blest Be the Tie That Binds," Fourth verse.

Chapter 6 THE WAR DECADE

1. William R. Maps, Jr., *Journal,* Nov. 10, 1865.
2. *Minutes,* 1862, 16, 17.
3. *Minutes,* 1863, 15.
4. HAM, II, 215.
5. HAM, II, 215, 216.
6. Williams, 160.
7. Nicholas Van Sant, *Sunset Memories,* 90, 91, Quoted in Williams, 160.
8. *Minutes,* 1865, 12.
9. Ibid., 24.
10. A. K. Street, *What I Think of Methodism After Fifty Years in the Itineracy,* 22, Italics mine.
11. Anderson, Chapters 5, 10.
12. Ibid., Chapters 4, 15.
13. Williams, 169.
14. E. H. Stokes, et. al., *The Earnest Minister,* 80.
15. James F. Rusling, "The War For the Union," *Methodist Quarterly Review,* April, 1864. Quoted in Williams, 170.
16. Williams, 172, 173. For a fuller discussion of New Jersey Methodists reaction to the Civil War see Robert J. Williams, "Slavery and Patriotism: New Jersey Methodists During the Civil War," *Methodist History,* July 1983.
17. William W. Sweet, *The Methodist Episcopal Church and the Civil War,* 192.
18. William R. Maps, *Journal,* March 10, 1862.
19. Frank B. Rose File, SNJ Conference Archives.
20. Rose letter, Conference Secretary's Files, 1865, SNJ Confrence Archives.
21. Sweet, 163, 164. See Appendix in Sweet for list of N. J. Conference delegates.
22. Ibid., 171, 172.
23. James P. Brawley, *Two Centuries of Methodist Concern: Bondage, Freedom and Education of Black People,* 81.
24. *Minutes,* 1867, 24.
25. *Enc. World Meth.,* I, 433.
26. Anderson, Chapter 4, 17.
27. HAM, II, 331.
28. *Minutes,* 1866, 31.
29. Gilmore, 33.
30. *Minutes,* 1866, 5.
31. *Minutes,* 1862, 9.
32. For an account of the struggle for lay rights in the N. J. Conference and lay activities in the 19th Century within the Conference, see Walter B. VanSant, "Lay Activities In the New Jersey Conference," *The Historical Trail,* 1962, 1963, 1964.
33. Information on Children's Day and its founding can be found in: Report on the "Origin of Children's Day," *Minutes,* 1892, pp. 72, 73. "The Origin of Children's Day," *Meth. Trail,* 47. Penny Moore, "Memories of Children's Day," *Hist. Trail,* 1980, 13, 14.

34. Simpson, *History of Bethel Church,* 129, 130.
35. *Minutes,* 1869, 17.
36. Ibid., 12.

Chapter 7   A FLOURISHING CHURCH

1. Winthrop S. Hudson, "The Methodist Age in America," *Methodist History,* April 1974, 15.
2. Donald G. Jones, *The Sectional Crisis and Northern Methodism,* 50.
3. John T. Cunningham, "The Story of New Jersey," *The New Jersey Almanac Tercentenary Edition,* 1964, 203.
4. Price, 132.
5. Ibid., 143.
6. Williams, 200.
7. Brawley, 133, 401.
8. 1884, *General Conference Journal.* Quoted in Barclay, III, 57.
9. *Minutes,* 1870, 25, 26.
10. *Methodist Trail,* 108. *Enc. World Meth.,* 2484, 2430.
11. *Minutes,* 1884, 15.
12. Ibid., 19.
13. *Minutes,* 1886, 39.
14. *Minutes of the N. J. Methodist State Convention,* Held in Trenton, N. J., September 27-29, 1870, 31.
15. Ibid., 105.
16. Homer L. Calkin, "The Methodists and the Centennial of 1876," *Methodist History,* January 1976, 95, 96. See also "Bishop Simpson's Centennial Prayer, 1876," *Methodist History,* October, 1976.
17. Ibid., 94.
18. *Minutes,* 1884, 49.
19. H. K. Carroll, W. P. Harrison, J. H. Bayliss, eds., *Proceedings of the Centennial Methodist Conference,* Baltimore, Md., December 9-17, 1884.
20. *Minutes,* 1886.
21. *Formal Fraternity,* 40.
22. *Proceedings of the Joint Commission,* typed transcript of original minutes in SNJ Conference Archives, 8.
23. Kenneth E. Rowe, "The Spirit of Cape May," *The Historical Trail,* 1977, 15.
24. *Minutes,* 1870, 13.
25. Ibid., 16.
26. VanSant, *Historical Trail,* 1964, 11.
27. Ibid., 12.
28. *Minutes,* 1872, 41.
29. VanSant, 12.
30. Ibid.
31. *Minutes,* 1898, 82.
32. Elaine Magalis, *Conduct Becoming to a Woman,* 105, 106.
33. Louise McCoy North, *The Story of the New York Branch of the WFMS of the M. E. Church,* 110.
34. Ibid., 156, 157.
35. Lewis Curts, *The General Conferences of the Methodist Episcopal Church from 1792 to 1896,* 184. Hilah F. Thomas and Rosemary Skinner Keller, eds., *Women in New Worlds,* I, 203.
36. *Minutes,* 1870, 22.
37. Notes in author's files supplied by Elizabeth Hawk. See list of Epworth League and Youth Fellowship Presidents in Appendix.
38. *Minutes,* 1896, 109-131.
39. Alphonso Alva Hopkins, *The Life of Clinton Bowen Fisk,* 147.
40. *Minutes,* 1900. See Statisticians Report.
41. *Minutes,* 1892, 22.
42. *Minutes,* 1893, 64.

43. *Minutes,* 1897, 19, 26, 27, 31.
44. *Minutes,* 1890, 18.
45. *Minutes,* 1887, 16.
46. *Minutes,* 1891, 20, 21.
47. *Minutes,* 1892, 21.
48. *Minutes,* 1895, 110.
49. Written by John Newton.

Chapter 8 CAMP MEETINGS IN SOUTHERN NEW JERSEY

1. Original in records of Goshen Church. Typescript of Minutes, June 7, 1834 to March 10, 1838 in SNJ Conference Archives. Typescript, 1.
2. Original Minute Book in private hands. Zerox copy in Archives of the SNJ Conference.
3. *Christian Advocate,* Sept. 14, 1865, 290.
4. Minutes of the 1765 Conference, quoted in Frank Bateman Stanger, *The Wesleyan Doctrine of Scriptural Holiness,* 2.
5. *The Book of Discipline of the United Methodist Church,* 1980, 66.
6. Quoted in HAM, II, 611.
7. Charles Edwin Jones, *Perfectionist Persuasion,* Appendix II, Appendix III. A good book for a discussion of the holiness movement. See also HAM, II, 608-627 and Norwood, *The Story of American Methodism,* 297-301.
8. John S. Inskip, *Penuel,* 8.
9. Ibid., 472.
10. Mr. & Mrs. Richard F. Gibbons, *History of Ocean Grove, 1869-1939,* 9.
11. *Minutes,* 1910, 98. 1907, 52.
12. Audrey G. Sullivan, *Nineteenth Century South Jersey Camp Meeting,* South Seaville, N. J., gives the date of 1863, 7. Robert W. Crowther, Jr., *Methodist Camp Meetings in Southern New Jersey,* says 1864 is considered the date of origin. It might have been that the Association was formed in 1863 and held their first camp in 1864.
13. Sept. 8, 1875. Quoted in Sullivan, 14, 15.
14. *Minutes,* 1890, 16.
15. Crowther (there are no page nos. on the zerox copy of Crowther's paper).
16. Ibid.
17. Gail A. Eisenlohr, *From Vision to Reality,* A History of Malaga Camp Meeting, 1869-1969, 1.
18. *Life and Times of Rev. J. B. Graw,* 1832-1901, 325.
19. Eisenlohr, 3.
20. Gibbons, 9.
21. Ibid., 11.
22. *Minutes,* 1878, 19.
23. *New Jersey Conference Camp Meeting Association,* 100 Year Anniversary Booklet, 1870-1970, 5, 6.
24. Ibid., 17.
25. Ibid., 9.
26. Ibid.
27. Harold Lee, *A History of Ocean City, N. J.,* 11.
28. Ibid., 17.
29. Ocean City Association, First Annual Report.
30. Ocean City Association, Third Annual Report, 24.
31. 100th Anniversary Program, 14, 20.
32. Ibid., 3.
33. Lloyd E. Griscom, "Ocean City, Once Peck's Beach," in *The Herald.* Also Union List of Methodist Ministers.
34. Minutes of the Delaware Conference of the Methodist Episcopal Church, 1893, 37.

35. This account of Delanco Camp is indebted to H. Raymond Hughes, *The History of Delanco Camp Meeting Association* written in 1961 and his updated history, *Looking Back,* written in 1984. See also his article on "Delanco Camp Meeting," *The Historical Trail,* 1984.
36. Hughes, *History,* 10.
37. Ibid., 12.
38. *Minutes,* 1908, 84. Quoted in Hughes, 28.
39. Hughes, 47.
40. Ibid., 53.
41. Ibid., 86.
42. Hughes, *Looking Back,* 5.
43. Ibid., 9.
44. pp. 196, 197.
45. Material on Island Heights in author's files. Also, Graw, 112-117.
46. *Hist. Trail,* 179.
47. *Minutes,* 1913, 77. 1935, 509.
48. Written by Cecil Frances Alexander.

Chapter 9 ENTERING A NEW CENTURY

1. Hudson, "The Methodist Age in America," 15.
2. Ransom E. Noble, Jr., quoted in Cunningham, 204.
3. *Minutes,* 1903, 84.
4. Defined by C. H. Hopkins, *The Rise of the Social Gospel in American Protestantism, 1865-1915.* This is the standard history of the movement. Quoted in Richard M. Cameron, *Methodism and Society in Historical Perspective,* 283.
5. Cameron, 285.
6. HAM, III, 388.
7. Quoted in HAM, III, 388.
8. *Discipline,* Methodist Episcopal Church, 479-481.
9. *Minutes,* 1911, 98.
10. *Minutes,* 1914, 96.
11. *Minutes,* 1912, 40, 47.
12. *Minutes,* 1914, 100-107.
13. *Minutes,* 1914, 96.
14. *Methodism and Society in the Twentieth Century,* Vol. 2, *Methodism and Society,* 66.
15. *Minutes,* 1900, 56.
16. *Minutes,* 1905, 55.
17. *Minutes,* 1910, 65.
18. Edmund Hewitt, *Minutes,* 1905, 55.
19. Clement Price, *Freedom Not Far Distant,* 135.
20. *Minutes,* 1909, 94.
21. *Minutes,* 1912, 170, 172.
22. *Minutes,* 1906, 95.
23. *Minutes,* 1914, 69.
24. *Minutes,* 1902, 23, 24.
25. *Minutes,* 1906, 58.
26. *Minutes,* 1907, 56.
27. *Minutes,* 1908, 99.
28. *Minutes,* 1900, 53.
29. Ibid., 59.
30. *Minutes,* 1904, 53.
31. *Minutes,* 1908, 73.
32. *Minutes,* 1915, 73.
33. Ibid., 79.

34. *Minutes,* 1916, 83.
35. Ibid., 82.
36. Ibid., 74.
37. *Minutes,* 1917, 46.
38. Ibid., 70, 71.
39. *Minutes,* 1901, 53.
40. *Minutes,* 1908, 82.
41. *Minutes,* 1909, 65, 66.
42. Ibid., 73.
43. *Minutes,* 1906, 46.
44. *Minutes,* 1904, 59.
45. Ibid., 54.
46. *Minutes,* 1910, 75.
47. *Minutes,* 1907, 31, 32.
48. *Minutes,* 1911, 122.
49. Samuel Wesley Lake, Trenton District Presiding Elder's Report, *Minutes,* 1900, 60.

Chapter 10 WORLD WAR I AND THE TURBULENT TWENTIES

1. Muelder, 117.
2. Sydney E. Ahlstrom, *A Religious History of the American People,* Vol. 2, 403, 404.
3. Cunningham, 205-207.
4. Price, 192.
5. *Minutes,* 1917, 35.
6. *Minutes,* 1918, 227.
7. *Minutes,* 1919, 469. Cunningham, 207.
8. *Minutes,* 1931, 508.
9. *Minutes,* 1961, 388, 369. *Enc. World Meth.,* II, 2173. Dorothy Kille Thomas, ed. *Haddonfield United Methodist Church:* A Sesquicentennial History, 1829-1979, 122-128.
10. Thomas, 129. Union List.
11. *Minutes,* 1954, 594.
12. Letter, July 27, 1984, Rev. David M. Finch to the author. List of General Conference Delegates. No memoir of William E. Massey appeared in the Conference Minutes.
13. *Minutes,* 1920, 632, 633, 673, 674. Paul A. Stellhorn and Michael J. Birkner, eds., *The Governors of New Jersey, 1664-1974,* 190-193.
14. Muelder, 118.
15. M. Miller, "A Footnote to the Role of the Protestant Churches in the Election of 1928," *Church History,* 25 (1956). Quoted in Muelder, 119.
16. Some relevant documents and studies of The Modernist Controversy are:
    Minutes, 1914, "Report of Committee on Publication," 100-107.
    Minutes, 1917, "Report on Course of Study," 107-118.
    Minutes, 1918, 280-293.
    Minutes, 1919, General Conference Memorial, 445, 446, 456.
    Minutes, 1920, 676.
    Minutes, 1921, Resolution Concerning the 1920 General Conference Decision on Course of Study, 36.
    Harold Paul Sloan material, Archives Drew University. Includes paper, "My Earliest Contacts with Modernism." Shows how the N. J. Protest began and how it developed. Tells what the N. J. Protest attempted. Copy in Sloan files, SNJ Conference Archives.
    "Harold Paul Sloan, Defender of the Faith," in Thomas, ed., *History of Haddonfield Church,* 122-128. Includes appointments held and books written.
    HAM, III, 270-273.
17. Sloan, "My Earliest Contacts with Modernism," 4.
18. *Minutes,* 1917, 45, 51, 60, 107-118.

19. *Minutes,* 1918, 280-293. Resolutions of Action, 289.
20. *Minutes,* 1919, 445, 446, 456.
21. *Minutes,* 1920, 670.
22. *Daily Christian Advocate,* May 20, 1920, p. 391. Quoted in HAM, 271. See also *Minutes,* 1921, 36.
23. Letter to Rev. William G. Burleigh, Elkins, West Virginia, March 13, 1928. Sloan correspondence, Drew University.
24. Thomas, 125.
25. Sloan, "My Earliest Contacts with Modernism," 14.
26. Williams, 316.
27. David M. Chalmers, *Hooded Americanism: The First Century of the Ku Klux Klan, 1865-1965.* Quoted in Williams, 306, 307.
28. Quoted in Williams, 311.
29. *Minutes,* 1926, 220.
30. *Minutes,* 1920, 629.
31. Ibid., 723.
32. *Minutes,* 1921, 44.
33. Ibid., 96.
34. *Minutes,* 1925, 26.
35. *Minutes,* 1928, 705.
36. *Minutes,* 1929, 30, 31.
37. Ibid., 164.
38. *Minutes,* 1923, 346, 347.
39. *Minutes,* 1917, 87, 88.
40. *Minutes,* 1922, 198.
41. *Minutes,* 1923, 363.
42. *Minutes,* 1925, 28.
43. *Minutes,* 1924, 514.
44. Edward S. Sheldon, "Recounted Miracles of Grace," No. 31. "The 1928 Revival in First Church Collingswood," 2.
45. Ibid., 4.
46. *Minutes,* 1920, 648.
47. *Minutes,* 1921, 55, 56.
48. *Minutes,* 1925, 48.
49. HAM, II, 524.
50. *Minutes,* 1929, 73.
51. *Minutes,* 1921, 37.
52. *Minutes,* 1926, 212.
53. Short, *Chosen to Be Consecrated,* various pages. See index. *Enc. of World Meth.,* II, 2014, 2015.

Chapter 11 THE METHODIST CHURCH IS BORN

1. Quoted in HAM, III, 403.
2. HAM, III, 406.
3. HAM, III, 417.
4. *Minutes,* 1925, 24.
5. *Minutes,* 1936, 34, 188.
6. An excellent summary is Frederick E. Maser, "The Story of Unification," HAM, III, Chapter 32, pages 407-478. For a Methodist Episcopal Appraisal see Paul N. Garber, *The Methodists Are One People.* Methodist Episcopal South, John M. Moore, *The Long Road to Methodist Union.* Methodist Protestant, James H. Straughn, *Inside Methodist Union.* A more recent work showing the southern perspective is Robert Watson Sledge, *Hands On the Ark,* The Struggle for Change in the Methodist Episcopal Church, South, 1914-1939.
7. Norwood, *The Story of American Methodism,* 410.

8. *Minutes,* 1933, 28. Churches who wish to know who their first lay delegates were can see the Conference *Minutes,* 1933, pages 183-187.
9. *Minutes,* 1933, 187.
10. Conference *Minutes.* Papers on file SNJ Conference Archives. Personal interviews with Helen Phillips Neary, April 13, 1984. Helen P. and Robert C. Neary, Sr., *Our Travels, Little Things We Remember and Rev. Helen P. Neary, A Lady Circuit Rider.*
11. *Minutes,* 1956, 139. N. J. Conference M. P. *Minutes,* 1908, 16.
12. *Minutes,* 1931, 449.
13. *Minutes,* 1932, 666.
14. *Minutes,* 1934, 283.
15. *Minutes,* 1936, 35.
16. *Minutes,* 1936, 44, 45.
17. *Minutes,* 1938, 193.
18. *Minutes,* 1939, 27, 28.
19. *Minutes,* 1937, 294.
20. Williams, 323, 324.
21. *Minutes,* 1930, 273, 274.
22. Methodist Sesqui-Centennial Souvenir Book.
23. *Minutes,* 1934, 374-376.
24. Ibid., 308.
25. *Minutes,* 1936, 54-56.
26. Ibid., 114, 115.
27. *Minutes,* 1933, pages 50-55.
28. *Minutes,* 1933, 35.
29. *Minutes,* 1934, 240.
30. *Minutes,* 1938, 526.
31. *Minutes,* 1937, 294, 364.
32. Union List of Ministers, SNJ Conference.

Chapter 12 THE METHODIST PROTESTANTS

1. This chapter is an expansion of the author's "Methodist Protestants: A 150 Year Old Legacy in Southern New Jersey," *Historical Trail,* 1979. It takes advantage of material not available at that time, much of which was placed in my hands by the Rev. J. Wesley Day, member of the Advisory Committee and former Methodist Protestant Missionary to China. Rev. Day's father, the late Rev. Roby F. Day, was one time President of the Eastern Conference of the Methodist Protestant Church.
2. Ethel Wolfe Born, "Who Were The Methodist Protestants?" *Response,* official program journal of United Methodist Women. November, 1983, 18.
3. For a discussion of the factors leading to the formation of the Methodist Protestant Church see: Ancel H. Bassett, *A Concise History of the Methodist Protestant Church.*

Douglas R. Chandler, "The Formation of the Methodist Protestant Church," HAM, I, 636-683.

Edward J. Drinkhouse, *History of Methodist Reform,* 2 Vols.

John B. Warman, "Our Methodist Protestant Heritage," *Methodist History,* January 1979.

The Methodist Protestant, Centennial Edition 1828-1928, Vol. 98, No. 20. May 16, 1928.
4. Warman, 71.
5. Ibid.
6. Ibid., 72.
7. *Enc. World Meth.,* II, 2256.
8. Warman, 73.
9. "Records of Matthias Barkalow, Independent Methodist Preacher, 1806-1827," *The Genealogical Magazine of New Jersey,* May 1964, 49-59.

10. Records of Old First United Methodist Church, West Long Branch, N. J. Quoted in Steelman, *Old First United Methodist Church,* West Long Branch, New Jersey, 1809-1984, 15, 16.
11. For an account of the Independent Methodists see Ibid., 14-16. "Records of Matthias Barkalow." James D. Peterson, *Matthias Barkalow* 1787-1827, Elder in the Independent Methodist Church of New Jersey. An unpublished paper.
12. Joseph Henry Bennett, *The Union Meeting House,* English Creek, N. J. Unpublished manuscript.
13. Steelman, *Old First UM Church,* 18. Information from Mrs. William Carlisle, genealogist of the Budd family.
14. *The Methodist Protestant,* Centennial Edition, p.i. contains a list of Representatives to the General Convention of 1828.
15. Manuscript Minutes, Drew University, pages 1-11.
16. *Methodist Protestant Discipline,* 1839, 13.
17. Ibid., 126.
18. Manuscript Minutes, 49.
19. Ibid.
20. *Our Young People,* Publication of the Methodist Protestant Church, 1892.
21. N. J. Conference, MP, Manuscript Minutes, 1843, 1.
22. Ibid.
23. Ibid., 5.
24. *Discipline,* 1904, 206.
25. 68.
26. *Minutes,* New Jersey Conference, MP Church, 1856, 5.
27. Ibid., 1892, 24.
28. *Our Young People.*
29. *Minutes,* 1892, 18.
30. Ibid., 17.
31. *Enc. World Meth.,* II, 2590.
32. E. G. Chandler, *History of the Woman's Foreign Missionary Society of the Methodist Protestant Church, 1879-1919,* 230.
33. Copy of a letter Dr. Roby F. Day to Dr. James R. Joy, Sept. 25, 1944. Also *Enc. World Meth.,* I, 941.
34. *Minutes,* 1911, 11.
35. *Minutes,* 1919.
36. *Minutes,* 1932, 38.
37. Ibid., 58.
38. *Minutes,* 1939, 22.
39. *Minutes,* 1939, 25.
40. 1953 *Minutes,* Eastern Conference of the Bible Protestant Church, 1.
41. The lists of churches and ministers comes from the 1939 *Minutes,* Eastern Conference MP Church and the 1939 *Minutes,* N. J. Conference The Methodist Church.
42. N. J. Conference *Minutes,* 1940, 223, 224.
43. *Our Young People,* 1892. HAM, II, 406. For the role of Appleget in defense of women's rights see William T. Noll, "Women As Clergy and Laity in the 19th Century Methodist Protestant Church," *Methodist History,* January 1977, 115ff.
44. *Our Young People,* 1892.
45. *Minutes,* Eastern Conf., 1939, 16, 17.

Chapter 13 MINISTERING TO CHILDREN AND YOUTH

1. Quoted in Miriam L. Coffee, "The Origin of Sunday Schools in England and in America," *The Historical Trail,* 1980, 3.
2. Quoted in *Enc. World Meth.,* II, 1979.
3. Ibid., 2277.

4. See above, page 74.
5. *Enc. World Meth.*, II, 2429, 2430.
6. Miriam Coffee, 10, *Enc. World Meth.*, II, 2277.
7. Figures on the chart are taken from the Conference Minutes for the years specified. Membership totals for all years include officers and teachers. 1838 is the first year statistics are given for the Conference. 1858 is the first year after the Conference was divided. 1945 is used to show the decline during the depression and war years. 1960 was the peak year for Sunday School attendance, but only about 3,200 more than 1929.
8. Miriam Coffee, 11.
9. *Minutes*, 1963, 726, 727.
10. See above, 88.
11. J. B. Graw, *Life and Times*, 87, 88.
12. HAM, II, 645.
13. Ibid., 646.
14. J. Bruce Behny & Paul H. Eller, *The History of the Evangelical United Brethren Church*, 242, 344, 371.
15. See above, 102. See Appendix VII for listing of Conference youth officers.
16. "The Echoes of Fifty Years, 1921-1970," Pennington Institute 50th Anniversary Program Book, 1.
17. SNJ Conference Archives Files and information supplied by Mrs. Burdelle (Betty) Hawk. Most of the information on Conference Institutes was gathered by Mrs. Hawk.
18. From information supplied by Rev. Carlton Bodine, Sr.
19. Much of the information provided by Dr. Earl Townsend Hann.
20. Letter to the author, containing notes of Seaville Camp and its Institutes, June 1984.
21. *Minutes*, 1952, 67.
22. *Minutes*, 1956, 68.
23. Albert E. Hartman, "The Methodist Conference Center at Mt. Misery," 25th Anniversary Historical Sketch, 3 pages mimeographed, October 3, 1971.
24. *Minutes*, 1963, 736. Note Delanco Camp is not included.
25. Notes provided by Betty Hawk.
26. Ibid.
27. Notes supplied by Rev. Donald T. Phillips, Sr.
28. See above, 153.
29. *Minutes*, 1948, 57.
30. *Minutes*, 1972, 77.
31. See above, 153.
32. *Minutes*, 1983, 178.
33. *Minutes*, 1963, 741.
34. Letter to the author, July 24, 1984.

Chapter 14 WAR AND PEACE

1. Colossians 3:16 (RSV).
2. Much of the material on our South Jersey Methodist gospel song writers comes from the Rev. F. Elwood Perkins, "They Love to Sing!" South Jersey's Heritage in Hymns and Gospel Songs, *The Historical Trail*, 1974.
3. *Minutes*, 1942, 721, 722. Quoted in Perkins, 9.
4. Perkins, 11.
5. Psalm 149:1.
6. Chorus of "Count Your Blessings," Johnson Oatman, Jr. Italics mine.
7. HAM, III, 550. See also *Enc. World Meth.*, I, 946, 947.
8. Norwood, 411.
9. Ibid.
10. HAM, III, 1293, 1294.

11. See Chapter 12. For list of churches not entering The Methodist Church see page 183.
12. See table, *Minutes,* 1940, pages 298-300.
13. *Minutes,* 1941, 438.
14. *Minutes,* 1940, 231, 232.
15. *Minutes,* 1941, 434.
16. *Minutes,* 1942, 600.
17. Ibid., 637.
18. *Minutes,* 1943, 841.
19. *Minutes,* 1944, 64.
20. Composite Report of District Superintendent A. C. Brady, *Minutes,* 1945, 258.
21. *Enc. World Meth.,* I, 608, 609.
22. *Minutes,* 1945, 259.
23. *Minutes,* 1946, 520.
24. *Minutes,* 1947, 674.
25. *Minutes,* 1948, 78.
26. *Minutes,* 1941, 403.
27. *Minutes,* 1942, 604.
28. Ibid., 605.
29. *Minutes,* 1943, 855.
30. Biographical Data, SNJ Conference Archives. *Enc. World Meth.,* I, 590, 591.
31. *Enc. World Meth.,* II, 1404, 1405. SNJ Conference, Union List of Ministers.
32. See above, page 58.
33. See above, pages 69, 82.
34. See above, page 187.
35. Union List. *Enc. World Meth.,* II, 2562.
36. *Enc. World Meth.,* II, 1851, 1852. Union List.
37. Stellhorn & Birkner, eds., *The Governors of New Jersey,* 217. Cunningham, *The Story of New Jersey,* 209.
38. A complete list of Conference women presidents and Conference Lay Leaders is in the Appendix.
39. Minutes of Special Session, 1945 *Minutes,* 394-396.
40. *Minutes,* 1946, 453.
41. See above, page 196. Also below, pages 277, 278.
42. *Minutes,* 1946, 476.
43. *Minutes,* 1950, 501, 511, 512.
44. *Minutes,* 1947, 675.
45. *Minutes,* 1950, 517.
46. *Minutes,* 1948, 68, 69.
47. *Minutes,* 1947, 644-648.
48. *Minutes,* 1948, 85.
49. *Minutes,* 1956, 142.
50. Ibid.

Chapter 15 WOMEN'S ROLE IN SOUTHERN NEW JERSEY METHODISM

1. See page 99.
2. See page 165.
3. *Minutes,* 1956, 139.
4. See Time Line in Elaine Magalis, *Conduct Becoming to a Woman. Enc. World Meth.,* I, 679. This gives her ordination date as 1896, but it was probably 1894. See also Norwood, *Story of American Methodism,* 352.
5. *Minutes,* 1921, 99.
6. See page 165.

7. *The United Methodist Newscope,* March 16, 1984, 2.
8. *Minutes,* 1974, 206. 1975, 200. 1977, 74.
9. See page 101.
10. *Enc. World Meth.,* II, 1367.
11. Steelman, *History of Old First United Methodist Church,* 55.
12. Title of an article in *Methodist History,* January 1980.
13. Keller, Ibid., 86.
14. See page 100.
15. Ibid., Keller, 87.
16. *Enc. of World Meth.,* II, 2588.
17. See page 180.
18. *Enc. World Meth.,* II, 2592.
19. *Committed to Mission Tomorrow, Building on Yesterday,* UMW pamphlet.
20. Louise McCoy North, *The Story of the New York Branch of the Woman's Foreign Missionary Society of the Methodist Episcopal Church,* 54.
21. Ibid., 110.
22. Ibid., 56.
23. Ibid., 57.
24. Ibid., 105.
25. *Minutes,* 1896, 7.
26. North, 331-333.
27. *Minutes,* 1879, 52, 53.
28. Records of Bridgeton District WFMS, SNJ Conference Archives.
29. Ruth Esther Meeker, *Six Decades of Service,* a History of the Woman's Home Missionary Society of the Methodist Episcopal Church, 1880-1940, 61.
30. For more about Jeannette Fisk and Hannah Garrison see page 104.
31. See chapter 7.
32. Meeker, 298.
33. More about the Deaconess Center will be told in Chapter 18.
34. See Meeker.
35. *Minutes,* 1896, 7.
36. *Minutes,* 1930, 273, 274.
37. E. G. Chandler, *History of the Woman's Foreign Missionary Society of the Methodist Protestant Church,* 230-234.
38. Ibid., 237.
39. This material and much that follows on the WSCS and UMW are from material provided by Mrs. Alice Detwiler, member of the history Advisory Committee. The material she supplied is on file in the SNJ Conference Archives.
40. "The Wesley Fellowship," 1976 program booklet.
41. Mary Agnes Dougherty, "The Methodist Deaconess," *Methodist History,* January 1983, 90-93.
42. Quoted in, Mary Agnes Dougherty, "The Social Gospel According to Phoebe," *Women in New Worlds,* I, 207.
43. See pages 134, 135.
44. Information from retired deaconess Helen Phillips Neary.
45. Information and records supplied by Deaconess Betty Ruth Goode, Program Assistant, Deaconess and Home Missionary Service of the General Board of Global Ministries. Information is in the SNJ Conference Archives.
46. For information on Deaconesses see the two articles by Dougherty above. Also Virginia Lieson Breriton, "Preparing Women for the Lord's Work," *Women in New Worlds,* I. *Enc. World Meth.,* I, 640ff.
47. Personal interview, April 13, 1984. Helen P. and Robert C. Neary, Sr., *Our Travels and a Lady Circuit Rider.*
48. Records through the 1984 appointments.

49. Material on Hazel Horner, Alice Detwiler and Matilda Winn, comes from biographical data collected by the UMW for a project, "100 Women in Mission."
50. See Appendix V for complete list with dates.
51. A notation in my notes on Women.
52. Written by Penny Moore, 1984.

Chapter 16 THE METHODIST CHURCH

1. *A Religious History of the American People,* II, 447.
2. Ibid., 448.
3. Ibid., 449.
4. Norwood, *The Story of American Methodism,* 413.
5. *Enc. World Meth.,* II, 2712.
6. Quoted in Ahlstrom, II, 596.
7. *Minutes,* 1963, 693.
8. *Minutes,* 1962, 488.
9. Ibid.
10. These statistics and those which follow are taken from the Conference *Minutes* for the years indicated.
11. *Meth. Trail.*
12. *Minutes,* 1954, 469.
13. *Minutes,* 1955, 719.
14. *Minutes,* 1959, 676.
15. *Methodist Relay,* December 1962, 2.
16. *Meth. Trail,* 143.
17. *Meth. Trail,* 258, 259.
18. *Minutes,* 1963, 722.
19. *Minutes,* 1966, 62.
20. *Minutes,* 1952, 67, 68.
21. *Minutes,* 1955, 741, 742.
22. *Minutes,* 1956, 41.
23. *Minutes,* 1960, 68.
24. *Minutes,* 1959, 693-695.
25. *Minutes,* 1961, 238.
26. *Minutes,* 1968, 97.
27. *Minutes,* 1963, 717.
28. *Minutes,* 1965, 323.
29. *Minutes,* 1968, 89.
30. *Minutes,* 1955, 728.
31. *Methodist Relay,* Feb. 1956, 4.
32. See pages 97, 98.
33. See 1961 *Minutes,* and *Methodist Relay,* October, 1961.
34. *Minutes,* 1961, 336, 337.
35. Albea Godbold, ed. *Forever Beginning, 1766-1966,* Historical Papers presented at American Methodism's Bicentennial Conference, Baltimore, Md., April 21-24, 1966.
36. *Methodist Relay,* April, 1966, 1.
37. The text of his address is printed in the 1966 *Minutes,* pages 74-81.
38. *Minutes,* 1966, 67.
39. Bishop Matthew Simpson had a summer home on the beachfront at Long Branch, given him by some of his lay friends.
40. *Enc. World Meth.,* II, 2315, 2316. Biographical notes in Conference Archives. Prince A. Taylor, Jr., *The Life of My Years.*

41. The accurate listing is found in *Delaware Conference Minutes,* 1965. Churches, pages 228, 229. Ministers, pages 51-53. Retired ministers, page 109. Widows, pages 109, 110. Retired supply, page 111. See also *N. J. Conference Minutes,* 1965. Churches, page 296. Ministers, page 299. Omitted from this list are Charles W. S. Cannon, Lucius E. Jordan and Cyrus W. Perry. Another list is on pages 262, 263. There are inaccuracies here.

42. The official name change from the N. J. to the SNJ Conference was effective July 1, 1965. See *Minutes,* 1965, 282.

43. *Minutes,* 1965, 271.
44. *Minutes,* 1952, ii, iii.
45. *Minutes,* 1953, 405, 406.
46. *Minutes,* 1959, 627.

Chapter 17 OUR ETHNIC CHURCHES

1. *Minutes,* 1965, 307.
2. *Minutes,* 1837, published in *Hist. Trail,* 1983, 7.
3. *Minutes,* 1856, 6.
4. See page 76. C.f. Licorish, "Delaware Conference." *Enc. World Meth.,* I, 652. Tees, *Methodist Origins,* 137. See also Licorish, "Brief History of the Delaware Conference," Delaware Conference *Minutes,* 1965, 196, 197.
5. Licorish, *Enc. World Meth.,* I, 652.
6. *Minutes,* Delaware Conference, 1864, 5. A microfilm copy of all the Delaware Conference *Minutes* is in the SNJ Conference Archives.
7. Ibid., 6. The number in parenthesis indicates the number of years they had been traveling as a Local Preacher.
8. Ibid., 3.
9. Ibid., 12.
10. *Minutes,* Delaware Conference, 1865, 27.
11. *Minutes,* Delaware Conference, 1864, 11.
12. *Minutes,* Delaware Conference, 1965, 194, 195.
13. Ibid., 209.
14. *Enc. World Meth.,* II, 1666, 1667.
15. Ibid., 2347. Ralph H. Jones, *Charles Albert Tindley,* 16.
16. Approved Supply Pastor.
17. Part Time Supply Pastor.
18. The list of transferred Churches, *Minutes,* Delaware Conference, 1965, pages 238, 239. The list of appointments is in Ibid., 59.
19. *Minutes,* 1967, 35.
20. Delaware Conference *Minutes,* 1965, 109, 110. N. J. Conf. *Minutes,* 1965, 438, 439.
21. The United Methodist *Newscope,* July 27, 1984, 1.
22. Ibid.
23. *Minutes,* 1982, 120.
24. Ibid., 121.
25. *Minutes,* 1955, 728.
26. *Minutes,* 1956, 74.
27. *Minutes,* 1958, 461, 473.
28. *Minutes,* 1961, 285.
29. *Minutes,* 1967, 61.
30. As of 1985.
31. *Minutes,* 1983, 109.
32. *Newscope,* July 27, 1984, 4.
33. *Minutes,* 1977, 60.
34. *Minutes,* 1978, 61.
35. *Minutes,* 1979, 101.

36. *Minutes,* 1980, 63.
37. See pages 155, 156.
38. Galatians 5:1 (RSV).
39. Galatians 3:26, 28 (RSV).

Chapter 18 INSTITUTIONS OF THE CHURCH

1. See page 55.
2. Kenneth Anderson, *History of Pennington School,* 9.
3. See above, page 68.
4. Page 69.
5. Pages 69, 70.
6. Page 69.
7. Anderson, Chapter 4, p. 17.
8. *Semi-Centennial Pennington Seminary,* 7.
9. Anderson, Chapter 5, p. 1.
10. Ibid., 5.
11. *Minutes,* 1891, 30.
12. Anderson, Chapter 7, p. 8.
13. Anderson, Chapter 8.
14. Ibid., Chapter 9, p. 1.
15. Ibid., 11.
16. Ibid., Chapter 10, pages 1-4.
17. Ibid., Chapter 11, p. 1.
18. Ibid., 5, 6.
19. *Minutes,* 1932, 50-55.
20. Anderson, Chapter 11, p. 5.
21. Ibid., Chapter 12, pages 1, 2.
22. Ibid., 4.
23. *Minutes,* 1953, 405, 406.
24. Anderson, Chapter 13, pages 3-10.
25. Ibid., 12.
26. *Minutes,* 1959, 694.
27. *Minutes,* 1964, 102.
28. Convocation Program.
29. *United Methodist Relay,* Feb. 1980, 1, 4.
30. Report in 1867 Conference Sec. Files, SNJ Conf. Archives.
31. Paper in Conf. Institute File, SNJ Conf. Archives.
32. *Minutes,* 1875, 22.
33. Mrs. Charlotte Myers, "History of the New Jersey Memorial Home for Disabled Soldiers, Sailors, Marines and their Wives and Widows, Vineland, N.J." The *Vineland Historical Magazine,* July 1941, pages 122-125.
34. Mission Statement. 1983 Annual Report. The United Methodist Homes of New Jersey.
35. *Minutes,* 1889, 25.
36. *Minutes,* 1890, 31.
37. 75th Anniversary Program, Methodist Home, Collingswood, N. J., 4.
38. Ibid., 4.
39. *Minutes,* 1892, 21.
40. 75th Anniv. Program, 4.
41. *Minutes,* 1904, 56.
42. 75th Anniv. Program, 4, 6.
43. Paul A. Friedrich, *A History of The United Methodist Homes,* 7.
44. Ibid.
45. *Minutes,* 1907, 31.

46. Friedrich, 4.
47. Mary T. Evans, *History of The United Methodist Homes of New Jersey,* 75th Anniversary, 1907-1982, 10.
48. See pages 169, 170.
49. Friedrich, 4.
50. Ibid.
51. Ibid., 5.
52. Ibid.
53. Ibid., 6.
54. Ibid., 7.
55. Ibid., 8.
56. Meeker, *Six Decades of Service,* 210, 211.
57. Ibid., 211.
58. Interview with Helen Phillips Neary.
59. *Minutes,* 1967, 81.
60. *Minutes,* 1913, 69.
61. *Minutes,* 1914, 69.
62. *Minutes,* 1925, 50.
63. *Minutes,* 1926, 215.
64. See above, pages 213, 214.
65. Albert E. Hartman, "The Methodist Conference Center at Mt. Misery," 25th Anniversary Pamphlet, 2.
66. See above, page 197.

Chapter 19 THE UNITED METHODIST CHURCH

1. The information which follows in this section on the EUB tradition comes primarily from two sources: J. Bruce Behney and Paul H. Eller, *The History of the Evangelical United Brethren Church,* 1979. Also, Norwood, *The Story of American Methodism,* 1974. In Norwood see particularly Chapter 9, "Origins of the United Brethren," Chapter 10, "Origins of the Evangelical Association" and Chapter 36, "The Evangelical United Brethren." For a brief monograph on Otterbein see Paul W. Milhouse, *Philip William Otterbein,* "Pioneer Pastor to Germans in America," 1968.
2. A brief record of Martin Boehm is: Abram W. Sangrey, *Martin Boehm,* "Pioneer preacher in the Christian faith and practice, among the first German speaking colonists, in Pennsylvania, Maryland, Virginia," 1976.
3. Behney & Eller, 39.
4. Norwood, 111.
5. Behney & Eller, 230.
6. Ibid., 357.
7. Ibid., 18.
8. *Minutes,* 1968, 62.
9. *Minutes,* 1969, 48.
10. Microfilm *Journal,* Bishop John Seybert (Bishop of the Evangelical Association, 1839-1860.)
11. Information for this part of the History was provided by the Rev. Edward Ohms, largely from the *Minutes* of the Eastern Pennsylvania Conference of the Evangelical Association and the *Minutes* of the Northeastern Conference of the Evangelical United Brethren Church. Rev. Ohms is compiling the history of the former Atlantic Conference. The Conferences involved are: Eastern Pennsylvania Conference of the Evangelical Association, 1840-1875. Atlantic Conference of the Evangelical Association, 1875-1922. Atlantic Conference of the Evangelical Church, 1922-1946. Atlantic Conference of the Evangelical United Brethren Church, 1946-1957. Northeastern Conference of the EUB Church, 1957-1963. Eastern Conference of the EUB Church, 1963-1968. From, John H. Ness, Jr. "Table of Evangelical United Brethren Annual Conferences." *Methodist History,* October 1969.

12. Mimeographed History of the Evangelical United Methodist Church, Clarksboro, N. J., 2.
13. Above material from the History of Evangelical Church.
14. Information on these two Churches from Ohms.
15. *Minutes,* 1968, 101.
16. Ibid., 68.
17. *Minutes,* 1971, 61.
18. Ibid., 72.
19. See above pages 12-14.
20. The 1969 issue of *The Historical Trail* is a special Pilmore-Boardman Bicentennial Issue. The program is on pages 63, 64.
21. Bishop Taylor's address is printed in *The Historical Trail,* 1972. See also *The Historical Trail,* 1971, A Bishop Francis Asbury Bicentennial Issue.
22. *Minutes,* 1978, 152.
23. *Minutes,* 1982, 100.
24. *Minutes,* 1971, 49.
25. Ibid., 81.
26. *Minutes,* 1972, 90, 91.
27. Ibid., 111.
28. *Minutes,* 1974, 16. Attributed to Richard Cardinal Cushing.
29. *United Methodist Relay,* June 1976, 1.
30. *Minutes,* 1977, 120.
31. *Minutes,* 1979, 69.

Chapter 20 LOOKING BACK - LOOKING AHEAD

1. John Emory, ed. *The Works of the Rev. John Wesley, A.M.* Vol. VII. New York: J. Emory and B. Waugh, 1831, 315.

APPENDIX I

CONFERENCE SESSIONS 1837 - 1985

New Jersey Conference, Southern New Jersey Conference,
Methodist Episcopal, Methodist, United Methodist Church

Year	Date	Place	Bishop
1837	Apr. 26	Newark - Halsey Street	Waugh
1838	Apr. 25	Bridgeton - Commerce Street	Hedding
1839	Apr. 23	Trenton - Greene Street	Waugh
1840	Apr. 15	Burlington - Broad Street	Hedding
1841	Apr. 28	Newark - Halsey Street	Hedding
1842	Apr. 27	Camden - Third Street	Waugh
1843	Apr. 26	New Brunswick - Liberty Street	Hedding
1844	Apr. 17	Trenton - Greene Street	Morris
1845	Apr. 23	Mount Holly	Waugh
1846	Apr. 22	Newark - Clinton Street	Hedding
1847	Apr. 21	Salem - Walnut Street	Hamline
1848	Apr. 12	Paterson - Cross Street	Janes
1849	Apr. 18	Burlington - Broad Street	Morris
1850	Apr. 17	Camden - Third Street	Hedding
1851	Apr. 16	Jersey City - Trinity	Janes
1852	Apr. 7	Trenton - Greene Street	Janes
1853	Apr. 13	Bridgeton - Commerce Street	Morris
1854	Apr. 12	New Brunswick - Liberty Street	Waugh
1855	Apr. 11	Newark - Central	Janes
1856	Apr. 9	Newark - Broad Street	Simpson
1857	Apr. 8	Trenton - Greene Street	Scott
1858	Mar. 31	Camden - Third Street	Baker, O. C.
1859	Mar. 23	Mount Holly	Ames
1860	Mar. 14	Salem - Broadway	Morris
1861	Mar. 27	Bordentown - First	Simpson
1862	Mar. 19	New Brunswick - Liberty Street	Janes
1863	Mar. 18	Burlington - Broad Street	Scott
1864	Mar. 2	Bridgeton - Commerce Street	Simpson
1865	Mar. 22	Trenton - Greene Street	Ames
1866	Mar. 21	Camden - Third Street	Scott
1867	Mar. 20	Keyport	Janes
1868	Mar. 18	Lambertville	Scott
1869	Mar. 17	Millville - First	Clark
1870	Mar. 23	Long Branch - Centenary	Simpson
1871	Mar. 15	Salem - Broadway	Janes
1872	Feb. 28	Trenton - Central	Ames
1873	Mar. 13	Bridgeton - Trinity	Scott
1874	Mar. 18	Camden - Third Street	Ames
1875	Mar. 10	New Brunswick - Pitman	Simpson
1876	Mar. 29	Mount Holly	Wiley
1877	Mar. 24	Trenton - Greene Street	Peck
1878	Mar. 13	Burlington - Broad Street	Simpson
1879	Mar. 12	Keyport	Merrill
1880	Mar. 20	Camden - Third Street	Bowman
1881	Mar. 9	Salem - Broadway	Foster
1882	Mar. 8	Millville - First	Andrews

Year	Date	Place	Bishop
1883	Mar. 21	Long Branch - St. Luke	Wiley
1884	Mar. 12	Camden - Broadway	Harris, W. L.
1885	Mar. 19	New Brunswick - First	Warren
1886	Mar. 11	Bridgeton - Commerce Street	Hurst
1887	Mar. 10	Trenton - State Street	Foster
1888	Mar. 14	Camden - Broadway	Foss
1889	Mar. 6	Salem - First	Bowman
1890	Mar. 12	Millville - First	Goodsell
1891	Mar. 18	Trenton - Greene Street	Fitzgerald
1892	Mar. 16	New Brunswick - First	Vincent
1893	Mar. 15	Mount Holly	Walden
1894	Mar. 14	Camden - Broadway	Andrews
1895	Mar. 20	Burlington - Broad Street	Merrill
1896	Mar. 11	Bridgeton - Central	Joyce
1897	Mar. 24	Trenton - Central	Warren
1898	Mar. 30	Camden - First	McCabe
1899	Mar. 8	Atlantic City - Saint Paul	Foss
1900	Mar. 14	Millville - First	Hurst
1901	Mar. 6	Camden - Broadway	Mallalieu
1902	Mar. 12	Salem - Broadway	Andrews
1903	Mar. 18	Asbury Park - First	Fowler
1904	Mar. 9	Trenton - State Street	Merrill
1905	Mar. 8	Atlantic City - First	Cranston
1906	Mar. 14	New Brunswick - First	Goodsell
1907	Mar. 13	Red Bank - First	Warren
1908	Mar. 11	Millville - First	Wilson
1909	Mar. 10	Camden - First	Wilson
1910	Mar. 9	Atlantic City - Saint Paul	Spellmeyer, Neely
1911	Mar. 15	Ocean City - First	Hamilton, J. W.
1912	Mar. 13	Asbury Park - First	Berry
1913	Mar. 5	Atlantic City - First	Berry
1914	Mar. 11	Asbury Park - First	Berry
1915	Mar. 3	Atlantic City - St. Paul	Henderson
1916	Mar. 15	Asbury Park - First	Quayle
1917	Mar. 7	Atlantic City - First	Berry
1918	Mar. 6	Atlantic City - Saint Paul	Berry
1919	Mar. 12	Ocean Grove - Saint Paul	Shepard
1920	Mar. 13	Atlantic City - First	Berry
1921	Mar. 9	Asbury Park - First	Berry
1922	Mar. 8	Atlantic City - Saint Paul	Berry
1923	Mar. 14	Asbury Park - First	Leonard
1924	Mar. 5	Atlantic City - Central	Berry
1925	Mar. 4	Asbury Park - First	Leete
1926	Mar. 3	Atlantic City - First	Hughes, E. H.
1927	Mar. 8	Asbury Park - First	Anderson
1928	Mar. 6	Atlantic City - Saint Paul	Berry
1929	Mar. 5	Asbury Park - First	Richardson
1930	Mar. 4	Atlantic City - Central	Lowe
1931	Mar. 3	Asbury Park - First	Burns
1932	Mar. 1	Atlantic City - First	Richardson
1933	Mar. 8	Asbury Park - First	Richardson
1934	Sept. 27	Atlantic City - Saint Paul	Richardson
1935	Sept. 19	Asbury Park - First	Brown

Year	Date	Place	Bishop
1936	Sept. 23	Ocean City - First	Richardson
1937	Sept. 22	Asbury Park - First	Richardson
1938	Sept. 21	Atlantic City - Saint Paul	Mead
1939	Sept. 29	Ocean City - First	Richardson
1940	Oct. 3	Atlantic City - Saint Paul	Richardson
1941	Oct. 2	Asbury Park - First	Richardson
1942	Oct. 1	Ocean City - First	Oxnam
1943	Sept. 24	Ocean City - First	Richardson
1944	Sept. 22	Ocean City - First	Corson
1945	Sept. 27	Ocean City - First	Corson
1946	Sept. 26	Ocean City - First	Corson
1947	Sept. 25	Ocean City - First	Corson
1948	Sept. 23	Ocean City - First	Corson
1949	Sept. 22	Ocean City - First	Corson
1950	Sept. 21	Ocean City - First	Martin, P. E.
1951	Sept. 27	Ocean City - First	Corson
1952	Sept. 17	Ocean City - First	Corson
1953	Sept. 16	Ocean City - First	Reed
1954	Sept. 22	Ocean City - First	Corson
1955	Sept. 21	Ocean City - First	Corson
1956	Sept. 19	Ocean City - First	Corson
1957	Sept. 18	Ocean City - First	Corson
1958	Sept. 17	Ocean City - First	Smith, A. F.
1959	Sept. 16	Ocean City - First	Corson
1960	Sept. 14	Ocean City - First	Corson
1961	Sept. 20	Ocean City - First	Corson
1962	Sept. 19	Ocean City - First	Corson
1963	Sept. 18	Ocean City - First	Corson
1964	Sept. 16	Ocean City - First	Taylor
1965	June 9	Ocean City - First	Taylor
1966	June 15	Ocean City - First	Taylor
1967	June 14	Ocean City - First	Taylor
1968	June 12	Ocean City - First	Taylor
1969	June 18	Ocean City - First	Taylor
1970	June 15	Ocean City - First	Taylor
1971	June 14	Ocean City - First	Taylor
1972	June 12	Ocean City - First	Taylor
1973	June 11	Ocean City - First	Taylor
1974	June 10	Ocean City - First	Taylor
1975	June 9	Ocean City - First	Taylor
1976	June 14	Ocean City - First	Taylor
1977	June 13	Ocean City - First	White
1978	June 12	Ocean City - First	White
1979	June 11	Ocean City - First	White
1980	June 9	Ocean City - First	White
1981	June 7	Ocean City - St. Peter's	White
1982	June 14	Ocean City - St. Peter's	White
1983	June 13	Ocean City - St. Peter's	White
1984	June 11	Ocean City - St. Peter's	White
1985	June 10	Ocean City - St. Peter's	Irons

APPENDIX II
METHODIST PROTESTANT CONFERENCE PRESIDENTS

A. NEW JERSEY CONFERENCE

YEAR	PRESIDENT	PLACE OF MEETING
1843[1]	Herman Bruce	Glassboro
1856[2]	William B. Vanleer	Newport
1857	A. L. McCall	
1858		
1859	Thomas K. Witsil	
1860	William B. Vanleer	Union Valley
1861	William B. Vanleer	Manasquan
1862	William B. Vanleer	Bridgeton
1863	William B. Vanleer	Bridgeport
1864	Elias D. Stultz	Glassboro
1865	Elias D. Stultz	Pleasantville: Mt. Pleasant
1866	William B. Vanleer	Union Valley
1867	William B. Vanleer	Manasquan
1868	Taylor T. Heiss	Fair Haven
1869	Taylor T. Heiss	Bridgeton
1870	Elias D. Stultz	Pennsgrove
1871	Elias D. Stultz	South Amboy
1872	Elias D. Stultz	Glassboro
1873	Elias D. Stultz	Pleasantville: Mt. Pleasant
1874 (March)	Henry Watson	Manasquan
1874 (Oct.)	Taylor T. Heiss[3]	Pennsgrove
1875	Firth Stringer[4]	Bridgeton
1876	Elias D. Stultz	Union Valley
1877	Elias D. Stultz	Fair Haven
1878	Elias D. Stultz	Camden
1879	Louis D. Stultz	Pennsgrove
1880	Louis D. Stultz	
1881	Louis D. Stultz	Scullville
1882	Louis D. Stultz	South Amboy
1883	John L. Watson	Manasquan
1884	John L. Watson	Bridgeton
1885	John L. Watson	Fair Haven
1886	John L. Watson	Glassboro
1887	John L. Watson	Fair Haven
1888	Thomas B. Appleget	Manasquan
1889	Thomas B. Appleget	Bridgeton
1890	Thomas B. Appleget	Pennsgrove
1891	Thomas B. Appleget	Atlantic City
1892	Charles D. Sinkinson	South Amboy
1893	Charles D. Sinkinson	Bridgeton
1894	Charles D. Sinkinson	Lake Como
1895	Charles D. Sinkinson	Leesburg
1896	Charles D. Sinkinson	Fair Haven
1897	James H. Clarke	Manasquan

YEAR	PRESIDENT	PLACE OF MEETING
1898	James H. Clarke	Bridgeton: Laurel Hill
1899	James H. Clarke	Allenwood
1900	James H. Clarke	Camden
1901	James H. Clarke	Manasquan
1902	William D. Stultz	Pleasantville: Mt. Pleasant
1903	William D. Stultz	Westville
1904	William D. Stultz	Glassboro
1905	William D. Stultz	Fair Haven
1906	William D. Stultz	Lake Como
1907	Louis D. Stultz	Millville: Broad Street
1908	Louis D. Stultz	Atlantic City: Trinity
1909	Louis D. Stultz	Bridgeton: Laurel Hill
1910	Louis D. Stultz	Lake Como
1911	Louis D. Stultz	Allenwood

B. EASTERN CONFERENCE

YEAR	PRESIDENT	PLACE OF MEETING
1912	Charles D. Sinkinson	Brooklyn: Grace
1913	Charles D. Sinkinson	Atlantic City: Christ
1914	Charles D. Sinkinson	Atlantic City: Christ
1915	Frederick W. Varney	Lynbrook, N. Y.
1916	Frederick W. Varney	Lake Como
1917	Frederick W. Varney	Atlantic City: Christ
1918	Frederick W. Varney	Manasquan
1919	Frederick W. Varney	Shickshinny, Pa.
1920	Clifford S. Kidd	Millville: Broad Street
1921	Clifford S. Kidd	Glassboro
1922	Clifford S. Kidd	Inwood, L. I., N.Y.
1923	Clifford S. Kidd	Millville: Broad Street
1924	Clifford S. Kidd	Westville
1925	Roby F. Day	Bridgeton: Laurel Hill
1926	Roby F. Day	Lynbrook, L. I., N.Y.
1927	Roby F. Day	Westville
1928	Roby F. Day	Ventnor
1929	Roby F. Day	Ventnor
1930	George D. Jones	Ventnor
1931	George D. Jones	Shickshinny, Pa.
1932	George D. Jones	Ventnor
1933	George D. Jones	Westville
1934	George D. Jones	Ventnor
1935	Clifford S. Kidd	Ventnor
1936	Clifford S. Kidd	Ventnor

YEAR	PRESIDENT	PLACE OF MEETING
1937	Clifford S. Kidd	Atlantic City: Christ
1938	Clifford S. Kidd	Bridgeton: Laurel Hill
1939	Clifford S. Kidd	Atlantic City: Christ

1. The first session of the N. J. Conference was held in 1843.
2. The first published *Minutes* was in 1856.
3. Henry Watson died during the year and his place as President was taken by Taylor T. Heiss. Rev. Heiss was ill during Conference and died shortly afterward.
4. Firth Stringer transferred to the North Illinois Conference two months before the 1876 Conference was held. The N. J. Conference thought it was irregular for him to sign his own transfer.

APPENDIX III

DISTRICT SUPERINTENDENTS 1837-1985

(The name was changed from Presiding Elder to District Superintendent in 1908.)

Manning Force			Isaac N. Felch	
Newark	1837-40		Paterson	1845-8
Paterson	1841-4		Burlington	1852-5
Newton	1852-5		George F. Brown	
Waters Burrows			Rahway	1845-8
Paterson	1837-40		Camden	1849-51
Rahway	1841-4		Burlington	1856-9
			Trenton	1860-2
Richard W. Petherbridge				
Trenton	1837-40		Isaac Winner	
Burlington	1848-51		Trenton	1845-8
			Rahway	1849-51
Thomas Neal			Rahway	1855-6
Camden	1837-40		John K. Shaw	
Burlington	1841-4		Camden	1845-8
John S. Porter			Trenton	1849-52
Newark	1841-4			
Burlington	1845-7		Thomas Sovereign	
Paterson	1853-5		Newark	1848-51
Newark	1856		Bridgeton	1853-5
Daniel Parrish			William A. Wilmer	
Trenton	1841-4		Paterson	1849-52
Newark	1845-7		Trenton	1853-6
Charles T. Ford			Thomas McCarroll	
Camden	1841-4		Newark	1852-5
			Paterson	1856

Caleb A. Lippincott
Rahway — 1852

Benjamin Day
Newton — 1856

Samuel Y. Monroe
Bridgeton — 1856-9
Camden — 1864(part)

Abram K. Street
Trenton — 1857-9
Camden — 1860-3

George Hughes
Burlington — 1860-2

William E. Perry
Bridgeton — 1860-2
Trenton — 1863-6
Bridgeton — 1871-3

Jefferson Lewis
Burlington — 1863-6
Camden — 1867-70

Charles H. Whitecar
Bridgeton — 1863-6
Trenton — 1873-4
Camden — 1875-6

Joseph B. Dobbins
Camden — (1864 part)-5-6
Trenton — 1867-70

Elwood H. Stokes
New Brunswick — 1867-70
Camden — 1871-4

Aaron E. Ballard
Bridgeton — 1867-70
New Brunswick — 1871-4

Samuel VanSant
Burlington — 1867-70
Trenton — 1871-2
Trenton — 1876-7
New Brunswick — 1878-81 (part)

Jacob B. Graw
Burlington — 1871-4
New Brunswick — 1875-7
Camden — 1881-4
Trenton — 1885-90
Bridgeton — 1898-1900

John S. Heisler
Bridgeton — 1874-7

Thomas O'Hanlon
Trenton — 1875

Samuel E. Post
Burlington — 1875-6
Camden — 1877-80

William W. Moffett
Trenton — 1878-80
New Brunswick — 1884-7

Charles E. Hill
Bridgeton — 1878-81

David H. Schock
Trenton — 1881-4

Edmund Hewitt
New Brunswick — (part) 1881-83
Bridgeton — 1901-5

William Walton
Bridgeton — 1882-5

John S. Gaskill
Camden — 1885-6

George L. Dobbins
Bridgeton — 1886-91
Camden — 1899-1904

Milton Relyea
Camden — 1887-92

James Moore
New Brunswick — 1888-91
Camden — 1905-7(part)

George Reed
Trenton — 1891-6

Wm. P. C. Strickland
New Brunswick — 1892-6

George B. Wight
Bridgeton — 1892-7

Daniel B. Harris
Camden — 1893-8

S. Wesley Lake
Trenton — 1897-99 (1900 part)

Joseph L. Roe			Joseph B. Kulp	
New Brunswick	1897-1902		Bridgeton	1925-31
William P. Davis			Sherman G. Pitt	
Trenton	1901-7		Trenton	1925-28
	(1900 part)			
John B. Haines			Charles I. Fitzgeorge	
New Brunswick	1903-8		Camden	1926-32
Nomer J. Wright			George W. Yard	
Bridgeton	1906-11		Trenton	1929-32
Alfred Wagg			Thomas J. J. Wright	
Trenton	1907-11		Bridgeton	1931-36
Bridgeton	1918-22			
New Brunswick	1923-24		Edwin F. Hann	
			Camden	1932-34(part)
J. Morgan Read				(part)1935-41
Camden	(part 1907)-1908		Leon Chamberlain	
			Trenton	1933-(part) 1934
Sanford M. Nichols			New Brunswick	(part) 1934-39
Camden	1909-14			
			Harold Paul Sloan	
John Handley			Camden	1934-35 (part)
New Brunswick	1909-12			
Camden	(part 1924)-26(Part)		Thomas S. Brock	
			Trenton	(part) 1934-39
George H. Neal				
Bridgeton	1912-17		Charles D. Whitton	
James W. Marshall			Bridgeton	1937-43
Trenton	1912			
New Brunswick	1913-18		Albert L. Baner	
			New Brunswick	1940
Percy Perinchief			Camden	1941-45(part)
Trenton	1913-14			
			W. Rolland Raver	
Furman A. DeMaris			Trenton	1940-46
Camden	1915-18			
New Brunswick	1929-34(part)		A. Corbin Brady	
			New Brunswick	1941-47
Melville E. Synder				
Trenton	1915-24		W. W. Payne	
Trenton (acting)	(part) 1928		Bridgeton	1943-49
			Benjamin F. Allgood	
Alexander Corson			Camden	(part)1945-1951
Camden	1919-24(part)			
Trenton	(part)1932		Ira S. Pimm	
			Trenton	1946-1951
James D. Bills				
New Brunswick	1919-22		Herbert J. Smith	
			New Brunswick	1947-1952
Herbert J. Belting				
Bridgeton	1923-24		W. Neal Raver	
New Brunswick	1925-28		Bridgeton	1949-1952

Franklin T. Buck
  Camden
	1951-1956	Hooker D. Davis
		  Southwest
			1969-74

William R. Guffick
  Trenton
  New Brunswick
	1951-1955
	1958-1964
		Edward B. Cheney
		  Northwest
			1970-75

		Charles W. Marker Northeast	1970-75

Albert S. Layton
  Bridgeton
	1952-1957	C. Wesley Crossley
		  Southeast
			1974-77

B. Harrison Decker
  New Brunswick
	1952-1958	Carl W. Halversen
		  Camden
			1974-79

Nelson M. Hoffman
  Trenton
  Camden
	1955
	1956-60
		Lawrence E. Moore
		  Central
			1974-78

F. Elwood Perkins, Jr.
  Trenton
	1956-62	Donald T. Phillips, Jr.
		  Southwest
			1975-80

Charles R. Smyth
  Bridgeton
	1957-58	Robert J. Beyer
		  Northeast
			1976-81

Marvin R. Guice
  Bridgeton
	1958-64	David M. Finch
		  Northwest
			1976-81

Ernest W. Lee
  Camden
  Southeast
  Camden
	1960-64
	1968-69
	1970-73
		Robert K. Smyth
		  Southeast
			1978-82

George R. Propert
  Trenton
	1962-67	M. Russell Shivers
		  Central
		  Northwest
			1979-81
			1982-84

Robert E. Acheson
  Bridgeton
  Southwest
	1964-67
	1968
		Champion B. Goldy
		  Camden
		  Central
			1980-81
			1982-

Lawrence G. Atkinson
  Camden
	1964-69	John L. Ewing
		  Southwest
			1981-

Paul A. Friedrich
  New Brunswick
  Northeast
	1964-67
	1968-69
		Charles Wilcock
		  Northeast
			1982-

L. Burdelle Hawk
  Northwest
  Southeast
	1968-69
	1970-73
		George T. Wang
		  Southeast
			1983-

Albert V. Lang
  Central
	1968-73	David N. Cousins
		  Northwest
			1985-

(Note: Because of the different times a Superintendent assumed office, there was often an overlapping in the years served.)

APPENDIX IV
DELEGATES TO GENERAL AND JURISDICTIONAL CONFERENCES

1840   Baltimore, Md.
Charles Pitman, Manning Force, Richard W. Petherbridge, Isaac Winner, John S. Porter. Reserve: John K. Shaw

1844   New York, N.Y.
Isaac Winner, John S. Porter, John K. Shaw, Thomas Neal, Thomas Sovereign. Reserve: John McClintock.

1848   Pittsburg, Pa.
Charles Pitman, George F. Brown, John K. Shaw, Isaac Winner, Manning Force, Isaac N. Felch, David W. Bartine. Reserves: Thomas McCarroll, John S. Porter.

1852   Boston, Mass.
John McClintock, George F. Brown, Daniel P. Kidder, John S. Porter, Jefferson Lewis, James Ayres, Thomas McCarroll, Isaac Winner.

1856   Indianapolis, Ind.
George F. Brown, John McClintock, John S. Porter, Samuel Y. Monroe, Jefferson Lewis, Isaac N. Felch, John S. Swain, William A. Wilmer, John L. Lenhart. Reserves: James M. Tuttle, Nicholas VanSant.

1860   Buffalo, N.Y.
Samuel Y. Monroe, George F. Brown, Abram K. Street, George Hughes. Reserves: Charles H. Whitecar, Joseph B. Dobbins.

1864   Philadelphia, Pa.
Samuel Y. Monroe, Charles H. Whitecar, William E. Perry, Abram K. Street. Reserves: Elwood H. Stokes, Jefferson Lewis.

1868   Chicago, Ill.
Elwood H. Stokes, Samuel VanSant, John S. Heisler, Isaac Winner, Francis A. Morrell. Reserves: Joseph B. Dobbins, Aaron E. Ballard.

1872   Brooklyn, N.Y.
Clergy: Isaiah D. King, Jacob B. Graw, Charles E. Hill, Joseph B. Dobbins, Aaron E. Ballard. Lay: Samuel A. Dobbins, James Bishop. Reserves: T. V. F. Rusling, James F. Rusling.

1876   Baltimore, Md.
Clergy: Jacob B. Graw, Enoch Green, Thomas Hanlon, Charles W. Heisley. Reserves: Daniel P. Kidder, David H. Schock.
Lay: W. H. Bodine, C. E. Hendrickson. Reserves: W. S. Yard, G. D. Horner.

1880   Cincinnati, Ohio.
Clergy: Jacob B. Graw, William W. Moffett, George B. Wight, Charles E. Hill. Reserves: Jefferson Lewis, David H. Schock.
Lay: Clinton B. Fisk, Jesse H. Diverty. Reserves: William S. Yard, John W. Newlin.

1884   Philadelphia, Pa.
Clergy: Jacob B. Graw, David H. Schock, George B. Wight, William Walton. Reserves: Edmund Hewitt, Daniel P. Kidder.
Lay: Clinton B. Fisk, Benjamin F. Archer. Reserves: William S. Yard, John W. Newlin.

1888   New York, N.Y.
Clergy: J. Leander Sooy, Jacob B. Graw, George B. Wight, George L. Dobbins. Reserves: Philip Cline, William W. Moffett.
Lay: Clinton B. Fisk, William H. Skirm. Reserves: A. Emory Street, John W. Newlin.

1892   Omaha, Neb.
Clergy: Thomas Hanlon, George B. Wight, Jacob B. Graw, James Moore, Edmund Hewitt. Reserves: Daniel B. Harris, George Reed.
Lay: William H. Skirm, A. Emory Street. Reserves: Clement W. Shoemaker, M. F. Middleton.

1896   Cleveland, Ohio
Clergy: Jacob B. Graw, James R. Mace, George B. Wight, Joseph L. Roe, George Reed.
Reserves: Thomas Hanlon, William P. C. Strickland. Lay: Clement W. Shoemaker, James F. Rusling. Reserves: William H. Skirm, Caleb H. Butterworth.

1900   Chicago, Ill.
Clergy: Jacob B. Graw, George L. Dobbins, James W. Marshall, John Handley, James H. Payran. Reserves: William P. C. Strickland, Simon W. Lake.
Lay: William H. Skirm, Matthias Woolley, Ezra B. Lake, Caleb H. Butterworth, George B. Langley. Reserves: Joseph Elverson, John S. Turner, James E. Taylor, W. H. Heisler, W. P. Finlaw.

1904   Los Angeles, Calif.
Clergy: George L. Dobbins, J. Morgan Read, William P. Davis, William R. Wedderspoon, John B. Haines. Reserves: James W. Marshall, Edmund Hewitt. Lay: George H. Franklin, John Sykes, Caleb H. Butterworth, Benjamin Patterson, A. Emory Street. Reserves: L. L. Hand, Frank S. Wells, Charles W. Fisher, Alfred C. Graw, James E. Hewitt.

1908   Baltimore, Md.
Clergy: J. Morgan Read, John D. Fox, James W. Marshall, John Handley, Holmes F. Gravatt. Reserves: Alfred Wagg, Nomar J. Wright, John B. Haines.
Lay: William H. Heisler, Harry P. Bennett, Henry S. Springer, W. Holt Apgar, Henry Bradway. Reserves: John E. Rossell, Alfred C. Graw, Thomas M. Dickey.

1912   Minneapolis: Minn.
Clergy: Alfred Wagg, John Handley, Sanford M. Nichols, Edmund J. Kulp, Melville E. Snyder. Reserves: James W. Marshall, Holmes F. Gravatt, Daniel E. Clair.
Lay: Charles F. Repp, William S. Child, William H. Heisler, Charles C. Read, Harry P. Bennett. Reserves: A. G. Smith, E. N. Cole, James E. Hewitt.

1916   Saratoga Springs, N.Y.
Clergy: Melville E. Snyder, George H. Neal, Holmes F. Gravatt, James W. Marshall, Furman A. DeMaris. Reserves: Samuel H. Hann, John R. Mason, Alfred Wagg.
Lay: Harry P. Bennett, W. H. Cox, John E. Rossell, Charles F. Repp, William E. Massey. Reserves: William S. Child, Wilfred B. Wolcott, A. J. Tams.

1920   Des Moines, Iowa
Clergy: John R. Mason, Alfred Wagg, Melville E. Snyder, James D. Bills, Harold P. Sloan. Reserves: Alexander Corson, Furman A. Demaris, James W. Marshall.
Lay: Edward S. Sheldon, William E. Massey, Harry P. Bennett, Charles C. Read, Wilfred B. Wolcott. Reserves: William A. Sweeney, Elwood S. Johnson, Edgar Y. Dobbins.

1924   Springfield, Mass.
Clergy: Alexander Corson, Harold P. Sloan, Alfred Wagg, DeWitt C. Cobb, Furman A. Demaris, Reserves: Melville E. Snyder, Herbert J. Belting, Edward A. Wells.
Lay: Alvin C. Poffenberger, William J. Couse, William E. Massey, Franklin B. Platt, Harry P. Bennett. Reserves: Edgar Y. Dobbins, W. Holt Apgar, J. B. F. Morgan.

1928   Kansas City, Mo.
Clergy: Harold P. Sloan, Furman A. DeMaris, Herbert J. Belting, Thomas S. Brock, Edward A. Wells. Reserves: John Goorley, George H. Neal, Joseph B. Kulp. Lay: Alvin C. Poffenberger, William E. Massey, Edgar Y. Dobbins, Mark R. Reynolds, Howard I. Branson. Reserves: Willis T. Porch, Harry P. Bennett, Benjamin M. Woodward.

1932   Atlantic City, N.J.
Clergy: Thomas S. Brock, Furman A. DeMaris, Harold P. Sloan, Charles I. Fitzgeorge, Edward A. Wells, Thomas J. J. Wright. Reserves: John Goorley, Alexander Corson, Woodburn J. Sayre. Lay: Alvin C. Poffenberger, Edgar Y. Dobbins, Mark R. Reynolds, Harry P. Bennett, Willis T. Porch, George W. Scarborough. Reserves: LeRoy S. Champion, Elwood S. Johnson, T. Dowdney Clark.

1936   Columbus, Ohio
Clergy: Thomas S. Brock, Harold P. Sloan, Woodburn J. Sayre, Thomas J. J. Wright. Reserves: Leon Chamberlain, Edward A. Wells.
Lay: Frank C. Propert, LeRoy S. Champion, Harry P. Bennett, Helen Phillips.[1] Reserves: Mark Reynolds, Edgar Y. Dobbins, Elmer E. Matthews, Alfred E. Blakeman.

1939   Uniting Conference, Kansas City, Mo.
Clergy: Thomas S. Brock, Harold P. Sloan. Reserves: Edwin F. Hann, Leon Chamberlain. Lay: Frank C. Propert, Harry P. Bennett. Reserves: Alvin C. Poffenberger, Elmer E. Matthews.

1940   Atlantic City, N.J.
Clergy: Thomas S. Brock, Edwin F. Hann, Harold P. Sloan, Leon Chamberlain. Jurisdiction: George D. Jones, Henry L. Bradway, Charles D. Whitton, Furman A. DeMaris, Edward A. Wells. Reserves: Herbert J. Smith, Thomas J. J. Wright, Herbert J. Belting.
Lay: Frank C. Propert, Alvin C. Poffenberger, Mrs. George Yard, Harry P. Bennett. Jurisdiction: Edgar Y. Dobbins, Harry S. Jackson, Alice Detwiler, Helen Phillips, Leon Cossaboon. Reserves: Francis B. Stanger, Mark Reynolds, Mrs. Berryman McCoy.

1944   Kansas City, Mo.
Clergy: Albert L. Baner, Austin C. Brady, Benjamin F. Allgood, W. Rolland Raver. Jurisdiction: Charles D. Whitton, Henry L. Bradway, Edwin F. Hann, William W. Payne. Reserves: Marvin R. Guice, Ira S. Pimm.
Lay: Francis A. Stanger, Frank C. Propert, Alvin C. Poffenberger, Mrs. Henry Ebner.
Jurisdiction: Howard S. Stainton, Edgar Y. Dobbins, Mark Reynolds, Mrs. Benjamin F. Allgood. Reserves: Mrs. H. W. Bland Detwiler, J. H. Rogers.

1948   Boston, Mass.
Clergy: G. Ernest Thomas, Benjamin F. Allgood, Ira S. Pimm.
Jurisdiction: Everett W. Palmer, Harry F. Henry, Austin C. Brady, Charles R. Smyth, Henry L. Bradway. Reserves: Herbert J. Smith, William R. Guffick, Lynn H. Corson.
Lay: Frank C. Porpert, Mrs. Henry D. Ebner, Francis A. Stanger, George Bowen. Jurisdiction: George C. Ingling, Elmer E. Matthews, Howard S. Stainton, Hammell P. Shipps, Mark Reynolds. Reserves: J. H. Rogers, George W. Williams, Levi B. Sharp.

[1] First woman delegate from the New Jersey Conference.

1952 San Francisco, Calif.
Clergy: Herbert J. Smith, W. Neal Raver, Henry L. Bradway.
Jurisdiction: William R. Guffick, G. Ernest Thomas, Benjamin F. Allgood, Franklin T. Buck, Lynn H. Corson. Reserves: Carl W. Reamer, A. Lynn Gongloff, Frank B. Stanger.
Lay: Hammell P. Shipps, Evelyn Schalick, Frank C. Propert.
Jurisdiction: Howard S. Stainton, Francis A. Stanger, George Bowen, Anne Ebner, Helen Phillips. Reserves: Alvin Whiting, Carlton Hughes, Elmer E. Matthews.

1956 Minneapolis, Minn.
Clergy: Lynn H. Corson, William R. Guffick, Frank B. Stanger.
Jurisdiction: Carl W. Reamer, W. Neal Raver, Roger J. Squire, Albert S. Layton, B. Harrison Decker. Reserves: Charles Smyth, Nelson Hoffman, J. Stanley Wagg.
Lay: Mrs. George P. Marple, Howard Stainton, Elmer E. Matthews.
Jurisdiction: Frank S. Smith, Mrs. Ira Pimm, Mrs. Henry D. Ebner, Herbert J. Schoellkopf, Mark Reynolds. Reserves: Mrs. Orvil Schalick, Mrs. H. Bland Detwiler, Fred Applegate.

1960 Denver, Col.
Clergy: William R. Guffick, Lynn H. Corson, F. Elwood Perkins.
Jurisdiction: Charles R. Smyth, Frank B. Stanger, Marvin R. Guice, Neal Raver, Nelson Hoffman. Reserves: Robert Howe, G. Ernest Thomas, Carl W. Reamer.
Lay: Mrs. Emerson Gardner, Herbert J. Schoellkopf, William F. Egan, Jr.
Jurisdiction: Fred Applegate, Robert Mumford, Arthur Schalick, Jr., Howard Stainton, Mark Reynolds. Reserves: Walter B. VanSant, Charles Crabiel, LeRoy Fowler.

1964 Pittsburg, Pa.
Clergy: William R. Guffick, George R. Propert, Charles A. Sayre, Ernest W. Lee.
Jurisdiction: Robert Jenks, Frank B. Stanger, Marvin R. Guice, Robert B. Howe, W. Gordon Lowden. Reserves: Charles R. Smyth, W. Neal Raver, Franklin T. Buck.
Lay: Robert Mumford, Hammell P. Shipps, Mrs. Albert Stretch, Herbert J. Schoellkopf.
Jurisdiction: Frank Egan, Jr., Fred Applegate, Howard Stainton, Mrs. Charles Marker, Henry L. Backenson. Reserves: Mark Reynolds, Charles Lang, Walter B. VanSant.

1966 Chicago, Ill.
Same delegates.

1968 Uniting Conference, Dallas, Texas
Clergy: Charles Sayre, George Propert, William R. Guffick, Robert E. Acheson.
Jurisdiction: Hooker D. Davis, Paul Friedrich, Frank B. Stanger, Lawrence Atkinson, Robert B. Howe. Reserves: Edward Cheney, W. Neal Raver, Daniel Hulitt.
Lay: Robert J. Mumford, W. Frank Egan, Henry L. Backenson, Mrs. Carlton Nelson.
Jurisdiction: Walter B. VanSant,[1] Elwood Davis, LeRoy Fowler, Elmer Matthews, Leon R. McKelvey. Reserves: Mrs. Frederick Krill, Mrs. Edward Fiedler, Mrs. Harry Sibley.

1970 St. Louis, Mo.
Same delegates.

1972 Atlanta, Georgia
Clergy: Charles A. Sayre, Hooker D. Davis, Ernest W. Lee, Frank B. Stanger.
Jurisdiction: Edward Cheney, Charles Marker, Albert Lang, L. Burdelle Hawk,

---

[1]Frank Egan became ill and was unable to attend General Conference. His place was taken by Walter B. VanSant.

Robert Howe, Carl Halvorsen. Reserves: Stanley Menking, Russell Shivers.
Lay: Hammell P. Shipps, Leon E. Walker, Mrs. James Brogden, Edwin Hann, Jr. Jurisdiction: Ulysses Estilow, William Kirk, Kirk Schelling, Henry Backenson, Elwood Davis, Mrs. Frank Johnson. Reserve: William Mason.

1976 Portland, Or.
Clergy: Charles Sayre, Ernest Lee, Edward Cheney, Carl Halvorsen.
Jurisdiction: Ernest Lyght, Russell Shivers, Frank Stanger, Hooker Davis, David Finch, Stanley Menking. Reserves: Charles Marker, C. Wesley Crossley, Daniel Hulitt.
Lay: Elizabeth Brogden, William Mason, Ronald Beppler, Leon Walker.
Jurisdiction: Edwin Hann, Hammell P. Shipps, William Ritt, Gertrude Klein, Alice Moore, Elwood Davis. Reserves: Henry Backenson, Sudie Nichols, Ruth Tracy.

1980 Indianapolis, Ind.
Clergy: Charles Sayre, Ernest W. Lee, Hooker D. Davis, Carl Halvorsen.
Jurisdiction: David Finch, Stanley Menking, Robert Beyer, Leonard Rowell, Russell Shivers. Reserves: Julio Gomez, Frank Stanger, Robert Symth.
Lay: Ronald Beppler, Elizabeth Brogden, June McCullough, James Davison.
Jurisdiction: W. Astor Kirk, Leon Walker, William Mason, Hammell Shipps, Herman Carr, Reserves: Ruth Kappler, Gertrude Klein, Carl Still.

1984 Baltimore, Md.
Clergy: Charles A. Sayre, M. Russell Shivers, John L. Ewing, Robert K. Smyth, Carl Halvorsen.
Jurisdiction: Sydney Sadio, Sandra Murphy, David Finch, Stanley Menking. Reserves: Lanie Price, Charles Wilcock, Harry R. Stevenson, Jr.
Lay: William L. Weller, Ronald Beppler, June McCullough, Betty Ricards, James J. Davison.
Jurisdiction: Elizabeth Brogden, Carol Hann, William Mason, Ruth Kappler. Reserves: Leon Walker, Herman Carr, Charlotte Yerks.

APPENDIX V

CONFERENCE WOMEN PRESIDENTS

A. WOMAN'S FOREIGN MISSIONARY SOCIETY

(The title of the chief officer was Conference Secretary, originally called Corresponding Secretary.)

1872-1876	Mrs. James
1877-1882	Mrs. John Aber
1883-1895	Mrs. Dallas Lore
1896	Mrs. Dallas Lore
	Mrs. Kennard Chandler
1897-1898	Mrs. Dallas Lore
	Mrs. H. H. Hartranft
1899-1902	Mrs. H. H. Hartranft
1903-1910	Mrs. W. H. Reeves
1911	Mrs. L. V. Mulford
1912-1916	Mrs. H. P. Sayford
1917-1919	Mrs. L. K. Willman
1920-1922	Mrs. O. H. Willard
1923	Mrs. Joseph K. Sharp
1924-1934	Mrs. W. C. Petherbridge
1935-1939	Mrs. Walter B. Williams

B. WOMAN'S HOME MISSIONARY SOCIETY

1885-1896	Mrs. Clinton B. Fisk
1897-1905	Mrs. Charles F. Garrison
1906-1907	Mrs. H. L. Caminade
1908-1913	Mrs. J. Morgan Read
1914-1919	Mrs. M. E. Snyder
1920-1939	Mrs. George W. Yard

C. WOMAN'S SOCIETY OF CHRISTIAN SERVICE AND UNITED METHODIST WOMEN

1940-1942	Bessie Brady (Mrs. A. Corbin)
1943-1946	Anne Ebner (Mrs. Henry D.)
1947-1950	Ethel Janke (Mrs. O. C. F.)
1951-1954	Evelyn Schalick (Mrs. W. Orvyl)
1955-1958	Christine Marple (Mrs. George)
1959-1962	Marguerite Gardner (Mrs. E. Emerson)
1963-1966	Mabel Stretch (Mrs. Albert)
1967-1970	Dorothy Nelson (Mrs. Carlton)
1971-1975	Elizabeth Brogden (Mrs. James)
1976-1979	June McCullough (Mrs. William)
1980-1983	Betty Ricards (Mrs. Bruce)
1984-	Margaret Howell (Mrs. Wayne)

(Note. Because of the different times a president assumed office, some in September, some June, others January 1st, there was often an overlapping in the years served.)

D. SISTERHOOD AND WESLEY FELLOWSHIP

1903-1907	Hannah Garrison (Mrs. Charles F.)
1907-1908	Laura I. Handley (Mrs. John)
1908-1911	Estella B. Lilley (Mrs. William A.)
1911-1913	Mary C. Davis (Mrs. William P.)
1913-1915	Julia F. Senser (Mrs. George G.)
1915-1916	Frances Hewitt (Mrs. Edmund)
1916-1923	Estella B. Lilley
1923-1929	Ethel Sloan (Mrs. Harold P.)
1929-1933	Rena Smith (Mrs. Herbert J.)
1933-1937	Elsie Hann (Mrs. Edwin F.)
1937-1940	Anne Ebner (Mrs. Henry D.)
1940-1942	Elsie Hann
1942-1946	Elizabeth Reamer (Mrs. Carl W.)
1946-1950	Bernita Myers (Mrs. Stacy D.)
1950-1954	Henrietta Guffick (Mrs. William R.)
1954-1958	Sarah Hoffman (Mrs. Nelson M.)
1958-1962	Ethel Hayward (Mrs. J. Courtney)
1962-1966	Dorothy Nelson (Mrs. Carlton N.)
1966-1970	Lucile Sayre (Mrs. Charles A.)
1970-1974	Anne McClelland (Mrs. William R.)
1974-1978	Eleanor Long (Mrs. John M.)
1978-1980	Connie Shivers (Mrs. Russell M.)
1980-1984	Penny Moore (Mrs. Lawrence E.)
1984-	Leona Quigg (Mrs. Walter A.)

APPENDIX VI
CONFERENCE LAY LEADERS

A. **NEW JERSEY LAYMEN'S ASSOCIATION**

1913	Dr. G. H. Franklin
1914	Charles C. Read
1915-1916	Dr. Grafton E. Day
1917	H. S. Miner
1918	W. B. Wolcott
1919	Harold B. Wells
1920	William E. Massey
1921	Franklin B. Platt
1922-1923	C. W. Wanger
1924	E. S. Woodward
1925-1927	L. C. Ogden
1928-1931	A. C. Poffenberger
1932-1939	Harry S. Jackson

B. **CONFERENCE LAY LEADERS**

1940-1947	Francis A. Stanger
1948-1953	Dr. Hammell P. Shipps
1954-1962	Herbert J. Schoellkopf
1963-1967	Robert J. Mumford
1968-1971	Leon E. Walker
1972-1975	William G. Mason
1976-1979	James J. Davison
1980-1985	William L. Weller
1986-	June McCullough (Mrs. William)

APPENDIX VII
CONFERENCE YOUTH PRESIDENTS

A. EPWORTH LEAGUE

1892	Amos M. North
1893	Percy Perinchief
1894	George G. Senser
1895-1896	Henry J. Zelley
1897	James H. Batten
1898	Samuel M. VanSant
1899-1900	Marshall Owens
1901	James M. Read
1902	Joseph F. Shaw
1903-1904	Furman A. DeMaris
1905-1906	Thomas S. Brock
1907-1909	Sherman G. Pitt
1910	Joseph B. Kulp
1911-1912	George T. Harris
1913	Leon Chamberlain
1914	Frederick L. Jewett
1915	Archie Harris
1916	Frederick L. Jewett
1917	DeWitt C. Cobb
1918	Elbert M. Conover
1919	Herbert J. Root
1920	Leslie L. Hand
1921-23	W. B. Housel
1924-1926	Matthias Campbell
1927-1930	A. Corbin Brady
1931-1934	Ira S. Pimm
1935-1937	W. Lester Whitfield
1938-1941	Henry D. Ebner

B. METHODIST YOUTH FELLOWSHIP

1942	Stanley Hagaman
1943	G. Lester Whitfield
1944-1945	Virginia Long
1946-1947	Donald Pimm
1948-1950	Richard Case
1951-1953	Robert Shoemaker
1954	Janet Barbatto
1955	William Suiter
1956-1957	Barbara Carson
1958-1959	David White
1960	Jack Suiter
1961	Eddie Gatjen
1962	Francis Rousseau
1963	Paul Duffy
1964	Pat Hallowell
1965	Noel Hess
1966	Judy Broome

1967	Linda Brobst
1968	Jack Shaw
1969-1970	Linda Alvord
1971	Steve Harding
1972	Clark Fitchett
1973	Stanley E. McCleave
1974-1975	Cindy Horton
1976	Janice Bucco
1977	Linda Holdcraft
1978	Larry Potts
1979	Doug Moses
1980	Linda Conrad
1981	Gene McGrath
1982	Andrew Hoffman
1983	Lori Hunt
1984	Sara Thomas
1985	Joanna Lund
1986	Judith Smith

BIBLIOGRAPHY

Abbott, Benjamin. *Experiences and Gospel Labors,* ed. John Ffirth. New York: T. Mason and G. Lane, 1836 (first published 1809.)

Anderson, Kenneth. Manuscript *History of Pennington School, 1838-1970.* (A copy of the rough draft of the manuscript is in the office of the Alumni Director of the School. The completed manuscript was destroyed in the Pennington Fire.)

Asbury, Francis. *The Journal and Letters,* ed. Elmer T. Clark, J. Manning Potts, and Jacob S. Payton. 3 vols. Nashville: Abingdon Press, 1958.

Ahlstrom, Sydney E. *A Religious History of the American People.* 2 volumes. Garden City, N.Y.: Doubleday & Company, Inc., 1975.

Atkinson, John. *Memorials of Methodism in New Jersey.* Philadelphia: Perkinpine & Higgins, 1860.

Baker, Frank. "Captain Thomas Webb, Pioneer of American Methodism." *Religion and Life,* Summer 1965.

———. *John Wesley and the Church of England.* Nashville: Abingdon Press, 1970.

———. *From Wesley to Asbury.* Durham, N. C.: Duke University Press, 1976.

Barclay, Wade Crawford. *History of Methodist Missions,* Early American Methodism, 1769-1844, Vol. 1: "Missionary Motivation and Expansion." New York: The Board of Missions and Church Extension of The Methodist Church, 1949.

———. *History of Methodist Missions,* Early American Methodism, 1769-1844, Vol. 2: "To Reform the Nation." New York: The Board of Missions and Church Extension of The Methodist Church, 1950.

———. *History of Methodist Missions,* The Methodist Episcopal Church, 1845-1939, Vol. 3: "Widening Horizons," 1845-1895. New York: The Board of Missions of The Methodist Church, 1957.

Barkalow, Matthias. "Records of Matthias Barkalow, Independent Methodist Preacher, 1806-1827." *The Genealogical Magazine of New Jersey,* May 1964.

Bassett, Ancel, H. *A Concise History of the Methodist Protestant Church.* 2nd ed., rev. & enlarged. Pittsburg: James Robison and Baltimore: W. J. C. Dulaney, 1882.

Bates, E. Ralph. *Captain Thomas Webb.* London: World Methodist Historical Society, 1975.

Bennett, Joseph Henry. *Preaching Stations of Benjamin Abbott in the Jerseys.* Unpublished manuscript. No date. (In author's collection. Copy in Atlantic County Historical Society, Somers Point, N.J.)

———. *The Union Meeting House,* English Creek, N.J. Unpublished manuscript. No date. (In author's collection. Copy in Atlantic County Historical Society, Somers Point, N.J.)

Blackman, Learner. *Journal.* (Archives of the Mississippi Conference. Micro-film in SNJ Conference Archives.)

Born, Ethel Wolfe. "Who Were the Methodist Protestants?" *Response,* official program journal of United Methodist Women. November 1983.

Brawley, James P. *Two Centuries of Methodist Concern:* Bondage, Freedom and Education of Black People. New York: Vantage Press, 1974.

Brereton, Virginia Lieson. "Preparing Women For the Lord's Work." *Women in New Worlds,* I.

Bucke, Emory Stevens, ed. *History of American Methodism,* 3 vols. Nashville: Abingdon Press, 1964. (Cited in notes as HAM.)

Calkin, Homer L. "The Methodists and the Centennial of 1876." *Methodist History,* January 1976.

Cameron, Richard M. *Methodism and Society in Historical Perspective,* Vol. I, "The Methodist Church in Social Thought and Action." New York and Nashville: Abingdon Press, 1961.

Campbell, Barabara E. *In the Middle of Tomorrow.* New York: Women's Division of Global Ministries The United Methodist Church, 1975.

Carroll, H. K., Harrison, W. P., Bayliss, J. H., ed. *Proceedings, Sermons, Essays, and Addresses of the Centennial Methodist Conference,* held in Mt. Vernon Place M. E. Church Baltimore, Md., December 9-17, 1884. New York: Phillips & Hunt, 1885.

Chandler, Douglas R. "The Formation of the Methodist Protestant Church." *History of American Methodism,* I, 636-683.

Chandler, Mrs. E. G. (Rosalie Porter). *History of the Woman's Foreign Missionary Society of the Methodist Protestant Church, 1879-1919.* Pittsburg: Press of Pierpoint, Siviter & Co., 1920.

Coffee, John Hillman. *The New Jersey Conference, 1836-1861.* Unpublished thesis, The Philadelphia Divinity School, 1959.

―――― . "The Rev. Joseph Pilmore, D.D." *The Historical Trail,* 1969.

Coffee, Miriam L. "The Origin of Sunday Schools in England and in America." *The Historical Trail,* 1980.

Coke, Thomas. *Extracts of the Journals of the Late Rev. Thomas Coke, L.L.D.,* Comprising several visits to North America and the West Indies; His tour through a part of Ireland, and his nearly finished voyage to Bombay in the East-Indies: to which is prefixed a Life of the Doctor. Dublin: The Methodist Book-Room, 1816.

Committed to Mission Tomorrow, Building on Yesterday. United Methodist Women Pamphlet, 1983.

Conference Secretary's Files. New Jersey Conference, the Methodist Episcopal Church. SNJ Conference Archives.

Constitution and Discipline. Methodist Protestant Church, 1939. 3rd edition. Other dates.

Crowther, Robert W., Jr. *Methodist Camp Meetings in Southern New Jersey.* A Thesis, Princeton Theological Seminary, 1959.

Cunningham, John T. "The Story of New Jersey." *The New Jersey Almanac,* Tercentenary Edition. Trenton Evening Times, 1964.

Curts, Lewis, ed. *The General Conference of the Methodist Episcopal Church from 1792 to 1896.* Cincinnati: Curts & Jennings. New York: Eaton & Mains, 1900.

Doctrines and Discipline of the Methodist Episcopal Church, 1798, etc. (cited in notes as *Discipline.*)

Dougherty, Mary Agnes. "The Methodist Deaconess." *Methodist History,* January 1983.

―――― . "The Social Gospel According to Phoebe." *Women in New Worlds,* I.

Drinkhouse, Edward J. *History of Methodist Reform.* 2 Vols. Baltimore and Pittsburg: Board of Publication of the Methodist Protestant Church, 1899.

Earley, Charles. "John Early: Pioneer Methodist in New Jersey." *The Historical Trail,* 1963.

"The Echoes of Fifty Years, 1921-1970." Pennington Institute 50th Anniversary Program Book.

Ege, Ralph. *Pioneers of Old Hopewell.* Hopewell, N.J.: Race & Savidge, 1908.

Eisenlohr, Gail A. *From Vision to Reality.* A History of Malaga Camp Meeting, 1869-1969. Newfield, N.J.: West Jersey Grove Association, 1969.

Evans, Mary T. *History of The United Methodist Homes of New Jersey.* 75th Anniversary, 1907-1982. Ocean Grove, 1982.

Extracts of Letters Containing Some Account of the Work of God Since the Year 1800. Written by the Preachers and Members of the Methodist Episcopal Church, to their Bishops. New York: Cooper & Wilson, 1805.

Formal Fraternity. Proceedings of the General Conference of the Methodist Episcopal Church and of the Methodist Episcopal Church, South, in 1872, 1874, and 1876, and of the Joint Commission of the Two Churches on Fraternal Relations, at Cape May, New Jersey, August 16-23, 1876. New York: Nelson & Phillips. Nashville: A. H. Redford, 1876.

Friedrich, Paul A. *A History of The United Methodist Homes of New Jersey.* 70th Anniversary Issue, 1907-1977. Ocean Grove: Board of Trustees, 1977.

Gaines, Abner J. "New Jersey and the Fourteenth Amendment." Proceedings of the New Jersey Historical Society. Vol. LXX, No. 1, January 1952.

Garber, Paul N. *The Methodists Are One People.* Nashville: Cokesbury Press, 1939.

Gardner, D. H. "The Emancipation of Slaves in New Jersey." *Proceedings of the New Jersey Historical Society.* Vol. IX, No. 1, January 1924.

Gaustad, Edwin Scott. *Historical Atlas of Religion in America.* New York: Harper & Row, 1962.

Gibbons, Mr. & Mrs. Richard F. *History of Ocean Grove 1869-1939.* Ocean Grove: Ocean Grove Times, 1939.

Gilmore, Rev. Alexander. *Centenary Memorial Sermon.* Delivered Before the New Jersey Annual Conference, March 26, 1866. Camden: S. Chew, 1866.

Godbold, Albea. *Forever Beginning, 1766-1966.* Historical Papers presented at American Methodism's Bicentennial Conference. Baltimore, Md., April 21-24, 1966. Lake Junaluska, N.C.: Association of Methodist Historical Societies, 1967.

———. "Francis Asbury and His Difficulties with John Wesley and Thomas Rankin." *Methodist History,* April 1965.

Graw, A. C. *Life and Times of Rev. J. B. Graw, D.D., 1832-1901.* Pastor, Soldier, Reformer, Presiding Elder. Camden, N.J.: A. C. Graw, 1901.

Green, Harry F. "Historic Gloucester Point." *The Historical Trail,* 1969.

Griscom, Lloyd E. "Early American Methodism: The Unique Career of a Pioneer." Joseph Toy. *The Historical Trail,* 1984.

———. "First Methodist in New Jersey: Joseph Toy." *The Historical Trail,* 1968.

———. "Ocean City, Once 'Peck's Beach.' " *The Herald,* September, 1979. Clipping in files Archives SNJ Conference.

Hampton, Vernon Boyce, ed. *Newark Conference Centennial History, 1857-1957.* The Historical Society of the Newark Annual Conference of The Methodist Church, 1957.

Hanly, Mrs. Joanna P. R. *Memoirs of the late Rev. Joseph J. Hanly, M.D. of the New Jersey Conference.* Philadelphia: J. B. Lippincott & Co., 1861.

Harmon, Nolan B., ed. *The Encyclopedia of World Methodism.* 2 vols. Nashville: The United Methodist Publishing House, 1974.

Hartman, Albert E. "The Methodist Center at Mt. Misery." 25th Anniversary Historical Sketch. Mimeographed. 1971.

Hildebrand, Reginald F. "Methodist Episcopal Policy on the Ordination of Black Ministers, 1784-1864." *Methodist History,* April 1982.

The Historical Trail. 1962-1984. Yearbook of the Historical Society of the Southern New Jersey Annual Conference of The United Methodist Church.

———. Bishop Francis Asbury Bicentennial Issue, 1971.

———. Pilmore-Boardman Bicentennial Issue, 1969.

"History of the Evangelical United Methodist Church, Clarksboro, N.J." Mimeographed, 1980.

Hopkins, Alphonso Alva. *The Life of Clinton Bowen Fisk.* New York: Funk & Wagnalls, 1888.

Hopkins, Charles Howard. *The Rise of the Social Gospel in American Protestantism, 1865-1915.* New Haven: Yale University Press, 1940.

Hudson, Winthrop S. *Religion in America.* New York: Charles Scribner's Sons, 1965.

———. "The Methodist Age in America." *Methodist History,* April 1974.

Hughes, H. Raymond. *Looking Back.* An updated history of Delanco Camp Meeting. Unpublished, 1984. (Written at the request of the Commission on Archives and History, SNJ Conference and on file in their Archives.)

———. *The History of Delanco Camp Meeting Association, Delanco, N.J.* Unpublished, circa 1961. (Copy in files of Archives SNJ Conference.)

———. "The Purpose and a Brief History of Delanco Camp Meeting." *The Historical Trail,* 1984.

Jamison, Wallace N. *Religion in New Jersey.* Vol. 13, The New Jersey Historical Series. Princeton: D. Van Nostrand Company, Inc., 1964.

Jason, William C., Jr. "The Delaware Annual Conference of The Methodist Church, 1864-1965." *Methodist History,* July 1966.

———. "The History and Contribution of the Delaware Conference." *Official Journal and Year Book of the Delaware Annual Conference, The Methodist Church,* 1965. An Address given at the Annual Meeting of the Northeastern Jurisdictional Historical Association, Barratt's Chapel, Frederica, Delaware, April 29, 1965.

Jones, Charles Edwin. *Perfectionist Persuasion:* The Holiness Movement and American Methodism, 1867-1936. ATLA Monograph Series, No. 5. Metuchen, N.J.: The Scarecrow Press, 1974.

Jones, Donald G. *The Sectional Crisis and Northern Methodism.* A Study in Piety, Political Ethics and Civil Religion. Metuchen, N.J.: The Scarecrow Press, Inc., 1979.

Jones, Ralph H. *Charles Albert Tindley,* Prince of Preachers. Nashville: Abingdon Press, 1982.

Journal of the Philadelphia Conference of the Methodist Episcopal Church. Handwritten copy, 1800-1836, in Southern New Jersey Conference Archives.

Keller, Rosemary Skinner. "Creating a Sphere for Women in the Church." *Methodist History,* January 1980.

Kingston, William J. "Charles Pitman: New Jersey Apostle." *The Historical Trail.* In three parts, 1972, 1973, 1974.

Lednum, John. *A History of the Rise of Methodism in America.* Philadelphia: John Lednum, 1859.

Lee, Harold. *A History of Ocean City, New Jersey.* Ocean City: The Friends of the Ocean City Historical Museum, 1965.

Lee, Jesse. *A Short History of The Methodists.* Baltimore: Magill and Clime, 1810. Fascimile edition, Rutland, Vermont: Academy Books, 1974.

Licorish, Joshua E. "Brief History of the Delaware Conference." *Official Journal and Year Book of the Delaware Annual Conference, The Methodist Church,* 1965.

———. "Delaware Conference." *Encyclopedia of World Methodism,* I, 652.

Magalis, Elaine. *Conduct Becoming to a Woman.* Bolted Doors and Burgioning Missions. New York: Women's Division, Board of Global Ministries, The United Methodist Church, 1973.

Malmsbury, Caleb A. *The Life, Labors and Sermons of Rev. Charles Pitman, D.D.* Philadelphia: Methodist Episcopal Book Room, 1887.

Maps, William R., Jr. *Journal.* 1831-1843. 1852-1897. (Original two Journals are in private hands. Excerpts in the Museum of Old First United Methodist Church, West Long Branch, N.J.)

Maser, Frederick, E. *Robert Strawbridge,* First American Methodist Circuit Rider. Rutland, Vermont: Strawbridge Shrine Association, Inc. in cooperation with Academy Books, 1983.

———. "The Story of Unification." *History of American Methodism,* III, 407-478.

Mathews, Donald G. *Slavery and Methodism:* A Chapter in American Morality 1780-1845. Princeton: Princeton University Press, 1965.

McClintock, John. Letters. (Manuscript Collection. Drew University.)

McCormick, Richard P. *New Jersey from Colony to State 1609-1789.* New Brunswick: Rutgers University, 1964.

McLean, Revs. A. and Eaton, J. W. (official reporters of the General Conference of the M.E. Church), ed. *Penuel:* or Face to Face with God. New York: W. C. Palmer, Jr., Publisher, 1869. Tells the story of the National Holiness Camp Meetings at Vineland, Manheim and Round Lake.

Meeker, Ruth Esther. *Six Decades of Service.* A History of the Woman's Home Missionary Society of the Methodist Episcopal Church, 1880-1940. Published by the Continuing Corporation of the WHMS, M. E. Church, 1969.

Methodist History. Quarterly publication of the General Commission on Archives and History of The United Methodist Church. October 1962 to date.

Methodist Home. Collingswood, New Jersey. 75th Anniversary. 1890-1965.

Methodist Magazine, 1826.

The Methodist Protestant. Centennial Edition, 1828-1928. Volume 98. Number 20, May 16, 1928.

Methodist Protestant. *Manuscript Minute Book.* (Archives, Drew University.) Contains Minutes First Associated Methodist Churches East and North of the Chesapeake. Early Minutes of the Philadelphia, New York and New Jersey Conferences. Also Quarterly Minutes of the Glassboro and Centreville, New Jersey Circuits. Zerox copies of Minutes First Annual Conference Associated Methodist Churches and 1843 session of the New Jersey Conference in SNJ Conference Archives.

Methodist Relay. United Methodist Relay. Voice of the New Jersey Conference and New Jersey Area. 1956 to date.

Methodist Sesqui-Centennial. Baltimore: The American Methodist Historical Society, 1934.

Milhouse, Paul W. *Philip William Otterbein.* Pioneer Pastor to Germans in America. Nashville: The Upper Room, 1968.

Minutes. Atlantic Conference of the Evangelical Association, 1875-1922. Atlantic Conference of the Evangelical Church, 1922-1946.

Minutes. Cape May Circuit, June 7, 1834 to March 10, 1838. (Original records in Goshen United Methodist Church, Goshen, N.J. Typed copy in SNJ Conference Archives.)

Minutes. Delaware Conference of The Methodist Church, 1965. Other years as cited.

Minutes. Eastern Conference of the Evangelical United Brethren Church, 1963-1968.

Minutes. Eastern Conference, Methodist Protestant Church, 1912-1939.

Minutes. Eastern Pennsylvania Conference of the Evangelical Association, 1840-1875.

Minutes. Freehold Circuit, later Farmingdale Circuit, 1837-1867. Original in private hands. (Zerox copy in SNJ Conference Archives.)

Minutes. New Jersey Conference, Methodist Episcopal Church, 1838-1938. (Cited in notes as Minutes.)

Minutes. New Jersey Conference, The Methodist Church, 1939-1965. (Cited in notes as Minutes.)

Minutes. New Jersey Conference, Methodist Protestant Church, various dates.

Minutes. Northeastern Conference of the Evangelical United Brethren Church. 1957-1963.

Minutes of the New Jersey Methodist State Convention, Trenton, N.J., September 27-29, 1870. Trenton: W. T. Nicholson, 1870.

Minutes. Southern New Jersey Conference, The Methodist Church, 1966, 1967. (Cited in notes as Minutes.)

Minutes. Southern New Jersey Conference, The United Methodist Church, 1968-1984. (Cited in notes as Minutes.)

Moore, John M. *The Long Road to Methodist Union.* Nashville: The Methodist Publishing House, 1943.

Moore, Penny. "Memories of Children's Day." *The Historical Trail,* 1980.

Moss, Arthur Bruce. *Thomas Webb,* a Founder of American Methodism. New York: N. Y. Conference Commission on Archives and History, 1975.

Muelder, Walter G. *Methodism and Society in the Twentieth Century,* Vol. II, "The Methodist Church in Social Thought and Action." New York and Nashville: Abingdon Press, 1961.

Myers, Charlotte. "History of the New Jersey Memorial Home for Disabled Soldiers, Sailors, Marines and their Wives and Widows, Vineland, N.J." *The Vineland Historical Magazine.* July 1941.

Neary, Helen P. and Robert C., Sr. *Our Travels, Little Things We Remember and Rev. Helen P. Neary, A Lady Circuit Rider.* Privately Printed, 1978.

Ness, John H., Jr. "Table of Evangelical and United Brethren Annual Conferences." *Methodist History,* October 1969.

The New Jersey Almanac. Tercentenary Edition, 1964-1965. Trenton Evening Times, 1964.

New Jersey Conference Camp Meeting Association, 100th Anniversary, 1870-1970. Pitman Grove, 1970.

New Jersey Conference Memorial. Containing Biographical Sketches of all Its Deceased Members, including those who have died in the Newark Conference. Camden: Perkinpine & Higgins, 1865.

Noll, William, T. "Women As Clergy and Laity in the 19th Century Methodist Protestant Church." *Methodist History,* January 1977.

North, Louise McCoy. *The Story of the New York Branch of the Woman's Foreign Missionary Society of the Methodist Episcopal Church.* New York: N. Y. Branch, 1926.

Norwood, Frederick A., ed. *Sourcebook of American Methodism.* Nashville: Abingdon Press, 1982.

_____ . *The Story of American Methodism.* Nashville: Abingdon Press, 1974.

Ocean City Association Annual Reports, 1881, 1883. (Copies in the personal files of Dr. Robert J. Williams.)

Ocean City Tabernacle Association. *100th Anniversary Program Book,* 1979.

One Hundred Women in Mission. Biographical Data. United Methodist Women, SNJ Conference. Unpublished, 1984. (Copy in SNJ Conference Archives.)

"The Origin of Children's Day." *Methodist Trail in New Jersey,* 47.

"Origin of Children's Day." *N.J. Conference Minutes, M. E. Church,* 1892, 72, 73.

Our Young People. Publication of the Methodist Protestant Church, 1892. No further date. (Clipping in Manuscript Minute Book. Zerox copy SNJ Conference Archives.)

Perkins, F. Elwood. "They Love to Sing!" South Jersey's Heritage in Hymns and Gospel Songs. *The Historical Trail,* 1974.

Peterson, James D. *Matthias Barkalow 1787-1827,* Elder in the Independent Methodist Church of New Jersey. Unpublished Paper, 1983. (Copy in author's collection. Also in the Barkalow Homestead, Museum of the Wall Township Historical Society.)

Phoebus, George A. *Beams of Light on Early Methodism in America,* Chiefly drawn from the Diary, Letters, Manuscripts, Documents, and Original Tracts of the late Rev. Ezekiel Cooper. New York: Phillips & Hunt, 1887.

Pilmore, Joseph. *Journal,* ed. Frederick E. Maser and Howard T. Maag. Philadelphia: Message Publishing Company, 1969.

Price, Clement Alexander. *Freedom Not Far Distant,* A Documentary History of Afro-Americans in New Jersey. Newark: New Jersey Historical Society, 1980.

Proceedings of the Joint Commission of the Methodist Episcopal Church, and the Methodist Episcopal Church, South. In Session at Congress Hall Cape May, N.J. August 16th A.D. 1876. (Typed transcript of original Minutes in Archives SNJ Conference. Original in Library of Emory University, Atlanta, Georgia. Published Proceedings in *Formal Fraternity.*)

Rankin, Thomas. *Diary.* Manuscript. (Garrett Biblical Institute Library, Evanston, Ill.)

Raybold, George A. *Annals of Methodism,* Sketches of the Origin and Progress of Methodism in various portions of West Jersey. Camden: T. Stokes, 1847.

_____ . *Reminiscences of Methodism in West Jersey.* New York: Lane & Scott, 1849.

Rose, Frank B. (Manuscript File. SNJ Conference Archives.)

Rowe, Kenneth E. "The Spirit of Cape May." *The Historical Trail,* 1977.

Rusling, James F. "The War for the Union." *Methodist Quarterly Review,* April 1864.

Sangry, Abram W. *Martin Boehm.* Pioneer preacher in the Christian faith and practice, among the first German speaking colonists, in Pennsylvania, Maryland, Virginia. Ephrata, Pennsylvania: Science Press, 1976.

Semi-Centennial Pennington Seminary, 1890.

Seybert, John. *Journal.* Bishop of the Evangelical Association, 1839-1860. (Microfilm copy in SNJ Conference Archives.)

Sheldon, Edward S. "The 1928 Revival in First Church Collingswood." *Recounted Miracles of Grace.* No. 31. (Mimeographed copy SNJ Conference Archives.)

Shipps, Howard F. *The Forgotten Apostle of Methodism.* Philadelphia: Temple University School of Theology, Doctor of Sacred Theology Thesis, 1955.

———. "War Time Evangelism, A Chapter in the Life of Benjamin Abbott." *The Historical Trail*, 1978.

Short, Roy H. "Camp Meeting Movement." *Encyclopedia of World Methodism*, I, 382-384.

———. *Chosen to Be Consecrated.* The Bishops of The Methodist Church 1784-1968. Lake Junaluska, N.C.: Commission on Archives and History, The United Methodist Church, 1976.

Simpson, Hazel, B., Compiler. *History of Bethel M. E. Church Gloucester County, New Jersey.* Hurffville: Bethel Board of Trustees, 1945.

Simpson, Matthew. "Bishop Simpson's Centennial Prayer, 1876." *Methodist History*, October 1976.

Sledge, Robert Watson. *Hands On the Ark.* The Struggle for Change in the Methodist Episcopal Church, South, 1914-1939. Lake Junaluska, N.C.: Commission on Archives and History, The United Methodist Church, 1975.

Sloan, Harold Paul. Manuscript files, Drew University Archives. Includes "My Earliest Contacts with Modernism." (A copy is in the Sloan files, SNJ Conference Archives.)

Smith, Elizabeth M. "William Roberts: Circuit Rider of the Far West." *Methodist History*, January 1982.

Smith, Warren Thomas. "The Christmas Conference." *Methodist History*, July 1968.

Smyth, Charles R. "The Founding of Pennington School." *The Historical Trail*, 1962.

Sneath, Richard. "Journal," June 4, 1798-February 26, 1801. *History of Bethel M.E. Church.* Hurffville, N.J.: Bethel Board of Trustees, 1945.

Spellman, Norman W. "The Christmas Conference." *History of American Methodism*, Vol. I, 213-232.

Stanger, Frank Bateman. *The Life and Ministry of the Rev. Joseph Pilmore, D.D.,* Philadelphia: Temple University School of Theology, Doctor of Sacred Theology Thesis, 1942.

———, ed. *The Methodist Trail in New Jersey,* One Hundred and Twenty-Five Years of Methodism in the New Jersey Annual Conference, 1836-1961. Camden: The New Jersey Annual Conference of The Methodist Church, 1961.

———. *The Wesleyan Doctrine of Scriptural Holiness.* Paper given at Wesleyan Symposium, Haddonfield, N.J. United Methodist Church, March 3, 1984.

Steelman, Robert B. *Beginning of Methodism in Southernmost Jersey.* Philadelphia: Temple University, Master of Sacred Theology Thesis, 1962.

———. "Captain Thomas Webb, Founder of Methodism in New Jersey." *The Historical Trail*, 1976.

———. "Charter Members of the New Jersey Conference of the Methodist Episcopal Church." *The Historical Trail*, 1980.

———. "Learner Blackman." *Methodist History*, April 1967.

———. "Methodist Protestants: A 150 Year Old Legacy in Southern New Jersey." *The Historical Trail*, 1979.

———, ed. & transcriber. "Minutes of the New Jersey Conference of the Methodist Episcopal Church, 1837." *The Historical Trail*, 1983.

———. *Old First United Methodist Church,* West Long Branch, New Jersey, 1809-1984. Rutland, Vermont: Academy Books, 1984.

———. "The Rev. Richard Boardman." *The Historical Trail*, 1969.

Stellhorn, Paul A., Birkner, Michael J., ed. *The Governors of New Jersey 1664-1974.* Biographical Essays. Trenton: New Jersey Historical Commission, 1982.

Stevens, Abel. *A Compendious History of American Methodism.* New York: Phillips & Hunt, 1868.

———. "Scrapbook on Slavery and the M. E. Church." Book B. (Drew University Archives.)

Stewart, W. G. *A Memoir of the Life and Labors of the Rev. Thomas G. Stewart.* Philadelphia: Collins, Printer, 1858.

Still, William. *The Underground Railroad.* Philadelphia: Porter & Coates, 1872.

Stokes, E. H.; Hughes, George; Wallace, Adam. *The Earnest Minister.* A Record of the Life, Labors and Literary Remains of Rev. Ruliff V. Lawrence, for sixteen years an itinerant in the New Jersey and Philadelphia Conferences. Philadelphia: Adam Wallace, Publisher, Methodist Home Journal Office, 1873.

Straughn, James H. *Inside Methodist Union.* Nashville: The Methodist Publishing House, 1958.

Street, Rev. A. K. "Sketch of My Itinerate Life." *What I Think of Methodism after Fifty Years in the Itineracy.* Preached before the New Jersey Conference, Held in Salem, March 11th, 1881. Camden: S. Chew, Printer, 1881.

Strobridge, G. E. *Biography of the Rev. Daniel Parish Kidder,* New York: Hunt & Eaton, 1894.

Sullivan, Audrey G. *Nineteenth Century South Jersey Camp Meeting South Seaville, New Jersey.* Fort Lauderdale, Florida: Audrey G. Sullivan, 1980.

Swain, Rev. Richard. *Journal,* While on the Salem Circuit, N.J. March 19-September 22, 1792. Pages 99-207 of the Journal. Robert B. Steelman, ed. and transcriber. Rutland, Vt.: Academy Books, 1977. (Original handwritten Journal is in the Archives of the SNJ Conference.)

Sweet, William Warren. *The Methodist Episcopal Church and the Civil War.* Cincinnati: Methodist Book Concern Press, 1912.

Taylor, Prince A., Jr. "Asbury and American Methodism." *The Historical Trail,* 1972.

_____ . *The Life of My Years.* Nashville: Abingdon Press, 1983.

Tees, Francis H. *Methodist Origins.* Nashville: Parthenon Press, 1948.

Thomas, Dorothy Kille. *Haddonfield United Methodist Church:* A Sesquicentennial History, 1829-1979. Haddonfield: Haddonfield United Methodist Church, 1979.

Thomas, Hilah and Keller, Rosemary Skinner, ed. *Women in New Worlds:* Perspectives on the Wesleyan Tradition, I. Nashville: Abingdon Press, 1981.

"The Underground Railroad in New Jersey." Bulletin No. 9. *Stories of New Jersey,* New Jersey Writers Project, Work Projects Administration. Newark: 1939-41 Series. 6 page pamphlet.

Union List of United Methodist Ministers of the Southern New Jersey Conference, 1836-1986. Unpublished. (SNJ Conference Archives.)

The United Methodist Newscope. March 16, 1984. July 27, 1984.

Van Sant, Nicholas. *Sunset Memories.* New York: Eaton & Mains, 1896.

Van Sant, Walter B. "Lay Activities In the N.J. Conference." *The Historical Trail,* 1962, 1963, 1964.

Wakely, J. B. "One Hundred Years: A Centennial Discourse." *The Methodist Home Journal,* 1870.

Ware, Thomas. *Thomas Ware, A Spectator at the Christmas Conference.* A Miscellany on Thomas Ware and the Methodist Christmas Conference. William R. Phinney, Kenneth E. Rowe and Robert B. Steelman, ed. Rutland, Vermont: Academy Books, 1984.

_____ . *Sketches of the Life and Travels of Rev. Thomas Ware.* New York: T. Mason and G. Lane, 1839.

_____ . "The Christmas Conference." *Methodist Magazine and Quarterly Review,* January 1832.

Wesley, John. *Journal,* Standard Ed., ed. Nehemiah Curnock. 8 vols. London: Epworth Press, 1938.

Warman, John B. "Our Methodist Protestant Heritage." *Methodist History,* January 1979.

The Wesley Fellowship. 1976 Program Booklet.

Whitefield, George. *Journal.* London: The Banner of Truth Trust, 1965.

Williams, Robert John. *A Century of Compromise:* New Jersey Methodists on the Status and Role of Blacks in the Church and Society. Ph.D. Thesis, Drew University, 1983.

_____ . "Slavery and Patriotism: New Jersey Methodists During the Civil War." *Methodist History,* July 1983.

INDEX

Aber, Mrs. John, 101, 223
Abbot, Benjamin, 20, 22, 24, 26, 28, 32, 37, 38,39, 295
Abbott, William T., 83
Abrams, Margaret, 220, 231
Absecon, 31, 105
Acheson, Robert E., 247, 251
Adams, Mrs. W. T., 229
Adelphia (Bethesda), 30, 33, 108
Albright, Jacob, 281, 282, 283
Aldersgate, 2, 243
Aldine, 137
Alexander, Neil, 278
Allentown, 4
Allenwood, 179, 183
Allgood, Benjamin F., 215, 247
Allgood, Bertha, 200, 226
Allin, Mrs. Robert, 229
Alloway, 90, 280
Amboy, 4, 16
Ammerman, George, 164,184
Amwell, 4
Anderson, Charles E., 184
Anderson, Howard E., 255
Anderson, Kenneth 264, 266
Anderson, R. A., 208
Anderson, William, 274
Andrew, James O., 66
Appleget, Thomas B., 181, 184, 219
Archer, George, 139
Armenian Mission, 156
Arnold, Frederick D., 256
Asbury, Bishop Francis, 5, 8, 11, 14-19, 22, 23, 25, 26, 28, 29, 33, 34, 37, 38, 40, 43-47, 49, 55-57, 64, 157, 175, 186, 281-283, 289, 295
Asbury District, 47, 48
Asbury, N.J., 33, 48
Asbury Park, 91, 105, 106, 118, 119, 134, 138, 145, 152, 157, 166, 189, 212, 214, 224, 229, 247, 275, 287, 289
Ashton, Mary, 141
Assurance, 41
Atco, 224
Atkinson, L. G., 195, 247, 278
Atlantic City, 91, 107, 137, 138, 143, 145, 148, 166, 168, 180, 184, 185, 206, 219, 227, 237, 241, 248, 249, 253, 254, 259, 287, 288, 293
Atlantic City: Asbury, 253-257
Atlantic City: Central, 207, 237
Atlantic City: Christ, 162, 179-183, 185, 207, 227, 237
Atlantic City: First, 237
Atlantic City: Hamilton Memorial, 253, 256
Atlantic City: St. Paul's, 106, 141, 169, 170, 207, 237
Atlantic Highlands, 123, 126
Atwood, Anthony, 53, 61
Auburn, 33, 137
Audubon, 139, 238
Aura, 11, 45, 46, 284
Avalon, 139, 215
Avon, 184
Ayres, James, 60, 61

Bagwell, Clarence W., 256
Bailey, David, 121, 280
Bailey, William T., 271
Baird, Christiana, 108, 271

Baker, Eric W., 250
Baker, George C., 100
Ballard, A. E., 94, 112, 117, 120, 126
Bancroft, Henrietta, 274
Bancroft-Taylor Home, 104, 135, 225, 230, 272-275
Baner, Albert L., 209
Baner, Albert S., 145, 215
Bargaintown, 31, 33, 38, 48
Bargaintown Circuit, 47, 55, 56
Barkalow, Matthias, 175
Barnegat, 75, 108
Barnsboro, 31, 89, 120, 177, 179, 184, 225
Barratt's Chapel, 26, 27
Barrington, 152
Bartine, David, 56
Bascom, Henry, 60
Baskingridge, 4, 30
Batsto, 30, 31, 34, 75, 231
Bayonne, 230
Bayville, 108
Beach Haven, 86
Belleville, 48
Belmar, 204, 214
Bennett, Harry P., 146, 147, 215
Beppler, Ronald, 292
Bergen Circuit, 47
Berkley, 284
Berry, Adolphus A., 255
Berry, Charles, 121
Berry, Joseph F., 141, 145, 150, 158
Bethel Circuit, 11, 29, 31, 38, 47
Bewley, George, 292
Beyer, Robert J., 195, 242, 243, 260
Bible Protestant Church, 162, 183, 207
Billingsport, 181, 231
Bills, James D., 132
Bishop, James, 99, 164
Bishop, John E., 255
Black Horse, 9
Blackman, Andrew, 38
Blackman, David, 38, 46, 295
Blackman, Learner, 38, 41, 45, 52
Blackman, Mary, 38
Blackman, Nehemiah, 38
Blackman, Sarah, 38
Blacks, 76, 92, 93, 133, 134, 150, 161, 162, 167, 168, 209, 210, 251-258
Blackwood, 256
Blain, J. D., 73
Blair, John D., 195
Blairstown, 30
Blake, Lyman M., 144
Bloomsburg, 39
Boardman, Richard, 12-14, 18, 281, 288
Bodine, Carlton W., 207
Bodine, Carlton, Jr., 195
Bodine's (Wading River) 30, 31
Boehm, Henry 5, 43-46, 53, 56, 57, 282
Boehm, Martin, 56, 281-283
Booth, Evangeline, 206
Bordentown, 9, 13, 67, 70, 72, 90, 204, 223
Bowen, Dolores, 229
Bowen, Henry P., 182, 184
Bowman, Bishop Thomas, 285
Boyd, William A., 209
Boys Camp, see Tumethca

Bradley Beach, 192, 259
Bradway, Henry, 191, 249
Brady, A. C., 192, 194
Brady, Bessie, 212, 215, 226, 228, 233
Brakeley, John H., 70
Branchville: Methodist Manor, 272, 273
Brandt, Richard, 182, 184
Breck, Mrs. Frank O., 203, 204
Brewin, Mrs. Morris, 229
Bridgeport, 179
Bridgeton, 32, 37, 39, 45-48, 62, 75, 87, 133, 180, 183, 191, 204, 223, 225, 226, 253, 261, 269, 270, 284, 287, 288
Bridgeton: Central, 99, 106, 137, 145, 192, 214, 259, 261
Bridgeton District, 76, 88, 94, 102, 105, 108, 117, 120, 133, 135, 137-140, 154, 157, 166, 191, 224, 228, 252, 255, 269
Bridgeton: First, 37, 45, 80, 96, 97, 106, 137, 224
Bridgeton: Fourth, 137, 191, 224
Bridgeton: John Wesley, 255
Bridgeton: Laurel Hill, 101, 179, 180, 184, 222
Bridgeton: Trinity, 76, 191, 205
Brigantine, 139
Briggs, Lois, 226
Bright, Harry J., 184
Brighton, 253
Brindle, James, 177
Brinkley, Joshua, 253
Brock, Thomas S., 170, 192, 193, 215
Brogden, Elizabeth, 228, 233
Brooklawn, 152, 238
Brooks, Uriah, 178
Broomfield, John C., 162
Brown, George F., 58, 77
Brown, Margaret, 230
Browns Mills, 31
Brownstown, 30
Bruce, Herman, 178
Buck, F. T., 195, 196, 214, 247, 277
Buckley, James, 60
Buckley, John, 60
Budd, Samuel, 174-179, 185
Budd, William, 11, 25
Buddtown, 31, 214
Burlington, 4, 8-10, 13, 16-18, 22, 27, 28, 30, 31, 33, 39, 48, 67, 72, 80, 92, 106, 170, 174, 177, 223, 228, 253, 256, 287, 289, 295
Burlington Circuit, 28, 29, 31, 47, 56
Burlington District, 76, 88, 90, 107, 252
Burrell, William H., 122
Burrows, Waters, 53, 55, 58
Buxton, Leonard S., 286

Caldwell, Mabel, 196
Camden, 67, 72, 83, 86, 87, 134, 138, 139, 152, 166, 179, 181-183, 225, 226, 230, 237, 241, 242, 259, 261, 275, 284, 285, 287, 288
Camden: Asbury, 238
Camden: Bethany, 156, 204, 242
Camden: Broadway, 96, 102, 105, 106, 117, 136-138, 140, 152, 166, 204, 258, 266, 277

346

Camden: Centenary Tabernacle, 90, 97, 106, 108, 212, 226, 237, 242, 249, 268, 271
Camden District, 55, 88, 107, 133, 137-139, 145, 152, 154, 157, 166, 192, 214, 215, 228, 237, 247, 256, 269, 275
Camden: Eighth Street, 256
Camden: El Buen, 259
Camden: El Redentor, 259
Camden: Fairview, 152, 238, 259
Camden: Ferry Ave., 76, 252-256
Camden: First, 97, 99, 105, 106, 138, 152, 168, 170, 204, 226
Camden: Kaighn Avenue, 156, 261
Camden Metropolitan District, 291
Camden: St. George, 191
Camden: State Street, 137, 215
Camden: Union, 105, 106
Camden: Wiley, 166
Camp Meeting, 48, 49, 61, 89, 108, 110-128, 295, 297
Campbell, James, 56
Camphor, Alexander P., 254
Cannon, Charles W. S., 256
Cape May, 75, 90, 91, 96-98, 207, 244, 253, 259, 297
Cape May Circuit, 48, 110, 113, 115
Cape May Conference, 97, 98, 102, 160, 244
Cape May Court House, 21, 31, 72, 75, 76, 137
Cape May: Franklin Street, 205, 255
Carleton, Mary E., 224
Carlisle, Ephriam, 179
Carpenter, Andrew R., 177
Carter, Bertrand, 292
Cartwright, Peter, 86, 87
Cassville Circuit, 108
Cedarville, 90, 94, 102, 224
Center Square, 137
Centerton, 33, 45, 177-179
Central District, 291
Chapel Hill Circuit, 70, 71
Chalker, Richard A., 86
Chamberlain, Leon, 167
Chandler, Mrs. Kennard, 223
Chang, Dong-Chan, 260
Chase, Sue S., 223
Chatsworth, 139
Chattle, Joseph, 59
Chattle, Thomas G., 59
Cheney, Edward B., 240
Cheney, Lynn M., 220, 231
Cheney, Lucilla H. Green, 224
Cherry Hill, 229
Cherry Hill: First Korean, 260
Cherry Hill: Old Orchards, 240, 242, 260
Cherry Hill: St. Andrews, 237, 240
Chew, Jesse, 17, 21
Chews, 139
Children's Day, 88, 89, 198, 296
Chisholm, Thomas O., 204
Christine, John S., 177
Christmas Conference, 5, 26, 27, 29, 65, 111
Circuit Rider, 42, 43, 46, 47
Civil Rights, 235, 245
Civil War, 59, 79-85
Clarke, Mrs. C. T., 226
Clarksboro, 31, 57
Clarksboro: Zion Evangelical 284-286
Clayton, 34, 94, 107, 270
Clementon, 179

Clinton, 30
Clonmell, 31
Coate, Azail, 46
Coate, Samuel, 49
Coffee, Eugene M., 205
Coffee, J. Hillman, 158, 205, 243
Coffee, Miriam, 189
Cohansie, 4, 54
Coke, Thomas, 25-28
Cokesbury College, 10, 26
Collingswood, 138, 152, 154, 192, 224, 228, 231, 271, 287
Collingswood Home, 108, 271
Collins, Isabelle, 256
Collins, John, 38, 45, 52
Collins, Mary, 55
Colonial Manor, 152
Colonization Society, 54, 60, 61
Colt's Neck, 30, 175
Columbus, 75
Conant, N. C., 182, 183
Conference Archives, 242, 249, 269, 292,
Conference Center, 196, 197, 213, 214, 229, 241, 242, 250, 277, 278, 297
Conference Office, 229, 240-242, 249
Conger, Zenas, 174, 175
Conover, Elbert M., 156
Conover, Richard A., 143
Conrad: Wayne, 240
Conversion, 40, 41
Cooke, Edward, 68, 69, 263, 264
Cookstown, 47, 72
Cooper, Ezekiel, 30, 31, 46
Cooper, John, 30
Corson, Alexander, 152
Corson, Fred P., 116, 123, 198, 210, 211, 214, 239, 244, 249, 250, 258, 268, 273, 293
Corson, Lynn H., 153, 196, 209, 215, 247, 277
Corson, Paul M., 215
Cottrane, Leslie W., 256
Craig, Judtih, 217
Cramer Hill, 179
Cranbury, 30, 184, 225
Crane, Jonathan, 69, 75, 105, 264
Crompton, J. Rolland, 267, 268
Cromwell, James O. 23, 31
Cromwell, Joseph, 23, 31
Crossley, C. Wesley, 293
Cross, Mr., 4
Crosswicks, 30, 33
Crowther, Robert & Mary, 196
Cumberland, 33, 214
Cumberland Circuit, 47, 48, 76
Curtin, Carlton J., 278

Dale, Samuel, 253
Darakjian, Avedis S., 156
Dare, Alphonso, 116, 148, 154, 158, 195
Davis, Elwood, 257
Davis, Hattie F., 135, 275
Davis, Hooker D., 121, 246, 256, 257, 287
Davis, James, 253
Davis, Ralph, 292
Davis, Thomas, 176
Davison, James, 196
Day, Benjamin, 59
Day, J. Wesley, 181
Day, Roby F., 181
Deaconess, 134, 135, 165, 229-231

Deaconess Home (Neighborhood Center), 134, 135, 139, 157, 225, 230, 231, 275-277
Dean, Dorothy, 256
Decker, Mrs. George, 226
Decker, B. Harrison, 150, 247
Deerfield, 31, 137
DeHoff, Paul A., 284
Delair, 253, 256
Delanco, 214
Delanco Camp Meeting, 124-126, 154, 194, 195, 297
Delaware Conference, 81, 227, 229, 246, 247, 251-256
Delmont, 31
DeMaris, F. A., 145, 166, 168, 170
Denman, Harry, 162
Dennisville, 75, 76
Denny, Collins, 160
Derrickson, Cyrus W., 255
Detwiler, Alice 164, 182, 197, 198, 226-229, 231
Detwiler, Bland, 164, 184, 198
Dias Creek, 102
Dickerson, Josie, 256
Dickins, John 26, 28, 186
Diverty, Jesse H., 99, 113, 114
Dividing Creek, 76, 154
Dobbins, G. L., 107, 108, 126, 139
Dobbins, Joseph B., 83, 88, 120
Dobbins, Samuel A., 99, 164
Dorlan, Samual J., 184
Dorsey, Dennis B., 172
Doughty, Samuel, 60
Dover, 30
Drew University, 67
Dreisbach, John, 283
Dreisbach, Martin, 283
Duke, William, 9
Duncan, Joel, 292
Dunk, Ronald, 194
Dunn, Harold, 292
Dyson, Ronald, 194

Earley, D. A., 207
Early, John, 11, 45, 295
Early, Miriam Lee, 266
East Brunswick, 237, 240
East Jersey Circuit, 23, 29, 30, 56
East Jersey District, 47, 48
Eatontown, 145
Ebner, Anne, 226, 233
Ebner, Henry D., 192, 195
Ebner, Reba, 226
Eckersley, William, 144
Eden, Esther, 205
Edge, Walter E., 210
Edison, Mrs. Thomas A., 267
Edwards, Edward I., 147
Edwards, Jonathan, 4
Egg Harbor, 178
Eisenlohr, Gail, 116
Eldora, 31
Elizabeth, 4, 33, 60, 178
Elizabethtown Circuit, 28, 29, 48
Ellison, Lucy V., 230
Elsey, Wilmore, 253
Elwell, A. D., 164, 184
Elwood, 133
Embury, Philip, 5, 6, 55
Emley's Hill, 33
English Creek, 31, 33, 38, 45, 46, 175
English, John, 176
Englishtown, 139
Episcopal Churches, 25

347

Epworth League, 102, 115, 153, 190-192
Essex, 48
Estellville, 105
Estelow, Horace, 292
Estilow, Ulysses S., 286
Etra, 33
Evangelical Association, 101, 219, 223, 283-285
EUB Church, 223, 227, 236, 281-286, 294
Evans, David C., 158, 195
Evans, George W., 100
Everittstown, 30
Ewanville, 270
Ewing, John, 121

Fairhaven, 179, 181, 184, 198
Fairton, 32, 37, 82, 94
Farmingdale, 82, 90, 117
Farmingdale Circuit, 110
Farrell, Carl, 195
Felch, Isaac N., 59
Fidler, Daniel, 56
Fiedler, Mrs. Edward, 229
Finesville, 30
Fisher, Horace J., 256
Fisk, C. B., 84, 96, 97, 102, 103, 114
Fisk, Jeannette, 93, 101, 104, 225, 231, 232
Fisler, Benjamin, 45
Flaherty, Ruth, 228
Flanders, 30, 33
Flanders Circuit, 28, 29
Fleming, Dr. Arthur S., 273
Fletcher, John, 8
Fletcher, M. C. E., 124
Flint, Annie Johnson, 203
Force, Manning, 47, 54, 55, 58
Ford, Charles T., 59
Fordville, 253, 255
Fort, George F., 70, 264, 267
Fort Dix, 207
Fort Hancock, 207
Fort Monmouth, 207
Foss, Cyrus, 271
Fox, Mary Baird, 271
Frambes, Joseph D., 178
Frank, Audrey, 230
Frankford Plains, 30, 33
Franklin, George, 134
Franklin, Howard S., 256
Franklinville, 133
Freedmen's Aid Society, 84, 85, 92, 112, 134
Freehold, 4, 23, 30, 33, 110, 175
Freehold Circuit, 21, 29, 48, 75, 110, 174, 175
Frelinghuysen, Theodore, 4
Frey, J., 284
Friedrich, Paul A., 246, 247, 259, 271
Friendship, 11, 20, 31, 32, 33, 37, 45, 46, 179, 183
Friendship Finley, 184
Fullman, Stephen G., 256

Galvan, Elias G., 260
Garber, Paul N., 268
Gardner, Marguerite, 228, 233, 248
Garrettson, Catherine, 217
Garrettson, Freeborn, 19, 26, 217
Garrettson, Richard, 22, 23, 295
Garrison, Hannah, 101, 104, 134, 225, 229, 231
Gatch, Philip, 20

Geddis, George E., 256
Geeting, George Adam, 282
Gilbert, Grace, 8
Gilder, Richard W., 204
Gilder, William H., 70
Gill, William, 22, 295
Gilmore, Alexander, 47, 49, 61, 78, 85, 86
Gingrich, C. 284
Given, Robert, 83
Glassboro, 87, 107, 120, 133, 178-180, 183, 184, 211, 226, 284, 285
Glendale, 231
Glendola, 175, 179, 183
Gloucester, 4, 13, 16, 34, 107, 230
Gloucester Circuit, 47, 48, 115
Gloucester Point, 12, 288
Goff, John, 110
Gomez, Julio, 258, 259
Gonzalez, Esequiel, 259
Goodluck (Potter's Church) 21, 30, 31, 34, 46, 175
Goodson, Kenneth, 294
Goodwill Industries, 280
Goorley, John 195
Goshen, 75, 82, 102, 191, 253
Gospel Song Writers, 201-206
Goucher, John F., 161
Grace, Eugene, 266
Graham, Billy, 119
Graw, Jacob B., 83, 87, 89, 94, 96, 104, 105, 108, 114, 115, 120, 126
Gray, Walter L., 256
Green, Francis, 157, 267
Green Grove, 110
Greenley, Mrs. P. C., 226
Greenwich, 4, 13, 16-18, 29, 31, 33, 55, 67
Greiner, Newton, 196
Grenlock, 253
Groveville, 126
Grum, William, 202
Guffick, William R., 170, 247
Guice, Marvin R., 247

Hackettstown, 30
Haddon, Charles K., 150
Haddonfield, 16, 87, 112, 145, 152, 183, 189, 215, 229, 237, 238, 240, 247, 287, 291
Haddon Heights, 139, 214
Haines, John B., 139, 148, 267
Hamburg Circuit, 48
Hamilton (Shark River), 23, 46, 110, 175
Hamilton Township: St. Mark's, 287
Hamm, Dorothy W., 230
Hammel, G. Q., 124
Hammonton, 231
Hancock's Bridge, 94
Hand, F. E., 207, 208
Hand, Mrs. R. T., 226
Handley, John, 140, 143
Hankins, Charles, 194
Hanley, Joanna R., 75
Hanley, Joseph J., 75
Hann, Earl T., 195
Hann, Edwin F., 207, 266
Hann, Edwin F., III, 194
Hann, Samuel, 133
Hardingville, 179, 183
Hargrove, Robert K., 97
Harmon, Nolan B., 244
Harrington, Sylvia R., 224
Harris, Robert S., 88

Harrisonville, 94, 258
Hartranfft, Charles R., 83
Hartranft, Mrs. A. M., 223
Hawk, Betty, 200
Hawk, L. Burdelle, 192, 194
Hayes, Lucy Webb, 100, 222
Hazlet, 9, 295
Hazlet: St. John's, 11, 287
Head Of The River, 23, 32, 33, 38, 39, 45, 105
Heck, Barbara, 5, 6, 217
Hedding, Elijah, 21, 263
Heisler, John S., 96
Heisler, Sallie B., 134, 230
Heislerville, 32, 137, 191
Heisley, Charles W., 83
Helm, Mary, 256
Henson, Isaac, 253
Hewitt, C. A., 207
Hewitt, Edmund, 140
Hewlings, Elizabeth S., 174
Highland Park, 212, 261
Highlands, 139, 214
Hightstown, 30, 108, 134, 184, 261
Hill, Charles E., 83
Hill, James B., 73
Hill, Judson S., 93
Hillman, Jessie B., 134, 230
Historical Society, 158, 249
Hoboken, 167
Hoffman, Nelson M., Jr., 268
Hoffman, Nelson M., Sr., 195, 198, 207, 247, 258
Holdich, Joseph, 60
Holiness, 111-113
Holt, Ivan Lee, 244
Hoover-Smith Election, 147, 148
Hopewell, 9, 17, 30
Hopkey, Sophie, 2
Horner, Hazel, 229, 231, 232
Hosier, Harry, 27
Howard, Ernest, 181
Howard, William C., 164, 184
Howe, Robert B., 194, 249, 292
Howell, 284, 286
Howell, Margaret, 228, 233
Hudson, Winthrop, 4, 91, 129
Hugg, Mrs. Charles, 191, 224
Hughes, Edwin Holt, 163
Hughes, George, 112, 117
Hughes, Raymond, 125, 126
Hughes, Richard, 246
Huizer, John S., 184
Hulitt, Daniel, 197, 278, 279
Hulse, Homer C., 144
Hunter, E. S., 124
Hurffville: Bethel, 11, 31, 33, 34, 46, 89, 120, 295
Hurley, William R., 181
Hurst, John F., 96
Hutchinson, Sylvester, 176, 177

Independent Methodists, 50, 175
Indians, 28
Inskip, John S., 89, 111, 112, 117
Irons, Neil L., 269, 294
Island Heights, 126
Italian Missions, 156

Jackson, Dorothy, 256
Jackson, George H., 184
Jackson, Harry S., 165
Jacksonville, 90
Jacobstown, 72
James, John, 22, 23, 295

James, Joseph H., 83
James, Mrs., 101,. 223
Janes, Edmund S., 160, 253
Janke, Ethel, 233, 248
Jason, William C., Jr., 254
Jennings, Mrs. A. M., 226
Jericho, 256
Jersey City, 57, 72, 167, 230
Johnson, Lyndon B., 236, 244
Jones, George D., 164, 180, 181, 184
Jordan, Lucius E., 256
Joslin, Zacchaeus, 179
Juliustown, 48

Kappler, Ralph, 196, 277
Keansburg, 108
Keighley, Mrs., 224
Keller, Elwood F., 184
Keller, Rosemary S., 222
Kelley, W. V., 138
Kelloway, Ernest O., 196, 278
Kelly, Leontine T. C., 217
Kemp, Peter, 282
Kennedy, John F., 287
Keyport, 258, 259
Keyport: El Mesias, 259
Kiah, Charles E., 256
Kickasola, Louis, 292
Kidd, C. S., 182
Kidder, Daniel P., 73, 74, 186, 187
Kiessling, William F., 181
KKK, 150, 151, 155
Kim, In Hwan, 260
Kim, Sun Ryang, 260
King, Martin Luther, Jr., 287
Kingston, 30
Kinsley, Charles M., 150
Kirby, John B., Sr., 249
Kirk, William A., 257
Klein, Gertrude, 228
Knight, E. C., 271
Knight, Russell, 196
Knowles, Daniel C., 82, 264
Korean Churches, 260, 261
Kulp, J. B., 166, 194

Ladies Aid, 101, 135, 151, 221, 226
Landisville, 214
Lake, 156, 261
Lake Como, 179, 184
Lake, Ezra, 115, 122, 123, 130
Lake, James E., 122, 123, 126
Lake, S. Wesley, 122, 123, 137
Lake, Simon, 122
Lake, W. Elwell, 123
Lakehurst, 207
Lakewood, 258, 259
Lambertville, 77, 230
Lang, Albert V., 198
Laphew, R. C., 208
Larkin, Bessie, 220
Lawnside: Mt. Zion, 67, 76, 252, 253, 256, 257
Lawrence, Ananias, 126
Lawrence, Ruliff V., 82, 113, 117
Lawrenceville, 72
Lay Representation, 88, 97, 98, 134, 151, 152, 164, 165
Laws, Lillie, 256
Layton, A. Keyes, 196
Layton, Albert S., 196, 247
Layton, Rev. & Mrs. Warren, 196
Leap, S. Rusling, 215
Ledden, W. Earl, 210, 211, 293
Lee, Ernest W., 236, 247

Lee, Hoon K., 261
Lee, Jesse, 26
Lee, Walker, 244
Lee, Yhop Y., 261
Leech, Lida Shivers, 204
Leesburg, 39, 94, 137, 179, 191, 226, 230
Le Huray, Eleanor, 224
Lenhart, John L., 59, 61, 83
Lentz, Marjorie, 228
Leonard, Adna, 266, 267
Lewis, Jefferson, 59, 61, 96, 108
Lewis, Roy L., 143, 207
Lewis, Susan M., 275
Lewis, Thomas H., 160, 161
Leyva, Jorge, 258
Licorish, Joshua, 252
Lincoln, Abraham, 79, 80, 81, 85, 87
Linwood, 133, 137, 198, 237, 287
Lippincott, Benjamin C., 96
Lippincott, Caleb A., 77
Lipscomb, Mrs. S. A., 180, 222
Little, Walter I., 292
Lockwood, 30
Long Branch, 23, 33, 57, 79, 91, 138, 140, 175, 223, 259, 287
Long Branch: Asbury, 108, 214
Long Branch: St. Luke's, 59, 90, 106, 145
Longstreet, Derrick, 46
Lore, Dallas D., 74
Lore, Rebecca T., 74, 223, 231
Love, Edgar A., 244
Lovely Lane, 8, 17, 26, 289
Lowden, C. Harold, 204
Lowden, W. Gordon, 194, 208
Lower Bank, 31, 81
Ludlam, Reuben, 110
Luff, Ralph G., 123
Luff, William G., 123
Lumberton, 31, 46, 202
Lyght, Ernest, 257

MacDaniel, Frank, 267
McCarroll, Thomas, 59, 60
McClintock, John, 55, 67, 87, 111
McConnell, H. H., 184
McCullough, June, 228, 233
McCullough, William, 292
McGowan, James S., 164, 184
McIntyre, Carl, 182
McKeag, Wallace, 193
McKendree, William, 43, 46, 172
McKinley, William, 100, 119, 129
McMurray, George H., 256

Maderia, Eugene, 259
Magee, John W., 144
Magnolia, 231, 253
Major, H., 284
Malaga, 31, 76, 89, 115, 116, 133, 297
Malaga Summer Assembly, 195
Mallalieu, Wilard F., 122
Manahawkin, 9, 30, 31, 75, 76
Manasquan (Squan River) 23, 46, 179, 180, 183, 229
Mandeville, Mrs. A. R., 226
Manluff, John, 253
Mantua, 16, 17, 18, 45, 90, 139
Maps, Hannah, 140
Maps, William R., Jr., 79, 99, 110
Margerum, Mrs. E. A., 223
Marker, Bert, 228
Marple, Christine, 233, 248

Marsh, Mrs. Crowell, 225
Marshall, James W., 137, 140, 266
Marshall, Robert R., 240
Martinez, Ramon, 259
Martorano, Leon, 208
Maser, Frederick E., 288
Massey, William E., 147, 150
Matawan, 46, 90
Matthews, Marjorie, 129, 217
Matthews, Mrs. W. H., Jr., 226
Mauricetown, 191
Mays Landing, 21, 31, 34, 46, 75, 105, 261
Mead, Charles L., 169
Medford, 48, 56, 137, 178
Merchantville, 88, 204, 296
Merchantville: Asbury, 76, 252, 253, 256, 257
Merwin, J. D., 208
Metcalf, Henry, 23
M E Church, South, 64-66, 97, 98, 101, 160-163
Methodist Hospital, 279
Methodist Protestant, 50, 101, 160-163, 171-185, 197, 218, 219, 222, 225, 226, 231
MYF, 192, 193
Middletown, 240
Middletown Circuit, 110
Middletown Point, 30
Milbourne, O'Connell, 256
Miles, C. Austin, 121, 203
Miller, G. Donald, 268, 269
Miller, George, 283
Miller, Linwood, 158
Mills, Nathaniel B., 30, 31
Milltown, 191, 240
Millville, 75, 90, 133, 138, 157, 180, 191, 210, 226, 287
Millville: Broad Street, 179, 184
Millville: First, 105, 106, 137, 138, 215, 224, 284
Millville: Fourth, 137
Millville: Mt. Pleasant, 184
Millville: Second, 137, 156
Millville: Trinity, 210
Missions, 54, 70-74
Modernist Controversy, 148-150
Moffett, W. W., 96
Molyneaux, W. A., 208
Monmouth, 177
Monmouth County: Korean, 260
Monroe, Samuel Y., 86
Montgomery, Carolyn J., 220, 231
Moon, L. F., 182
Moore, Alice, 257
Moore, Frank, 266, 268
Moore, G. Nelson, 195
Moore, James, 56
Moore, John M., 160,163
Moore, Noah W., 254, 293
Moore, Penny, 158, 227, 234
Moorestown, 21, 31, 75, 179, 183, 226, 287
Morrell, Francis Asbury, 55
Morrell, Thomas, 28, 55
Morris, Charles, 266
Morris, George K., 96
Morristown, 48
Morristown College, 93, 104, 134, 225, 242
Mott, John R., 206
Mt. Ephriam, 214
Mount Holly, 9, 13, 17, 23, 25, 27, 30, 31, 41, 61, 67, 82, 107, 137,

349

174, 213, 253, 256
Mount Laurel, 67
Mount Pleasant, 23
Muelder, Walter G., 142
Mulliner, Joseph, 24, 25
Mumford, Robert J., 247
Munyan, Edward M., 249
Murphy, John, 20, 32, 37, 295
Murphy, Sandra, 220
Murphy, Thomas, 11, 295
Mutual Rights, 50

Nash, Mrs. A. W., 226
National Park, 123, 126
Naylor, George H., 184
Neal, George H., 137, 150, 157
Neal, Thomas, 58
Neely, Thomas, 141
Neidig, John, 282
Nelson, Carlton N., 200
Nelson, Dorothy, 228, 229, 233, 248
Nelson, Frances, 200
Nelson, Mae, 156
Neptune City, 214
Newark, 4, 28, 29, 48, 53, 58, 60, 61, 72, 77, 87, 141, 167, 178, 179, 186, 230, 254, 287, 295
Newark Conference, 57-59, 77, 78, 86, 267, 271
Newark District, 55, 58, 59
New Brooklyn, 179, 184
New Brunswick, 4, 33, 46, 48, 61, 67, 72, 77, 92, 118, 177, 178, 204, 223, 225
New Brunswick Circuit, 47
New Brunswick District, 47, 88, 103, 108, 117, 137-140, 148, 151, 154, 157, 165, 166, 228, 256, 271
New Brunswick: Korean, 260
New Brunswick: St. James, 139
Newburg Circuit, 30
Newcomb, Kathryn, 230
Newcombtown, 181, 184
Newcomer, Christian, 282
New Egypt, 56
Newell, James, 49
Newfield, 189
New Gretna (Bass River), 30, 31, 75
New Hanover, 177
New Jersey District, 40
Newman, Ernest W., 256
New Mills Circuit (Pemberton) 47, 56
Newport, 9, 31, 94, 137, 179
Newton, 30
Newton District, 68
New York, 4, 9, 13, 14, 16, 17, 26-28
New York: John Street Church, 6, 7, 11, 17, 43
Nichols, Hosea, 115
Nichols, S. M., 275
Nichols, Sudie, 257
Nickless, Eda, 192, 226
Nickless, Walter, 195
Nixon, C. R., 208
Nolte, John, 285
North, Amos M., 102, 190
North, Frank Mason, 131
Northeast District, 243, 260, 291
Northfield, 238
Northwest District, 291
Norwood, Frederick A., 66
Nutter, Emma E., 165, 219, 231

Oakhurst, 237
Oatman, Johnson, Jr., 202

Ocean City, 91, 106, 108, 112, 121-124, 133, 137, 141, 162, 169, 210, 227, 229, 243, 244, 246, 247, 249, 297
Ocean City: Homes, 272-274
Ocean City: Macedonia, 124, 253, 256
Ocean City: St. Peter's (First) 122-124, 139, 147, 224, 287, 294
Ocean Grove, 89, 91, 96, 106, 108, 110, 112, 117-119, 135, 138, 140, 151, 166, 202, 204, 215, 223, 225, 228, 274, 297
Ocean Grove: Francis Asbury Manor, 140, 153, 169, 214, 249, 271-273, 297
Ocean Grove: St. Paul's, 117, 119, 137, 140, 144, 152, 273
Oceanport, 90
Oceanville, 184
Ogden, George B., 184
Oglethorpe, Gen. James, 2
O'Hanlon, Thomas, 140, 264, 266
O'Kelly, James, 50, 171, 174
Old St. George's, 5, 8, 13, 16, 17, 43, 47, 174, 249
Oliver, A. C., Jr., 143, 207
Oliver, Anna, 100, 123, 218, 219
Old Stone Meeting House, Swedesboro, 11, 33
Olin, Stephen, 67
Osborn, Blanche D., 205
Osborn, Herbert, 205
Osborn, William B., 112, 113, 117-119
Osbornville, 179, 183
Oswald, Carl E., 182, 184
Otterbein, Philip W., 26, 281-283
Oxnam, G. Bromley, 208

Page, Edward, 53
Palmer, Everett W., 194, 209, 212
Palmer, Phoebe, 111, 217
Palmyra, 10, 74
Panico, Thomas, 292
Parish, Daniel, 58
Park, Ik Soo, 260
Park, Sung Eun, 260
Parker, Jennie, 140, 151, 169, 271
Parker, Joel, 86
Parsells, Miriam, 230
Parsons, Mrs. E. S., 223
Paterson, 72, 134, 230
Paterson Circuit, 48
Paterson District, 55, 58
Patterson, Benjamin, 100
Paullin, Norman W., 116
Paulsboro, 238, 284
Pearson, Thomas W., 178
Pedicord, Caleb, 23-25, 41
Pedrick, Evan C., 116
Peermont, 139
Pemberton (New Mills) 8, 9, 11, 13, 16, 17, 18, 21, 22, 28-31, 33, 48, 54, 56, 223, 295
Pennington, 9, 13, 17, 18, 30, 33, 47, 72, 215
Pennington, Chester A., 208
Pennington Institute, 153, 191, 193, 194
Pennington School, 47, 54, 58, 59, 68-70, 82, 85, 96, 103-105, 108, 130, 137, 140, 144, 147, 157, 169, 170, 197, 211, 215, 229, 241, 242, 247-250, 263-269, 295

Pennsauken, 250, 288
Pennsgrove, 179, 183, 214
Pennsville (Penns Neck) 31, 33, 46
Perez, Agripino, 258
Perfect Love, 41, 42
Perinchief, K. R., 208
Perkins, F. Elwood, 243, 247
Perkins, William, 178
Perkintown, 46
Perry, Cyrus W., 256
Perry, William A., 120
Peterson, O. C. T., 208
Petherbridge, R. W., 47, 55, 58, 61
Phieffer, Damon, 266
Philadelphia, 4, 8, 12, 13, 14, 28, 45, 86, 95, 137, 184, 253
Philipbar, Charles, 285
Phillips, Donald T., Jr., 185
Phillips, Donald T., Sr., 164, 184
Phillips, Mrs. Donald, Sr., 226
Phillips, Helen, 165, 218, 230, 231
Phillips, Richard C., 181
Phoebus, George, 30
Pierce, Jehu, 253
Pike, W. N., 208
Piles Grove, 4
Pilmore, Joseph, 12-14, 18, 281, 288
Pimm, Donald, 198
Pimm, Ethel, 226, 228
Pimm, Ira S., 194, 247, 250, 268
Pine, Harry R., 210
Pitman, 137, 152, 153, 203, 228, 237, 261, 287
Pitman Camp Meeting, 112, 120, 121, 215, 297
Pitman, Charles, 47, 61, 71, 72, 120, 295
Pitman Manor, 272, 277
Pitt, Sherman G., 143, 193, 194
Plainfield, 287
Pleasant Mills, 33, 46, 105
Pleasant Plains, 90
Pleasant Valley, 30
Pleasantville, 133, 179, 181, 184, 261
Pleasantville: Asbury, 253, 256
Pleasantville: Wesley, 231
Point Pleasant, 215
Pointville, 144, 213, 214, 277
Poling, Daniel A., 165
Pollett, Frost, 253
Pool, William C., 171, 172
Porchtown, 72
Port Elizabeth, 21, 31-34, 45, 75, 90, 94
Port Monmouth, 108
Port Norris, 158, 224, 253
Port Norris: John Wesley, 255
Port Republic, 31, 58
Port Washington, 110
Porter, John S., 58, 77, 95
Porter, Ruth, 205
Potter, Thomas, 46
Pottieger, R. J. C., 286
Powell, Parmelia, 219
Powell, Robert, 189, 207
Price, Carl F., 204, 205
Price, Clement, 92
Price, Ella, 256
Princeton, 13, 30, 67, 153
Prohibition (See Temperance), 142, 147, 148, 167
Propert, Frank C., 215, 216
Propert, George R., 247

Quarterly Meeting, 40

350

Quigg, Leona, 229
Quigg, Walter, 240
Quinton, 76, 94, 252, 255
Quist, Roy W., 278

Radcliffe, Arthur, 169
Rahway District, 59
Raikes, Robert, 186
Rainear, Mrs. Benjamin, 229
Ranch Hope For Boys, 280
Randolph, David, 245
Rankin, Thomas, 8, 9, 16, 17, 18, 20
Rauschenbusch, Walter, 130
Raver, W. Neal, 247
Raver, W. R., 207, 215
Raybold, George A., 59, 61, 177
Raynor, Dennis G., 184
Read, J. Morgan, 137, 266, 267
Read, John H., 144
Red Bank 145, 148, 157, 178, 260, 287
Reeves, Walter, 169
Reeves, Willis, 97
Reinard, H. M., 207
Relay, 228, 239, 242, 243
Relyea, Milton, 107
Remaly, Howard, 242
Repsher, Donald R., 284
Revival, 68, 90, 108, 136-138, 153-155, 236-240
Revolution, War of, 9, 11, 17-19, 22, 23, 25
Rhee, Mrs. On Kyong, 260
Rhodes, 253
Ricards, Betty, 233
Richardson, Ernest G., 158, 162, 165, 226
Richardson, Martha, 256
Richman, B. F., 115
Richman, Joshua, Sr., 115
Richwood, 284
Ridgeway, A. C., 124
Ridout, Daniel L., 205
Ridout, George, 124, 143, 145
Roadstown, 94
Roberts, William, 72, 73
Robertson, Rebecca, 230
Robertsville, 179, 183
Robinson, Charles, 191
Robinson, Mrs. George O., 274
Robinson, James W., 244
Robinson, Robert, 253
Rodriguez, James Luiz, 242, 258
Roe, Joseph L., 133, 139
Roebling, 139
Rogers, Elizabeth A., 277
Rojas, Jeremias, 259
Romero, Perfecto, 259
Roosevelt, F. D., 206, 208
Roosevelt, Theodore, 119, 129
Rose, Frank B., 83
Ross, Elizabeth, 176
Rowe, Kenneth, 98
Rubio, Emerson W., 258, 259
Rumson, 90, 102
Runnymeade, 181
Rusling, J. F., 82, 99, 100, 104, 139
Rusling, T. V. F., 99
Russian Mission, 156

Sadio, Sydney, 261
Sairs, Capt. David, 23
Salem, 4, 24, 31, 34, 46-48, 67, 270
Salem: Broadway, 107, 191, 224
Salem Circuit, 21, 22, 28, 29, 31, 32, 38, 39, 47, 49, 56
Salem: First, 24, 33, 39, 90, 107, 108
Salem: Mt. Hope, 76, 251-255
Salter, David B., 176
Sanborn, J. S., 115
Sanfiel, Francisco, 258, 259
Sandtown, 31
Sargent, Norman V., 145
Sawn, Walter, 292
Sayre, Charles A., 170, 189, 247, 287
Scarborough, H. H., 208
Schaff, Clyde, 189, 190, 249
Schalick, Evelyn, 233, 248
Schock, Edward S., 178
Schoellkopf, Herbert J., 244, 247
Schopp, Edgar, 292
Scott, Levi, 58, 59, 211, 251
Scullville, 175, 179, 182, 183
Sea Bright, 102-104
Seabrook, 156, 261
Sea Isle City, 195
Sears, Brad, 277, 278
Seaside Park, 139
Seaville, 89, 110, 111, 113-115, 195-197, 297
Seay, Joseph W., 267
Senser, Earl C., 143
Seybert, John, 284
Shadford, George, 8
Sharp, Fred R., 292
Sharp, Solomon, 40
Sharptown, 31, 33, 94, 112, 177
Shaw, Alexander, 130
Shaw, Anna H., 100, 114, 218, 219
Shaw, James E., 145
Shaw, John Knox, 53, 54, 58, 77, 263, 266
Sheets, John C., 178
Sheldon, Edward S., 125, 154, 194
Shepard, William A., 144
Sherman, Gilbert A., 255
Shim, Zae Uh, 261
Shinn, Asa, 50, 172, 174, 185
Shipps, Hammell P., 125, 247, 248
Shivers, Connie, 227
Shivers, M. Russell, 194
Showack, Gladys, 220, 231
Shrewsbury, 23, 30, 46, 67
Shropshire, Lois, 195
Shull, Archie, 292
Silverton (Kettle Creek), 31, 34, 46, 90, 108, 212
Simpson, Matthew, 85, 95, 112, 160, 270
Sinkinson, Charles D., 179-182, 184
Sisterhood, 134, 229
Slack, Gilbert, 100
Slater, T. H., 182
Slavery, 64-68, 79-84, 179
Sliker, Steven F., 184
Sloan, Harold Paul, 132, 144, 145, 148, 150, 169, 170, 192, 215, 297
Smith, A. A., 115
Smith, Eva, 225
Smith, Fay, 228
Smith, Gypsy, 119
Smith, Harrison, 253
Smith, Herbert J., 247
Smith, Mrs. H. J., 226
Smith, Lizzie R., 121
Smith, William, 57, 58
Smithville, 33
Smyth, C. R., 194, 247, 250, 268
Smyth, Robert K., 194
Sneath, Richard, 11, 31

Snedeker, S. A., 208
Snethen, Nicholas, 172, 176
Snyder, Garner R., 120
Snyder, George R., 95
Snyder, Melville, 140
Social Concerns, 153, 155, 248, 287, 288, 292
Social Gospel, 130, 132
Soderbom, Carl G., 181
Somers Point, 184, 214, 231
Soule, Joshua, 172
South Amboy, 145, 179, 184, 249
South Dennis, 102, 191
Southeast District, 261, 291
South Jersey Institute, 269, 270
South Jersey: Korean, 261
South Vineland, 137
Southwest District, 257, 291
Sovereign, Thomas, 60, 61, 83
Spanish Ministries, 242, 258-260
Sparks, John A., 267
Sparks, Mrs. M. J., 223
Speedwell Furnace, 30
Spellmeyer, Henry, 141
Spencer, Charles P., 256
Spring lake, 184, 215, 256
Springtown, 67, 76, 253, 256
Squankum, 110
Staats, Anne, 191
Stainton, Howard, 147, 248, 269, 273
Stanger, Francis A., 212, 213
Stanger, Frank B., 112, 158, 243, 244, 288
Stanger, Mrs. F. B., 226
Stanger, Louisa, 180, 226
Starsmeare, George, 292
Staten Island, 46, 56
Steelman, Robert B., 158
Stelz, A. S., 285
Stephens, William, 177
Sterling, James, 39, 295
Stevens, Kenneth, 195
Still, Carl, 257
Stites, Edgar Page, 204
Stockton, John H., 117, 201
Stockton, Thomas H., 174
Stockton, William, 292
Stockton, William C., 83
Stockton, W. S., 50, 172-176, 185
Stokes, E. H., 117, 118, 120, 202
Stone Harbor, 139
Stout, Mrs. Richard, 275
Stow Creek, 31, 34
Strahan, Ruth, 244, 288
Stratford, 238
Straughn, James H., 162, 163, 182
Strawbridge, Robert, 5, 174
Street, A. K., 82, 96
Stretch, Mabel, 228, 233, 248
Stroman, John A., 229
Struthers, A. C., 180
Stultz, Lewis D., 184
Stultz, W. D., 180
Sunday, Billy, 119, 120, 137, 138
Sunday Observance, 107, 135, 153, 180
Sunday School, 62, 68, 74, 186-190, 236, 238, 286, 287
Surtees, Robert E., 145
Swain, Dr. Clara, 222
Swain, Joab, 39
Swain, Judah, 39, 295
Swain, Nathan, 39, 45
Swain, Richard, 28, 32, 39
Swainton, 253, 255

351

Swedesboro, 31, 67
Swing, Michael, 37

Tabernacle, 197, 279
Taft, William H., 119
Tansboro, 31
Tasco, William M., 255
Taylor, Jack L., 274
Taylor, Martha, 274
Taylor, Prince A., 78, 244-247, 273, 288, 289, 293, 297
Taylor, William, 113
Teates, Chester, 182
Temperance (see Prohibition), 54, 60, 64, 93-95, 114, 132, 133, 179, 215
Templin, S. E., 207
Tennent, Gilbert, 4
Tennent, William, Jr., 4
Thatcher, William, 39
Thoburn, Isabelle, 222
Thompson, James, 292
Thompson, Mrs. S. H., 225
Thornley, Mrs. 117
Thorofare, 139
Throckmorton, Job, 23
Tindley, Charles A., 205, 254
Tippy, Worth M., 131
Tittle, Ernest F., 206
Titusville, 30
Toms River, 21, 23, 30, 31, 48, 75, 108, 137, 175, 287
Toy, Joseph, 8, 10, 11
Trenton, 4, 8-10, 13, 16-18, 21, 22, 27, 29, 30, 33, 47, 50, 61, 72, 81, 82, 87, 93, 95, 104, 137-139, 165, 174, 177, 223, 225, 230, 241, 259, 261, 285, 287, 288, 295
Trenton: Asbury, 256, 257
Trenton: Broad Street, 137
Trenton: Cadwalader, 139
Trenton: Central, 90, 93, 99, 138, 165, 230, 258
Trenton Circuit, 9, 21, 28-30, 48
Trenton: Clinton Avenue, 139, 230
Trenton District, 47, 55, 58, 88, 108, 123, 124, 136-139, 157, 170, 228, 230, 256, 258
Trenton: First 5, 16, 28, 33, 39, 48, 105, 106, 138
Trenton: Greenwood Avenue, 139, 230
Trenton: Hamilton Avenue, 156
Trenton: St. Paul's, 165, 230
Trenton: Spanish, 259
Trenton: State Street, 82, 97, 104, 141
Trenton: Trinity, 90, 106, 117, 137, 138, 165, 230
Trimnell, Teressa, 156
Tuckahoe, 21, 31, 75, 76, 102
Tuckerton, 21, 30, 31, 34, 46, 48, 56, 75, 76, 108
Tullar, Grant C., 204
Tumetcha, 197, 278-280
Turk, Gary, 195
Turner, John D., 89
Turner, John S., 100
Turner, Mrs. S. J., 225
Turnersville, 287
Tussey, Moro, 292

Underground Railroad, 66, 67
Union Societies, 50, 175
Union Valley, 179, 184
United Brethren, 56, 101, 219, 282, 283
United Methodist Homes, 270-274
UMW, 222, 227, 292

Vail, Stephan M., 69, 263, 264
Valentin, Antonio, 258
Vance, Robert B., 97
Van Cleef, Robin A., 242
VanCott, Maggie, 217, 219
VanHook, Carlton R., 148
VanLeer, William B., 179
VanNest, Peter, 47, 56
VanSant, James, 179
VanSant, Nicholas, 81
VanSant, Samuel, 90, 108, 126
VanSant, Walter B., 99, 100
VanSciver, Harvey, 205
Vasey, Thomas, 25, 26
Ventnor, 180, 181, 185, 219
Verga, 152
Vernon Township, 30
Vincent, J. H., 102, 186, 190, 211, 212
Vineland, 94, 106, 112, 115, 133, 138, 170, 184, 203, 204, 223, 224, 258, 270, 287, 297

Wagg, Alfred, 124, 139, 148, 150
Wakely, J. B., 12
Waldwick, 33
Walker, John, 44, 47, 55, 57
Wall, 50, 90, 175, 186
Walter, John 283
Walton, William, 94, 120
Wang, George T., 261
Wantage, 30
Ward, Harry E., 131
Ware, Lena, 224
Ware, Thomas, 23, 26, 27, 41, 46, 55
Waretown, 21, 30, 31, 46
Warman, John B., 173, 174, 185
Warren Circuit, 48
Warren Grove, 231
Washington, George, 7, 19, 28, 55
Waters, William, 292
Watson's Corner, 90
Watsontown, 184
Waugh, Beverly, 53, 263
Way, Samuel, 292
Webb, N. E., 180
Webb, Thomas, 6-19, 17, 18, 295
Weed, Benjamin, 77
Welch, Herbert, 131, 161, 211
Welch, T. B., 94
Wells, Mrs. G. M. P., 225
Wentworth, Erastus, 74
Wesley, Charles, 1, 2
Wesley, John, 1-3, 12, 13, 19, 25-27, 49, 111, 149, 186, 217, 243, 281, 298
Wesley, Samuel, 1
Wesley, Susanna, 2, 217, 289
Wesleyan Methodist Church, 65
Wesleyan Repository, 50
West Berlin, 179
West Creek, 75, 76, 110, 215, 231
West Jersey Circuit, 23, 29
West Jersey District, 47, 48, 251
West Long Branch, 30, 46, 50, 57, 175, 176
Westley, Eugene M., 278
Westmont, 256
Westville, 179, 183, 207, 210, 226, 231
Weymouth, 105
Whatcoat, Richard, 25, 26, 41, 42

White C. Dale, 260, 261, 269, 289, 290, 294
White, James, 83, 242
White, Peter, 46
White, Woodie W., 257
Whitecar, C. H., 96
Whitefield, George, 3, 4, 295
Whitefield, Mrs. George, 226
Whitesville, 137
Whittier, Mrs. A. J., 225
Whitton, Charles D., 208
Whitworth, Abraham, 20, 37
Wight, George B., 96, 104, 126
Wilberforce, William, 3
Wilcock, Charles, 240
Wildwood, 192
Wiley, Isaac W., 69, 82, 211, 264
Willard, Frances E., 93, 100
Williams, R. J., 60, 67, 82, 92, 150
Williams, Mrs. W. B., 223, 224, 226
Williamstown, 31, 137, 154, 215, 270
Willingboro, 237, 240
Willingboro: Church of the Good Shepherd, 284, 286
Willow Grove, 115
Wilmer, William A., 53, 59
Wilson, Clarence T., 149
Wilson, Luther B., 271
Wilson, Woodrow, 130, 143
Winn, Matilda S., 232
Winner, Isaac, 58
Wirta, Ellen, 220, 231
Wise, Keith B., 284
Wittenmeyer, Annie T., 101, 220
Wolcott, Dorothy, 242
Wolverton, Alma, 230
WCTU, 93, 104, 114, 132
WFMS, 74, 100, 101, 157, 180, 222-225
WHMS, 93, 100, 101, 104, 134, 135, 151, 168, 180, 222, 224, 225, 230, 274, 275
WSCS, 197, 199, 212, 222, 226-229, 232, 292
Women's Rights, 99-101, 134, 135, 151, 164, 165, 218-220
Wood, William B., 122
Woodbridge, 4
Woodbury, 46, 48, 67, 137, 212, 219, 284, 287
Woodbury: Colonial Manor, 238
Woodbury: Mt. Zion, 76, 253, 256
Woodland, 238
Woodlynne, 202
Woodruff, 31
Woodstown, 48, 191, 215, 270
Worth, Dorothy, 121, 228
Wright, Milton, 283
Wright, N. J., 135, 191
Wright, Richard, 14
Wright, Thomas B., 292
Wright, T. J. J., 167, 195
Wrightstown, 30, 33, 144

Yard, Mrs. George W., 218, 225, 226
Yard, Laura, 93
You, Jong Keun, 260
Young, Charles I., 256
Young, M. N., 207
Young, Nathan, 253

Zaring, Elbert R., 131
Zelley, Edward S., 242
Zelley, Henry J., 102, 202